W9-CAW-410

MACMILLAN first DICTIONARY

SIMON & SCHUSTER BOOKS FOR YOUNG READERS
An imprint of Simon & Schuster Children's Publishing Division
1230 Avenue of the Americas, New York, New York 10020

Conceived and produced by Weldon Owen Pty Ltd
61 Victoria Street, McMahons Point
Sydney, NSW 2060, Australia

Group Chief Executive Officer John Owen
President and Chief Executive Officer Terry Newell
Publisher Sheena Coupe
Creative Director Sue Burk
Senior Vice President, International Sales Stuart Laurence
Vice President, Sales and New Business Development Amy Kaneko
Vice President, Sales, Asia and Latin America Dawn Low
Administrator, International Sales Kristine Ravn

Editorial Director Helen Bateman
Manuscript Editors Anne Bateman; Robert Coupe; Klay Lamprell; Mark Lamprell; Kate McAllan; Margaret McPhee; Bronwyn Sweeney

Project Editor Barbara Sheppard
Editors, Features and Captions Kate McAllan; Barbara Sheppard

Senior Art Director Colin Wheatland
Senior Designer Michelle Cutler
Designers Dizign Pty Ltd; Alison Groves; Sarah Norton
Designer, Reference Section Amellia O'Brick
Image Coordinator Shirley Cachia-Baldwin
Photo Researchers Shirley Cachia-Baldwin; Joanna Collard
Publishing Coordinator Mike Crowton

Color reproduction by SC (Sang Choy) International Pte Ltd
Printed by Tien Wah Press (Pte) Limited
Manufactured in Singapore

A WELDON OWEN PRODUCTION

SIMON & SCHUSTER BOOKS FOR YOUNG READERS is a trademark of Simon & Schuster, Inc.
The text for this book is set in Gotham and ITC Stone Informal.
10 9 8 7 6 5 4 3 2 1
Cataloging-in-publication data for this book is available from the Library of Congress.

ISBN-13: 978-1-4169-5043-1
ISBN-10: 1-4169-5043-5

MACMILLAN first DICTIONARY

GENERAL EDITOR
Christopher G. Morris

Simon & Schuster Books for Young Readers
New York London Toronto Sydney

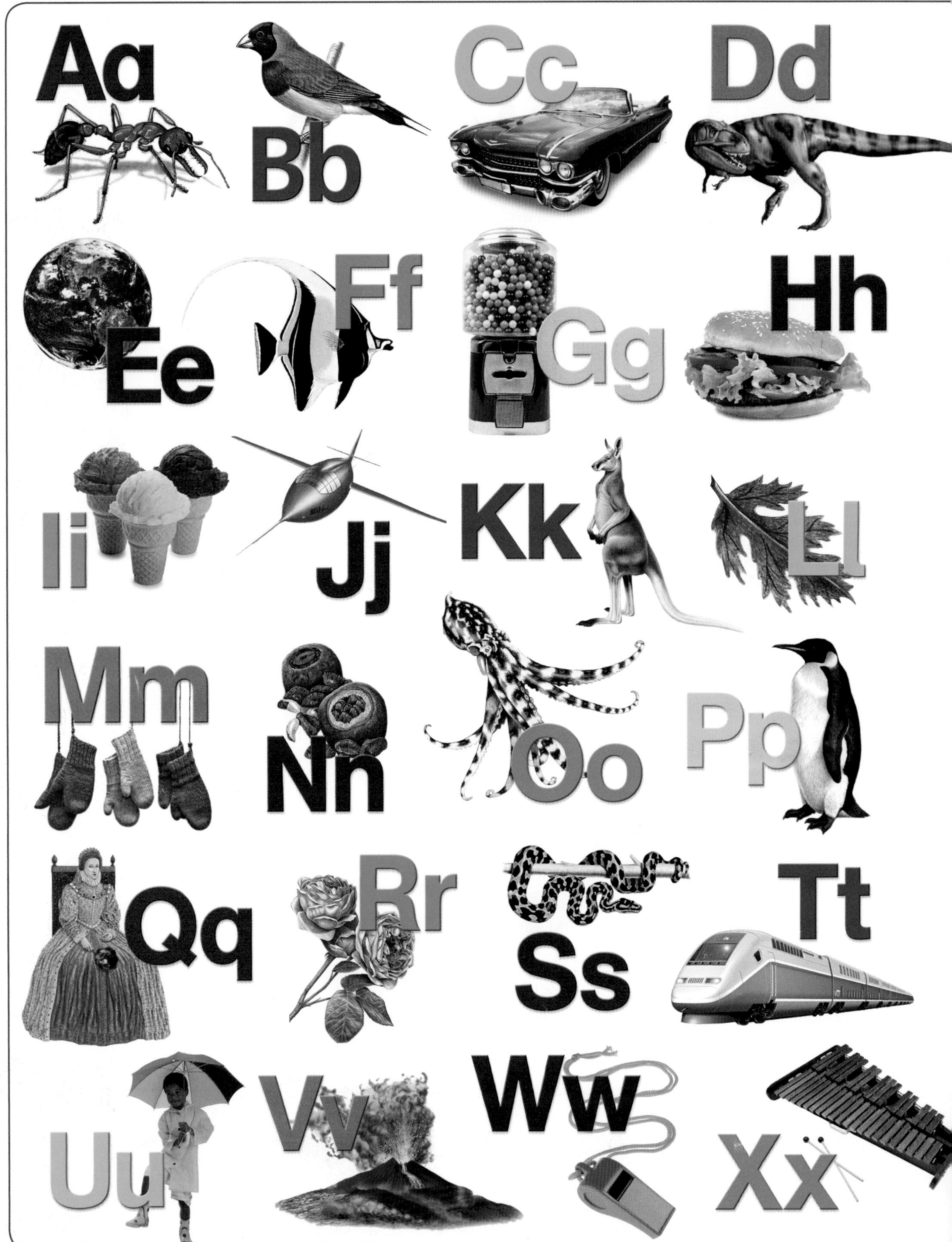
Aa
Bb
Cc
Dd
Ee
Ff
Gg
Hh
Ii
Jj
Kk
Ll
Mm
Nn
Oo
Pp
Qq
Rr
Ss
Tt
Uu
Vv
Ww
Xx

Contents

Yy

Zz

How to Use Your Dictionary

Welcome to this new edition of the *Macmillan First Dictionary.* All kinds of information about words is waiting for you in these pages. You can find the meaning of words you read or hear. You can learn how to spell words and where they come from. You can learn more about words by studying the illustrations and photos. The information here will help you understand how to get the most out of your dictionary.

Letter introduction
This shows the capital and lowercase form of the **letter**.

Illustrations and photos
The dictionary contains more than 1,400 **illustrations** and **photos**.

Guide words
These help you find entries by showing the **first** and **last word** on each spread.

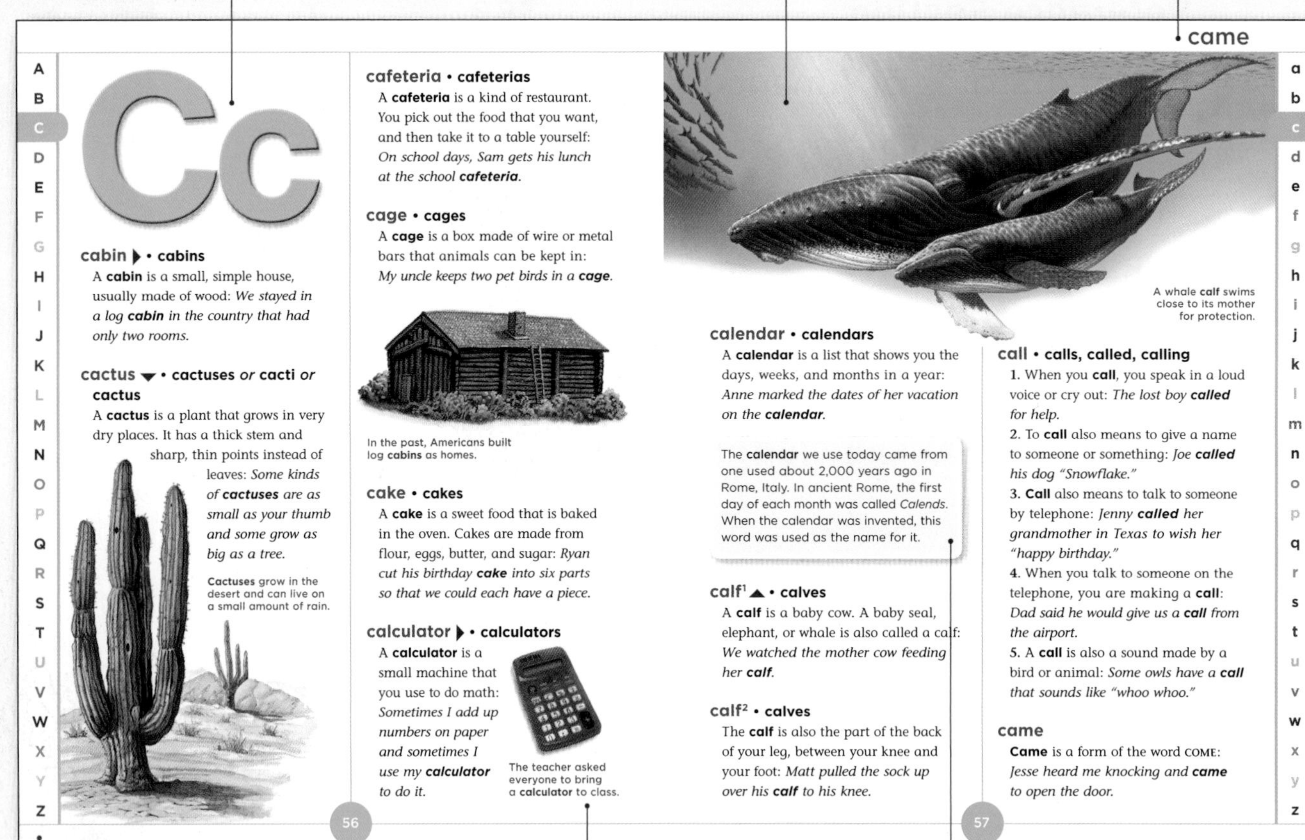

came

A B C D E F G H I J K L M N O P Q R S T U V W X Y Z

Cc

cabin • **cabins**
A **cabin** is a small, simple house, usually made of wood: *We stayed in a log **cabin** in the country that had only two rooms.*

cactus • **cactuses** *or* **cacti** *or* **cactus**
A **cactus** is a plant that grows in very dry places. It has a thick stem and sharp, thin points instead of leaves: *Some kinds of **cactuses** are as small as your thumb and some grow as big as a tree.*

Cactuses grow in the desert and can live on a small amount of rain.

cafeteria • **cafeterias**
A **cafeteria** is a kind of restaurant. You pick out the food that you want, and then take it to a table yourself: *On school days, Sam gets his lunch at the school **cafeteria**.*

cage • **cages**
A **cage** is a box made of wire or metal bars that animals can be kept in: *My uncle keeps two pet birds in a **cage**.*

In the past, Americans built log **cabins** as homes.

cake • **cakes**
A **cake** is a sweet food that is baked in the oven. Cakes are made from flour, eggs, butter, and sugar: *Ryan cut his birthday **cake** into six parts so that we could each have a piece.*

calculator • **calculators**
A **calculator** is a small machine that you use to do math: *Sometimes I add up numbers on paper and sometimes I use my **calculator** to do it.*

The teacher asked everyone to bring a **calculator** to class.

56

A whale **calf** swims close to its mother for protection.

calendar • **calendars**
A **calendar** is a list that shows you the days, weeks, and months in a year: *Anne marked the dates of her vacation on the **calendar**.*

The **calendar** we use today came from one used about 2,000 years ago in Rome, Italy. In ancient Rome, the first day of each month was called *Calends.* When the calendar was invented, this word was used as the name for it.

calf[1] • **calves**
A **calf** is a baby cow. A baby seal, elephant, or whale is also called a calf: *We watched the mother cow feeding her **calf**.*

calf[2] • **calves**
The **calf** is also the part of the back of your leg, between your knee and your foot: *Matt pulled the sock up over his **calf** to his knee.*

call • **calls, called, calling**
1. When you **call**, you speak in a loud voice or cry out: *The lost boy **called** for help.*
2. To **call** also means to give a name to someone or something: *Joe **called** his dog "Snowflake."*
3. **Call** also means to talk to someone by telephone: *Jenny **called** her grandmother in Texas to wish her "happy birthday."*
4. When you talk to someone on the telephone, you are making a **call**: *Dad said he would give us a **call** from the airport.*
5. A **call** is also a sound made by a bird or animal: *Some owls have a **call** that sounds like "whoo whoo."*

came
Came is a form of the word COME: *Jesse heard me knocking and **came** to open the door.*

57

a b c d e f g h i j k l m n o p q r s t u v w x y z

Alphabet guides
Color **alphabet guides** help you find letters quickly.

Captions
The **captions** for illustrated words provide extra information.

Where words come from
Many words have interesting **histories**. These are presented in colored feature boxes.

The main entry, or **headword**, is in blue.

bump • bumps, bumped, bumping

1. If you **bump** something, you hit it or knock it sharply: *Megan* ***bumped*** *the cup and it fell over.*

2. A **bump** is something rounded that sticks up higher than the area around it: *Ryan has a* ***bump*** *on his leg where the baseball hit him.*

These show **other forms** of the word. For nouns, they show plurals. For verbs, they show different tenses.

This is the **definition**, or meaning, of the word. Some words have more than one definition.

The red arrow points to an **illustration** of the word.

bunch ▶ • bunches

A **bunch** is a group of things that are like each other and are together: *Mom bought a* ***bunch*** *of grapes at the store.*

This is an **example sentence** to show how the word is used.

Feature panels
These colored **panels** provide more information about interesting words.

airplanes

The first airplane flight took place in 1903, in a plane built by brothers Wilbur and Orville Wright. Today, airplanes range in size from small propeller planes that carry one person to large jets that hold hundreds of passengers and can travel long distances.

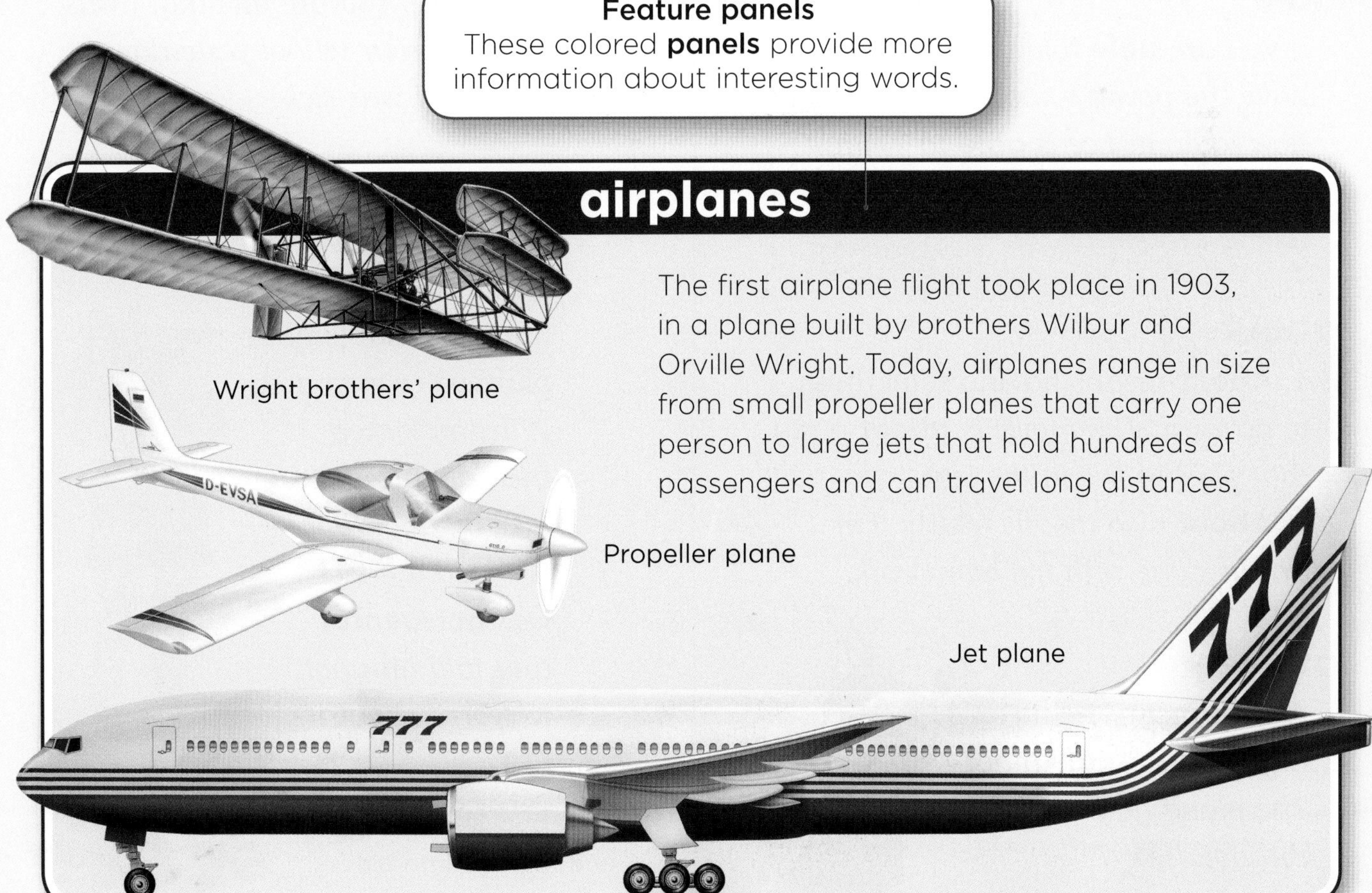

Wright brothers' plane

Propeller plane

Jet plane

Aa

The kite is flying high **above** the ground.

a

1. You say **a** when you mean one: *We have **a** dog at home.*
2. You also use **a** when you mean each: *I eat cereal once **a** day.*

able

If you are **able** to do something, you have the power to do it or you know how to do it: *Lee is **able** to swim across the pool underwater without taking a breath.*

about

1. About means having something to do with: *The movie is **about** a pig that goes to live in the city.*
2. About also means nearly: *I'm **about** done with my homework.*

above ▶

Above means being higher than something: *The plane flew **above** the clouds.*

absent

If you are **absent**, you are not in a place. You are missing: *I was **absent** from school yesterday because I was sick.*

accident ▼ • accidents

An **accident** is something that happens that is not planned or expected: *Winston kicked the ball into the lake by **accident**. We said the kick was **accidental** and told him not to worry about it.*

Jenny dropped the flower pot by **accident** and it broke into pieces.

An **acrobat** performs tricks while swinging on a bar.

acrobat ▲ • acrobats

An **acrobat** is a person who does special tricks, such as walking on a wire called a tightrope hanging high above the ground: *We saw **acrobats** turning somersaults at the circus.*

across ▼

If you go **across** something, you go from one side to the other: *Alexander walked **across** the street.*

act • acting, acted

1. When you **act**, you do something: *After the engine caught fire, the pilot **acted** quickly to land the plane. The pilot's **actions** saved many lives.*
2. To **act** also means to take part in a play: *Effie **acted** in the school play last night. She played the part of Snow White.*

activity ▶ • activities

An **activity** is something that you do: *Dad's favorite **activity** is playing golf. Mom says that it's good for him to keep **active** that way.*

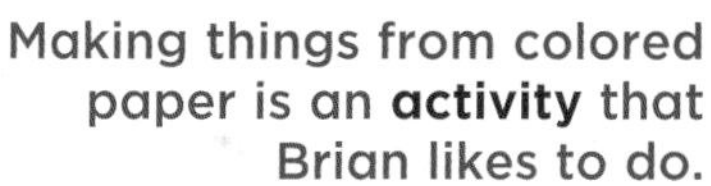

Making things from colored paper is an **activity** that Brian likes to do.

Herds of animals often swim **across** a river to get to the other side.

We learned to **add** numbers during math class.

actor • actors

An **actor** is someone who is in a play, movie, or on television. A female actor is called an **actress**: *The **actor** who played the part of the lost boy was good at crying.*

actual

Actual means real and not imaginary: *"Hot Coffee" is the name of an **actual** city. It is **actually** in Covington County, Mississippi.*

add ▲ • added, adding

1. To **add** means to put two or more numbers together to find the total: *When I **add** two and three, I get five. When I add these numbers together, this is **addition**.*
2. **Add** also means to put one thing with another: *Sean **added** an extra scoop of ice cream to his dessert.*

address ▼ • addresses

Your **address** is the number of the house and the name of the road and town where you live: *Grandma's **address** is 25 Potts Street, Jonesville, Florida.*

A package needs a complete **address** and stamps before it can be mailed.

adjective • adjectives

An **adjective** is a word that tells about a person, place, or thing. In the sentence *My shoes are black and muddy,* the words "black" and "muddy" are adjectives. An **adverb** is another kind of word that does this. It tells how something is done. In the sentence *I quickly cleaned my shoes before coming indoors,* the word "quickly" is an adverb.

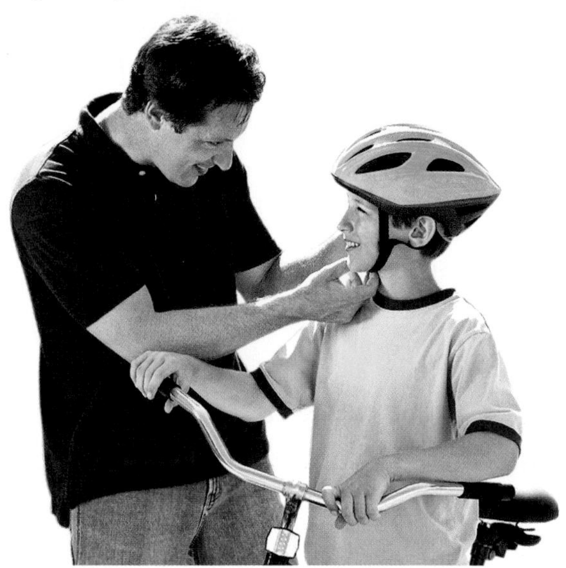

Joe asked an **adult** to help him put on his safety helmet.

adopt • adopted, adopting

When you **adopt** a child, it means that you choose a child to belong to your family after he or she has already been born: *Mr. and Mrs. Anderson are **adopting** a three-month-old girl. They are very excited about the **adoption**.*

adult ▲ • adults

An **adult** is someone who is a grown-up and not a child: *I am allowed to swim in the pool only when I have an **adult** with me.*

The lioness runs **after** the gazelle to try to catch it.

adventure ▶ • adventures

An **adventure** is an exciting activity that is different from other things that you normally do: *Camping in the Grand Canyon with my family was a real* ***adventure****.*

advertisement • advertisements

An **advertisement** is a notice that tells you about something for sale or somewhere to go to: *There are lots of* ***advertisements*** *on TV for cars. Car makers also* ***advertise*** *on the Internet and put* ***ads*** *in newspapers.*

advice

Advice is helpful information that someone else gives you, when you do not know what to do about something: *Her mom gave her some* ***advice*** *about which car to buy.*

afraid

If you are **afraid**, it means you are frightened or scared: *Robert is* ***afraid*** *of spiders and never wants to go near one.*

after ◀

1. **After** means later in time: *Mom is picking up my friend and me* ***after*** *our swimming lesson.*
2. **After** can also mean chasing someone or something: *The neighbor's dog always runs* ***after*** *our cat.*

afternoon • afternoons

Afternoon is the part of the day between lunchtime and evening: *We spent all* ***afternoon*** *playing at the park and didn't get home until dinnertime.*

Many people enjoy the **adventure** of climbing rocks.

again

If you do something **again**, it means you do it one more time: *The teacher was angry because we were late to school **again** this morning. This was the third time this week that we were late.*

Belinda leans **against** the box to write on it.

against ▲

1. When you are **against** someone or something, you are on the opposite side to them: *I played a game of soccer **against** my friends on Saturday.*
2. Against can also mean touching or leaning on something: *Ben pressed his face **against** the window so he could look outside.*

age • ages

Your **age** is how old you are: *I am six years of **age**.*

ago

Ago means back in the time before now: *Mom and Dad got married nine years **ago**.*

agree • agreed, agreeing

To **agree** means to think or feel the same way that someone else does: *We all **agreed** that Casey would make a good class president. The teacher was also in **agreement** with our choice.*

ahead ▼

If you are **ahead** of someone or something, it means that you are in front of them: *I ran **ahead** of the others so that I could be the first in line.*

The man in the yellow shirt is **ahead** of the other riders in the bicycle race.

airplanes

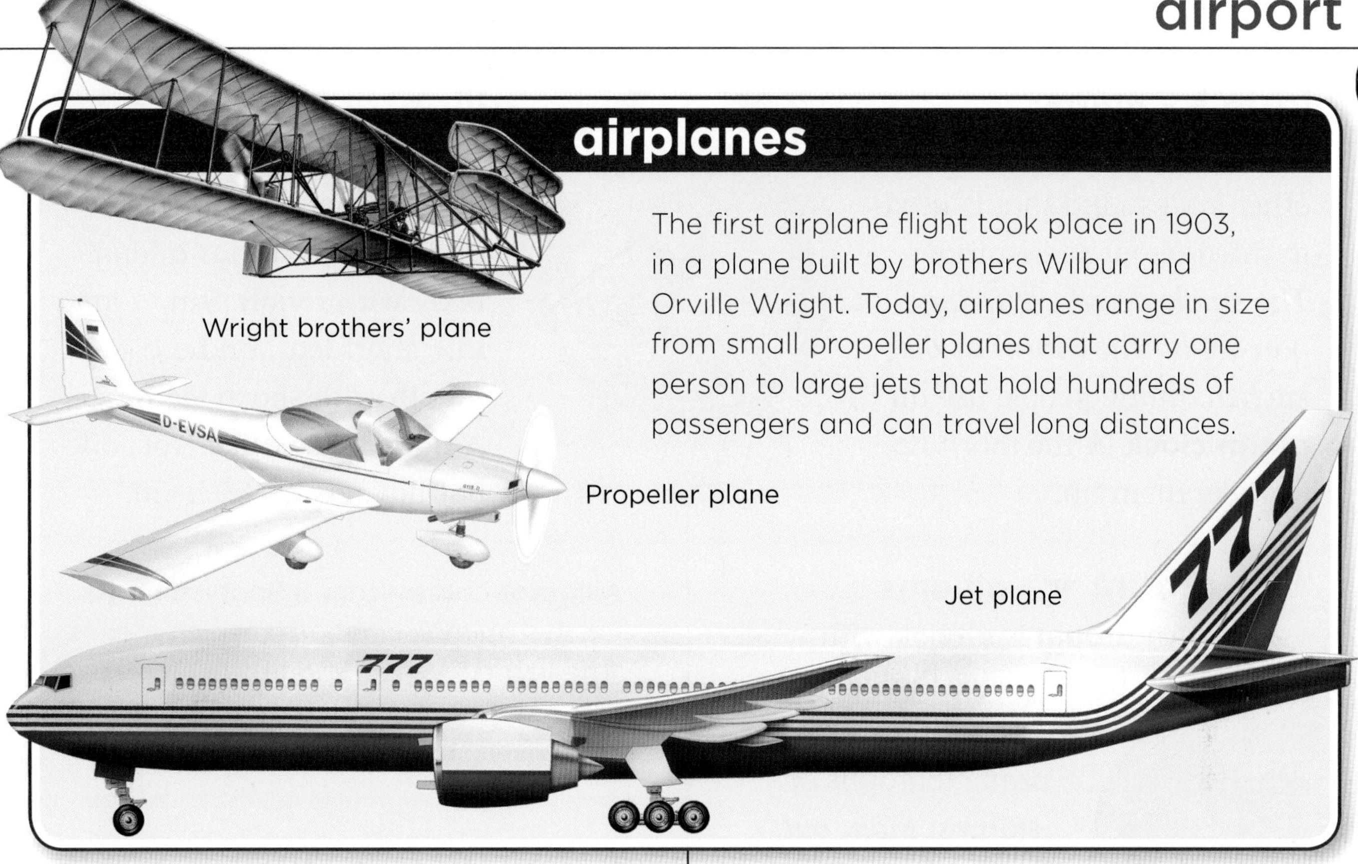

The first airplane flight took place in 1903, in a plane built by brothers Wilbur and Orville Wright. Today, airplanes range in size from small propeller planes that carry one person to large jets that hold hundreds of passengers and can travel long distances.

aim ▶ • aimed, aiming

To **aim** means to point something at someone or something else: *Mom **aimed** the camera carefully before taking the family Christmas photo.*

The man is teaching the boy how to **aim** straight.

air

Air is the gas all around us that we breathe in, but cannot see: *I opened up the window to let in some fresh **air**.*

air conditioner

An **air conditioner** is a machine used in cars and buildings to make the air cool: *It was a hot day, so Mom turned on the **air conditioner** as soon as we got in the car.*

airplane ▲ • airplanes

An **airplane** is a machine with wings and an engine, that can fly through the air from place to place. An airplane can carry people or things: *I traveled by **airplane** to visit Grandpa in Chicago.* An airplane is a type of **aircraft**.

airport • airports

An **airport** is a large, flat place where airplanes take off and land. There are some buildings at the airport where you can wait for people, and other buildings where the airplanes are fixed: *My dad's plane was late, so we had dinner while we waited at the **airport**.*

alarm ▶ • alarms

An **alarm** is a bell or some other loud sound that is used to warn about something: *The smoke from the frying pan set off the **alarm** in the kitchen.* Many people use an **alarm clock** in the morning to wake them up.

Dad sets my **alarm clock** every night so I wake up in time for school.

album ▼ • albums

An **album** is a book with blank pages that you use to keep things such as photographs or stamps: *Mom put the photos of my new baby sister in an **album**.*

Lauren sorts her vacation pictures and puts them in an **album**.

alike ▶

If things are **alike**, it means they look the same: *All the players on the team wear uniforms that are **alike**.*

alive

When people, plants, or animals are **alive**, it means that they are living: *I feed my goldfish every day to keep him **alive**.*

all

All means the whole of everything or everyone: *Jeremy kept eating until **all** of the chocolate chip cookies were gone.*

alligator ▶ • alligators

An **alligator** is a large animal that lives in rivers and swamps. It has a long body with rough skin, a long tail, short legs, and a big mouth with sharp teeth. Alligators look like crocodiles but have a shorter head.

Alligator comes from a Spanish name for this animal, *el legarto*, which means "the lizard." When Spanish explorers first saw this animal, they thought it was a very big type of lizard.

allow • allowed, allowing

When you **allow** something, it means that you let someone do something that they want to: *I was really excited when Mom said I was **allowed** to go to Tracy's birthday party.*

These twin brothers look **alike** because they have similar faces and the same kind of hair.

Female **alligators** are gentle when they carry babies in their mouth.

allowance • allowances

An **allowance** is a sum of money given to someone: *My brother gets a bigger **allowance** from our parents than I do, because he's older.*

all right

When something is **all right**, it is OK or good enough: *Jamie twisted his ankle playing soccer yesterday, but he is **all right** today.*

almost

Almost means nearly: *My younger sister is **almost** as tall as I am.*

alone

When you are **alone**, there is no one else with you: *Now that I am older, Mom lets me walk to school **alone**.*

along ▼

1. Along means in a line from one end to the other: *We walked **along** the beach.*

2. Along also means to have someone or something with you: *I brought some food **along** for the class picnic.*

Trees grow in a line **along** both sides of the road.

There are 26 letters in the English **alphabet**.

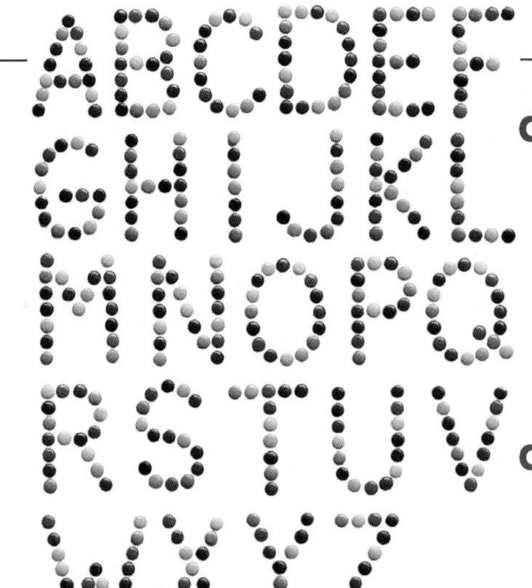

alphabet ▶ • alphabets

The **alphabet** is the set of letters we use to write words, put in a special order: *The third letter in the **alphabet** is "C."* When something has been arranged in this order, we say that it is in **alphabetical** order.

In the Greek language, the first two letters are *alpha* and *beta*, which are like the English letters "a" and "b." When people named the set of letters for the English language, they used a Greek word for this, **alphabet**.

already

Already means by now: *I turned on the TV as soon as we got home, but my favorite show was **already** over.*

also

Also means as well or too: *We own two dogs, and we **also** have a cat.*

although

Although means even though: ***Although** everyone likes Kate, she didn't get many votes for class president.*

always

Always means each time or all the time: *Water **always** runs downhill, never uphill.*

am

Am is a form of the word BE and is used with the word I: *I **am** three years older than my little brother.*

amaze • amazed, amazing

When you **amaze** someone, you surprise them greatly: *The magician **amazed** the crowd when he pulled a rabbit out of his hat.*

ambulance ▼ • ambulances

An **ambulance** is a special kind of car used to take sick or hurt people to the hospital: *The **ambulance** turned on its siren so that other cars would move out of the way.*

The word **ambulance** means "a walking hospital." The first kind of ambulance was when doctors would walk along with an army so that they could help soldiers who were hurt or sick.

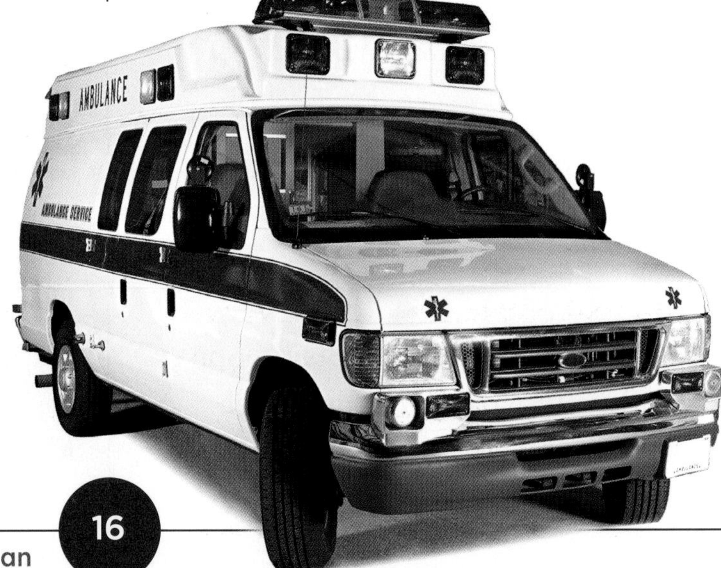

My sister went to the hospital in an **ambulance** when she broke her arm.

Every year, many people visit the Statue of Liberty in the **American** city of New York.

American ▶ • Americans

1. A person who lives in the United States, North America, or South America is called an **American**.
2. When something comes from **America** or has something to do with America, we say that it is **American**: *The school principal raises the **American** flag each morning.*

among ▼

1. Among means in the middle of: *We found a bird's nest **among** the thick branches of the tree.*
2. Among also means that something is shared: *Mom divided the candy **among** the three of us.*

A red tulip grows in a field **among** many yellow tulips.

amount • amounts

An **amount** is how much there is of something: *Brad poured only a small **amount** of juice into his glass, just in case he didn't like it.*

an

An is used instead of **a** before words that start with the letters *a, e, i, o, u,* and sometimes *h*: *Mom put **an** apple and an orange in my lunch box.*

ancient ▼

If something is **ancient**, it lived or happened a long time ago: *The **ancient** Egyptians lived along the Nile River more than five thousand years ago.*

and

1. And means also or as well as: *Rosie had a peanut butter **and** jelly sandwich for her lunch.*
2. Another meaning for **and** is added to or plus: *Six **and** two equals eight.*

angry • angrier, angriest

When you are **angry** you are very cross or mad at someone or something: *The man was **angry** when another car took the parking space he wanted. His **anger** went away when he found another space closer to the store.*

People in **ancient** Egypt made special buildings called pyramids.

animals

Animals come in many shapes and sizes. They can grow much larger than people, or be much smaller. Animals can have skin, feathers, scales, or fur covering their body. Some animals, such as whales, live in the sea. Others, such as birds, make nests in trees.

animal ◀ • **animals**
An **animal** is any creature that is alive and can move, but is not a plant. People, monkeys, deer, fish, and parrots are all kinds of animals.

ankle • **ankles**
The **ankle** is the part of your body that joins your foot to your leg: *Sally twisted her **ankle** when she was playing basketball.*

anniversary ▲ • **anniversaries**
An **anniversary** is a day on which something important happened in an earlier year: *August 21st this year is my grandparents' fortieth wedding **anniversary**.*

announce • **announced, announcing**
When you **announce** something, you tell other people about it: *The football coach **announced** that he would be choosing a new captain for the team. We were all very excited about his **announcement**.*

another
Another means one more: *I ate one piece of the pie and then asked if I could have **another**.*

answer ▼ • **answers, answered, answering**
1. When you **answer** someone, you say or write something to them after they have asked you a question, or called you or written to you: *The teacher asked why I was late, and I **answered** that the school bus had broken down. We **answer** the phone by saying "hello."*
2. It is called an **answer** when you say or write something to someone who has asked you something or called or written to you: *The **answer** to "What is five times two?" is "ten." I wrote a letter to my friend, and she sent an **answer** right away.*

Tom knew the **answer** to the question, so he raised his hand.

Ants have six legs like all other insects.

ant ▲ • ants

Ants are small insects that live under the ground in large groups: *The hungry **ants** crawled onto the picnic blanket looking for tiny crumbs.*

any

1. **Any** means one, but it does not matter which one: *Mom says that I can choose **any** color I like to paint my bedroom.*
2. **Any** also means some: *Do you have **any** money left to buy some candy?*
3. **Any** also means each and every: ***Any** child in our class is allowed to ask the teacher for help.*

anyone

Anyone means any person at all: ***Anyone** can go to watch the Thanksgiving Day parade. Have you asked **anybody** to go with you?*

anything

Anything means a thing, but it does not matter what it is: *Did you do **anything** exciting during summer vacation?*

apart ▼

1. **Apart** means away from each other: *The animals at the zoo are kept **apart** in different cages.*
2. If you take something **apart**, you separate it into bits and pieces: *Daniel pulled the watch **apart** to see how it worked.*

apartment • apartments

An **apartment** is a room or set of rooms that people live in: *My best friend lives in the **apartment** next to ours.*

Joan took the toy **apart** so she could build it again.

ape ▶ • apes

An **ape** is a large monkey that does not have a tail. Apes use their arms to swing through trees.

appear • appeared, appearing

When something **appears**, it means that you can see it: *The sun **appeared** from behind the rain clouds. Its **appearance** warmed us up for the rest of the afternoon.*

appetite • appetites

The feeling that you want to eat is called an **appetite**: *My brother has a big **appetite**. He eats three sandwiches for lunch each day.*

I gathered **apples** and put them in my basket.

apple ▶ • apples

An **apple** is a juicy round fruit that grows on trees. Apples can have red, yellow, or green skin.

aquarium ▶ • aquariums

An **aquarium** is a glass container in which live fish and other underwater animals can be kept. Some aquariums are big enough to hold large animals such as sharks and whales.

are

Are is a form of the word BE: *We **are** walking by ourselves to school today.* **Aren't** is a shorter way of saying "are not": ***Are** you leaving for school now? No, we **aren't** ready to go yet.*

area • areas

An **area** is a smaller part of a large place: *The park has one **area** for children to play in, and another area for dogs.*

argue • argued, arguing

When you **argue** with someone, you talk to them in a loud and angry way because they do not agree with you: *I **argued** with my sister about which movie we should see. Mom told us that she would decide for us because she was sick and tired of our **argument**.*

My science class went to the **aquarium** and we saw lots of fish.

apes

Apes live in some parts of Africa and Asia. Orangutans, gibbons, gorillas, and chimpanzees are all apes. They are very smart and can make simple tools to use.

Orangutan

Gibbon

Gorilla

A knight and his horse wore **armor** for protection.

arithmetic

When you use **arithmetic**, you work things out with numbers. For example, you can add or subtract them: *The teacher gave us* ***arithmetic*** *problems for homework every night.*

2+9=11
11-9=2

Addition and subtraction are both examples of **arithmetic.**

arm • arms

1. The **arm** is the part of your body that joins your shoulder to your hand: *Grandma put her* ***arms*** *around me and gave me a big hug.*
2. Other things can also have **arms**, such as the arms of a chair or the arms of a jacket: *Dad rested his glass on the* ***arm*** *of the chair while he was watching TV.*

armor

Armor is special metal clothing that soldiers and their horses used to wear in old times long ago, to keep from getting hurt during a battle: *You can see knights dressed in their* ***armor*** *at the museum.*

army • armies

An **army** is a large group of people who are trained to fight on land in a war: *In the Revolutionary War the American* ***army*** *fought against the British.*

Soldiers riding horses formed **armies** in ancient times.

around

1. **Around** means on all sides of something or in all directions: *We have a high fence* ***around*** *our backyard.*
2. **Around** can also mean in the opposite direction or on the other side: *Dad turned the car* ***around*** *because we were driving the wrong way.*
3. **Around** can also mean moving in a circle: *The dog kept spinning* ***around*** *to try to catch his tail.*
4. **Around** can also mean near to: *I've been on this street before—I think my friend lives* ***around*** *here somewhere. We're going to have lunch at* ***around*** *1 o'clock.*

The **arrow** on the sign bends to the left.

arrive • arrived, arriving

When you **arrive**, you come to a place that you were trying to get to: *Sam* ***arrived*** *fifteen minutes late to class because he had missed the bus.*

arrow ▲ • arrows

1. An **arrow** is a thin stick with a sharp point at one end and feathers at the other end. Arrows are shot from a bow and are used as weapons.
2. An **arrow** is also a sign used to point the right way to go: *The light was red, but the green* ***arrow*** *below meant it was OK to turn right.*

art ◀

Art is something beautiful made by someone, such as a painting, drawing, or a statue: *There is a great work of* ***art*** *in France known as the Mona Lisa.*

article • articles

An **article** is a piece of writing in a newspaper, magazine, or book: *Tiffany wrote an* ***article*** *about health food for the school newspaper.*

artist ▼ • artists

An **artist** is someone who makes beautiful things, such as paintings, drawings, and statues: *Famous* ***artists*** *get to show their paintings in museums.*

An **artist** paints a picture of trees and buildings.

The bear fell **asleep** after climbing up the tree.

as

We use the word **as** when we compare things: *Henry is almost* ***as*** *tall as his older brother.*

ashamed

When you feel **ashamed**, you feel sad or guilty about something you have done: *Emily felt* ***ashamed*** *that she had cheated on her math test.*

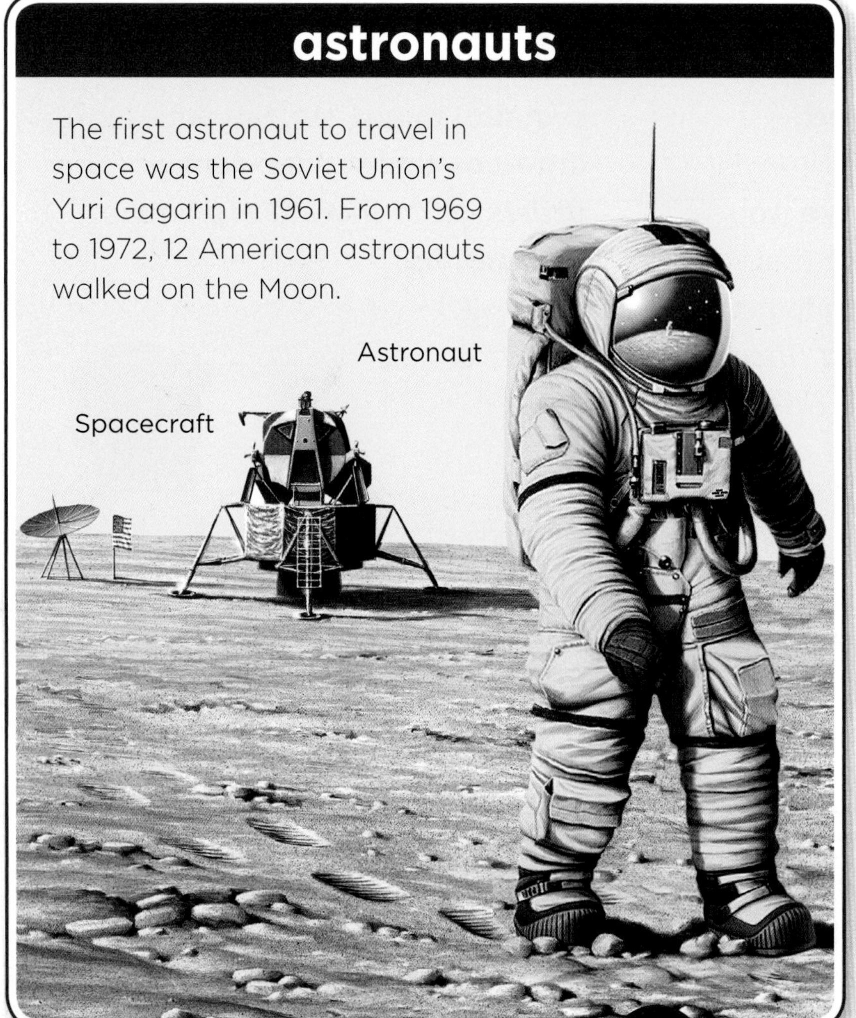

astronauts

The first astronaut to travel in space was the Soviet Union's Yuri Gagarin in 1961. From 1969 to 1972, 12 American astronauts walked on the Moon.

ask • asked, asking

1. You **ask** a question when you want to know something: *I* ***asked*** *my friend what he did during summer vacation.*
2. You also **ask** a question when you want something or need some help: *The teacher* ***asked*** *the students to move their tables to the back of the room.*

asleep

When you are **asleep**, you are not awake. You are sleeping: *The baby fell* ***asleep*** *in the back of the car and her mom had to carry her into bed.*

astronaut • astronauts

An **astronaut** is someone who travels in a spacecraft and explores space: *Neil Armstrong is a famous* ***astronaut*** *who walked on the Moon on July 20, 1969.*

The word **astronaut** comes from two words that mean "a star" and "a person who travels in a ship." Astronauts really do go into space, but they do not travel as far as the stars.

at

1. We use **at** to tell us where something or someone is: *Sarah missed school this morning because she was **at** the dentist.* **2.** We also use **at** to say when something is happening: *Our soccer game will start **at** 10 o'clock in the morning.*

ate

Ate is a form of the word EAT: *We **ate** pork chops for dinner last night.*

atmosphere • atmospheres

The **atmosphere** is the air all around Earth: *The smoke and gas from the factory is polluting the **atmosphere**.*

attach ▼ • attached, attaching

To **attach** means to fasten or join to something: *Dad **attached** a light to the front of my bicycle. He put on this **attachment** so that I could ride home in the dark.*

Joy **attached** her dog's leash to the pole so she could go into the store.

attack • attacks, attacked, attacking

1. When you **attack**, you start to fight: *Our dog **attacked** the neighbor's cat, but stopped after the cat scratched him.* **2.** An **attack** is a fight or battle: *The war began when the army made an **attack** on another country.*

attention

When you pay **attention**, you keep your mind on what is going on, and you watch and listen carefully: *The teacher told Jimmy to stop looking out the window and pay **attention** to math class.*

attic ▲ • attics

The **attic** is the space or room inside the roof of a house: *Mom stores our old baby clothes in the **attic**.*

A B C D E F G H I J K L M N O P Q R S T U V W X Y Z

audience ▼ • audiences
An **audience** is a group of people who have come together to watch or listen to something: *The* ***audience*** *cheered and clapped at the end of our school play.*

audio ▶
If something is **audio**, it has something to do with sound that is recorded or broadcast: *There was so much noise that we couldn't hear the* ***audio*** *announcements during the baseball game.*

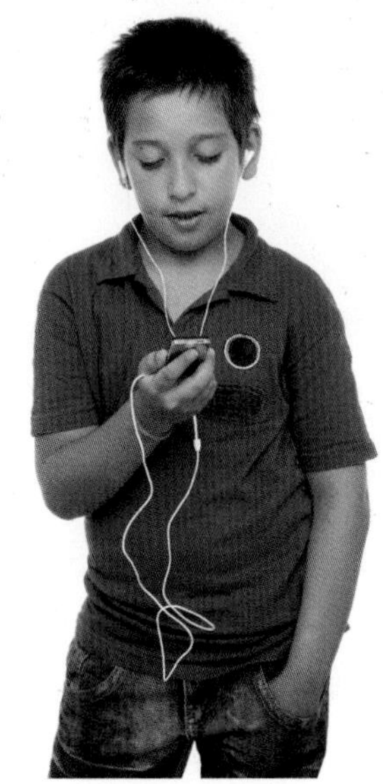
Antonio listens to music on his **audio** equipment.

My teacher drives a fast **automobile.**

aunt • aunts
Your **aunt** is your mother's or father's sister, or your uncle's wife.

author • authors
An **author** is someone who has written something, such as a story, a book, or an article in a newspaper: *Herman Melville was a famous American* ***author*** *who was born almost two hundred years ago.*

automobile ▲ • automobiles
An **automobile** is a motor car. Most automobiles have four wheels, can carry passengers, and have an engine that runs on gasoline. An automobile can also be called an **auto.**

In the past, **audiences** often watched plays in outdoor theaters.

autumn ▼ • autumns

Autumn is the season of the year after summer and before winter. This season is also called **fall**: *In **autumn** the weather becomes cooler and leaves fall from the trees.*

available

If something is **available**, you can get it, buy it, or use it: *Tickets for the basketball game will be **available** next week.*

During **autumn,** leaves turn beautiful colors, such as yellow, orange, and red.

average

1. **Average** means ordinary or not special: *Mario is an **average** runner. He doesn't win the race or come in last, but usually finishes somewhere in the middle.*
2. **Average** can also mean the number or measurement that most things in a group are near: *There are eighty students in four classes, so the **average** number of children in each class is twenty.*

The infant is **awake** and wants to get out of the crib.

awake ▲

When you are **awake**, you are not asleep: *I was **awake** this morning before sunrise.*

award • awards

People get **awards** when they do something special or do very well: *Henry received an **award** for being the best basketball player on the school team.*

away

1. **Away** means somewhere else: *My uncle is **away** on a business trip and will be back in two weeks.*
2. **Away** also means at a certain distance: *We live in New York, but my cousin William lives hundreds of miles **away** in Virginia.*
3. **Away** can also show that you have gotten rid of something: *Juan threw **away** some old newspapers.*

awful

Something is **awful** if it is very bad or frightening, or if people do not like it at all: *There was an **awful** wind last week that blew down three trees in our yard.*

We packed several **backpacks** to take on our camping trip.

Bb

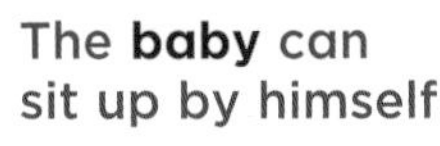

The **baby** can sit up by himself.

baby ◀ • babies
A **baby** is an infant or very young child who cannot yet walk or talk: ***Babies** cry when they are hungry or feel unhappy.*

baby-sit • baby-sat, baby-sitting
A person who **baby-sits** for babies or young children looks after them while their parents are away for a short time: *My older sister often **baby-sits** our neighbors' young children. She is their favorite **baby-sitter**.*

back ▶ • backs
1. Your **back** is the part of your body below your shoulders and behind your chest: *When John turned around I could see his **back**, but not his face.*
2. The **back** of something is the part opposite to the front: *We went around to the **back** of the house because the front door was locked.*
3. When you take something **back**, you take it to where you got it: *I must take this book **back** to the library.*

backpack ▲ • backpacks
A **backpack** is a bag with shoulder straps that you carry on your back. People who go camping often carry their food and other things they need in a backpack: *I carry my books to school in a red **backpack**.*

backward
Backward means the opposite way to the front: *Veronica quickly stepped **backward** when she saw the car coming toward her.* This word is sometimes spelled **backwards**.

The girls went into the water with their **back** toward me.

The man has just **baked** some bread in the oven.

bacteria

Bacteria are very tiny living things that you can see only under a special tool called a microscope. There are bacteria in the food we eat and in our body: *Sometimes **bacteria** in our food can make us feel sick, but other kinds of bacteria help to keep us healthy.*

Bacteria are too small to see unless you use a microscope. When people first saw bacteria under a microscope, they thought they looked like tiny sticks. So they made up the name *bacteria* from a word that means "a stick."

bad • worse, worst

1. If something is not good, we say it is **bad**: *The team played a **bad** game today and lost 7-0.*
2. If someone does not behave well, we say they are **bad**: *My mom said I was a **bad** boy because I didn't do my homework.*
3. We also call something **bad** if it is very strong and can hurt us: *Our teacher went home early today because he had a **bad** headache.*

bag • bags

A **bag** is a container that you carry things in. Bags can be made of paper, plastic, or other materials. You throw some bags away after you use them: *Jeremy always brings his lunch to school in a brown paper **bag**.*

bake ◀ • baked, baking

You **bake** bread, cakes, and other food when you cook them in a hot oven: *Some people **bake** their own bread. Other people buy their bread from a **bakery**.*

balance ▼ • balanced, balancing

You **balance** something when you hold it even so that it does not fall to the ground: *It is hard to **balance** a ball on the end of your finger.*

bald • balder, baldest

Someone who is **bald** has no hair on the top of their head: *Dad has thick, curly hair, but Grandpa is **bald**.*

You need to **balance** carefully to do tricks while riding on a bicycle.

A B C D E F G H I J K L M N O P Q R S T U V W X Y Z

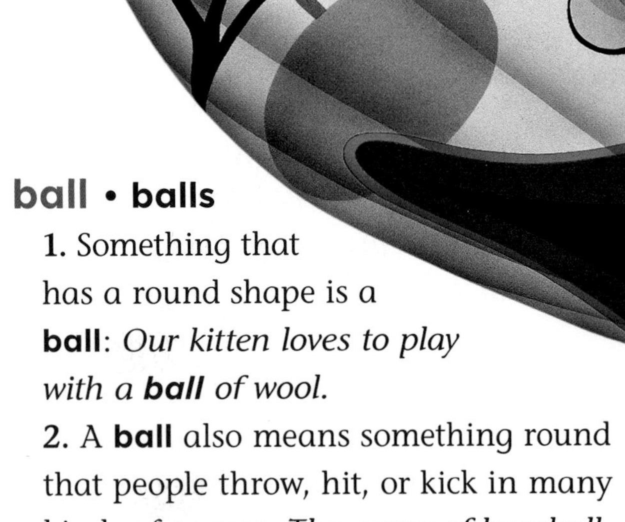

The family takes a ride in a hot air **balloon.**

ball • balls

1. Something that has a round shape is a **ball**: *Our kitten loves to play with a **ball** of wool.*

2. A **ball** also means something round that people throw, hit, or kick in many kinds of games: *The game of baseball is played with a white, hard **ball**.*

ballet ◀ • ballets

Ballet is a kind of dance with music in which the dancers move in special ways that often tell a story: *Melanie goes to classes after school to learn **ballet**.*

The **ballet** Swan Lake is popular around the world.

balloon ▲ • balloons

1. A **balloon** is a small rubber bag with a narrow tube at its open end. You blow into the tube and the balloon grows big like a ball and will float in the air: *Children like to have lots of **balloons** at birthday parties.*

2. A **balloon** can also be a kind of aircraft that is full of hot air and that is blown by the wind. People can travel in a large basket that is under the balloon.

banana ▼ • bananas

A **banana** is a yellow fruit that grows about six inches long and is narrow and curved. Bananas grow in bunches on trees in warm places: *Before you eat a **banana**, you need to peel off the thick, yellow skin.*

Bananas are green on the tree before they are ripe enough to eat.

Musicians in this **band** play drums and instruments called bagpipes.

band ▶ • bands

A **band** is a group of musicians who play together: *I want to learn to play the drums so that I can join the school **band**.*

A **bandage** can be wrapped around your arm or leg.

bandage ◀ • bandages

A **bandage** is a piece of clean cloth that you place over or tie around a cut, scratch, or bruise to protect it or help it to get better: *Amanda's mother tied a **bandage** around her cut hand to stop it from bleeding.*

bang • bangs, banged, banging

1. A **bang** is a short, sudden, loud noise or exploding sound: *Fireworks make loud **bangs** when they explode.*
2. You **bang** something when you hit it hard and it makes a loud noise: *Samantha **banged** on the door until someone opened it.*

We are **barbecuing** food for our dinner tonight.

bank ▼ • banks

1. A **bank** is a place where people put their money so that it will be safe. Banks also lend money to people: *My brother Tim put twenty dollars into the **bank** yesterday.*
2. A **bank** is also the name of a container where children keep small amounts of money: *Eleanor has saved up two dollars in her little green **bank**.*

I keep my allowance in a piggy **bank**.

bar • bars

A **bar** is a long, thin piece of something. Wooden and metal bars are used to protect windows and doors: *There are iron **bars** over the windows at the front of our house.*

barbecue ◀ • barbecued, barbecuing

When you **barbecue**, you cook a meal out of doors over a fire: *Last night, Dad **barbecued** some meat and vegetables in our backyard.*

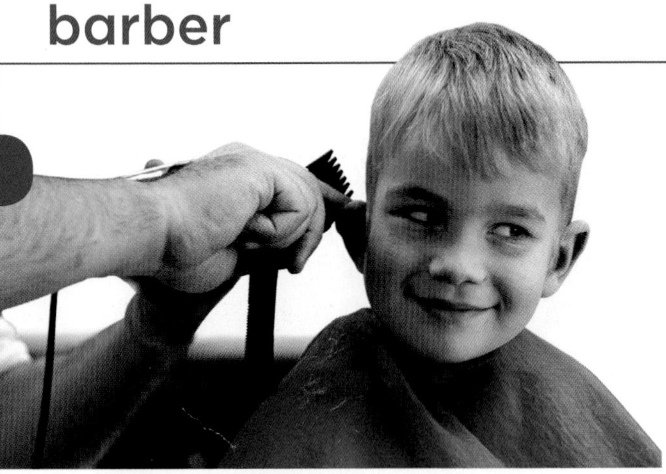

Dad asked the **barber** to cut my hair short on the sides.

barber ▲ • barbers

A **barber** is a person whose job is to cut people's hair: *When my hair grows long, Mom takes me to the **barber** to get it cut.*

bare ▼ • barer, barest

Something is **bare** if there is nothing that covers it: *We took off our shoes and walked along the beach with **bare** feet.*

The tree branches were **bare** after all the leaves fell off.

bargain • bargains

A **bargain** is something you buy for much less than it usually costs: *The movie tickets were only a dollar each—they were a real **bargain**.*

bark[1] • barks

Bark is what covers the outside of a tree trunk: *In winter, the **bark** of some trees falls off and leaves the tree trunks bare.*

The **barn** on my grandparents' farm is painted red and has a white roof.

bark[2] • barked, barking

To **bark** means to make a loud, sharp sound, like the noise a dog makes: *The dog next door **barked** all night and kept us awake.*

barn ▲ • barns

A **barn** is a large building on a farm where cows and other animals are kept, as well as food for them: *We fed the horses in the **barn** on my uncle's farm.*

This wooden **barrel** has no top.

barrel ▶ • barrels

A **barrel** is a large container that is used for storing food or liquids such as water or oil. Most barrels have flat tops and curved sides and are made of wood or metal.

base • bases

1. The **base** of something is the lowest part of it: *A lamp has a wide **base** so that it will not fall over.*
2. A **base** is also one of the four positions on a baseball field: *If a baseball player hits the ball hard enough, he may run to first, second, or third **base**.*

baseball ▼ • baseballs

1. **Baseball** is a bat and ball game played by two teams of nine players on a field with four bases. Players hit the ball with the bat and run from one base to the next: *I play **baseball** at school and watch baseball games on TV.*
2. A **baseball** is also the name of the ball that is used in this game: *Mark's dad gave him a new **baseball** for his birthday.*

basement • basements

A **basement** is the lowest inside part of a building and is usually below the ground: *We keep boxes of old books and papers in the **basement** of our house.*

basket ▶ • baskets

A **basket** is a container made of grasses, twigs, straw, wire, or other material: *Mom keeps her knitting wool in a large **basket**.*

The **basket** is filled with lemons.

A player reaches high in the air to try to catch the **baseball**.

A
B
C
D
E
F
G
H
I
J
K
L
M
N
O
P
Q
R
S
T
U
V
W
X
Y
Z

basketball ▸ • basketballs

1. **Basketball** is a game played by two teams of five players each. Players score points by throwing a large, round ball through a goal, which is called a **basket**: *You need a lot of energy to play **basketball**, because it is a very fast game.*
2. The ball used in this game is also called a **basketball**: *My parents are going to buy me a new **basketball** for my birthday present.*

The game of **basketball** was invented and named in 1891 by Dr. James Naismith of Springfield, Massachusetts. For the goal, he actually used a basket—an empty wooden basket that had been used to hold peaches.

The player on the blue team is about to put the **basketball** through the basket.

bat[1] • bats

A **bat** is a long, hard piece of wood or metal that you use to hit a ball in baseball, softball, and some other games.

Bats use their claws to hang upside-down from branches.

bat[2] ▲ • bats

A **bat** is also a small flying animal that has a body like a mouse and wings of thin skin: ***Bats** fly around and hunt during the night.*

bath • baths

When you take a **bath**, you wash yourself in a tub of water: *I take a shower every day, and I also take a warm **bath** once a week. There is a very large **bathtub** in our **bathroom**.*

bathing suit

A **bathing suit** is what you wear when you go swimming: *My older sister gave me her old **bathing suit** when she got a new and bigger one.*

battery ▸ • batteries

A **battery** has materials in it that make electricity for flashlights, radios, car engines, watches, and many other machines: *My watch has stopped—it needs a new **battery**.*

You need to use **batteries** in many electric games.

battle • **battles**

A **battle** is a fight between armies, ships, airplanes, or other groups who use weapons to hurt or kill each other: *The* ***battle*** *between the armies lasted for two days.*

bay • **bays**

A **bay** is a part of a sea or a lake that has land around some or most of it: *The waves are never too high in this* ***bay****.*

be • **was, were, been, being**

Be is a special word that we use very often. We use it to show where something is or what something is like: *My cousin Jenny will* ***be*** *here next week.*

beach • **beaches**

A **beach** is an area of sand or small rocks along the edge of an ocean, river, or lake: *During summer I go the* ***beach*** *every week and swim in the ocean.*

beak ▶ • **beaks**

The hard, pointed part of a bird's or a turtle's mouth is its **beak**: *An eagle has a strong, curved* ***beak****.*

bean • **beans**

A **bean** is a seed that you can eat as a vegetable. Beans grow in long, thin cases called pods: *I sometimes have hamburger and* ***beans*** *for dinner.*

bear ▲ • **bears**

A **bear** is a large, strong animal with thick fur, a very short tail, and sharp claws: *Some* ***bears*** *can be very dangerous when they are angry or frightened.*

The **beak** of a toucan is very colorful.

beard • beards

A **beard** is the hair that grows on a man's cheeks and chin: *Our school principal has a thick, long, red **beard**.*

beast • beasts

Any animal that has four legs is a **beast**: *Dogs, cats, and elephants are **beasts**, but birds are not.*

Beast now means any four-legged animal, but at first the word meant only one kind—a wild deer. In England long ago, deer were thought to be the most important wild animals that lived there. This is because they were the main animals that people hunted for food.

Beavers build homes and dams with branches and trees.

The musicians played the song by **beating** on the drums.

beat ▲ • beat, beaten *or* beat, beating

1. If you **beat** something, you hit it and then keep hitting it: *A drummer **beats** a drum with a stick.*
2. You **beat** someone if you win against them in a game or contest: *We **beat** their team in the final game.*

beautiful

We say something is **beautiful** if it is very nice to look at, or if it makes us happy when we see, hear, or think about it: *Mom said that the picture I drew of her was **beautiful**. Dad said my picture was a thing of **beauty**.*

beaver ◀ • beavers

A **beaver** is an animal with a wide, flat tail and webbed back feet for swimming. Beavers eat bark and leaves and live in water.

because

You say **because** when you want to give a reason for something: *I couldn't go to the party **because** I had a cold.*

become • became, becoming

You use **become** when something starts to be or grows to be: *I was not good at baseball when I started to play, but I have **become** better this year.*

bed ▸ • beds

A **bed** is used for sleeping on or resting: *I have two **beds** in my **bedroom**.*

There are around 20,000 kinds of **bees**.

bee ▲ • bees

A **bee** is an insect with four wings and black and yellow stripes on its round, hairy body. Some bees make honey.

beef

The meat from an animal called a cow, steer, or bull is **beef**: *Hamburgers are made with **beef**.*

Our pets have a special **bed** to sleep on.

been

Been is a form of the word BE: *Sally has **been** swimming in the lake with her brother.*

beetle ▼ • beetles

A **beetle** is an insect with hard wings that open when it flies and close up again when it stops.

before

Before means ahead of or in front of: *The number two comes **before** the number three. I ate breakfast **before** I left for school.*

beg • begged, begging

To **beg** means to ask for gifts of money, food, or help: *We saw a poor, homeless man **beg** for money.*

begin • began, begun

To **begin** means to start something: *My tennis lessons **begin** this weekend. This Saturday will be the **beginning** of my classes.*

Two male Hercules **beetles** fight near a female.

The man pulls on ropes to make the **bells** ring.

behave • behaved, behaving

1. To **behave** means to do things in the right way or act in a good way: *The teacher told us to **behave** when she left the room.*

2. To **behave** also means to act in a certain way: *My parents told me to **behave** well at Grandma's house. My good **behavior** made Grandma happy.*

behind

Behind means at the back of: *The baby ducks followed **behind** their mother.*

being • beings

1. **Being** is a form of the word BE: *I laughed because Dave was **being** really funny.*

2. A **being** is an animal or person: *We are human **beings**.*

believe • believed, believing

When you **believe**, you feel sure that something is real or true: *I **believe** we can win the game if we all play our best. My **belief** is that we can win the game.*

bell ◀ • bells

A **bell** makes a ringing sound when it is hit or shaken: *I rang my bicycle **bell** to make the dog get out of the way.*

belong • belonged, belonging

1. If something **belongs** to you, it means that it is yours and that you own it: *This book **belongs** to me, but you can borrow it.*

2. When something **belongs** somewhere, that is its proper or usual place: *Put the forks in the top drawer, where they **belong**.*

below ▼

When something is **below**, it is in a lower place: *At camp, Jimmy's bed was **below** mine.*

The red shoes are **below** the black shoes on the stairs.

belt • belts

A **belt** is something that keeps pants or a skirt from falling down: *Amy is wearing a pink **belt** around the waist of her blue jeans.*

We have a wooden **bench** in our yard.

bench ▲ • benches

A **bench** is a long seat: *We sat together on a wooden **bench** beside the river.*

bend ▶ • bent, bending

To **bend** something is to change it from being straight: *I **bent** down to tie my shoelaces.*

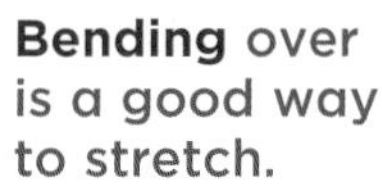

Bending over is a good way to stretch.

beneath

Beneath means below something or someone: *The water of the river flowed **beneath** the bridge.*

berry ▼ • berries

A **berry** is a small, round, soft fruit with seeds. Some kinds of berry plants are the strawberry, raspberry, and blueberry: *Every summer, we pick **berries** at Uncle Bob's farm.*

We ate the **berries** we picked for dessert.

beside ▼

Beside means next to: *Jo sits **beside** Alex in class.*

best

When something is **best**, it is better than all the others: *The **best** mark you can get on the test is 100, if you answer every question right. The Sharks are the **best** team in our Little League and have won all their games.*

bet • bets, betted, betting

1. When you **bet**, you make a guess about something that is going to happen: *Mom **bet** with Dad about who would win the game.*
2. A **bet** is an agreement to pay money or give away something special if you are wrong about your guess: *Jamie made a **bet** of two baseball cards that he could hit a home run in the next game.*

The two dogs are sitting **beside** each other.

better
Better is more of something that is good: *I studied hard for the test and got a **better** mark than I did on the last one. The team plays **better** now than they used to, because they have several good new players.*

between ▶
Something is **between** when it is in the middle: *In the photo I am standing **between** my dad and my mom.*

beyond
Beyond means on the other side of or far away from: *The library is **beyond** the park.*

bicycle ▼ • bicycles
A **bicycle** has two wheels, one in front of the other. It is moved along by pushing down with the feet on two flat parts called pedals. A short word for bicycle is **bike**.

Emma rides her **bicycle** to work every day.

The vanilla ice cream is **between** the strawberry and the chocolate.

big • bigger, biggest
When something is **big**, it is large or there is a lot of it: *That shirt is too **big** for me—I need a smaller size.*

The largest **bills** now printed in America are worth 100 dollars.

bill ▲ • bills
1. A **bill** is a piece of paper money: *Grandma gave me a five-dollar **bill** for helping her in the garden.*
2. A **bill** is also a piece of paper showing how much money has to be paid: *When you eat in a restaurant, they give you a **bill** for the food you have.*

biography • biographies
A **biography** is the story of a person's life written by someone else: *This book is a **biography** of President George Washington.*

biology
Biology is a science. It is the study of life and all living things. A **biologist** can study things like how animals and plants live, or the places where they live.

bird ▶ • birds
A **bird** is an animal with wings and feathers. Birds lay eggs. Most birds are able to fly. A chicken, an eagle, and a robin are kinds of birds.

birds

There are more than 9,000 kinds of birds. The smallest bird is the tiny bee hummingbird. The largest bird, the ostrich, is taller than a basketball player. Most birds can fly but some, such as penguins, cannot fly.

Many kinds of birds live in city parks.

birthday • birthdays
A **birthday** is the day you are born. Your **birth** is remembered on your birthday each year: *My cousin and I were born on the same day, so each year we share a party for our **birthday**.*

bit • bits
A **bit** is a small piece or a small amount: *Ted gave me a **bit** of his hamburger.*

bite ▶ • bites, bit *or* bitten, biting
1. When you **bite**, you use your teeth to cut into something: *The dog **bit** off a piece of the beef bone.*
2. A **bite** is the small piece taken with the teeth: *Jamie took a **bite** of his sandwich.*

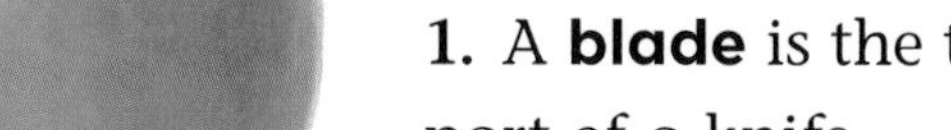

I took a **bite** of the apple.

bitter
Something is **bitter** if it has a sharp or sour taste: *The lemon juice tasted very **bitter**.*

black
Black is a very dark color. Black is the color of night or coal.

blade ▼ • blades
1. A **blade** is the thin, flat, sharp part of a knife.
2. The thin, flat part of something else, such as a fan, is also called a **blade**.

blame • blamed, blaming
When you **blame** someone, you say that they have done something bad or wrong: *Rory **blamed** the bus driver for making him late for school.*

The spinning **blades** on helicopters make them fly.

blanket ▶ • **blankets**

A **blanket** is a cover that people use to keep warm when they are sleeping: *Our cat sleeps on an old **blanket** in a basket.*

bleed • **bled, bleeding**

To **bleed** means to lose blood: *Jenny was **bleeding** from the cut on her finger.*

Some trees **bloom** every spring.

blind

When you are **blind** you cannot see. Blind people read special books that have raised dots that they can feel instead of letters.

block ▶ • **blocks**

1\. A **block** is hard and it has flat sides: *We built a castle with our wooden **blocks**.*

An igloo is a small building made with **blocks** of ice.

2\. A **block** is also an area inside four streets. You can also talk about a block between two streets: *We live four **blocks** from the shopping center.*

blood

Blood is the red liquid that goes inside your body. Blood is pushed through your body by your heart.

bloom ◀ • **bloomed, blooming**

When a tree or plant is **blooming**, it has flowers or **blossoms** on it: *The rose bushes in our garden are **blooming** now.*

blouse • **blouses**

A **blouse** is a piece of clothing like a shirt, made for girls and women.

blow ▼ • **blew, blowing**

1\. When you **blow**, you put air into something: *Mom asked me to **blow** up the balloons for the party.*

2\. To **blow** also means to move something with air: *Sam **blew** the dust off the old books we found in the attic.*

Isaac is **blowing** on the dandelion.

A
B
C
D
E
F
G
H
I
J
K
L
M
N
O
P
Q
R
S
T
U
V
W
X
Y
Z

boats

Boats are used to carry people and things across water. Sailboats are pushed along by the wind, while people use oars or paddles to move rowboats and canoes. Boats can be used for fun, for fishing, or for taking things from one place to another.

blue

Blue is a color. Blue is the color of the sky in the daytime, when there are no clouds.

board • boards

1. A **board** is a flat, long piece of wood. Boards are used in building houses, fences, and furniture.
2. A **board** is also a flat piece of stiff paper. This kind of board is used for drawing and for games: *We took our **board** games on vacation.*

boat ▲ • boats

A **boat** is used to travel on water. Some boats have sails and are moved by the wind. Some boats have motors.

body ◀ • bodies

A **body** is all the parts of a person, animal, or other kind of creature: *A bird's **body** is covered with feathers.*

We wear clothes to keep our **body** warm.

My parents read many **books**.

boil • boiled, boiling

1. To **boil** means to make a liquid very hot: *When water **boils**, it makes bubbles and steam.*

2. Boil also means to cook something in boiling water: *Dad **boiled** the carrots in a big pot of water.*

bomb • bombs

A **bomb** is something that is made to blow up. A bomb is used to hurt people, animals, and houses.

bone ▼ • bones

Bone is the hard part inside a person's body. The bones in your head have a round shape. The bones in your legs and arms are long and thin.

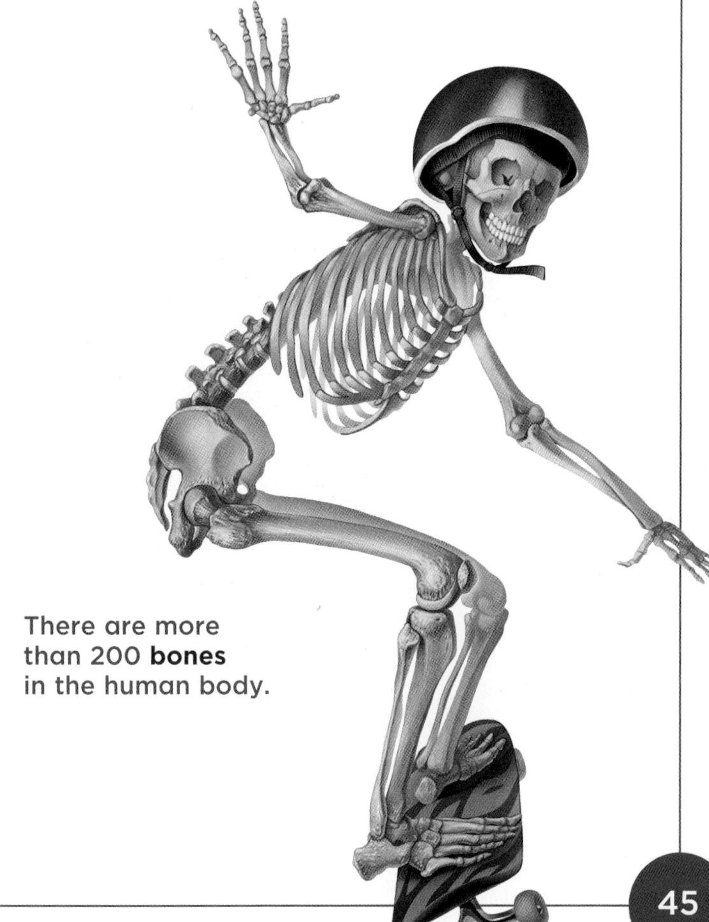

There are more than 200 **bones** in the human body.

book ◀ • books

A **book** has pieces of paper inside two covers. The pieces of paper inside a book are called pages. The pages of a book have words and sometimes pictures too.

boot ▶ • boots

A **boot** is a shoe that covers your foot and the bottom part of your leg: *Dad is buying me new **boots** to wear on our camping trip.*

My uncle has owned his cowboy **boots** for years.

born

When you are **born**, you start your life in the world: *We watched our puppies being **born** yesterday.*

borrow • borrowed, borrowing

To **borrow** means to take something from someone and then give it back: *My sister let me **borrow** her bike while she was at camp.*

boss • bosses, bossed, bossing

1. A **boss** is a person who runs a business or who is in charge of other people: *The **boss** of the company says he is going to move their office to another city.*

2. To **boss** is to tell others what to do: *I wish my older brother would stop **bossing** me around.*

both

Both means not just one, but two people or things: *Cats and dogs **both** make good pets.*

bother • bothered, bothering

If you **bother** people, you cause trouble for them or make them upset: *The noisy birds outside my window **bothered** me and made it hard to sleep.*

bottle ▲ • bottles

A **bottle** is a container that holds liquids: *The orange juice is in a glass **bottle** on the table.*

bottom ▼ • bottoms

The **bottom** of something is its lowest part: *Mark had chewing gum stuck to the **bottom** of his shoe.*

bought

Bought is a form of the word BUY: *Yesterday I went to the pet store and **bought** a goldfish.*

Crabs live in the sand on the **bottom** of rivers and oceans.

Tina is **bouncing** her ball on the ground.

bounce ▶ • bounced, bouncing

To **bounce** means to move back quickly after hitting something: *You can **bounce** a basketball before taking a shot at the basket.*

bow ▼ • bows

1. A **bow** is a special type of knot: *Tie your shoelace in a **bow** to make it easy to undo.*
2. A **bow** is also a thin strip of wood that is bent by a string tied to each end. It is used to shoot arrows: *The hunter used a **bow** and arrows to kill the deer.*

We tied the gold ribbon in a **bow** on Malcolm's present.

bowl • bowls

A **bowl** is a rounded dish with high sides. It is usually used to hold food or a liquid: *Nathan ate a **bowl** of cereal for breakfast.*

box • boxes

A **box** is a container that usually has four flat sides. Boxes can be made of cardboard, wood, or plastic: *Sarah keeps her rings in a jewelry **box**.*

boy • boys

A **boy** is a male child who grows up to be a man: *My brother, Alan, is the only **boy** in our family.*

brace • braces

1. A **brace** is something that holds the parts of a thing together or helps it to stand up or stay up: *After Annie fell off her horse, she had to wear a neck **brace** for a while.*
2. **Braces** are also wires that are put on your teeth to help make them straight: *I will have to get **braces** because my teeth are not straight.*

bracelet ▶ • bracelets

A **bracelet** is a piece of jewelry worn around the arm: *Rosa lost her **bracelet** when it slipped off over her hand.*

I made this **bracelet** for my little sister.

braid ▼ • braids, braided, braiding

1. When you **braid** something like hair or silk, you divide it into three bunches and put these over and under each other.
2. A **braid** is a long strip of hair or other things that have been braided: *Today I wore my hair in **braids**.*

Claudia had her hair **braided** when she was on vacation.

A B C D E F G H I J K L M N O P Q R S T U V W X Y Z

brand • brands

A **brand** of a product is one of a particular name: *Dad buys that **brand** of toothpaste because it tastes nice. Coca-Cola and Pepsi are well-known **brands** of soda.*

Some animals can wrap their tail around a **branch** and hang upside-down.

brain • brains

The **brain** is an important part inside the head of people and animals. It controls how they think, feel, and move: *When you touch something hot, your nerves send a message to your **brain** to tell you to take your finger away.*

brake • brakes

A **brake** is something that makes a car, truck, or other vehicle go more slowly or stop. Some brakes work by using a hand control, but others use a foot control: *The bus driver put her foot on the **brake** when she saw the red light.*

branch ▲ • branches

A **branch** is part of a tree or bush growing out from the main trunk that has leaves growing on it: *The **branches** of the apple tree hung low because they had so many apples growing on them.*

brave • braver, bravest

If you are **brave**, you can face danger without being afraid or showing fear: *Brandon was **brave** and jumped into the water to save the little boy who could not swim.*

bread ▼ • breads

Bread is a food made by mixing together and then baking flour, water, and other things: *Would you please give me the **bread** so I can make a sandwich?*

My grandmother buys **bread** at the bakery to serve at dinner.

The shell **broke** when the egg dropped on the floor.

break ▶ • **broke, broken, breaking**
1. When you **break** something, you make it separate into two or more pieces: *I saw the window* ***break*** *when a rock hit it.*
2. If something **breaks**, it does not work anymore: *We couldn't watch the TV because it was* ***broken****.*

The warm **breeze** helped the laundry on the line dry quickly.

breakfast • **breakfasts**
Breakfast is the first meal that you eat after you wake up in the morning: *Alicia ate an egg for her* ***breakfast****.*

The word **breakfast** comes from an old saying, "to break the fast." A "fast" is when you do not eat any food for a long time. So your breakfast "breaks the fast" after you have not eaten overnight.

breath • **breaths**
Your **breath** is the air you take into your body and breathe out again: *It was such a cold morning that Nick could see his* ***breath*** *in the air.*

breathe ▼ • **breathed, breathing**
To **breathe** is to take air into your body and then let it out: *It was hard to* ***breathe*** *because the air was filled with smoke.*

breeze ◀ • **breezes**
A **breeze** is a light, gentle wind: *At the end of the hot day, the cool* ***breeze*** *made us feel better.*

brick • **bricks**
A **brick** is a block of clay that has been baked. Bricks are used in building: *The builder made the garden wall out of* ***bricks****.*

Divers use special equipment so they can **breathe** underwater.

a b c d e f g h i j k l m n o p q r s t u v w x y z

A B C D E F G H I J K L M N O P Q R S T U V W X Y Z

bridge ▸ • bridges

A **bridge** is built over a river, road, or railroad line to let people cross from one side to the other: *We rode our bikes over the **bridge** to get to the other side of the river.*

The stone **bridge** was built across the river.

bright ▾ • brighter, brightest

1. Something that is **bright** gives out a lot of light or is full of light: *I put on my sunglasses because the sun was so **bright**.*
2. If you are **bright**, you are smart: *When Elizabeth got all her math problems right, her teacher said she was a **bright** girl.*

New York City has many **bright** lights.

bring • brought, bringing

To **bring** means to take something or someone with you to go somewhere: *Hank forgot to **bring** his towel with him to the beach.*

broke

Broke is a form of the word BREAK: *I dropped the glass of milk and it **broke**.* When something breaks into pieces or no longer works, it is **broken**.

broom ▸ • brooms

A **broom** is a brush that has a long handle. You use a broom to sweep with: *Jake cleaned up the dirt on the kitchen floor with a **broom**.*

Dad used a **broom** to sweep up the broken plate.

brother ▸ • brothers

A **brother** is a boy or man who has the same mother and father as you: *Mom and Dad took my **brother** and me to see a movie.*

Stephanie and her two **brothers** are watching the game.

brought

Brought is a form of the word BRING: *I **brought** my umbrella because it looked like it was going to rain.*

brown • browner, brownest

Brown is the color that is darker than yellow but not as dark as black: *Natalie's eyes are as **brown** as dark chocolate.*

The **bucket** is filled with things used for cleaning.

brush • brushes, brushed, brushing

1. A **brush** is a tool with stiff hair or wire set in a block of something hard, such as wood. Sometimes a brush has a short handle. Brushes are used for painting, cleaning, or to make your hair neat: *After you have finished your painting, wash the **brush** that you used.*
2. You **brush** something when you use a brush to clean it or make it neat: *Matthew **brushed** his hair before he went to school.*

bubble ▾ • bubbles

A **bubble** is small ball of air in a liquid or inside a drop of something: *There were lots of **bubbles** in the lemon soda.*

bucket ◂ • buckets

A **bucket** is a round, open container with a flat bottom and a handle: *Danny carried water from the pond in a **bucket**.*

Natasha is blowing **bubbles**.

buffalo ▼ • **buffaloes** *or* **buffalos** *or* **buffalo**

1. A **buffalo** is a large animal from North America with short horns and a coat of thick brown hair. It is also called a bison: *Wild* ***buffaloes*** *once lived on the plains of North America.*

2. **Buffaloes** are also oxen from Africa and Asia: *A* ***buffalo*** *pulled the cart.*

bug ▶ • **bugs**

A **bug** is an insect with four wings and a mouth that can bite: *Damian caught a* ***bug*** *and put it in a jar to look at, then he let it go again.*

Stink **bugs** make a strong smell to keep enemies away.

build • **built, building**

When you **build** something, you make it from other things: *Dad helped us* ***build*** *a tree house out of wood.*

When I visited Charleston, South Carolina, I saw beautiful **buildings** next to a park.

building ▲ • **buildings**

A **building** is something people make to work, live, and do other things inside: *In our town there are houses, stores, schools, churches, and many other kinds of* ***buildings****.*

bulb ▶ • **bulbs**

1. A **bulb** is the rounded part of some plants that is under the ground. New plants grow from bulbs: *Steve planted flower* ***bulbs*** *that will grow in spring.*

2. A **bulb** is also anything with a rounded shape like the bulb of a plant: *The light* ***bulb*** *broke, so Mom put in a new one.*

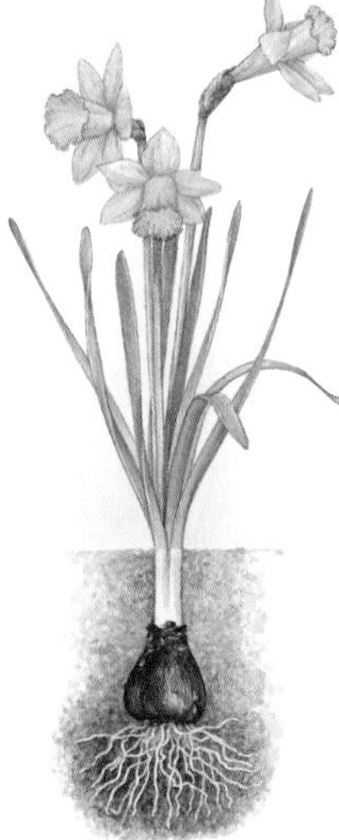

Daffodils grow from **bulbs.**

American **buffaloes,** also called bison, live in herds.

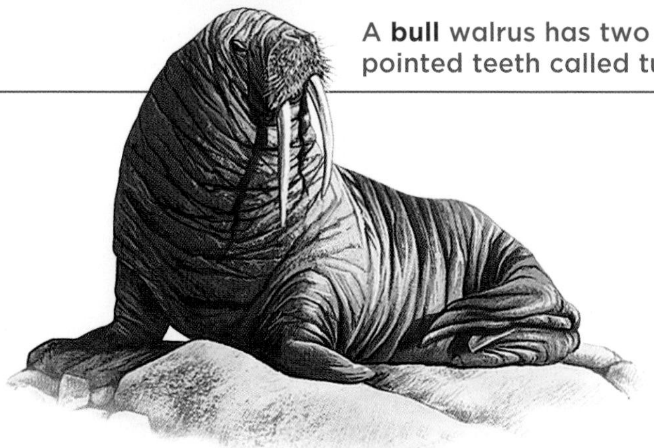

A **bull** walrus has two long pointed teeth called tusks.

bull ▲ • bulls

1. A **bull** is the adult male of cattle: ***Bulls** are usually much bigger than cows.*

2. A **bull** is also the adult male of certain animals, such as elephants, whales, or seals: *The two **bull** elephants hurt each other when they had a fight.*

bulldozer ▼ • bulldozers

A **bulldozer** is a big kind of vehicle with a wide, curved blade in front. Bulldozers are used to move dirt and rocks: *The land was made flat with a **bulldozer** before the house was built.*

bully • bullies

A **bully** is a person who tries to scare or be mean to another person. Bullies often pick on people they think are not as strong as they are.

Bulldozers are used on farms and to prepare the land for new buildings.

bump • bumps, bumped, bumping

1. If you **bump** something, you hit it or knock it sharply: *Megan **bumped** the cup and it fell over.*

2. A **bump** is something rounded that sticks up higher than the area around it: *Ryan has a **bump** on his leg where the baseball hit him.*

When the fire started in the forest, the dry branches **burned** quickly.

bunch • bunches

A **bunch** is a group of things that are like each other and are together: *Mom bought a **bunch** of grapes at the store.*

burn ▲ • burned *or* burnt, burning

1. To **burn** means to be on fire: *When the house was **burning**, a fire engine came to put out the flames.*

2. To **burn** also means to be hurt by something hot: *Hank **burned** his hand on the hot stove.*

I ride the school **bus** every morning and afternoon.

A B C D E F G H I J K L M N O P Q R S T U V W X Y Z

bury • buried, burying

When you **bury** something, you put it under the ground: *The dog **buried** the bone in some dirt in the yard.*

bus ▲ • buses

A **bus** is a big vehicle that can carry lots of people: *The whole class went to the zoo on a **bus**.*

Three years ago, we planted this **bush** in our yard.

bush ◀ • bushes

A **bush** is a large plant with lots of branches that is shorter than a tree: *Blueberries grow on **bushes**.*

business ▶ • businesses

1. **Business** is the work someone does to earn money: *Selling computers is a big **business** in this country.*
2. A **business** is also a place like a store, factory, restaurant, or farm where people work to earn money: *The **business** in that building on the corner is a pet store.*

busy ▶ • busier, busiest

If you are **busy**, you are doing something and cannot do anything else: *Dad cannot come to the phone because he is **busy** washing the car.*

Wayne cannot watch TV because he is **busy** doing his homework.

but

1. **But** is a word that is used to show how things or people are different to each other: *That book is about horses, **but** this one is about fish.*
2. **But** can also be used to mean except: *Everyone in the class **but** Peter got that question wrong.*

butter

Butter is a yellow food that is made from the fat in milk: *Megan spread **butter** on her toast.*

Erica and her brother set up their lemonade **business** on weekends.

butterflies

Butterflies live in most parts of the world. They travel to different places during the year in search of warmer or colder temperatures. A butterfly egg changes into a caterpillar before eventually turning into an adult butterfly.

White admiral

Monarch

Painted lady

88 butterfly

Swallowtail

butterfly ▲ • butterflies
A **butterfly** is an insect with four large wings that usually have bright colors.

button ▶ • buttons
1. A **button** is a small object that holds parts of clothing together. Buttons are often round: *It was cold, so Roy did up the **buttons** on his jacket.*
2. A **button** is also a small part that you turn or press to make something work or stop: *Theo pressed the elevator **button** to make it go to the fifth floor.*

Mom keeps some extra **buttons** in a sewing kit.

buy • bought, buying
When you **buy** something, you get it by paying money for it: *Grandma is going to **buy** me a new bicycle for my birthday.*

by
1. **By** means close to or beside: *When you come into the house, please leave your shoes **by** the door.*
2. **By** also means to be not later than: *Georgia has to go to bed **by** 8 o'clock.*

a b c d e f g h i j k l m n o p q r s t u v w x y z

cabin ▶ • **cabins**

A **cabin** is a small, simple house, usually made of wood: *We stayed in a log **cabin** in the country that had only two rooms.*

cactus ▼ • **cactuses** *or* **cacti** *or* **cactus**

A **cactus** is a plant that grows in very dry places. It has a thick stem and sharp, thin points instead of leaves: *Some kinds of **cactuses** are as small as your thumb and some grow as big as a tree.*

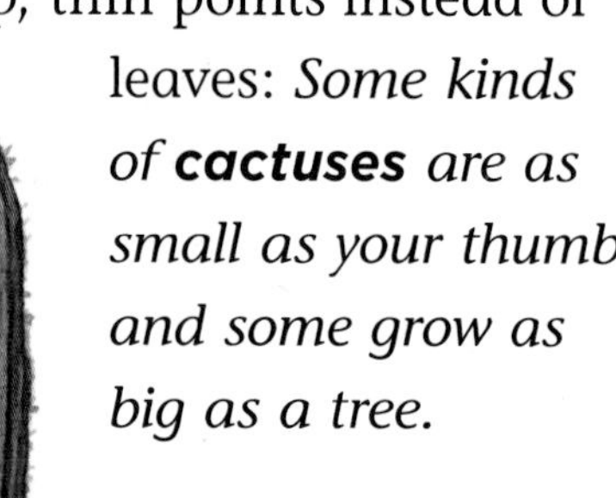

Cactuses grow in the desert and can live on a small amount of rain.

cafeteria • **cafeterias**

A **cafeteria** is a kind of restaurant. You pick out the food that you want, and then take it to a table yourself: *On school days, Sam gets his lunch at the school **cafeteria**.*

cage • **cages**

A **cage** is a box made of wire or metal bars that animals can be kept in: *My uncle keeps two pet birds in a **cage**.*

In the past, Americans built log **cabins** as homes.

cake • **cakes**

A **cake** is a sweet food that is baked in the oven. Cakes are made from flour, eggs, butter, and sugar: *Ryan cut his birthday **cake** into six parts so that we could each have a piece.*

calculator ▶ • **calculators**

A **calculator** is a small machine that you use to do math: *Sometimes I add up numbers on paper and sometimes I use my **calculator** to do it.*

The teacher asked everyone to bring a **calculator** to class.

A whale **calf** swims close to its mother for protection.

calendar • calendars

A **calendar** is a list that shows you the days, weeks, and months in a year: *Anne marked the dates of her vacation on the **calendar**.*

The **calendar** we use today came from one used about 2,000 years ago in Rome, Italy. In ancient Rome, the first day of each month was called *Calends*. When the calendar was invented, this word was used as the name for it.

calf[1] ▲ • calves

A **calf** is a baby cow. A baby seal, elephant, or whale is also called a calf: *We watched the mother cow feeding her **calf**.*

calf[2] • calves

The **calf** is also the part of the back of your leg, between your knee and your foot: *Matt pulled the sock up over his **calf** to his knee.*

call • calls, called, calling

1. When you **call**, you speak in a loud voice or cry out: *The lost boy **called** for help.*

2. To **call** also means to give a name to someone or something: *Joe **called** his dog "Snowflake."*

3. Call also means to talk to someone by telephone: *Jenny **called** her grandmother in Texas to wish her "happy birthday."*

4. When you talk to someone on the telephone, you are making a **call**: *Dad said he would give us a **call** from the airport.*

5. A **call** is also a sound made by a bird or animal: *Some owls have a **call** that sounds like "whoo whoo."*

came

Came is a form of the word COME: *Jesse heard me knocking and **came** to open the door.*

Allegra often **camps** in the forest because she likes to spend time outdoors.

camel ▼ • **camels**

A **camel** is a tall animal with a long neck and either one or two large bumps on its back. Camels can go for a long time without water: ***Camels*** *are used to carry people and things across the desert.*

camera ▶ • **cameras**

A **camera** is an object that you use to take photographs or to make movies: *Charles has a* ***camera*** *that takes photos underwater.*

camp ◀ • **camps, camped, camping**

1. A **camp** is place with tents or cabins where people live for a short time: *The Boy Scouts spent the week at a* ***camp*** *in the mountains.*
2. When you **camp**, you live in a tent and cook outdoors for a short time: *Last summer our family* ***camped*** *by the lake and went fishing every day.*

Ben used his new **camera** to take pictures of his friends.

can[1] • **could**

If you **can** do something, it means you know how to do it: *Emily* ***can*** *play the piano very well. My baby sister* ***can*** *stand up by herself.*

Long ago in China, people rode **camels** to travel around the country.

can[2] ▸ • cans

Mom opened a **can** of corn to heat for dinner.

A **can** is a container made of metal. Cans are used to hold food, drink, and other things: *Daniel had a* ***can*** *of soda with his lunch.*

candidate • candidates

A **candidate** is a person who runs in an election. A candidate wants people to vote for him or her: *Nicole was the most popular* ***candidate*** *in the election for school president.*

candle • candles

A **candle** is a long, thin piece of wax with a piece of string through the middle of it. A candle gives light when it burns: *Aaron blew out the* ***candle*** *and the room went dark.*

candy ▾ • candies

A **candy** is a sweet food. A chocolate bar is a kind of candy: *Every child at the party got a small bag of* ***candy****.*

can't

Can't is a shorter way of saying "cannot," which means that you are not able to do something or that you do not know how to do it: *I* ***can't*** *undo this knot. I* ***cannot*** *work out how you tied it.*

A lollipop is a kind of hard **candy** that has a stick to hold on to.

canyon ▾ • canyons

A **canyon** is a deep, narrow valley with high, straight sides: *Many* ***canyons*** *have a river at the bottom.*

cap • caps

A **cap** is a small round hat with a piece at the front: *I wear a* ***cap*** *to keep the sun out of my eyes. Baseball players wear* ***caps*** *as part of their uniform.*

The Grand **Canyon** in Arizona is about one mile deep.

capital • capitals

1. The **capital** of a country or state is the city where the government has its main buildings and offices: *The* ***capital*** *of the United States is Washington, D.C.*
2. A **capital** is also the bigger form of a letter of the alphabet. You use a capital for the first letter of a sentence and for a proper name, such as *Maria, California,* or *Lake Michigan*: *A, B, and C are the* ***capitals*** *for the letters a, b, and c.*

A B C D E F G H I J K L M N O P Q R S T U V W X Y Z

cars

In 1908, Henry Ford started making the Model T in his factory in Detroit, Michigan. Its price was $850 and it was the first car that many people had enough money to buy. Now, a lot of families own more than one car, and racing cars is a popular sport.

Ford Model T

Volkswagen Beetle

Cadillac convertible

Le Mans race car

Indy 500 race car

captain • captains

1. A **captain** is the person in charge of a boat or ship: *The **captain** steered the sailboat out of the harbor into the ocean.*
2. A **captain** can also be a person who is in charge of a group: *Morgan is the **captain** of our basketball team.*

car ◀ • cars

A **car** is a machine that you ride in on a road. It has four wheels and a motor: *Mom drives us to school in her **car**.*

card • cards

A **card** is a piece of thick paper with words, pictures, or numbers on it: *Grandma sent me a "get-well" **card** when I broke my arm.*

cardinal ▶ • cardinals

A **cardinal** is a bird with a thick beak, and feathers that stand up on its head. The male cardinal is mostly red.

Cardinals eat insects, seeds, and fruits.

care • cared, caring

If you **care** about something, you worry or think about it because it is important to you: *I **care** about my school grades and I want to do well.*

careful

If you are **careful**, you are thinking about what you are doing and you want to do it right: *I was **careful** not to go over the lines when I was coloring in the picture.*

careless

If you are **careless,** you are not thinking about what you are doing and you may not do it in the right way: *He was **careless** while pouring the milk, and he spilled some.*

carnival ◀ • carnivals

A **carnival** is a special kind of party with food, music, dancing, and games. Some carnivals also have a parade: *There will be clowns and pony rides at the **carnival**.*

Carnival comes from *carne*, a word that means "meat." The first type of carnival was a Christian holiday when people ate a lot of meat. This holiday was on the day before they were not supposed to eat any meat for 40 days.

carriage • carriages

A **carriage** is a vehicle with wheels for carrying people: *The king left the castle in a **carriage** pulled by six white horses.*

We bought **carrots** at the farmers' market.

carrot ▲ • carrots

A **carrot** is a plant with a long, orange-colored root that people eat as a vegetable: *You can eat **carrots** raw or you can cook them.*

carry ▶ • carried, carrying

If you **carry** something, you hold it and take it from one place to another: *Rosie helped her brother **carry** the food to the table.*

cart • carts

1. A **cart** is a wagon with two wheels. A cart is usually pulled by an animal: *The old farmer took his vegetables to the market on a **cart**.*
2. A **cart** is also a small wagon with four wheels that people use in a supermarket to carry the things they are going to buy: *He pushed the **cart** of groceries out to the car.*

carton • cartons

A **carton** is a container made of strong, stiff paper. Some food is sold in cartons: *Jan bought a **carton** of eggs at the store.*

cartoon • cartoons

A **cartoon** is a drawing that is funny or tells a story. There are cartoons in newspapers and magazines, and other cartoons on television and at the movies: *The children are watching a Rugrats **cartoon**.*

The women **carry** coffee beans in baskets.

carve • **carved, carving**
1. If you **carve** something like wood or stone, you cut it to make a shape: *The old sailor **carved** a tiny whale out of a piece of wood.*
2. **Carve** also means to cut meat into pieces: *Uncle Bill **carved** the roast beef for our dinner.*

case[1] • **cases**
A **case** is one example of something: *The police say that it was a **case** of murder.* **In case of** means if there is: *We took our umbrellas **in case of** rain.*

case[2] • **cases**
A **case** is also a box for holding something: *My brother bought a **case** to carry his computer when he goes away on business trips.*

cash • **cash**
Cash is money in the form of bills or coins: *Mom went to the bank to get some **cash**.*

cast • **casts**
A **cast** is a bandage covered with a paste that gets very hard when it dries. A cast is put around a broken bone to protect it: *My friends drew pictures on the **cast** on my broken arm.*

castle ◀ • **castles**
A **castle** is a large building with towers and high, strong walls to keep enemies out. In old times many years ago, kings and queens lived in castles.

cat ▶ • **cats**
1. A **cat** is an animal with fur and a long tail. Many people have a cat as a pet: *Jim gave his **cat** a dish of milk.*
2. Some kinds of **cats** are large and wild: *Lions, leopards, and tigers are **cats**.*

Castles were built to keep people safe from enemies.

cats

All cats have sharp claws and teeth. They are good hunters. Cats see well in the dark and often hunt at night. Small cats, such as house cats, catch mice and birds. Big cats, such as lions, hunt large animals for food.

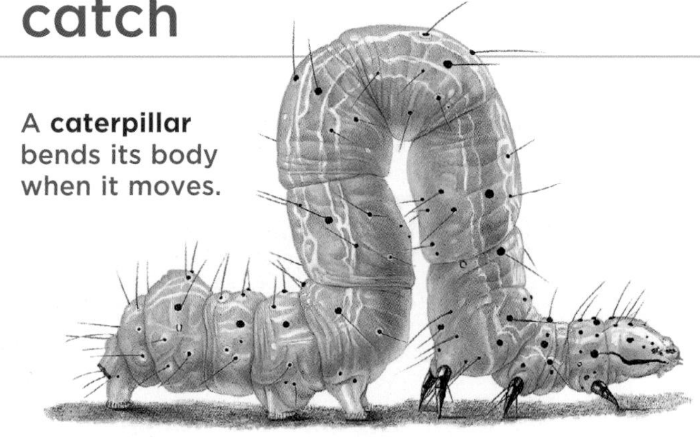
A **caterpillar** bends its body when it moves.

catch • caught, catching

To **catch** means to grab hold of something that is moving: *Jonathan moved quickly to **catch** the football.* *In baseball, the **catcher** is the player whose job is to catch the ball when the pitcher throws it.*

caterpillar ▲ • caterpillars

A **caterpillar** looks like a short, fat worm. A caterpillar will turn into a moth or butterfly: *Grandpa doesn't like **caterpillars** because they eat the leaves of his plants.*

The word **caterpillar** may come from two old French words that mean "cat" and "hair." When people first saw this insect, they thought it looked like a tiny cat covered with hairs.

catsup • catsups

Catsup is a thick liquid food made from tomatoes that you eat with other foods: *Josh put some **catsup** on his hamburger.* This word is sometimes spelled **ketchup**.

cattle ▼

Cattle are large animals that people use for meat and for milk. Cows and bulls are cattle: *Matt wants to be a cowboy when he grows up, and look after **cattle** on a ranch.*

caught

Caught is a form of the word CATCH: *Haley **caught** the dog by the collar before it could run away.*

cause • causes, caused, causing

1. To **cause** means to make something happen: *The thick fog **caused** several accidents on the road.*

2. A **cause** is a person or thing that makes something happen: *The **cause** of the forest fire was lightning hitting a dead tree.*

Every morning, the farmer puts his **cattle** out in the field.

cave ▶ • caves

A **cave** is a large, hollow space in a rocky place. Caves can be under the ground or in the side of a mountain: *Some bears live in **caves** in the winter.*

cavity • cavities

A **cavity** is a hole in a tooth: *The dentist filled a **cavity** in my tooth.*

I store computer data on a **CD**.

CD ◀ • CDs

A **CD** is a small plastic disk that has music or information on it: *Oliver listened to a music **CD** while he cleaned his room.*

ceiling • ceilings

A **ceiling** is the top inside part of a room: *Zach lay in bed and looked up at the **ceiling**.*

celebrate ▶ • celebrated, celebrating

When you **celebrate** something, you do things to show that it is important or special: *The family had a party to **celebrate** Hannah's birthday. They all enjoyed the birthday **celebration**.*

celebrity • celebrities

A **celebrity** is a famous person who is often seen on television or written about in newspapers and magazines: *Movie stars and sports stars are **celebrities**.*

You can go inside the **cave** on a raft or in a small boat.

cell • cells

1. A **cell** is a small room in a police station or prison: *The prisoners are locked in their **cell** at night.*
2. A **cell** is also one of the very tiny parts of something that is alive. Every animal or plant is made up of millions of cells. Cells are so small you can see them only with a microscope.

Henry's family help him **celebrate** his birthday.

Some kinds of **cell phones** can take pictures.

cell phone ▶

A **cell phone** is a small telephone that does not have wires. You can take a cell phone with you anywhere to make or get calls: *The girl sitting in front of me on the bus was talking on her **cell phone**.*

center ▼ • centers

The **center** is the middle part of something: *The statue of George Washington stood in the **center** of the park. The park is in the **central** part of the city.*

The arrow hit the **center** of the target.

century • centuries

A **century** is one hundred years: *In just one **century**, from 1870 to 1970, the small village grew into a large city.*

cereal ▼ • cereals

Cereal is a food made from wheat, rice, corn, or other plants. People eat cereal for breakfast: *Jasmine likes milk and sugar on her **cereal**.*

Long ago in Rome, people believed in gods and goddesses. They thought that the goddess *Ceres* watched over farmers and farming. Her name was given to **cereal,** which was the most important food that the Romans ate.

A bowl of **cereal** with milk is a healthy breakfast.

certain

If you are **certain,** you are very sure about something: *I am **certain** that this road goes to the city, because the sign says so. An elephant is **certainly** a very big animal.*

chain ▶ • chains

A **chain** is a row of rings that are joined together: *She kept the gate shut with a metal **chain** and a lock.*

I bought a gold **chain** at the store.

Chairs are made in lots of different shapes and sizes.

chair ▶ • chairs

A **chair** is a piece of furniture for one person to sit on. It has four legs and a back: *Mark sat in his **chair** at the dinner table.*

chalk ▼ • chalks

Chalk is a stick of soft, light-colored rock that is used for writing or drawing: *She used white **chalk** to draw a picture on the sidewalk.*

chalkboard • chalkboards

A **chalkboard** is a hard, smooth board that can be written or drawn on with chalk, and then erased. Chalkboards can be green or black: *The new teacher wrote his name up on the **chalkboard**.*

chance • chances

1. A **chance** is a time when you can do something: *Everyone in the class will get a **chance** to use the new computer.*
2. A **chance** also means something that might happen: *There is a good **chance** that we'll go camping on Saturday, if it doesn't rain.*

change • changed, changing

To **change** means to become different or to make something different: *Sally **changed** into her soccer uniform for the game this afternoon. Dad had to **change** the tire and put on a new one because the old one was flat.*

channel • channels

A television has lots of **channels**. Each channel has a different number and shows different programs: *Mom wanted to watch the news on **Channel** 4, but Dad kept putting on the football game instead.*

chapter • chapters

A **chapter** is a part of a book: *Granny read two **chapters** of my Harry Potter book to me last night.*

character • characters

A **character** is a made-up person in a story, play, or movie: *Spiderman is a **character** in a movie.*

Brittany uses **chalk** to draw a game of hopscotch at the playground.

charge • charged, charging

1. To **charge** means to ask a set amount of money for something: *That store will **charge** you two dollars for an ice-cream cone.*

2. Charge also means to buy something now, but pay for it later: *Mom didn't pay cash for the new computer—she **charged** it to her credit card.*

3. If you are **in charge** of something, you have control of it: *Mrs. Stanton is the boss of the company, so that means she is **in charge** of the business.*

chase ▶ • chased, chasing

To **chase** means to follow something quickly and try to catch it: *My cat likes to **chase** the birds that come into our yard.*

The big fish **chases** the little fish.

cheap • cheaper, cheapest

1. If something is **cheap**, it costs only a little money, or less than other things of the same kind: *To fly from New York to Los Angeles, he got a **cheap** ticket that cost only two hundred dollars.*

2. Cheap can also mean that something is not well made and does not last long: *It was a **cheap** toy and it broke only two days after we got it.*

The board is set up to play **checkers**.

cheat • cheated, cheating

If you **cheat**, you act in a way that is not honest: *She tried to look at my answers so she could **cheat** on the test.*

check • checks, checked, checking

1. To **check** means to test if something is correct or the way it should be: *Dad **checked** to make sure that we had all put on our seat belt.*

2. A **check** is a mark (✓) that is used to show that something is correct or has been noted: *The teacher put a **check** next to all the answers that José got right.*

checkers ◀

Checkers is a game for two players. Each player has twelve pieces, which they move over the squares on a board: *She beat her brother at **checkers** today.*

cheek • cheeks

Your **cheek** is the side of your face below your eye: *He filled his **cheeks** with air to blow out the candles on his birthday cake.*

cheer ▶ • cheered, cheering

To **cheer** means to shout because you are happy or you want something to happen: *The fans **cheered** when their team won the game.*

cheerful

If you are **cheerful**, it means that you feel happy: *Annelise is **cheerful** today because she is going to her best friend's house for a party.*

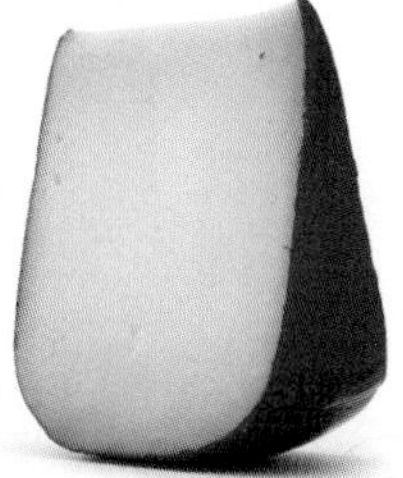

Swiss and Edam are two kinds of **cheese**.

cheese ▲ • cheeses

Cheese is a food made from milk: *I would like a **cheese** and tomato sandwich for lunch, please.*

chemical • chemicals

A **chemical** is something that is found in, on, or above Earth. It can be a gas, a liquid, or a solid object: *Oxygen, salt, water, and gold are all **chemicals**. **Chemistry** is the science where people study chemicals.*

cherry ▼ • cherries

A **cherry** is a small, round, red fruit that grows on trees. Cherries taste sweet: *When I eat **cherries**, I always take out the hard stone in the middle.*

You should wash **cherries** before you eat them.

chess ▼

Chess is a board game for two people. Each player has sixteen pieces that can be moved in different ways: *To win a game of **chess**, you must trap the other player's main piece, the king.*

chest • chests

1. Your **chest** is the front part of your body, between your neck and waist: *The undershirt keeps my **chest** warm.*
2. A **chest** can also be a big box that you use to store things in: *The pirates buried their gold in a wooden treasure **chest**.*

chew • chewed, chewing

When you **chew**, you break up or cut something with your teeth: *She **chewed** the peach with her mouth wide open.*

Leo is learning the rules of **chess** from his father.

chicken ▶ • chickens

A **chicken** is a bird that lays eggs. People eat the eggs and the meat from chickens: *A baby* ***chicken*** *is called a chick.*

This **chicken** has six chicks.

chief ▼ • chiefs

A **chief** is a person who is the leader of a group of people: *Sitting Bull was the* ***chief*** *who led the Lakota American Indian tribe.*

A Native American **chief** wears clothes made from leather and feathers.

child • children

A **child** is a young boy or girl: *The woman pushed the* ***child*** *on the swing.*

chill • chills

A **chill** is a feeling of cold: *We put on our coats and gloves to keep warm in the winter* ***chill****. It is very* ***chilly*** *walking in the snow.*

These houses have **chimneys** on their roof.

chimney ▲ • chimneys

A **chimney** is built on the roof of a building to take smoke to the outside from a fireplace, furnace, or stove. It is hollow: *When they made a fire in the cabin, the smoke went up the* ***chimney****.*

chimpanzees

Chimpanzees live together in family groups. They are intelligent and use a kind of language with each other. Chimpanzees eat fruits, leaves, eggs, insects, and some small animals.

A chimpanzee's arms are longer than its legs.

A chimpanzee uses a stick as a tool to get food.

chimpanzee ▲ • chimpanzees

A **chimpanzee** is a small ape with brownish-black fur that lives in forests in Africa: *The **chimpanzees** swung from tree to tree, looking for ripe fruits to eat.*

chin • chins

Your **chin** is the part of your face below your mouth: *The baby spilled her food down her **chin**.*

chip • chips

A **chip** is a small piece of something that is broken or cut off: *There were wood **chips** all over the yard after the men chopped down the big tree.*

chocolate ▶ • chocolates

Chocolate is a sweet brown food used to make cakes, candies, and drinks: *The cookies I like best have **chocolate** on top.*

Chocolate is my favorite candy.

choose • chose, chosen, choosing

When you **choose**, you pick out something as the one you want: *Which flavor of ice cream are you going to **choose**? There's so much of a **choice** of flavors that I can't decide.*

chop ▼ • chopped, chopping

To **chop** means to cut into small pieces: *The cook **chopped** some carrots for the stew.*

chorus • choruses

A **chorus** is a group of people who sing or dance together: *The **chorus** sings the last song at the end of the show.*

My uncle **chopped** wood for the fire.

Christmas

In countries all around the world, many people decorate trees indoors at Christmas time and put presents for each other around them. People first started decorating pine trees for Christmas in Germany about 500 years ago.

The acrobats at the **circus** are doing tricks.

circus ▲ • circuses

A **circus** is a show in a big tent with clowns, acrobats, and animals. Circuses travel from town to town: *They watched the clowns run across the wire that was hanging high above the ground at the* ***circus****.*

Christmas ▲ • Christmases

Christmas is December 25th, the day **Christians** celebrate the birthday of Jesus **Christ**. Jesus started the Christian religion more than two thousand years ago.

church ▶ • churches

A **church** is a building where Christians pray and learn about God: *We went to* ***church*** *on Sunday.*

circle • circles

A **circle** is a round shape: *A bicycle wheel is a* ***circle****.*

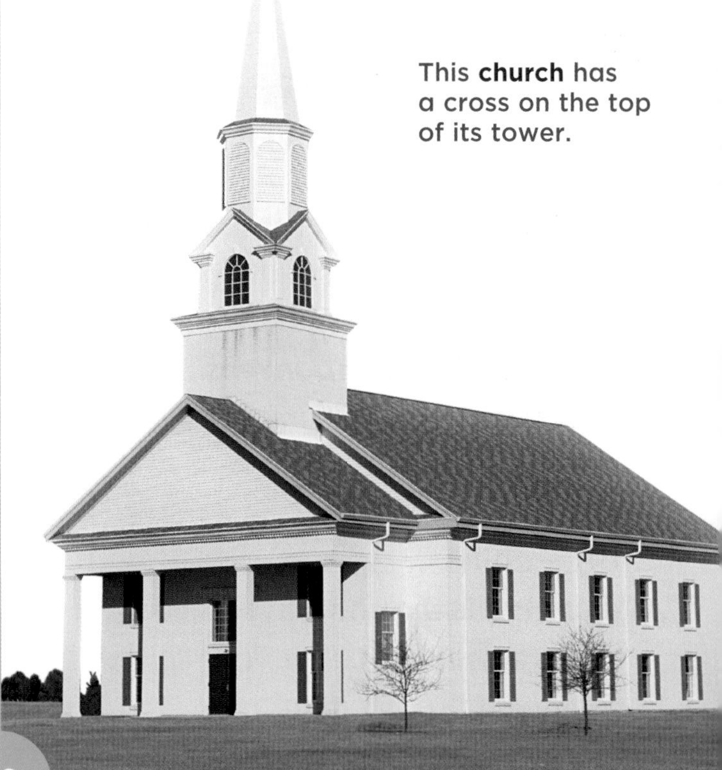

This **church** has a cross on the top of its tower.

citizen • citizens

A **citizen** is a person who belongs to a country: *I was born in the state of Texas, so I am a **citizen** of the United States of America.*

city • cities

A **city** is a big place where many people live and work. Cities are larger than towns: *New York **City** is the biggest city in the United States, with lots of tall buildings.*

class • classes

A **class** is a group of students who are taught together: *Mike is learning about frogs in science **class**. The teacher brought a box with live frogs to the **classroom**.*

claw • claws

A **claw** is a sharp, curved nail on the foot of an animal or bird: *She cried when the cat scratched her with its **claws**.*

clay • clays

Clay is a kind of dirt. Wet clay is easy to shape into pots or bricks. It gets hard when it is dried or baked: *I made a long snake out of **clay** in art class.*

There are many tall buildings in the **city** of Singapore.

clean • cleaner, cleanest, cleaned, cleaning

1. If something is **clean**, it has no dirt on it: *He washed the floor with soap and water and it is **clean** now.*
2. To **clean** means to wash something or to get rid of dirt: *My friend has to **clean** his room before he can play.*

claws

Animals use their claws for fighting and to catch other animals. They also use them to dig, to climb trees, and to scratch.

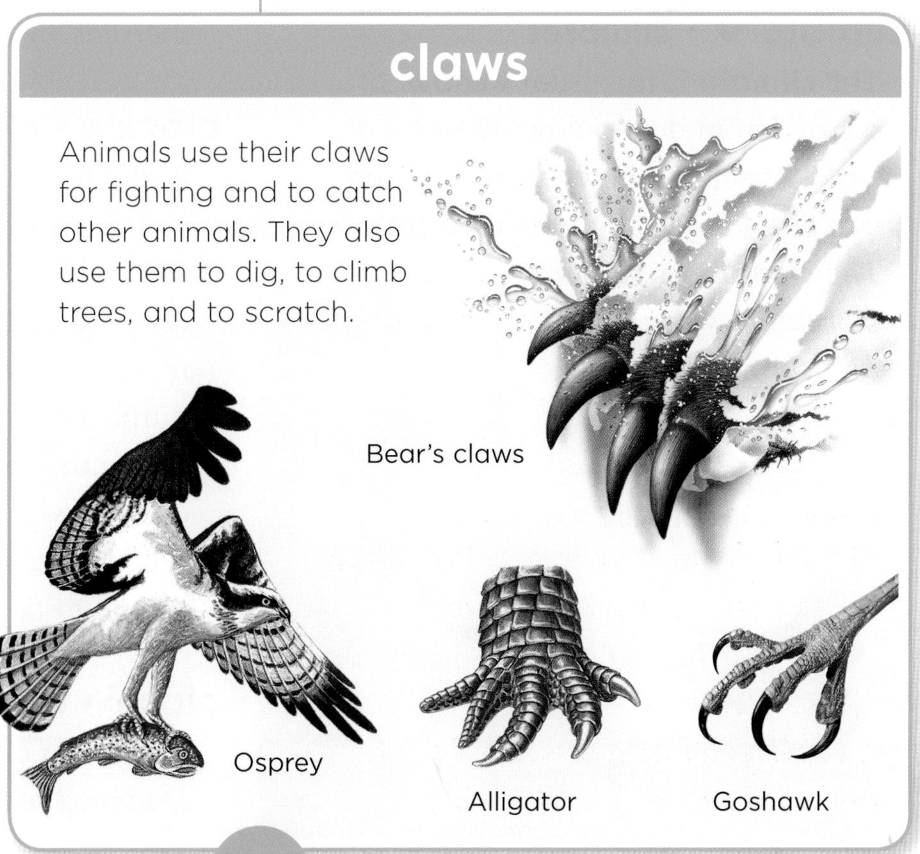

clear ▼ • **clearer, clearest**

1. **Clear** means that something is easy to see through: *A glass window is* ***clear****.*

2. **Clear** also means that something is easy to understand: *The coach called out our names in a strong,* ***clear*** *voice.*

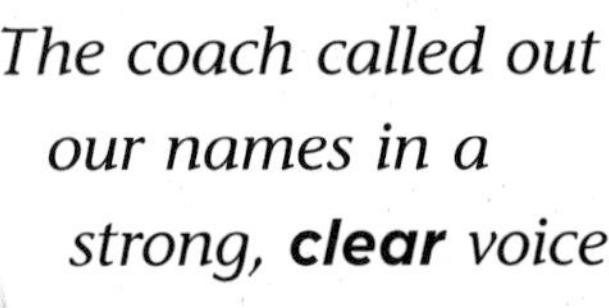

I can see the fish through the **clear** glass bowl.

clever • **cleverer, cleverest**

If you are **clever**, you are a quick thinker and can use your mind well: *Julian is so* ***clever****—he always gets good marks in school.*

climate ▼ • **climates**

The **climate** is the usual weather of a place from day to day over a long time. It includes how much rain and sun a place gets, and the temperature: *The* ***climate*** *in Miami, Florida, is warm and sunny.*

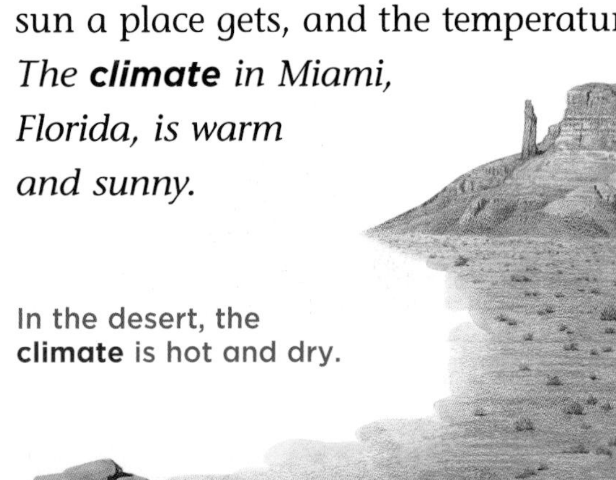

In the desert, the **climate** is hot and dry.

Caitlin wears safety equipment and a helmet to **climb** the wall.

climb ▲ • **climbed, climbing**

When you **climb**, you go up or over something using your hands and feet: *The little girl can* ***climb*** *to the top of the slide by herself.*

clock ▶ • **clocks**

A **clock** shows you the time. Some clocks have two hands that move around the numbers. Some have numbers that change with the time: *The* ***clock*** *in the kitchen says 9 o'clock, so it's time for me to go to bed.*

The **clock** is showing four minutes to three.

close[1] • **closed, closing**

When you **close** something, you shut it: *I stopped reading and* ***closed*** *the book.*

close[2] • closer, closest

When you are **close** to something, you are near it: *The basketball court is **close** to his house and he can walk there in five minutes.*

closet • closets

A **closet** is a small room where you can keep clothes and other things: *We packed our toys away in the **closet**, then shut the door.*

cloth • cloths

Cloth is material that clothes and other things are made from. Cotton, silk, wool, and nylon are used to make cloth: *The dressmaker will use yellow silk **cloth** to make Karen's new dress.*

The **clouds** in the sky might drop more snow on the mountains.

clothes ▶

Clothes are things you wear to cover your body. Pants, shirts, dresses, and coats are types of clothes: *Bobby's favorite **clothes** are his basketball shirt and his jeans. His parents like him to wear nice, neat **clothing** to church.*

The kinds of **clothes** people wear have changed over time.

cloud ▼ • clouds

A **cloud** is white or gray and it floats high in the sky. Clouds are made of tiny drops of water or ice: *Thick gray **clouds** filled the sky. Dad didn't need to wear his sunglasses because it was so **cloudy**.*

The **coast** is rocky and has beaches.

clown ▶ • **clowns**

A **clown** is a person who does tricks and silly things to make people laugh: *The **clown** with the bright green hair kept falling over her big shoes.*

The **clown** did a funny dance to make us laugh.

club • **clubs**

1. A **club** is a group of people who meet together because they like the same hobby or the same thing: *I belong to the Simpsons fan **club**.*
2. A **club** is also a heavy stick that is often thicker at one end. A club can be used as a weapon.

clue • **clues**

A **clue** is something that helps you find an answer to a puzzle or mystery: *The marks on the back door were the **clue** that showed how the man got in the house to steal the money.*

coach ▼ • **coaches**

A **coach** is someone whose job is to show people how to play a sport, and to tell them what to do when they play: *The **coach** told our soccer team to get a good night's sleep before the big game tomorrow.*

The **coach** gives his team instructions before the game.

coal • coals

Coal is a black or dark brown rock that you burn for heating or to make electricity: *People dig mines deep in the ground to find and take out **coal**. When we went camping, Dad cooked breakfast each morning over the hot **coals** of the campfire.*

coast ◀ • coasts

The **coast** is the land next to the ocean: *We spent our summer vacation at a beach house on the **coast**.*

coat • coats

A **coat** is a piece of clothing with long sleeves that you wear over other clothes to keep warm: *It was cold outside so I put on my **coat** and hat.*

coffee ▶ • coffees

Coffee is a dark brown drink that is made from the crushed roasted beans of a plant. It is usually served hot: *Mark likes to have a cup of **coffee** with milk and sugar at breakfast.*

Coffee beans are often stored in cloth bags.

coin • coins

A **coin** is a small, flat piece of metal used as money. Coins are marked in a certain way to show what country they are from and how much they are worth: *A quarter is a **coin** worth twenty-five cents.*

cold ◀ • colds, colder, coldest

1. **Cold** means not warm: *It was so **cold** outside in the snowy weather that the water in the lake turned to ice.*
2. When you have a **cold**, you feel sick and you might sneeze and cough and have a runny nose: *Andrew stayed in bed for three days because he was sick with a **cold**.*

It was so **cold** that there was frost on the ground.

a b c d e f g h i j k l m n o p q r s t u v w x y z

A B C D E F G H I J K L M N O P Q R S T U V W X Y Z

collar ▸ • collars

1. A **collar** is the part of your clothes that goes around the neck: *Mom ironed the **collar** of my shirt so that it was flat.*
2. A **collar** is also a leather band or chain that you put around an animal's neck: *Nick had to grab his dog by its **collar** to stop it from chasing the cat.*

The puppy is wearing a **collar**.

collect ▾ • collected, collecting

Collect means to bring or get a lot of things together into one place: *Sebastian likes to **collect** stamps. He has hundreds of different stamps in his **collection**.*

We **collect** shells as we walk on the beach.

college • colleges

College is a school that you can go to for more study and learning after you finish high school: *Penny is starting **college** in the spring and she wants to become a doctor.*

color ▸ • colors, colored, coloring

1. **Color** is one reason why things of the same kind can look different from others. There are lots of different colors, such as red, blue, green, pink, and yellow: *Today the sky is a bright blue **color**.*
2. When you **color** something, you use your pens and pencils to make a picture: *Nathan **colored** the picture of the sun with his new yellow and orange crayons.*

comb ▸ • combs

A **comb** is a piece of plastic or metal with a row of thin teeth sticking out on one side. Combs are used to put your hair in place and make it look nice and neat: *Grandma always keeps a **comb** in her handbag in case she needs to fix her hair.*

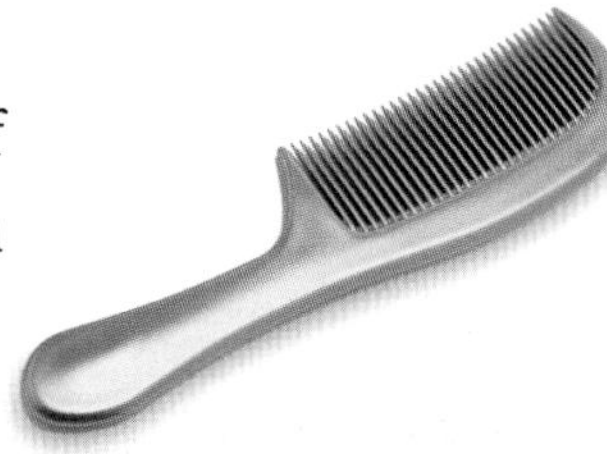

Use a **comb** to get the knots out of your hair.

come • came, come, coming

To **come** means to move toward someone or something: *My dog will **come** running over to me when I call his name.*

colors

The three main colors are yellow, blue, and red. You can make new colors by mixing colors together. For example, blue mixed with red makes purple.

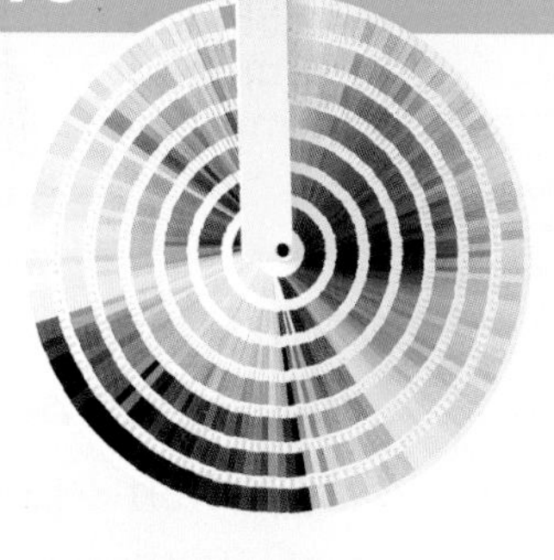

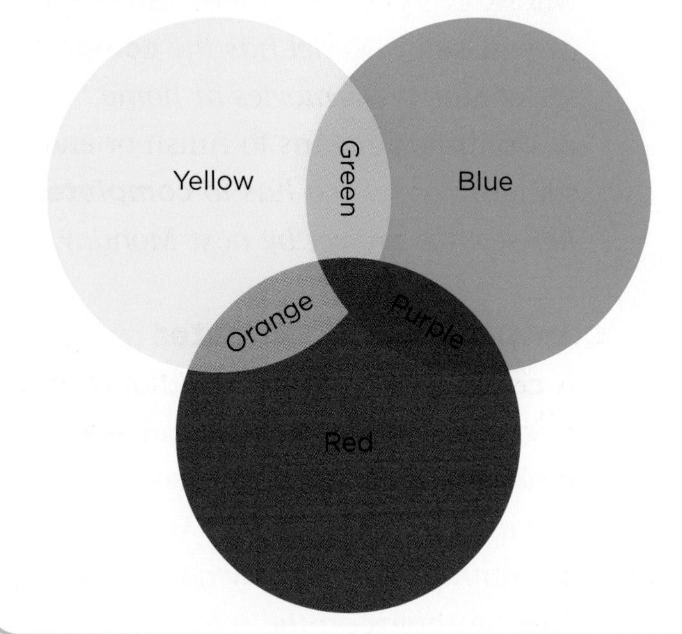

comfortable

When something is **comfortable**, it makes you feel nice and relaxed: *Lucy liked going to sleep at night because her bed was so soft and* ***comfortable****.*

comic • comics

1. **Comic** means funny or amusing: *It was a* ***comic*** *sight to see my little sister singing and dancing in front of the mirror.*
2. **Comics** are a set of cartoons in a row that tell a story: *I went to the store to buy the new Superman* ***comic****.*

comma • commas

A **comma** is a mark (,) that is used in writing to make a small break in a sentence. This sentence has four commas: *When we went to the zoo, we saw monkeys, tigers, elephants, and lots of other animals.*

comment • comments

A **comment** is something that you say or write about a person or thing: *The teacher wrote a nice* ***comment*** *on my report card about my good behavior in class.*

commercial • commercials

A **commercial** is an advertisement on radio or television that is meant to make you want to buy or use something: *The food* ***commercials*** *on TV always make me feel hungry.*

common

If something is **common**, it means it happens a lot: *It's* ***common*** *for it to rain here in the spring, and last month it rained almost every day.*

Rory is reading in a **comfortable** chair.

A B C D E F G H I J K L M N O P Q R S T U V W X Y Z

company • companies

1. A **company** is a group of people who work together in the same business: *The Ford Motor **Company** is famous for making cars and trucks.*
2. You say that you have **company** when you have guests visiting: *Mom told us to change clothes for dinner because we had **company** coming.*

A bicycle is slow **compared** to a motorcycle.

compare ▲ • compared, comparing

Compare means to look at things to see how they are the same, and how they are different: *Joe and Sean **compared** the size of their hands and saw that Sean's hands were bigger. The teacher showed us pictures of a coyote and a wolf and made a **comparison** of the two animals.*

complain • complained, complaining

If you **complain**, you tell someone about all the things that are bothering you or making you unhappy: *The neighbors **complained** that our dog was barking too much at night. After their **complaint**, Mom let the dog sleep inside with us.*

Sacha and her dad are using the **computer** to search for information.

complete • completed, completing

1. When something is **complete**, it is whole. Everything is there and no parts are missing: *Daniel has the **complete** set of Star Wars movies at home.*
2. **Complete** means to finish or end something: *Jessica has to **complete** her science project by next Monday.*

computer ▲ • computer

A **computer** is a machine that can hold a lot of information and work out problems faster than a person can: *Lee uses his **computer** to write stories, do math problems, play games, and look up things on the Internet.*

concert ▼ • concerts

A **concert** is a show of music for people to come and listen to: *The school band is giving a **concert** on Sunday afternoon.*

Jordan and his band played a song at the school **concert**.

condition • conditions

Condition means the way someone or something is: *My shoes are in bad **condition** because they are dirty and have holes in them.*

cone ▶ • cones

Pine **cones** contain seeds for pine trees.

1. A **cone** is a shape with a round, flat bottom, and sides that come together in a point at the top.
2. A **cone** is also anything that is shaped like a cone: *Tim had two scoops of chocolate chip ice cream in a **cone**.*

confuse • confused, confusing

1. To **confuse** means to mix up or make hard to understand: *The teacher sometimes **confuses** me when she talks fast and uses big words.*
2. **Confuse** also means thinking that things are the same when they are different: *Some people **confuse** my voice with my mom's voice. That can cause **confusion** when I answer the phone instead of her.*

Congress ▶

Congress is the part of the United States government that makes the laws. There are two groups in **Congress**, the **Senate** and the **House of Representatives**: ***Congress** held a meeting to talk about a new law that would give more money to schools.*

consonant • consonants

A **consonant** is any letter of the alphabet except for *a, e, i, o,* and *u*, which are called VOWELS.

consumer • consumers

A **consumer** is any person who buys and uses things: ***Consumers** spend a lot of money shopping for presents at Christmas time.*

The box **contains** a hammer and other tools.

contain ▶ • contained, containing

When something is **contained**, it is held inside: *My school bag **contains** my books, a sweater, and my lunch box. I use my lunch box as a **container** to hold my food.*

contest • contests

A **contest** is a race or game that people try to win to get a prize: *Josh came in second in the pie-eating **contest** at the school fair.*

Congress meets in the United States Capitol building.

Dad **cooks** vegetables to serve with dinner.

continent ▼ • **continents**
A **continent** is one of the large areas of land on Earth. There are seven continents in the world: Asia, Africa, North America, South America, Europe, Antarctica, and Australia.

continue • **continued, continuing**
If something **continues**, it keeps happening. It goes on and on: *The rain **continued** to fall for three days straight.*

continents

Most of the land that makes up the seven continents is in the northern half of our planet. The continents were once joined together and then they separated over a long time.

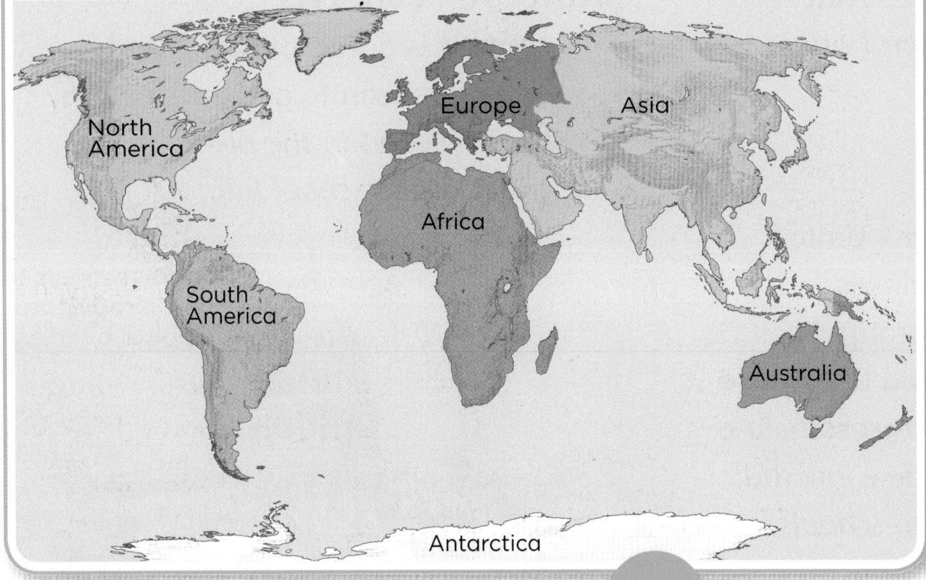

control • **controlled, controlling**
When you **control** something, you are in charge of it and you make it work or run the way you want it to: *The pilot is **controlling** the airplane.*

cook ◀ • **cooked, cooking**
To **cook** means to heat food until it is ready to eat: *Mom **cooks** spaghetti and meatballs on Sundays.*

We keep our **cookies** in a glass jar.

cookie ▲ • **cookies**
A **cookie** is a small, flat, sweet cake: *Grandma baked chocolate chip **cookies** as a special surprise.*

cool • **cooler, coolest**
Cool means fairly cold. Something cool is not warm, but not very cold either: *I splashed some **cool** water onto my face after I had been running.*

copy • copies, copied, copying

1. To **copy** means to do or make something that is exactly the same as something else: *The teacher told us to **copy** the list of words she wrote on the board.*

2. A **copy** is something that is the same as something else: *You can use this machine to make a **copy** of your letter before you mail it.*

corn

Corn is a yellow, sweet-tasting vegetable that can be cooked and eaten: *We had fresh **corn** for dinner.*

We bought ears of **corn** at the farmers' market.

corner • corners

A **corner** is the point where two lines, sides, or edges meet: *I folded down the **corner** of the page in my book.*

correct • corrected, correcting

1. **Correct** means without any mistakes: *The teacher was pleased because the student gave the **correct** answer.*

2. To **correct** means to show someone the mistakes they have made: *The teacher **corrected** our tests with a red pen.*

The soft, white part of the **cotton** plant is ready to be picked when the seeds open.

The children dressed up in **costumes** for the Halloween party.

cost • costs, cost, costing

1. The **cost** of something is the amount of money you need to buy it: *The **cost** of one ticket to the school play is five dollars.*

2. **Cost** also means you have to pay a certain amount of money to buy something: *Dad bought me a computer game that **cost** eighty dollars.*

costume ▲ • costumes

A **costume** is special clothes you wear to dress up or pretend to be something else: *Laura wore a chicken **costume** for Halloween.*

cotton

Cotton is light material made from part of a plant: *Dad wears white **cotton** shirts to work in the yard, so that he doesn't get too hot.*

couch ▸ • couches

A **couch** is a large, soft piece of furniture with enough room for two or more people to sit on at the same time: *The children sat on the* ***couch*** *with a big bowl of popcorn to watch their favorite television show.*

cough • coughed, coughing

When you **cough**, you make air come out of your throat with a loud and sudden noise: *I* ***coughed*** *several times when a peanut got stuck in my throat.*

could

Could is a form of the word CAN. It is used when you talk about what someone or something was able to do: *When I was on summer vacation, I* ***could*** *stay up and watch television.* **Couldn't** is a shorter way of saying "could not": *Mom said I* ***couldn't*** *watch that movie on TV because it was too scary.*

There are sheep in the field in the **country.**

The dog should not be sitting on the **couch.**

count ▾ • counted, counting

1. To **count** means to add up the number of things that there are: *The teacher told everyone to sit still while she* ***counted*** *how many children were there.*
2. **Count** also means to say numbers in order, one after the other: *Tony's little sister can* ***count*** *up to twenty.*

Ian **counted** his marbles to find out how many he had.

country ◂ • countries

1. **Country** means the land that is away from cities and towns: *We went away for a weekend in the* ***country****, riding horses and going on mountain walks.*
2. A **country** is also an area of land where people live that has its own government: *I was born in the United States, but my best friend was born in another* ***country*** *called Australia.*

We saw a **couple** of birds sitting together on a branch.

couple ▶ • couples

A **couple** is two people or two things: *Liz put a* ***couple*** *of apples in her backpack for us to eat later.*

courage

Courage means being strong to do something, even though you are afraid: *Kieryn showed* ***courage*** *when she swam out into the water to save the drowning boy.*

court ▼ • courts

1. A **court** is a place that is used for matters having to do with the law: *When he got a ticket for driving too fast, he had to go to* ***court*** *to pay a fine. Everyone in the* ***court*** *had to stand up when the judge walked in.*
2. A **court** is also an area where some sports are played: *Let's meet over by the tennis* ***courts*** *before the game.*

Cindy and her uncle go to the basketball **court** on weekends.

cousin • cousins

Your **cousin** is your aunt's or uncle's child: *Our* ***cousins*** *came to stay with us for summer vacation.*

cover • covers, covered, covering

1. To **cover** means to put one thing over all of another thing: *When the baby fell asleep, her mom* ***covered*** *her with a blanket.*
2. A **cover** is something that is put over another thing to protect it: *This book about birds has a picture of an eagle on the* ***cover****.*

The **cowboy** watches his cattle.

cow • cows

A **cow** is a large animal that we use for milk and meat. A cow is a female animal and the male of this animal is called a bull: *On our trip to the farm, our class was shown how to milk* ***cows****.*

cowboy ▲ • cowboys

A **cowboy** is a man who works with cattle on a ranch: *There were* ***cowboys*** *and* ***cowgirls*** *riding horses at the rodeo.*

The **coyote** has thick fur and a long tail.

coyote ▲ • coyotes

A **coyote** is a wild animal, of the same family as a wolf or dog: *When we went camping, we could hear the **coyotes** in the woods at night.*

crab ▼ • crabs

A **crab** is a sea animal that has a hard flat shell, eight legs, and two claws: *Harry found some **crabs** hiding under the rocks at the beach.*

A **crab** swims in the water.

The mirror has large **cracks** in it.

crack ▲ • cracks

A **crack** is a narrow space or line you can see in something when it has a small break in it: *Dad wanted to hide the **crack** in the wall by hanging a picture in front of it.*

cracker ▶ • crackers

A **cracker** is a thin, flat, hard kind of food, usually made by baking some kind of flour: *We had cheese and **crackers** for a snack.*

These **crackers** taste salty.

crane ▶ • cranes

1. A **crane** is a large machine with a long swinging arm for lifting and moving heavy things: *The **crane** lifted the huge piece of stone and moved it out of the way of the other workers.*
2. A **crane** is also a tall bird with long legs and a long neck. Cranes have a long beak and walk around in the water looking for food.

crash • **crashes, crashed, crashing**
1. To **crash** means to hit or break something with a very loud noise: *The car **crashed** into a tree when it went off the road.*
2. A **crash** means a loud and sudden noise: *We heard a **crash** in the kitchen when the shelf fell and some dishes broke.*

My baby sister has learned to **crawl**.

crawl ▲ • **crawled, crawling**
To **crawl** means to move along on your hands and knees: *A baby will **crawl** along the floor before it learns how to walk.*

The **crane** lifts the heavy metal bar to the top of the new building.

Lola got new **crayons** for her birthday.

crayon ▲ • **crayons**
A **crayon** is a colorful stick of wax used for writing, drawing, or coloring: *Maria used her new **crayons** to color the picture.*

crazy • **crazier, craziest**
When you are acting **crazy**, you are likely to do silly things: *Eating six pieces of apple pie at one time was a **crazy** idea.*

cream ▶
Cream is the thick, yellow-looking part that you find at the top of milk: *Mom bought some **cream** to have with the strawberries.*

Nana puts **cream** in her coffee.

create • **created, creating**
To **create** means to make: *Louis **created** a special birthday card for his dad using a piece of cardboard, a ribbon, some seashells, and his colored pencils.*

crocodiles

Crocodiles lie in the water when they hunt, with only their eyes, nose, and ears sticking out. When an animal comes to the water to drink, the crocodile grabs it, pulls it in, and drowns it.

Nile crocodile

A crocodiles waits under the water.

creature • creatures
A **creature** is any animal that is living: *Whales and fish are **creatures** that live in the sea.*

credit
Credit is a way of paying for something after you buy it: *Gina bought a new dress on **credit**. She used her **credit card** again later to buy some shoes to go with it.*

crime • crimes
A **crime** is something a person does that is against the law: *Stealing a car is a **crime**. **Criminals** who are caught stealing are often put into jail.*

crocodile ▲ • crocodiles
A **crocodile** is a large animal that lives in rivers and lakes. It has a long body with rough skin, a long tail, short legs, and a long, thin mouth with sharp teeth. Crocodiles look like alligators, but have a longer head.

You can **cross** the street when the light turns green.

cross ◀ • crossed, crossing
To **cross** means to go from one side of something to the other side: *Charlie **crossed** over the river by using the bridge.*

crow ▶ • **crows**

A **crow** is a large bird with shiny black feathers: *The **crow** called out as it flew around searching for food.*

Crows live in the park near my school.

crowd ▼ • **crowds**

A **crowd** is a large number of people in one place: *There was a big **crowd** at the football game.*

Large **crowds** go to the state fair every year.

The queen's **crown** has many jewels.

crown ◀ • **crowns**

A **crown** is a circle of gold, silver, and jewels that kings and queens wear on their head like a hat: *The **crown** was made with diamonds and other expensive stones.*

cruel • **crueler, cruelest**

If you are **cruel** to someone, you are very mean to them on purpose: *It was **cruel** of that boy to say she was fat. Some people think that it is **cruel** to hunt animals for sport.*

crust • **crusts**

The hard outside layer of something is called its **crust**: *Mom was mad because I ate the soft middle part of the piece of bread and left the **crust** on my plate.*

crutch ▼ • **crutches**

A **crutch** is a long stick with a soft top that fits under your arm to help you walk: *Sarah used **crutches** for four weeks after she broke her ankle.*

cry • **cried, crying**

If you **cry**, you have tears come out of your eyes because you are sad or hurt: *Patrick **cried** when his dog Chester died.*

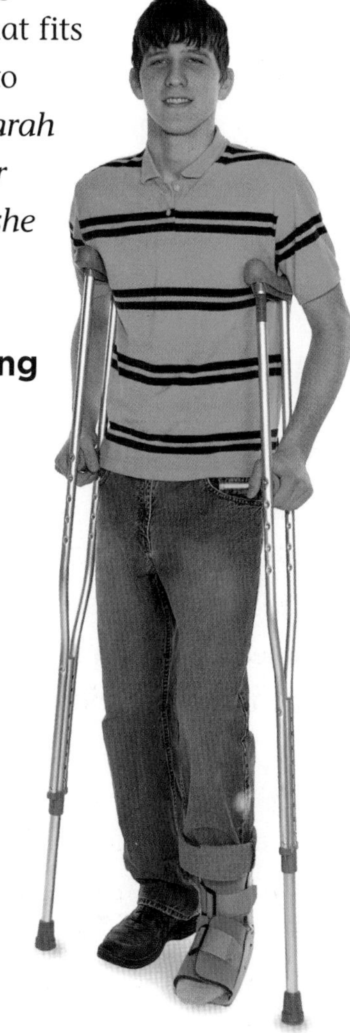

Max has **crutches** because he hurt his foot.

A B C D E F G H I J K L M N O P Q R S T U V W X Y Z

The polar bear **cub** plays in the snow.

cub ▲ • cubs

A **cub** is a young bear, lion, tiger, or wolf: *The mother bear watched her **cub** play in the water.*

cube ▶ • cubes

A **cube** is a solid object like a block, with six equal square sides: *Hannah put two **cubes** of ice into her glass of water.*

Mom likes sugar **cubes** in her coffee.

cup ▼ • cups

1. A **cup** is a small, round container used for drinking: *Liz washed out her coffee **cup** and put it back on the shelf.*

2. A **cup** is also a container for measuring liquids: *The recipe says to add one and a half **cups** of milk.*

Margaret used a measuring **cup** to get the right amount of liquid.

curious ▼

If you are **curious**, you want know or learn about something: *Frank was **curious** about where butterflies came from and looked on the Internet to find out about this.*

curl • curls

A **curl** is a piece of hair shaped in a circle: *The baby has black **curls** all over her head. Her mom and dad also have **curly** hair.*

current • currents

1. **Current** means at the present time: *Your **current** address is where you are living right now.*

2. A **current** is a flow of water, electricity, or air: *The logs were sent down the river by the strong **current**.*

Molly is **curious** about what is on the other side of the fence.

The stream **curves** around the tree.

curtain ▼ • curtains

A **curtain** is a piece of cloth that hangs from the top of a window or at the front of a stage: *The **curtains** closed, so we knew that the play was over.*

The window in our living room has **curtains.**

curve ▶ • curves, curved, curving

1. A **curve** is a line that bends around with no points or corners: *The letter "S" has **curves**.*
2. To **curve** means to go in a way that is not straight: *The road is straight where it goes past our house, but then it **curves** to the right.*

cushion • cushions

A **cushion** is a kind of pillow filled with soft material: *Uncle Graham sat down on the couch and leaned back on the big, blue **cushions**.*

customer ▶ • customers

A **customer** is someone who buys things from other people: *The **customers** waited in a line at the post office to buy stamps.*

The **customer** shops for fruits at the market.

cut • cut, cutting

1. To **cut** means to divide something into smaller pieces: *Rosie **cut** the cake so that everybody could have a piece.*
2. To **cut** also means to make something shorter or smaller: *I asked the hairdresser to **cut** my hair because it was getting into my eyes.*
3. To **cut** also means to hurt yourself with something sharp: *Amanda **cut** her finger on the broken glass.*

cute • cuter, cutest

Cute means that something looks pretty: *The baby looks very **cute** in her little pink dress.*

I picked a **daisy** to give to my friend.

Dad, dad • **Dads, dads**

Dad or **Daddy** is what you call your father: ***Dad*** *sometimes plays ball in the park with me.*

daisy ▲ • **daisies**

A **daisy** is a small flower with a yellow center and white petals: *Emma picked some* ***daisies*** *from the garden.*

The word **daisy** was made up by putting together the words *day* and *eye*. "The day's eye" was a name used for the Sun, and people thought that the bright color of a daisy looked like the Sun.

dam ▼ • **dams**

A **dam** is a wall that is built across a river to stop and hold water: *Our town uses a* ***dam*** *to collect drinking water.*

Dams store water that we need for businesses and for our homes.

damp • **damper, dampest**

If something is **damp**, it is a little bit wet: *The grass is still* ***damp*** *from all the rain last night.*

dance ▼ • **dances, danced, dancing**

1. To **dance** is to move your body to the sound and rhythm of music: *Lots of my friends* ***danced*** *at the party, but Shelly was the best* ***dancer*** *out of everyone.*

2. A **dance** is a set of actions you do to particular music: *Jason knows how to do lots of* ***dances****, like the tango and the waltz.*

People around the world **dance** in many different ways.

danger ▲ • **dangers**

Danger means that there is a chance that something bad could happen, something that might hurt you: *There is a **danger** that the tornado might come this way. Tornadoes are very **dangerous**. They can break up houses and hurt people.*

dark • **darker, darkest**

1. **Dark** means without any light: *When all the lights are off, the room is very **dark**.*
2. **Dark** is also not light-colored: *The teacher wore a **dark** blue suit with a red tie.*

January 1 is the **date** of the first day of the year.

data

Data is facts and information about something: *I put together a lot of **data** about grasshoppers for my school project. This computer has room for a lot of **data**.*

date ▼ • **dates**

1. A **date** is the day, month, and year when something happens: *I marked the **date** of my sister's birthday on the calendar.*
2. The **date** is also the words or numbers that tell the day, month, or year: *Today's **date** is June 21st.*

daughter • **daughters**

A **daughter** is someone's female child: *Rachel took her son and two **daughters** to the beach.*

day • **days**

1. **Day** is the time between sunrise and sunset when it is light: *The family spent the whole **day** at the beach.*
2. A **day** is also a time of twenty-four hours. Seven days make one week: *Sunday is my favorite **day** of the week because that is when I visit my grandmother.*

dead

If something is **dead**, it is no longer living: *Martha threw away the **dead** flowers and picked some new ones from the garden.*

deaf • **deafer, deafest**

If a person or an animal is **deaf**, they cannot hear at all, or cannot hear very well: *Our old dog Buster is **deaf** and can't hear us when we call him.*

dear • dearer, dearest

If something is **dear** to you, you like it very much: *Our grandmother says that my brother and I are very **dear** to her.*

decide ▼ • decided, deciding

Decide means to choose to do something instead of something else: *Aunt Moira **decided** to buy the blue dress instead of the green one. She said it was a hard **decision** to make, because both were very nice.*

It is hard to **decide** which candy to take.

deck • decks

1. A **deck** is a flat area like a floor on the outside of a boat or ship: *All the people on the ship came out on **deck** to watch the whales swim by.*
2. A **deck** also means one of the levels on a boat or ship: *This ship has five **decks** and it has a swimming pool on the top deck.*
3. A pack of playing cards that people use for different games is also called a **deck**: *We will have to buy a new **deck** because some of the cards in this one are missing.*

Divers explore a ship that is **deep** under the ocean.

deep ▲ • deeper, deepest

Deep means a long way down: *We had to dig a very **deep** hole to plant the tree.*

deer ▼ • deer

A **deer** is a large animal that can run fast. Deer have four long legs and short brown fur. Male deer have long horns.

define • defined, defining

When you **define** something, you explain what it means. A dictionary defines thousands of words: *You can **define** the word "difficult" as "something that is hard to do." You can look in the dictionary for the **definition** of this word.*

Male **deer** use their horns to fight with each other.

delicious

Something that you really enjoy tasting or smelling is **delicious**: *Jill says that her mother cooks **delicious** food.*

A man **delivers** a package.

deliver ◀ • delivered, delivering

If you **deliver** something, you take it to a place or give it to a person: *The store will **deliver** the new TV set to our house. They say the **delivery** will come at about 10 o'clock Friday morning.*

democracy • democracies

A **democracy** is a country where people vote in elections to decide who will be in the government: *The United States is a **democracy** because people can vote to choose the President and other people in the government. A country like this has a **democratic** form of government.*

In the Greek language, the word for "people" is *demos.* Greece was the first place where we know that people used **democracy** as a way to rule a country.

den ▶ • dens

A **den** is a place where a wild animal sleeps or rests, and where it feels safe: *Some bears sleep in their **den** all through the winter.*

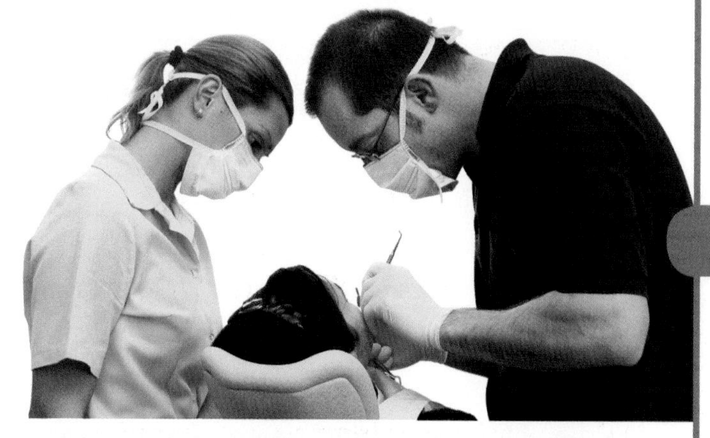
Sophie had her teeth cleaned by the **dentist**.

dentist ▲ • dentists

A **dentist** is a person who takes care of people's teeth and gums: *Mom takes me to the **dentist** every six months to make sure my teeth are healthy.*

department • departments

A **department** is part of a government or of a large organization such as a hospital, business, or college: *When Luis broke his leg he went to the X-ray **department** at the hospital.*

depend • depended, depending

If you **depend** on someone, you need them to help you in some way, or you trust them to do something: *My parents **depend** on me to keep my room neat and clean.*

The lizard is leaving its **den**.

deserts

Deserts do not have much water, so only a few kinds of plants grow there. Some animals, like camels, can live in the desert because they can go for a long time without food or water. People often ride camels and use them to carry things.

describe • described, describing
You **describe** something when you tell what it looks like, sounds like, or feels like: *Sandra **described** her cat Cuddles as a large, friendly animal with black and white fur. That's a very good **description** of Cuddles.*

desert ▲ • deserts
A **desert** is a very dry area where it does not rain much and where not many kinds of plants can grow. There is a lot of sand in most deserts: *People who travel through a **desert** must take along water to drink, because there is almost no water in the desert.*

design • designs, designed, designing
1. A **design** is a plan of what something will look like when it is made: *Anne's mom drew a **design** for the new dress before she started to make it.*
2. If you **design** something, you draw or paint what it should look like when it is made: *When Mr. Wilson **designed** his new garden, he made a plan of where he would plant the different trees and flowers.* A person who designs clothes or other things is called a **designer**.

desk ▼ • desks
A **desk** is a piece of furniture like a table where people read, write, or use computers: *Dad sits at his **desk** when he is writing a letter or working at his computer.*

dessert • desserts
Dessert is the food you eat at the end of a meal: *I sometimes have ice cream and fruit for **dessert** at dinnertime.*

detective • detectives
A **detective** is a kind of police officer who tries to find out who has done things that are against the law: *When the **detectives** found the missing money, they were able to find out who stole it.*

Simon works on his homework at his **desk**.

Diamonds can be made into jewelry.

develop • **developed, developing**

You **develop** something if you plan it and then make it or invent it: *Scientists have **developed** machines called robots that can work in factories and do many other jobs. Scientists are working on the **development** of many other new kinds of machines.*

dial • **dials**

1. A **dial** is the part of an instrument that shows a how much there is of something, such as time, temperature, or speed: *The clock on our kitchen wall has a large **dial**, but my watch has a very small dial.*

2. Some television and radio sets have a **dial** on the front that you use to select the channel you want to watch or the program you want to hear: *When the radio news program started, Francesco turned the **dial** to find another station with music.*

diamond • **diamonds**

1. A **diamond** is a very hard, clear or pale stone that is found under the ground. Diamonds are jewels that cost a lot of money: *Pam has a gold ring with a beautiful **diamond** in it.*

2. A **diamond** is also a shape that has four sides and four corners at the top, bottom, and sides: *A baseball field is shaped like a **diamond**.*

dictionary • **dictionaries**

A **dictionary** is a book that tells what words mean and how you should spell them: *If you read a word you don't know, you can look it up in a **dictionary** to find out what it means.*

did

Did is a form of the word DO: *Joanna **did** her homework before she went out to play.* **Didn't** is a shorter way of saying "did not": *It **didn't** rain for weeks and the ground was very dry.*

The pilot checks the **dials** to see how high he is flying.

A B C D E F G H I J K L M N O P Q R S T U V W X Y Z

die • died, dying

To **die** means to stop being alive: *Our cat Ginger was very old and sick and she **died** last week.*

diet • diets, dieted, dieting

1. Your **diet** is the kind and amount of food and drink that you usually have: *Fruits and vegetables are an important part of our **diet**.*
2. A **diet** also means a smaller amount of food and drink than a person usually has: *Aunt Freda wants to lose weight, so she is on a **diet**.*
3. If you **diet**, you eat and drink less than you usually do: *My uncle **dieted** for three months and lost more than ten pounds.*

different ▼

Different means not the same as, or not like, something: *An elephant and a mouse are both animals, but they are very **different**, because one is very big and the other is tiny. There is a big **difference** between them.*

difficult

Difficult means not easy to do or to understand: *The last question on the test was very **difficult** and almost all the students got it wrong. My little sister has **difficulty** playing the piano because her hands are so small.*

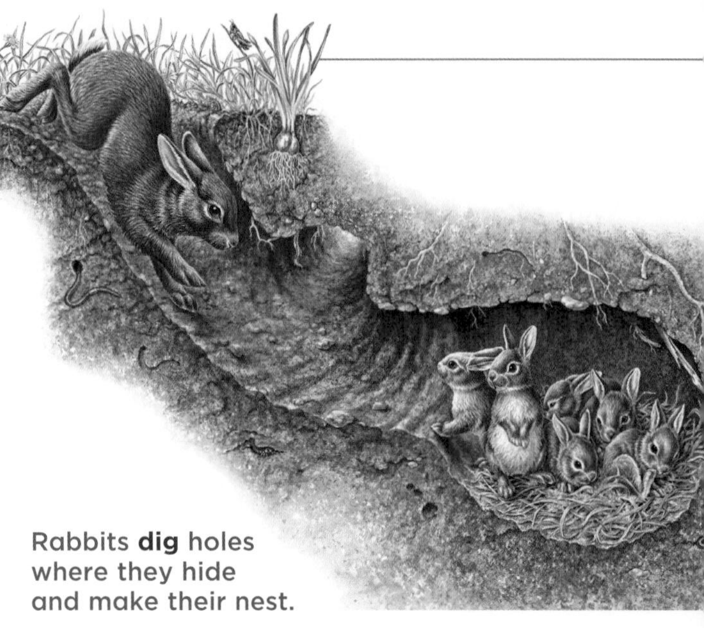

Rabbits **dig** holes where they hide and make their nest.

dig ▲ • dug, digging

To **dig** means to make a hole, usually in the ground: *Squirrels can **dig** holes in the ground and bury food in them.*

dinner • dinners

Dinner is the main meal of the day. Most people eat dinner in the evening: *In winter we have **dinner** indoors, but on summer evenings we sometimes eat outdoors.*

dinosaur ▶ • dinosaurs

Dinosaurs were animals that lived many millions of years ago. No dinosaurs are alive today. Some dinosaurs were very big and some were small. Some kinds of dinosaurs would kill and eat other animals, while others ate only plants.

These instruments make **different** kinds of sounds.

dinosaurs

Many different kinds of dinosaurs once lived on Earth. They all died long ago, maybe because Earth was hit by a huge rock from space or because the climate changed.

direct • **directed, directing**

1. **Direct** means going in a straight line or by the shortest way you can: *If I walk the **direct** way home from school, I don't pass by the store. If I want to buy something at the store, I don't go **directly** home. I go over to Main Street.*

2. If you **direct** someone to do something, you tell them how to do it, or you tell them that they must do it: *The teacher **directed** the children to write a story about their vacation.*

The sailor points in the **direction** of land.

direction • **directions**

1. A **direction** is the way you go to get somewhere: *When we left school, Marjorie went in one **direction** toward her house, and I went in another direction toward mine. If we drive in this **direction**, we will be going north.*

2. A **direction** is also a way of doing something or getting to a place: *The teacher gave the children **directions** about how to work the computer.*

dirt

1. **Dirt** is anything that makes a thing not clean: *Megan had to change her dress because there was **dirt** on it. Later, she washed the **dirty** dress to get it clean.*

2. **Dirt** also means loose earth, as in a garden: *The dog dug a hole in the **dirt**, then buried the bone.*

Dad needs to clean his **dirty** boots.

disappear • **disappeared, disappearing**

If something **disappears**, you cannot see it any longer: *The car **disappeared** from our view when it turned the corner.*

disappoint • **disappointed, disappointing**

If something **disappoints** you, it makes you feel sad that it happened: *David was **disappointed** when his team lost the game.*

discover ▲ • **discovered, discovering**
To **discover** means to learn something you did not know, or to find something you did not know was there: *When we looked in the closet we **discovered** a box full of old books. It was a very surprising **discovery**.*

disease • **diseases**
When people, animals, or plants have a **disease**, it means they are not healthy. People who have a disease may feel very sick. If someone has **heart disease**, it means their heart does not work the way it should.

dish ▶ • **dishes**
A **dish** is a container that you put food in. You can also eat food out of a dish: *At breakfast we eat our cereal out of small **dishes**, and there is also a large dish of fruits on the table.*

disk • **disks**
1. Something that is flat, thin, and has a round shape is a **disk**: *Our dog Joey has a metal **disk** on his collar that has his name and where he lives written on it.*
2. A **disk** is also a thin, hard, round piece of plastic that stores computer information: *If you put this **disk** into your computer you'll be able to see some photos of our new house.* This word is sometimes spelled **disc**.

distance • **distances**
If you measure how far apart two things or places are, you find out the **distance** between them: *New York and California are a great **distance** apart, about three thousand miles. New York City and San Francisco are very **distant** from each other.*

Please bring the butter **dish** to the table.

Janice **dived** into the water.

A B C **D** E F G H I J K L M N O P Q R S T U V W X Y Z

dive ▸ • dived *or* dove, dived, diving

When you **dive**, you throw yourself into water with your arms straight out in front of your head: *Karen can **dive** into the pool from the high diving board. She is an excellent **diver.*** Another sort of **diver** wears special clothing and uses special equipment to breathe underwater for long periods of time.

divide ▾ • divided, dividing

1. To **divide** means to separate something into two or more parts or groups: *A wooden fence **divided** the field into two parts. There were sheep on one side of this **division** and cattle on the other.*
2. **Divide** also means to show how many times one number is contained in another: *If you **divide** twelve by two, the answer is six.*

divorce • divorces, divorced, divorcing

1. If a husband and wife **divorce**, they stop being married to each other: *Victoria's parents **divorced** and now she lives with her father.*
2. A **divorce** is the end of a marriage by law: *Rick's parents got a **divorce** last year.*

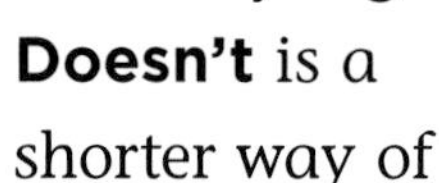

do • did, done, doing

1. To **do** something is to work at it or to make it happen: *Every day after school I **do** my homework.*
2. **Do** also means to act or behave in a certain way: *When I asked Mario what he **did** on Saturday, he said he played tennis.*

doctor ▾ • doctors

A **doctor** is a person whose job it is to keep people healthy and who helps them get better if they are sick: *Fernando had the flu last week and the **doctor** gave him some medicine to help him feel better.*

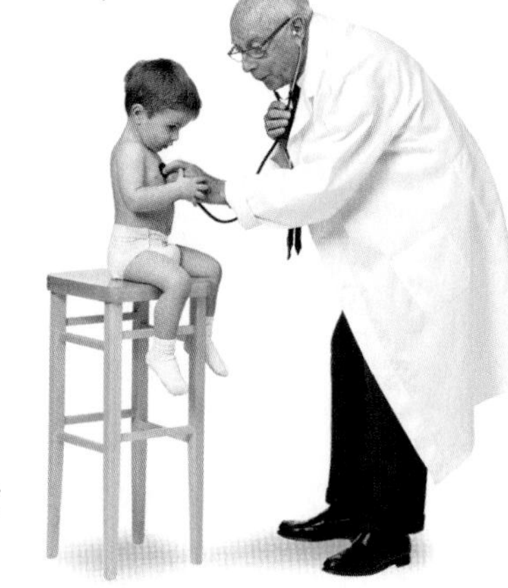

The **doctor** listens to Bobby's heart.

does

Does is a form of the word DO and is used with HE, SHE, or IT: *My sister **does** all her homework on Friday night.* **Doesn't** is a shorter way of saying "does not": *She **doesn't** want to be worrying about it over the weekend.*

dog ▸ • dogs

A **dog** is an animal with four legs and a tail. Dogs eat meat and most dogs bark. People keep many kinds of dogs as pets: *Our **dog** Buster is very friendly, but he scares some people when he barks.*

I **divided** my money into different kinds of coins to count it.

dogs

There are many different animals in the dog family. Some are wild, such as foxes and wolves. Others are tame, such as Chihuahuas and Dalmations, and people keep them as pets.

The calls of a group of wolves can be heard for about six miles.

Chihuahua

Dalmation

Arctic fox

Dingo

Red wolf

Samoyed

African wild dog

Coyote

Golden jackal

Knock on the **door** to see if anybody is home.

doll • dolls

A **doll** is a child's toy that is made to look like a baby, an older child, or an adult: *My small sister has names for all her* ***dolls*** *and she pretends they are real people.*

The **doll** has a pretty dress and a hat.

done

1. **Done** is a form of the word DO and is used with HAS, HAVE, or HAD: *Fatima says that she has already* ***done*** *the shopping.*
2. **Done** also means finished or complete: *The job I started yesterday is now* ***done****.*

don't

Don't is a shorter way of saying "do not": *We will need to buy some eggs because we* ***don't*** *have any.*

door • doors

A **door** is something that you open or close when you enter or leave a space such as a room or a building. You can lock a door if you do not want people to be able to go in: *The front* ***door*** *to our house is made of wood, but the door to our garage is made of strong metal.*

dot • dots

A **dot** is a very small round mark: *Dad's tie is red with white* ***dots****.*

Mia's and Georgia's dresses are covered in **dots**.

double • doubled, doubling

1. To **double** means to make twice the amount: *Last week Helga made ten dollars, but this week she **doubled** that and made twenty dollars.*
2. Double means twice as much or twice as many of something: *Jason was really hungry, so he asked for a **double** helping of the beef stew.*

The children go **down** the water slide quickly.

doubt • doubts, doubted, doubting

1. If you **doubt** something, you think it may not be true: *Melanie **doubts** that her mother will let her go to that movie because it starts so late.*
2. A **doubt** is a feeling that something may not be true: *There is some **doubt** that our friend Antonio will be able to come to visit us next week, because he does not have his plane ticket yet.*

down ▲

If you go **down**, you go from one place to a lower one: *I climbed **down** from the tree.*

Each one of the **dozen** eggs is a different color.

dozen ▲ • dozens *or* dozen

A **dozen** is a group of twelve: *We bought a **dozen** cookies at the store.*

drag • dragged, dragging

Drag means to pull something along the ground: *Frank **dragged** the heavy chair across the kitchen floor.*

dragon ▼ • dragons

A **dragon** is a make-believe monster that looks like a giant lizard with wings and sharp claws. Dragons are supposed to be able to shoot out fire from their mouth.

drain • drains, drained, draining

1. Drain means to take water or another liquid away from something: *We **drained** the fish tank to clean inside it.*
2. A **drain** is a pipe used to move water or liquid away from something: *Dad called in a plumber to fix the blocked **drain** in the sink.*

The **dragon** has a long red and yellow body.

draw ▶ • **drew, drawn, drawing**
To **draw** means to do a picture of something: *Jean used her colored pencils to **draw** a picture of her house.*

David and Ari are **drawing** pictures in the notebook.

drawer • **drawers**
A **drawer** is a box that can slide in and out of a piece of furniture: *I opened the bottom **drawer** of my desk to get some more paper.*

drawing • **drawings**
A **drawing** is a picture that you make with a pencil or crayon: *Emily did a **drawing** of her mom for Mother's Day.*

dream • **dreams, dreamed** *or* **dreamt, dreaming**
1. A **dream** is a story that you can see happening when you are asleep: *I had a **dream** last night that I was flying through the air.*
2. When you **dream**, you can see a story happening while you sleep: *Gina **dreamed** that she was a princess who was locked in a tall castle.*

Nana's **dresser** has lots of drawers to store her clothes.

dress ▶ • **dresses, dressed, dressing**
1. A **dress** looks like a skirt and blouse joined to make one piece: *My sister got a new **dress** for her birthday party.*
2. When you **dress**, you put on clothes: *Matt jumped out of bed and got **dressed** for school.*

Constance is done sewing her **dress**.

dresser ◀ • **dressers**
A **dresser** is a piece of furniture with shelves and drawers. A dresser is used to store things like clothes: *There is a mirror on top of Yvonne's **dresser**.*

drill ▼ • **drills, drilled, drilling**

1. Drill means to make a hole in wood, metal, or other material: *She **drilled** a hole in the wall so that the wire could go through.*

2. A **drill** is a tool that makes holes in wood, metal, or other material: *Dad used a **drill** to make holes for the screws.*

3. A **drill** is also a way of learning something by doing it over and over again: *The teacher says that doing spelling **drills** helps us to learn new words.*

Men use a **drill** to make a hole in the rock.

drink ▼ • **drank, drunk, drinking**

Drink means to swallow a liquid, such as water or milk: *Brian likes to **drink** orange juice with breakfast. Kate **drank** two glasses of water because she was so thirsty.*

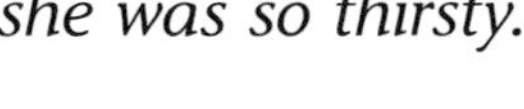

The cat **drinks** milk from a bowl.

The worker is careful when he **drives** the bulldozer.

drive ▲ • **drove, driven, driving**

Drive means to steer a car, bus, or train and make it move the way you want: *Mom is going to **drive** our car to the airport to pick up Dad on the 4 o'clock flight.*

drop ▶ • **drops, dropped, dropping**

1. To **drop** means to let fall: *Jack **dropped** his bag on the ground.*

2. A **drop** means a small amount of liquid: *A **drop** of rain fell on my head.*

Drops of water sit on the window.

drown • **drowned, drowning**

Drown means to die because you cannot breathe underwater: *A boy almost **drowned** in the big waves at the beach.*

The river is **dry** because no rain has fallen for a long time.

drug • drugs

1. A **drug** is a medicine used to make you feel better when you are sick, or to keep you from getting sick: *Aspirin is a* ***drug*** *Mom takes if she has a headache. She buys it from the* ***drugstore****.*

2. There is another kind of **drug** that is not a medicine. It can hurt your body and make you feel sick. It is against the law to use this kind of drug.

drum ▶ • drums

A **drum** is a musical instrument that you hit with your hand or with a stick to make a sound: *Jessica played the* ***drum*** *in the concert at school.*

dry ◀ • drier, driest, dried, drying

1. **Dry** means without water. Dry is the opposite of wet: *The desert is very* ***dry*** *and hot.*

2. To **dry** something means to get water out of it to make it dry: *After the storm had finished, we* ***dried*** *our wet clothes in the sun.*

The baby **ducks** swim close to their parents.

duck ▲ • ducks

A **duck** is a bird that lives on the water. Ducks have webbed feet to help them swim: *A family of* ***ducks*** *used to visit the pond near my uncle's house.*

dug

Dug is a form of the word DIG: *We* ***dug*** *a hole in the garden to plant a tree.*

The man hits the **drum** and makes a loud noise.

dull • duller, dullest

1. **Dull** means not sharp: *The scissors were too **dull** to cut the string.*
2. **Dull** also means boring: *Mom said that the movie was so **dull** she and Dad left before it was over.*

dump • dumped, dumping

If you **dump** something, you drop it in a rough way on the ground, the floor, or some other place: *I **dumped** my books on the table.*

during

During means happening in that time: *A noise woke the girls **during** the night.*

dust • dusted, dusting

1. **Dust** means tiny, dry pieces of dirt: *There was lots of **dust** in the old house. The old piano was very **dusty**.*
2. To **dust** means to wipe dust away: *Mom **dusts** the dining room table every few days.*

DVD • DVDs

A **DVD** is a plastic disk that has movies, music, or other things on it. You can play a DVD on a computer or DVD player: *We have lots of **DVDs** of old movies.*

Store **DVDs** in plastic cases so they will not get scratched.

The wind blows red **dust** over the town.

A B C D E F G H I J K L M N O P Q R S T U V W X Y Z

Each **ear** of wheat contains many seeds.

Ee

Rabbits use their long **ears** to listen for danger.

each

1. **Each** means every one person or thing in a group: ***Each** pupil will be asked ten questions on the test.*
2. **Each** also means for one: *These candies cost five cents **each**.*

eagle ▶ • eagles

An **eagle** is a large, strong bird with a curved beak. It hunts small animals, birds, and fish. Eagles can fly very high: *The **eagle** made its nest in a tall tree.*

ear[1] ▲ • ears

You have an **ear** on each side of your head, near your eyes. People and animals hear sounds through their ears: *Our dog's **ears** stood up when it heard Dad's car coming down the road.*

Eagles use their claws to catch animals to eat.

ear[2] ▶ • ears

An **ear** is also the part of some plants where the seeds grow: *Mom cooked four **ears** of corn for lunch.*

early • earlier, earliest

1. **Early** means near the start of something: *On school days Ross gets up **early** in the morning, at about 6 o'clock.*
2. **Early** also means before the usual time: *The other team did not show up for the game, so we came home **early**.*

earn • earned, earning

1. When you **earn**, you get paid for the work you do: *My sister **earns** money by washing Mom's car.*
2. **Earn** also means getting a reward for doing something well: *Her good work **earned** her a gold star.*

Much of **Earth** is covered in water, so it looks blue from space.

Earth ▶

1. **Earth** is the planet we live on. It takes one year to go around the Sun: *You can see the Moon from **Earth**.*
2. The word **earth** also means dirt: *He dug up the **earth** in the front yard to plant a tree.*

earthquake ▼ • earthquakes

When there is an **earthquake**, the ground shakes and large pieces of earth move. Sometimes things break and buildings fall down.

east ▼

East is the direction you face to see the sun rise in the morning. North, south, east, and west are the four main directions. East is opposite west: *We drove **east** from California to visit my uncle in Arizona. When we got to the **eastern** part of the state, we crossed over a river to get to Arizona.*

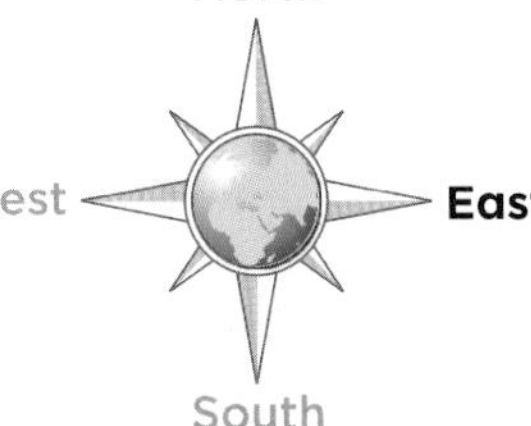

The compass shows the direction for **east.**

earthquakes

Earthquakes happen very suddenly. They can make buildings fall down and roads crack. Broken water pipes may make it hard for firefighters to put out fires.

A B C D E F G H I J K L M N O P Q R S T U V W X Y Z

Easter ▼ • Easters

Easter is a Christian holiday that is on a Sunday in March or April. It celebrates the death of Jesus and his return to life: *We gave each other **Easter** eggs at Easter.*

The word **Easter** probably comes from the name of a goddess of long ago. Her holiday was held in spring. When the Christian holiday of Easter was started, it was held at the same time of year.

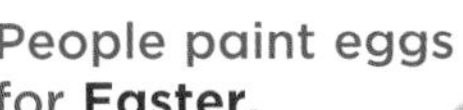

People paint eggs for **Easter.**

easy • easier, easiest

Something is **easy** if it is not hard to do: *This picture book is **easy** to read.*

eat ▶ • ate, eaten, eating

Eat means to chew and swallow food: ***Eat** your lunch or you will be hungry later.*

echo • echoes

An **echo** is a sound that bounces off a hard surface, such as a stone wall or mountain. You hear the sound over and over, but it gets softer each time you hear it: *The climbers shouted when they reached the top of the mountain and the **echoes** reached the people down below.*

The children sit on the **edge** of the pool to practice kicking.

edge ▲ • edges

The **edge** of something is the part where it begins or ends: *He put the glass too close to the **edge** of the table and it fell off onto the floor. The yard has grass in the middle and flowers growing at the **edges**.*

A praying mantis **eats** a butterfly.

The mother snake is protecting her **eggs**.

education • educations

When you learn something, you are getting an **education**: *As part of our **education** on the subject of animals, the teacher took us to the zoo. The talk about tigers at the zoo was very **educational**.*

egg ▲ • eggs

Female birds, insects, and many animals can grow **eggs** inside their body from which their babies are born: *For breakfast, people often eat **eggs** from chickens.*

either

1. You use **either** when you are talking about one of two things: *I would like to play a sport next year, **either** baseball or soccer.*
2. You can use **either** when you mean also: *Sarah didn't like the movie very much, and I didn't **either**.*

elbow • elbows

An **elbow** is the part of an arm where it bends: *I bumped my **elbow** on the corner of the desk.*

elect • elected, electing

When you vote for someone, you **elect** them: *The team **elected** Jules as captain. He'll be the captain until they have another **election** next year.*

electric

Electric means powered by electricity: *In some poor countries, most people don't have **electric** lights or other **electrical** things like refrigerators and washing machines.*

electricity ▼

Electricity is a kind of energy that makes light and heat. It also makes machines go: *Televisions need **electricity** to make them work.*

The bright city lights need **electricity** to work.

elephants

There are two kinds of elephants. African elephants are bigger than Asian elephants. Elephants have long teeth called tusks. They use their trunk to breathe and to bring food and water to their mouth.

African elephant

Asian elephant

An elephant uses water stored in its trunk to take a shower.

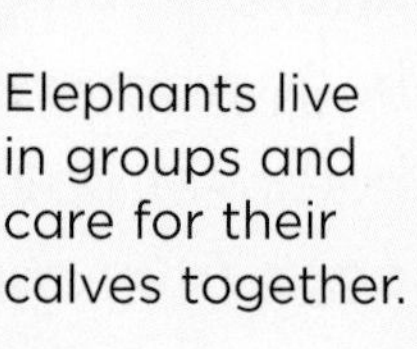

Elephants live in groups and care for their calves together.

elementary school

An **elementary school** teaches the first six or eight grades: *After **elementary** school, I will go to junior high school and then to high school.*

elephant ▲ • elephants

Elephants are the largest animals that live on land. They have a huge body, large ears, and a long nose called a trunk.

elevator ◀ • elevators

An **elevator** is a machine with a small room that carries you up or down from one floor of a building to another floor.

You can see out of glass **elevators** as you ride up and down.

else

1. Else means not the same, or different: *I don't like this food, so can I please have something **else**?*
2. Else also means as well: *Who **else** wants a piece of cake?*
3. Else also means if not: *Hurry up, or **else** you will miss the bus.*

e-mail • e-mails

An **e-mail** is a message that you get or send using a computer: *My friend Jenny sent me an **e-mail** to tell me about the movie she saw last night.*

emergency ▼ • emergencies

An **emergency** is when something dangerous happens very fast and you need to act quickly. A forest fire or a car crash is an emergency.

empty ◀ • emptier, emptiest

If something is **empty**, it has nothing in it: *He drank all his milk and his glass was **empty**.*

We have an **encyclopedia** that has 10 books in the set.

encyclopedia ▲ • encyclopedias

An **encyclopedia** is a book, or set of books, about lots of different things. Encyclopedias usually go from A to Z: *Benjamin opened the "S" part of the **encyclopedia** and read about snakes.*

There was an **emergency** because of the flood.

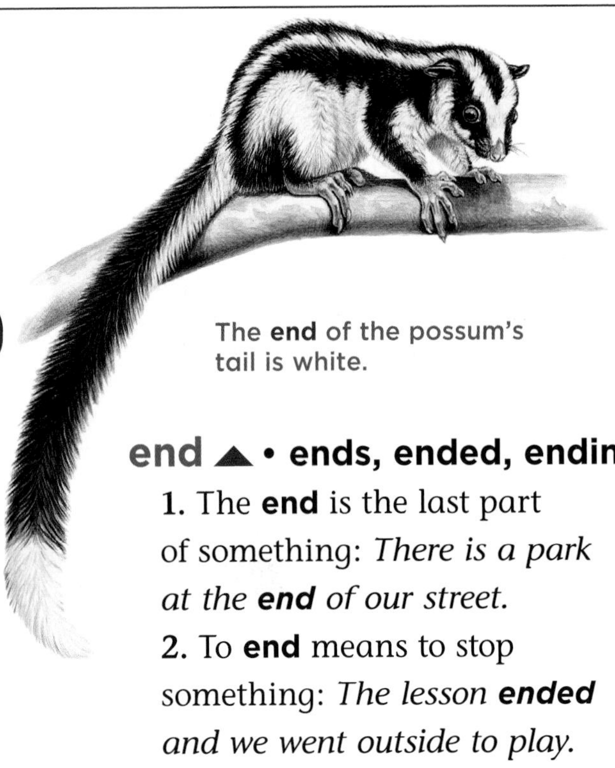
The **end** of the possum's tail is white.

end ▲ • ends, ended, ending

1. The **end** is the last part of something: *There is a park at the **end** of our street.*

2. To **end** means to stop something: *The lesson **ended** and we went outside to play.*

enemy ▼ • enemies

1. An **enemy** is someone who hates another person and wants to hurt them: *The **enemies** of the king took away his power and put him in prison.*

2. An **enemy** is also a country at war with another country: *During World War II, Japan was the **enemy** of the United States, but now the two countries are friends.*

energy

Heat, light, and electricity are kinds of **energy**. Energy is the power that makes machines work. Cars burn gasoline for the energy to make them go. You use your own energy when you run or jump or skip.

The word **energy** was first used in ancient Greece to mean "trying to do something" or "being at work." When a thing, such as a car, uses energy, it is doing work that is useful to people.

engine ▶ • engines

1. An **engine** is a machine that uses energy to make something move: *To drive a car, the first thing you do is start the **engine**.*

The steam **engine** pulls the train.

2. An **engine** is also the part of a train that pulls the rest of the train along: *The **engine** pulled the train up the hill.*

The soldiers sink the ship of their **enemies** during the battle.

engineer ▶ • engineers

1. An **engineer** is a person who plans how to make things like roads, bridges, engines, and machines: *The **engineer** told them how to build the bridge.*
2. An **engineer** is also a person who drives a train engine: *The **engineer** sounds the horn to let us know the train is coming.*

The **engineer** checks on the building project.

English

English is the language people speak in the United States and many other countries around the world. It was first used in the country of England.

The first meaning of the word **English** was "of the Angles." Long ago, a group of people called the Angles went to the country of England. At that time, England was called "Angle-Land," meaning "the country of the Angles."

enjoy • enjoyed, enjoying

Enjoy means to like. When you enjoy something, it makes you feel good and you like to do it: *I **enjoy** going to the movies.*

Before you mail the letter, close the **envelope**.

enough

If you have **enough** of something, you have as many or as much as you need: *Andy had **enough** eggs to bake a cake. I did not have **enough** time to finish my work and will do the rest tomorrow.*

enter ▶ • entered, entering

If you **enter** a place, you go into it: *Mom asked me to **enter** the room quietly because the baby was sleeping. The way into a building is called its **entrance**.*

The sign shows the way to **enter**.

entertainment • entertainments

An **entertainment** is something that people watch for fun: *There was a clown at Melinda's party as part of the **entertainment**.*

entire

If something is **entire**, it is whole with nothing left out: *He ate the **entire** sandwich and there wasn't one bit left over. It has rained the **entire** day and the streets are flooded.*

envelope ◀ • envelopes

An **envelope** is a piece of folded paper. Letters and cards are mailed inside envelopes: *Betty sent her friend a birthday card in an **envelope** with love hearts drawn on it.*

environment ▼ • environments

The **environment** is everything around you, such as the air, water, land, and living plants and animals: *The camp leader told us not to leave garbage behind when we left the camp, or we would be hurting the* ***environment****.*

equal • equaled, equaling

1. If two things are **equal**, they are the same in number or size as each other: *He cut the apple into four* ***equal*** *pieces and gave one to each child.*
2. To **equal** means to be the same as or to add up to: *Ten plus ten* ***equals*** *twenty.*

Many different animals live together in this **environment** in Africa.

equipment

A piece of **equipment** is a tool or other thing you need to do a job or play a sport: *The* ***equipment*** *Jay needed to fix the gate was a hammer and some nails. A ball, a bat, and a glove are part of the* ***equipment*** *used to play baseball.*

You can get rid of pencil marks with an **eraser.**

erase ▲ • erased, erasing

If you **erase** something, you get rid of it by rubbing it out or taking it away: *Hoshi didn't like the way her drawing looked, so she* ***erased*** *it. Eloise borrowed my* ***eraser*** *to clean the pencil marks off her page.*

People ride up and down on the **escalators** in the shopping mall.

escalator ▲ • escalators

An **escalator** is a set of moving stairs that can go up or down: *In the mall, Isaac and his mom went up the **escalator** to go to the shoe store.*

escape • escaped, escaping

If you **escape** from something, you get away from it: *When Annie left the door of her mouse's cage open, it **escaped** and ran out the door.*

especially

Especially means more than usual or in a special way: *I like to swim in the ocean, **especially** on days when the waves are not too high.*

even

1. Something that is **even** is flat or smooth: *The ice on the frozen pond was **even**, so it was easy to skate on.*
2. Also, a number that is **even** is one that can be divided in two with none left over: *Twenty can be divided into two groups of ten, so it is an **even** number.*
3. If something is **even**, it also means it is the same height or length as something else: *The table kept leaning to one side, because its legs were not **even**.*

evening ▼ • evenings

Evening is the time around the end of the day when it is becoming night: *They usually have dinner at about 6 o'clock in the **evening**.*

ever

Ever means at some time or at any time: *Have you **ever** seen a kangaroo in the zoo?*

We turn on the lights at our house in the **evening**.

every

Every means each person or thing in a group: ***Every*** *child in the class has their own desk to sit at.*

everyone ▼

Everyone means every person in a group: *At the end of the year, Mr. Jones gave* ***everyone*** *in his class their report card. He also gave* ***everybody*** *a copy of a book about animals to read.*

everything

Everything means all the things that are in a group: *Jasmine packed* ***everything*** *she was taking on her trip in one bag.*

everywhere

Everywhere means in all places: *Ben could not find his jacket, even though he had looked* ***everywhere*** *in the house for it.*

evil

Someone who is **evil** is very bad or causes harm on purpose: *In a story that I read, an* ***evil*** *man put the princess to sleep for a hundred years.*

Donkeys, pikas, and rhinoceroses are **examples** of animals that do not eat meat.

exact

If something is **exact**, it is true or done without a mistake: *I guessed that about a hundred people were there, and it turned out the* ***exact*** *number was ninety-two. Kelly said she had been sick all week, but that isn't* ***exactly*** *true because I saw her at the mall yesterday.*

example ▲ • examples

An **example** is something that shows you what other things of the same kind are like: *Swans and ducks are* ***examples*** *of birds that can swim.*

Everyone on the team wears a red hat and a white shirt.

excellent

Something that is **excellent** is very, very good. It is much better than most other things of the same kind: *Tanya baked an **excellent** banana cake and we ate it all right away.*

except ▶

Except means everything apart from just one: *All of the ponies were black, **except** one, which was brown.*

excited

If you are **excited**, you feel happy about something and are interested in it: *Fiona couldn't sit still because she was **excited** about going to the zoo. It was **exciting** because she was going to see the new baby giraffe.*

The men **exercise** by playing a game called squash.

All of the seats are blue **except** for the one that is red.

excuse • excuses, excused, excusing

1. To **excuse** means to let someone off from doing something: *James was **excused** from swimming class because he had a cold.*
2. To **excuse** also means to forgive someone: *Grandma **excused** me for breaking her dish because it was an accident.*
3. An **excuse** is a reason for being let off or forgiven: *Sue's **excuse** for being late was that her alarm clock didn't go off.*

exercise ◀ • exercises, exercised, exercising

1. **Exercise** is something you do to stay in good health and to feel good: *Walking, running, swimming, and playing a sport are all good kinds of **exercise**.*
2. If you **exercise**, you use your body to do something to stay in good health: *My Aunt Kate **exercises** by riding her bike each day.*

exit ▶ • **exits**

An **exit** is a way to go out of somewhere: *At the library, each door that goes to the outside has a big sign saying "**EXIT**" above it. To go to Grandma's house, we will get off this road at **Exit** 42.*

expect • **expected, expecting**

If you **expect** something, you think it is likely to happen: *Adam **expects** to do well on the spelling test tomorrow, because he has been studying a lot.*

The gold and diamond watch is **expensive**.

expensive ▲

If something is **expensive**, it costs a lot of money: *Max could not buy the model airplane he wanted because it was too **expensive**.*

experience • **experiences**

1. An **experience** is something you do that you remember well: *The **experience** of singing on stage was very exciting for Chloe.*

2. **Experience** is also what you have if you have been doing something for a long time: *Ben got that job because he already has three years' **experience** working in a restaurant.*

experiment ▼ • **experiments, experimented, experimenting**

1. An **experiment** is a test you do to find out if something is true or not: *Hannah's **experiment** was to see what would happen if she added water to flour. In science, people will do **experiments** to test if a certain idea is really a fact.*

2. If you **experiment**, you try something out: *Ethan **experimented** with his paints and made different colors by mixing them.*

explain • **explained, explaining**

If you **explain** something, you make it easy to understand or give its meaning: *When I found the word "eternal" in a book I was reading, Mom **explained** what it meant. Her **explanation** was very clear. Eternal means "lasting forever."*

Bronwyn measured how much water to give each plant for her **experiment**.

explode ▶ • exploded, exploding

To **explode** means to suddenly blow apart with a loud noise: *The balloon* ***exploded*** *when Rachel blew too much air into it.*

explore ▼ • explored, exploring

If you **explore**, you look around somewhere to find out new things: *The astronaut set off in a rocket to* ***explore*** *Mars. James Cook was a famous* ***explorer*** *who was one of the first people to sail all over the Pacific Ocean.*

explosion • explosions

An **explosion** is what happens when something explodes: *The* ***explosion*** *of the gas bottle started a fire at the back of the house.*

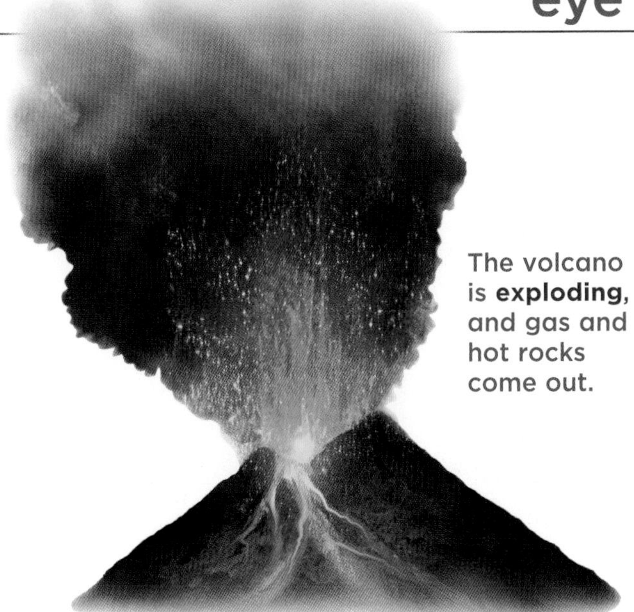

The volcano is **exploding**, and gas and hot rocks come out.

extra • extras

When you have something **extra**, you have more than you need: *Gus took a bottle of water on his bike ride for himself, and an* ***extra*** *one in case his friend wanted one.*

eye • eyes

The **eye** is the part of the body that an animal uses to see: *Penny woke up, then opened her* ***eyes*** *to look at the clock.*

The ships set sail to **explore** the world.

Ff

Trevor's **face** is painted like a lion.

face ◀ • faces, faced, facing

1. The **face** is the front of an animal or person's head. Your face is where your eyes, nose, and mouth are: *When the baby ate her dessert, she got ice cream all over her **face**.*

2. To **face** means to have the front of your body turned toward something: *The teacher asked Jill to **face** the class when she gave her report.*

fact • facts

A **fact** is something that people know is true: *It is a **fact** that it gets dark earlier in winter than in summer.*

factory ▶ • factories

A **factory** is a building or group of buildings where people use machines to make lots of things: *Hundreds of motorcycles are made every week in the **factory** where my dad works.*

There is a **fair** in our town every summer.

fair[1] • fairer, fairest

If you are **fair**, you treat different people in the same way as each other: *To be **fair**, Tom gave each of his friends a turn to ride his new bike.*

fair[2] ▲ • fairs

A **fair** is a place where people sell things they have made or grown. There is also music at fairs, along with games and rides: *At the **fair**, Tina bought a necklace from a man selling jewelry that he had made.*

The machines in the **factory** are making cars.

Katie wrote a story about two **fairies** for class.

fairy • fairies

A **fairy** is a very small person who has magical powers and wings to fly with. Fairies are make-believe, not real: *In the story Ella read, the **fairy** had a magic wand.*

fall • falls, fell, fallen, falling

1. To **fall** means to go from a higher place to a lower one: *Be careful when you go up in the tree, so that you don't **fall** out.*
2. A **fall** is when a person or thing suddenly comes down hard on the ground or floor: *Cathy broke her arm when she had a **fall** from her pony.*
3. **Fall** is also the season between summer and winter: *In the **fall**, the leaves of the maple trees change color and fall to the ground.*

false • falser, falsest

Something that is **false** is not true or correct: *It is **false** that insects have seven legs, but true that they have six.*

We use a **fan** to keep cool during summer.

family • families

1. Your **family** is the group of people who are your relatives. Your mother, father, brothers, or sisters are your close family. Your grandparents, uncles, aunts, and cousins are also a part of your family: *My mom had a new baby, so now there are four people in our **family**.*
2. A **family** is also a group of things that are similar to each other: *The wolf and the fox belong to the same **family** of animals.*

This is a photo of my whole **family**.

famous

Something or someone **famous** is known about by lots of people: *The Grand Canyon is a **famous** place in the United States. Elvis Presley was a **famous** singer.*

fan[1] • fans, fanned, fanning

1. A **fan** is a thing that you use to move air to make a place cooler: *Mom switched on the ceiling **fan** because it was hot in the house.*
2. To **fan** means to move air backward and forward: *The wind **fanned** the forest fire and made it get bigger.*

a b c d e f g h i j k l m n o p q r s t u v w x y z

fan[2] • fans

A **fan** is a person who likes some person or thing very much, such as a movie star, a sport, or a certain sports team: *David is a big baseball **fan** and really likes to watch his favorite team, the Boston Red Sox.*

The word **fan** comes from the word *fanatic*. A fanatic is someone who thinks about a certain thing a lot, as if it is more important than anything else.

far • farther, farthest

1. **Far** means not close: *My best friend Jennifer has moved **far** away to another state, but I will still be able to talk to her on the phone.*
2. **Far** is also used to talk about the distance between places: *It is not **far** from my house to school, and I walk there every day.*

The wrestler is **fat**, but he is also very strong.

farm ▶ • farms

A **farm** is a place where animals are raised and plants are grown to use for food: *Kevin's parents have a **farm** where they keep cows that they get milk and cheese from. His parents are both **farmers**.*

farther

Farther is a form of the word FAR: *It is **farther** from here to Ben's house than it is to Daniel's.*

fast ▲ • faster, fastest

If you are **fast**, it means you are moving quickly: *I ran as **fast** as I could, but I couldn't get the ball before it rolled down the hill.*

fat ◀ • fatter, fattest

1. A **fat** person or animal is heavier than it should be in order to be healthy: *I had to stop feeding my dog so much food, because she was getting too **fat**.*
2. If something is **fat**, it is thick or wide: *It took Lara a long time to read that **fat** book.*

My grandparents' **farm** has a big barn where the animals sleep.

father • fathers

A **father** is a male parent: *Usually when birds lay eggs, the **father** brings food to the mother while she sits on the eggs in the nest.*

faucet • faucets

A **faucet** is something on the end of a pipe that is used to turn water on and off: *Turn the **faucet** off all the way or it will drip.*

fault • faults

If something is your **fault**, you are the one who made something wrong happen. You are to blame for it: *It was Julie's own **fault** that she missed the school bus, because she got out of bed too late.*

favor • favors

A **favor** is something kind or nice that you do for someone to help them: *I did Mom a **favor** by doing the laundry.*

favorite • favorites

Your **favorite** thing or person is the one you like best: *Meg took her **favorite** teddy bear with her when she had to stay in the hospital.*

fear • fears, feared, fearing

1. **Fear** is the strong feeling that something bad may happen: *Beth has a **fear** of big dogs.*
2. If you are afraid of something, you **fear** it: *James **feared** he would fall off the ladder and hurt himself.*

feast ▼ • feasts

A **feast** is a large, special meal for many people: *Our friends prepared a **feast** to celebrate Chinese New Year, with many different kinds of foods.*

Native Americans often use **feathers** when they make special hats.

feather ▶ • feathers

A **feather** is one of the light, soft parts that cover a bird's body. Feathers protect the bird's skin, keep the bird warm, and help it to fly: *Janine's pet parrot has bright green **feathers**.*

The people have a **feast** with many kinds of food.

feed • **fed, feeding**
When you **feed** a person or animal, you give them food to eat: *It's my job to **feed** our cat every day.*

feel • **felt, feeling**
1. When you **feel** something, you put your hand or another body part on it. You touch it or it touches you: ***Feel** how hard this rock is.*
2. **Feel** also means to know in your mind how you are: *I **feel** happy when I play with my dog.*
3. The **feel** of something means the way it is when you touch it: *I like the **feel** of a kitten's soft fur.*

feeling • **feelings**
1. A **feeling** is the way you are in your mind about something. Being happy, sad, or afraid are feelings: *I had a **feeling** that something was wrong from the look on Jan's face, and she told me her team lost the big game.*
2. If you hurt someone's **feelings**, you make them unhappy: *Bruce's **feelings** were hurt because we didn't invite him to our party.*

feet
You say **feet** for more than one FOOT: *I put both **feet** in the water.*

fell
Fell is a form of the word FALL: *The book **fell** off the table onto the floor.*

felt
Felt is a form of the word FEEL: *I **felt** afraid when I saw the spider.*

The **female** kangaroo has a baby.

female ◀ • **females**
A **female** is a person or animal that can have babies or lay eggs. A female is the opposite of a male: *Women and girls are **females**.*

fence ▼ • **fences**
A **fence** is something like a wall that is built to keep things in or out, or to go between one place and another: *There is a wooden **fence** between our yard and our neighbor's yard. The best hit in baseball is one that goes over the **fence** for a home run.*

The horses look over the **fence**.

fern ▶ • ferns

A **fern** is a plant with green leaves and no flowers. Ferns grow in damp places where the sun does not shine much.

Ferns can either grow tall or grow low on the ground.

ferry ▼ • ferries

A **ferry** is a boat that takes people across water: *We took the **ferry** to the other side of the lake.*

Some **ferries** can carry cars and trucks.

festival ▼ • festivals

A **festival** is a special time with music and food when people feel happy: *The town has a **festival** every year to celebrate the start of summer.*

fever • fevers

When you have a **fever**, your body temperature is higher than it should be and your body feels hot. If you have a fever, you are sick: *The doctor took my temperature with a thermometer, and it showed I had a **fever**.*

The word **fever** comes from an old word meaning "a fire" or "to burn." In old times, people thought that someone with a bad fever had a fire burning inside their body to make them hot.

few • fewer, fewest

A **few** means not many: *Hailey is getting excited because it is only a **few** more days until her birthday.*

fiction • fictions

Fiction is a story that is made up by the writer. It is not about real people and things that really happened: *This story about a wolf that can drive a car is **fiction**. The book I am reading about how wolves hunt for food is **nonfiction**.*

There are lion dances at the **festival** for Chinese New Year.

a b c d e f g h i j k l m n o p q r s t u v w x y z

A B C D E F G H I J K L M N O P Q R S T U V W X Y Z

field ▼ • fields

1. A **field** is an area of land where there are no trees: *The farmer planted corn in the **field**.*

2. A **field** is also an area of land where you can play a sport or game: *The football players ran onto the **field** to start the game.*

There are fences around the **fields** on my aunt's farm.

fierce ▶ • fiercer, fiercest

If something is **fierce**, it is wild, strong, and dangerous: *The **fierce** dog guarding the yard barked at us through the fence, and then he jumped up and tried to bite us.*

fight • fights, fought, fighting

1. When people **fight**, they are mad at each other. They shout and push and hit and want to hurt the other person: *My friend was **fighting** with his brother and punched him on the nose.*

2. A **fight** is when people do not agree about something, and shout and argue a lot about it: *Jocelyn had a **fight** with her parents about doing her homework.*

figure • figures

A **figure** is a sign that you use for a number: *We write the **figure** "6" for "six."*

The man **fills** the container with grapes.

fill ▲ • filled, filling

When you **fill** something, you put as much into it as it will hold: *Rachel asked me to **fill** her glass with milk, all the way to the top.*

The **fierce** alligator catches the bird.

The shark has white tips on its **fins**.

film • films

1. A **film** is a very thin covering on the top of something: *There is a **film** of oil on the water.*
2. Film is also a special, very thin plastic that is used in some cameras to make photographs or movies: *Lawrence bought some **film** to use in his old camera.*
3. A **film** is also a movie: *"Star Wars" was a very popular **film**.*

fin ▲ • fins

A **fin** is one of the flat, pointed parts that sticks out of the body of a fish. Dolphins and whales also have fins. Fins help the fish to keep its balance and to move through the water.

final

If something is **final**, it is the last thing and comes at the end: *December is the **final** month of the year. We waited an hour for the bus, and then it **finally** came.*

find • found, finding

When you **find** something, you discover where it is: *Jack was lucky to **find** a ten-dollar bill in his old coat.*

fine[1] • finer, finest

1. If something is **fine**, it is very good: *90 out of 100 is a **fine** mark on a test.*
2. If you are **fine**, you are feeling well and healthy: *I was sick last week, but I'm **fine** now.*

fine[2] • fines

A **fine** is money that has to be paid for doing something wrong: *My uncle had to pay a **fine** for parking his car in the bus stop.*

finger ▼ • fingers

A **finger** is one of the five long, thin, end parts of your hand. One of these fingers is your thumb: *I pushed my **fingers** into my glove.*

You can use your **fingers** to make shadows that look like animals.

The first horse to **finish** the race will win.

finish ▲ • finished, finishing

Finish means to come to an end: *I've nearly **finished** reading this book—just six pages more to go.*

fire • fires

A **fire** is the light, heat, and flames made by something that is burning: *When we camped out, we made a **fire** to cook some hamburgers.*

fire engine

A **fire engine** is a truck that takes firefighters to a fire. It also carries hoses and ladders and other things to help put out the fire and save people: *Most **fire engines** are red and have bright lights, so people can see them and get out of their way.*

firefighter ▼ • firefighters

A **firefighter** is someone whose job is to put out fires and to go to where a person is sick or hurt to help them there: *The **firefighter** carried the girl down the ladder from the burning building.*

The **firefighters** use water to put out the fire in the building.

A **firefly** has a light that flashes on and off at the end of its tail.

firefly ▶ • **fireflies**

A **firefly** is a small flying insect that gives off light in the dark. Fireflies live in wet places in the woods and you can see them only at night.

fireplace • **fireplaces**

A **fireplace** is a place in a room where you can burn a fire indoors. It has a chimney above it to take away the smoke: *Dad started a fire in the **fireplace** to warm the room.*

fireworks ▼

Fireworks burn or explode to make loud noises or bright, colored patterns of light: *Amy stayed up late to watch the **fireworks** on New Year's Eve.*

Fireworks light up the night sky.

first

If someone or something is **first**, they are before anyone or anything else: *Neil Armstrong was the **first** person to stand on the Moon.*

first aid ▶

If someone gets sick suddenly or has been hurt in an accident, the help that is given to them before they can get to a doctor is called **first aid**: *The coach gave John **first aid** when he hurt his leg playing football.*

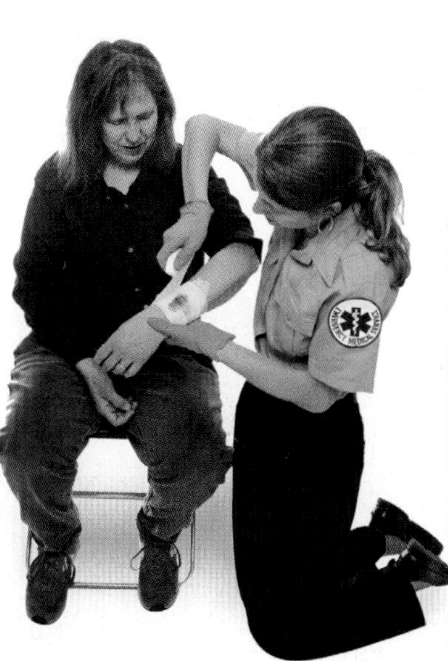

Mom needs **first aid** because she cut her arm.

fish

There are thousands of different kinds of fish. Some live in salt water and others live in fresh water. Most fish have scales that cover and protect their body. Some fish, such as sharks, hunt other fish to eat.

Moorish idol

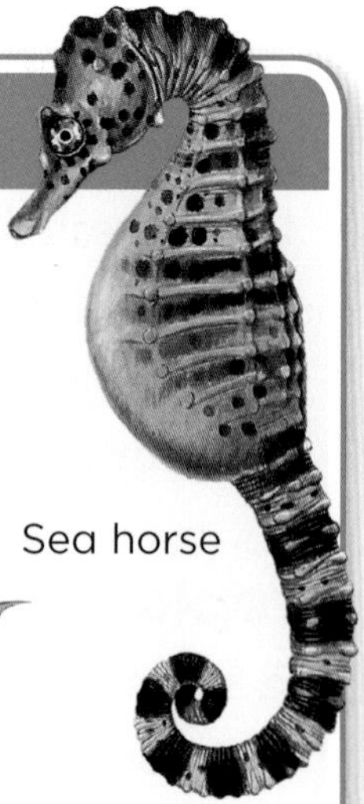

Sea horse

Salmon

Purplequeen

Loach

Hagfish

Leopard shark

Butterflyfish

Mandarin fish

Anemonefish

Hammerhead

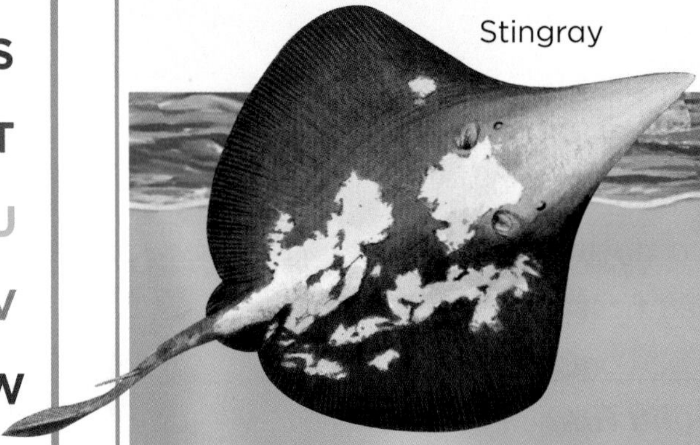

Stingray

Piranha

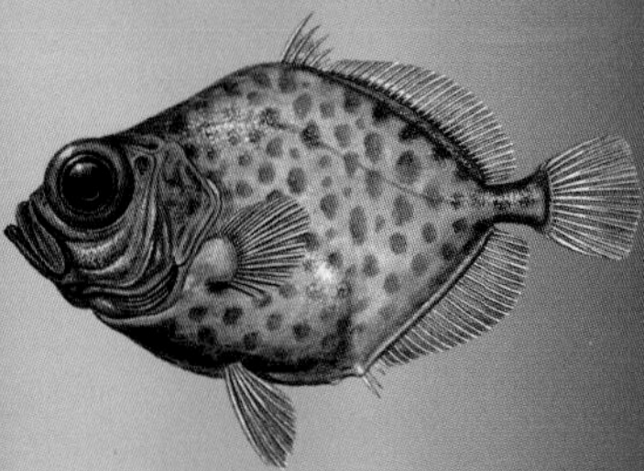

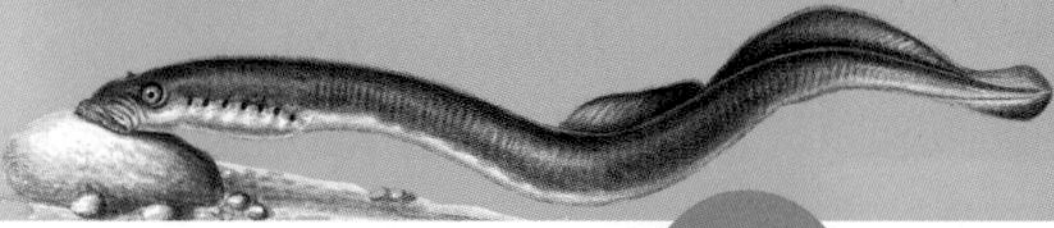

Lamprey

Spotted oreo

The United Kingdom's **flag** is called the Union Jack.

fish ◀ • **fish** *or* **fishes, fished, fishing**
1. A **fish** is an animal that lives in the water. Many different kinds of fish live in the ocean and in lakes and rivers. People often eat fish as food: *__Fish__ swim with their fins and can breathe under the water.*
2. To **fish** means to catch or try to catch fish: *We __fished__ from the boat. Uncle Giorgio likes to go __fishing__, but sometimes he doesn't catch any fish.*

fist • **fists**
Your **fist** is your hand with the fingers closed into a tight ball: *The angry man shouted and shook his __fists__.*

fit • **fitted, fitting**
To **fit** means to be the right shape or size: *I like this shirt and it __fits__ me well. Will this chair __fit__ into the back seat of the car, so that we can bring it home?*

fix ▼ • **fixed, fixing**
When you **fix** something that is broken or not working, you repair it or make it work again: *Dad helped me __fix__ the broken wing on my toy plane and now I can fly it again.*

Melissa needs glue to **fix** the broken bowl.

flag ◀ • **flags**
A **flag** is a piece of cloth with a special design on it that is the sign of a country. Every country has its own flag. The flag of the United States is red, white, and blue with fifty stars and thirteen stripes.

flame • **flames**
A **flame** is the hot, yellow light you see when something is burning: *Daniel poured some water on the campfire and the __flames__ went out.*

flashlight • **flashlights**
A **flashlight** is a small light you can carry around in your hand. A battery makes it work: *Jim put on his __flashlight__ when he went into the dark cave, to see if anything was there.*

Linda rolled out the cookie dough to make it **flat**.

flat ▲ • **flatter, flattest**
If something is **flat**, it is smooth and level: *The top of this table is __flat__.*

flavor • **flavors**
Flavor is the taste that something has: *Which __flavor__ of ice cream do you want—chocolate or vanilla?*

Haley and Ryan do the puzzle on the **floor.**

flew
Flew is a form of the word FLY: *The duck opened its wings and **flew** away.*

float • floated, floating
1. To **float** means to stay on the top of the water, without going down into it: *If I throw this empty plastic bottle into the swimming pool, I think it will **float**.*
2. **Float** also means to move slowly and gently through the water or the air: *A feather **floated** down from the bird's nest.*

flood • floods, flooded, flooding
1. A **flood** is a lot of water that covers land that is usually dry: *We had a **flood** last year because there was so much rain that the river went over its sides and into the town.*
2. To **flood** means to cover with water: *When Will forgot to turn off the faucet, the water **flooded** the bathroom floor.*

floor • floors
1. The **floor** is the level surface of a room that you walk on or stand on: *The cup rolled off the table and fell onto the **floor**.*
2. A **floor** is also all the rooms that are at the same level of a building: *The doctor's office is on the third **floor**.*

flour • flours
Flour is a powder made from wheat or from other grain. Flour is used to make bread, biscuits, and cakes: *Chris measured out two cups of **flour** to make the cake.*

flow • flows, flowed, flowing
1. If something **flows**, it moves along in a smooth way, without any breaks in it: *The river **flowed** from the top of the mountain to the valley below.*
2. A **flow** is the smooth moving along of something, such as a liquid like water.

The bridge is in danger of being washed away in the **flood.**

flower ▼ • flowers

A **flower** is the part of a plant that makes seeds and fruits. Flowers come in many colors and are usually good to smell: *We picked **flowers** from our garden to give to Grandma on her birthday.*

flu • flus

The **flu** is an illness like a bad cold, but much worse. When someone has the flu, they feel sore in parts of their body and get a fever: *When Joe had the **flu**, he was very sick and had to stay in bed for more than a week.*

Some **flies,** such as the deer fly, bite.

fly[1] • flew, flown, flying

1. To **fly** is to move through the air: *Birds can **fly** from one tree to another tree.*

2. Fly also means to move about in the air: *A flag was **flying** from the top of the ship.*

fly[2] ▲ • flies

A **fly** is an insect with two wings: *Ali waved her hands to keep the **flies** away from the picnic table.*

flowers

Flowers come in lots of different colors, shapes, and sizes. They grow on trees, bushes, and other plants. Insects and birds feed on flowers. Many people grow plants in their gardens especially for their beautiful flowers.

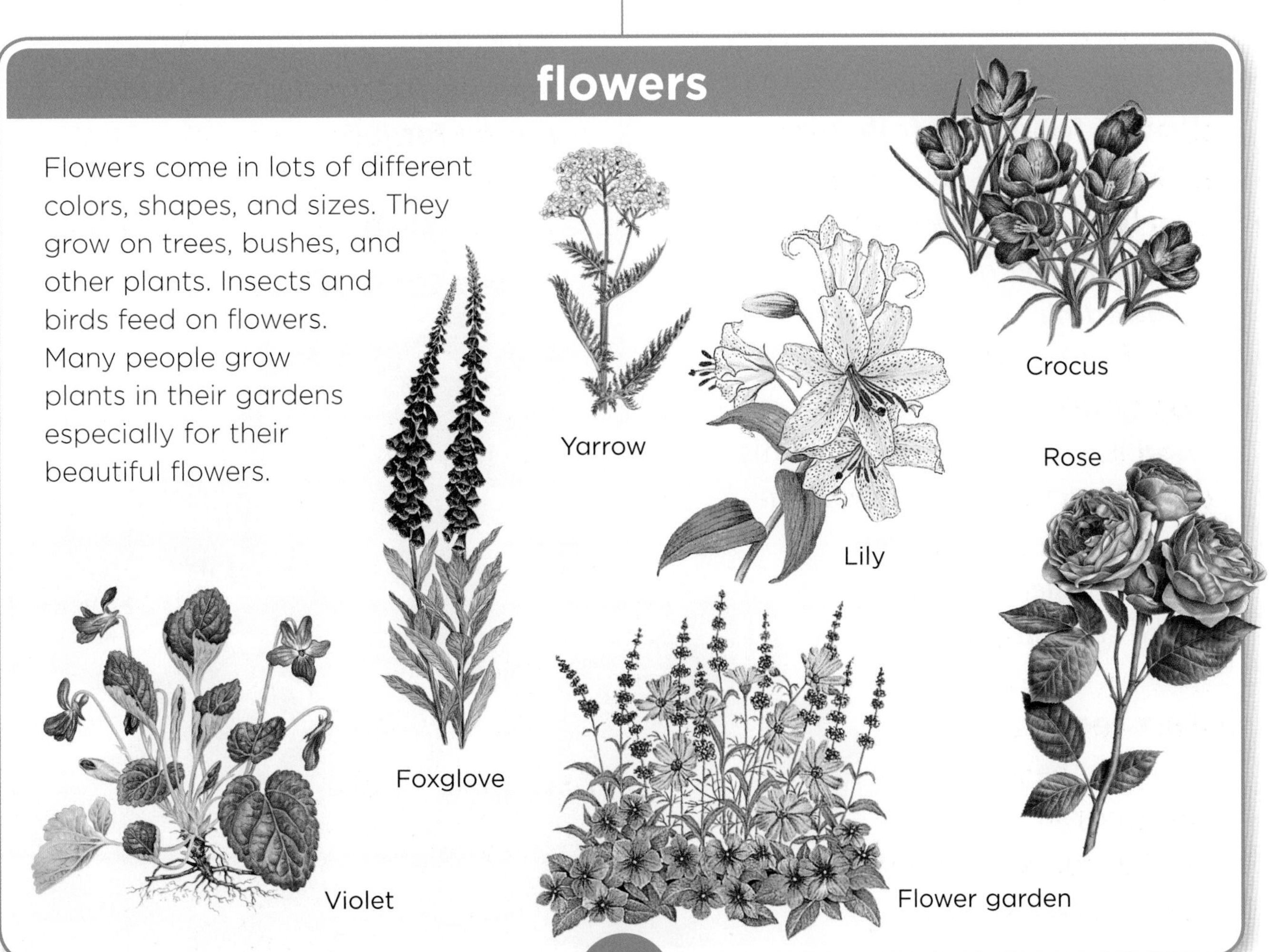

A B C D E F G H I J K L M N O P Q R S T U V W X Y Z

fog • fogs

Fog is tiny drops of water in the air that make a thick cloud close to the ground: *The tops of the building were covered in a **fog**.*

fold ▶ • folded, folding

When you **fold** something, you bend it over so that it becomes smaller: *This bed and chair **fold** up, so you can put them away in the closet. Patti keeps pictures of her pet dog in a special **folder** she made from stiff paper.*

Colleen has **folded** all of the towels.

follow • followed, following

Follow means to go or come after something or somebody: *Megan let her big brother go first, then she **followed** him down the narrow path.*

food • foods

Food is what people and animals eat to keep them alive: *Katherine eats all types of **food**, but her little sister does not like to eat fish.*

foot • feet

A **foot** is the part of your body at the end of your leg: *Lisa hopped along on one **foot**.*

football ▼ • footballs

1. **Football** is a game that two teams play on a large field with a goal at either end. Each team has eleven players. The players on one team try to score points by throwing, carrying, or kicking the ball over the other team's goal. The other team tries to stop them.
2. The ball you use to play this game is also called a **football**.

for

1. You say **for** when you are talking about something lasting through a certain time, distance, or amount: *The party went on **for** two hours.*
2. You also use **for** when something is meant for a person or purpose: *I got the red sweater as a birthday present **for** Julia.*

The player running with the **football** is trying to score.

The nurse touches Marcy's **forehead** to see if it feels warm.

forehead ▲ • foreheads
Your **forehead** is the top part of your face, above your eyes and below your hair: *He wore a cap to keep the sun off his eyes and **forehead**.*

foreign
If something is **foreign**, it comes from another country that is not your country: *Patricia learns a **foreign** language, Japanese, at school.*

forest ▶ • forests
A **forest** is a large area of land covered by trees: *We went for a walk in the **forest**.*

forever
Forever means that something will last for all time: *Mom and Dad tell me that they will love me **forever**.*

forget • forgot, forgotten *or* **forgot, forgetting**
If you **forget**, you do not remember something: *Did you **forget** to bring your umbrella? You're going to get really wet in this rain.*

forgive • forgave, forgiven, forgiving
Forgive means to stop being mad at someone or thinking they are wrong about something: *My sister said she would **forgive** me for breaking her necklace, because I said I was sorry.*

fork • forks
A **fork** is a small tool that you eat food with. Forks have a handle at one end and long, thin points at the other end: *I use a knife and **fork** to eat my dinner.*

form • forms, formed, forming
1. **Form** is the shape that something has: *George's birthday cake was in the **form** of a football.*
2. To **form** means to make or shape something: *The teacher told the children to **form** two straight lines.*

Dan enjoys walking in the redwood **forest**.

fossils

Fossils of bones tell us how big the animals were, what they looked like, and what they ate. Fossil footprints tell us how the animals walked, and about the groups they lived in.

Fish fossil

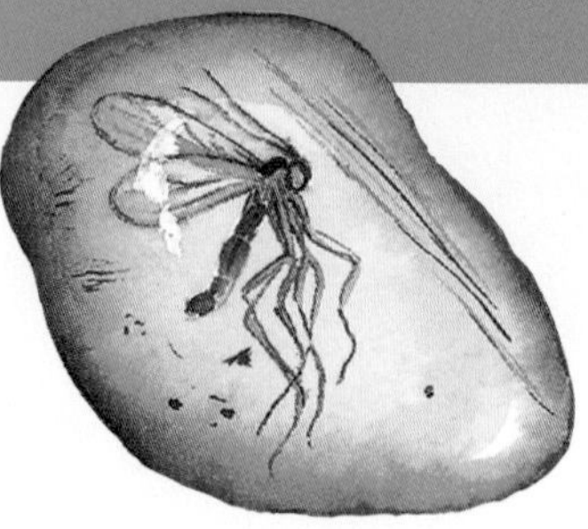

Insect fossil

Scientists use tools to remove fossils from the ground.

fort ▼ • forts

A **fort** is a strong building that is hard for an enemy to get into: *The soldiers used large, heavy guns to blow a hole in the thick stone walls of the **fort**.*

This **fort** is easy to protect because it is on top of a mountain.

forward

Forward means toward a place or time ahead: *The parade moved **forward** along Main Street. My watch was running slow, and I had to set it **forward** by twenty minutes.*

fossil ▲ • fossils

A **fossil** is a part or print of an animal or plant that died a long time ago and became hard. Fossils are found in rock: *Those **fossils** of the dinosaur's teeth and bones are millions of years old.*

found

Found is a form of the word FIND: *Mrs. Martinez gave a reward to the boy who **found** her purse.*

fountain • fountains

A **fountain** sends a small stream of water up into the air. Some fountains are nice to look at. Others are for drinking water from: *The **fountain** in the middle of the pond shot water high up into the air from a statue.*

Fourth of July ▶

The **Fourth of July** is an American holiday that honors the day when the United States first became a country. That day was July 4, 1776. This holiday is also called **Independence Day**.

There are big celebrations on the **Fourth of July** in the United States.

fox ▼ • foxes

A **fox** is a small wild animal that looks like a dog. Foxes have thick, reddish fur, a long, bushy tail, and a thin head with large, pointy ears: *The **fox** jumped on the rabbit and killed it.*

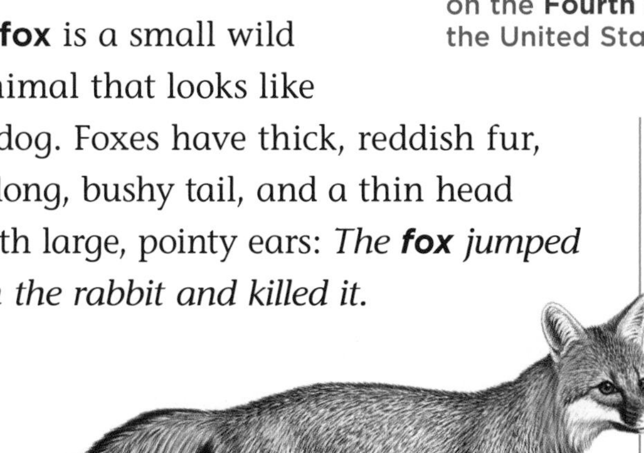

The gray **fox** is good at climbing trees.

Popsicles are desserts that have been **frozen** and are nice to eat on hot days.

free • freer, freest

1. If something is **free**, it costs no money: *The Fourth of July concert in the park was **free**, and anyone could come to listen without paying any money.*
2. **Free** also means to be able to do what you want and not be held back: *The birds are **free** to fly wherever they want.*

freeze ▲ • froze, frozen, freezing

Freeze means to get hard and solid because it is very cold: *Water **freezes** and turns into ice. I took the ice cream out of the **freezer** for dessert.*

fresh • fresher, freshest

1. If something is **fresh**, it is new. It has just been made or done: *Tony did not like what he wrote, so he got a **fresh** piece of paper and started again.*
2. Also, if water is **fresh**, it is not salty: *The Great Lakes have **fresh** water, but the Atlantic and Pacific Ocean have salt water.*

friend ▸ • friends

A **friend** is a person whom you like and who likes you. Friends like doing things together and spending time with each other: *Lisa and Melanie became **friends** when they went to the same dance class. The class was very **friendly** toward the new girl.*

frighten ▾ • frightened, frightening

Frighten means to scare or make afraid: *When Paul jumped out of the closet and yelled "Boo!," he **frightened** me. What he did was really **frightening** to me.*

The balloon pops and the loud noise **frightens** the boy.

My **friends** and I like to go to the beach on weekends.

frog ▸ • frogs

A **frog** is a small animal that lives in or near water. Frogs have toes that are joined together and long back legs that they use to hop about on land or to swim in water.

from

1. You say **from** to show where or when something starts: *The plane flew **from** Chicago to New York.*

2. You also use **from** when something starts at a person, thing, or place: *Jennifer got a phone call **from** her grandpa.*

3. You also use **from** for a distance away: *Their house is two blocks **from** the playground.*

front • fronts

The **front** is the part that faces forward or is seen first: *A big sign at the **front** of the store said "Sale Today." The driver of a car sits in the **front** seat on the left.*

A B C D E F G H I J K L M N O P Q R S T U V W X Y Z

frogs

Frogs spend a lot of time on land, but they die if they dry out. They lay their eggs in water. Most frogs eat insects, but a few can catch larger animals, such as mice. Frogs call to each other. Each kind of frog has its own special call.

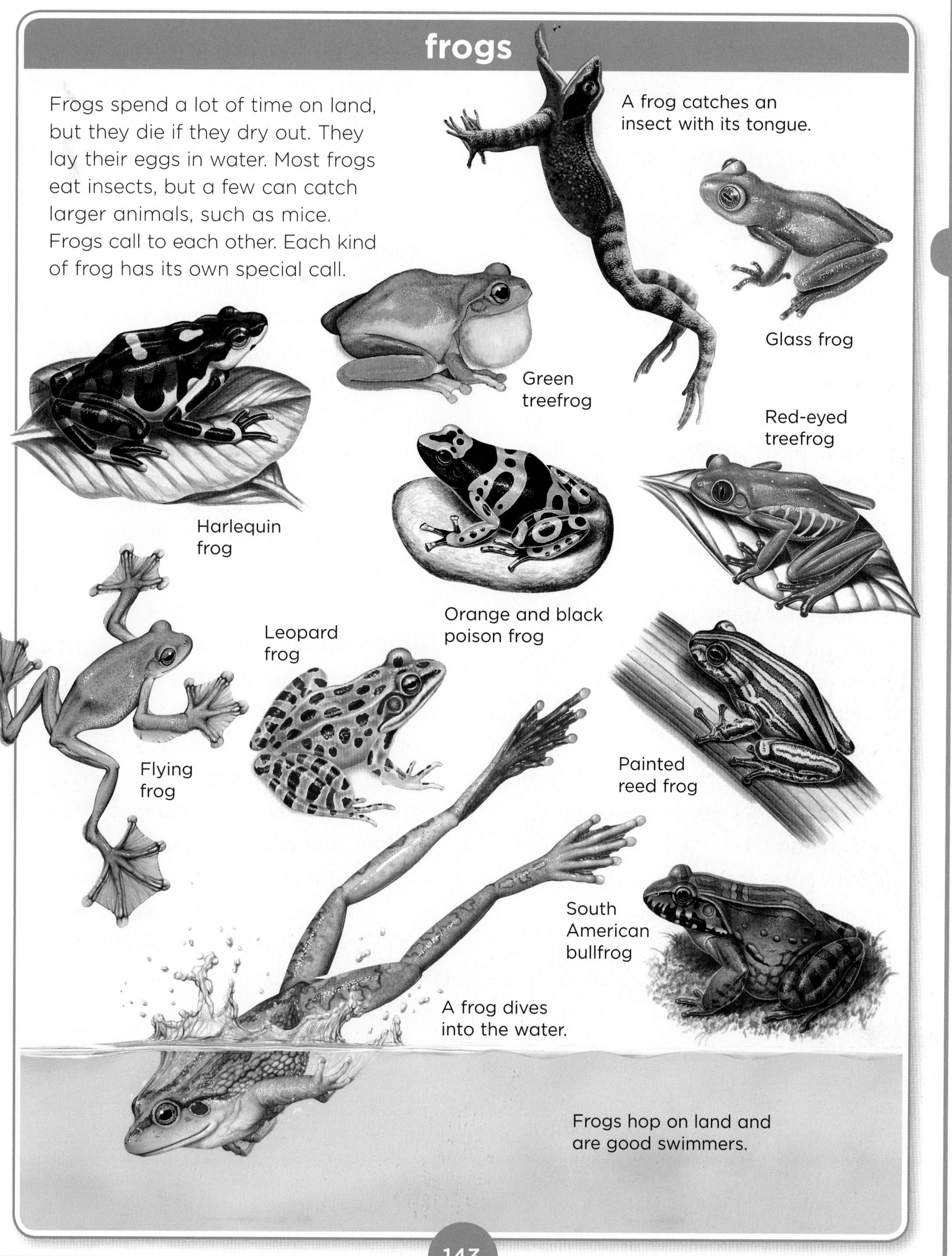

a b c d e f g h i j k l m n o p q r s t u v w x y z

It is good to eat two or three pieces of **fruit** every day.

frost ▼ • frosts

Frost is the white layer of tiny bits of ice that forms on very cold mornings: *The front lawn is covered in* ***frost****.*

frown • frowns, frowned, frowning

1. **Frown** means to have lines on your forehead because you are worried, mad, or thinking hard: *The teacher* ***frowned*** *at me because Oliver and I kept talking in class.*

2. A **frown** is the way a person's face looks when they are worried, angry, or thinking hard: *That unfriendly girl always has a* ***frown*** *on her face.*

fruit ◀ • fruits

Fruit is the part of a plant that holds the seeds. You can eat some fruits, such as oranges, pears, and cherries: *Dan loves to eat a piece of* ***fruit*** *after school.*

fuel • fuels

Fuel is anything that you burn to give heat or to make an engine work. Coal, wood, and gasoline are fuels: *We used sticks and branches as* ***fuel*** *for the campfire.*

The word **fuel** comes from an old word meaning "a fireplace." A fireplace is used to burn wood, which was the only kind of fuel that people used for heat in earlier times.

full ▶ • fuller, fullest

Full means that something holds as much as it can or it is complete. Nothing more will fit into something that is full: *My stomach is* ***full*** *from all the cakes I ate at the party.*

The bucket is **full** of candy.

It was cold last night, and in the morning **frost** covered the leaves and grass.

fun
A person or thing that is **fun** makes you have a good time and be happy: *Riding our sleds in the snow is a lot of **fun**.*

A polar bear's white **fur** helps it hide on ice and snow from other animals.

funeral • funerals
A **funeral** is a special ceremony for someone who has died. At funerals, people come together and share their sad feelings.

funny • funnier, funniest
A person or thing that is **funny** makes you laugh: *Jake couldn't stop laughing at the **funny** cartoon on TV.*

fur ▲ • furs
Fur is the thick, soft hair that covers the body of some animals: *My cat has shiny, black **fur**.*

furnace • furnaces
A **furnace** is a large, heavy box that holds a fire inside it. Furnaces are used to heat buildings or to melt metals: *The **furnace** in the basement keeps our house warm in winter.*

furniture ▶
Chairs, beds, tables, and dressers are different types of **furniture**: *The new house has no **furniture** yet, so we sat on the floor when we went to look at it.*

further
You say **further** when you mean more: *I don't know enough about whales yet for my report, so I have to do some **further** reading.*

future
1. **Future** means the time ahead that has not come yet: *There is no hospital in our town, so we hope they will build one in the **future**.*
2. **Future** also means happening in the time ahead: *The coat is too big for me right now, and my mom put it away for **future** use.*

I got new **furniture** for my room, including a desk, shelves for books, and a dresser.

The balloons are filled with a **gas** called helium that is lighter than air.

Gg

garden ▼ • gardens

A **garden** is a place to grow flowers, vegetables, and other plants: *Camille picked some daisies from the **garden**.*

The tree in our **garden** blooms every spring.

game ▼ • games

A **game** is something you play for fun. Many games have rules that you have to follow to win the game. Football, basketball, chess, and hide-and-seek are all games.

garage • garages

A **garage** is a building where you keep a car. You can also store things in a garage, such as tools for the garden: *Mr. Davis parked his car in his **garage**.*

The girls play a board **game** together.

garbage

Garbage is the food bits and other waste that people throw away: *I put the skin from my orange in the **garbage**.*

gas ◀ • gases

1. A **gas** is something that is very light and fills up all the space that it is inside. Usually, you cannot see a gas, but you can sometimes smell it: *Mrs. Lee turned on the **gas** and lit the stove, so she could cook some eggs.*
2. Gas is also the liquid that you put in a car or truck so that it goes: *Mom told Dad that the car needed **gas**. He filled the car up with **gasoline** at the gas station.*

The word **gas** comes from an old word meaning "air." Everything in the world is either a *solid* (such as a rock), a *liquid* (such as water), or a *gas*.

The front **gate** is shut so our puppy cannot run away.

gate ▲ • gates

A **gate** is a type of door in an outside wall or fence: *I waited for my brother at the school **gate**.*

gather ▼ • gathered, gathering

Gather means to bring together or to come together: *The children **gathered** the nuts that had fallen from the tree.*

gave

Gave is a form of the word GIVE: *I **gave** Tom a DVD for his birthday.*

These women **gather** tea leaves from bushes.

geese

You say **geese** for more than one GOOSE: *The **geese** honked as they flew in the sky.*

general ▼ • generals

1. If something is **general**, it is usual, or it happens for most people: *The **general** feeling among parents who have seen the new "Batman" movie is that it is too scary for small children. Mom **generally** sees a movie with her friend every Thursday night.*
2. A **general** is a leader in the army: *The **general** gave orders to the soldiers.*

This statue of **General** George Washington riding his horse is in Washington, D.C.

genius • geniuses

A **genius** is a very smart person who can think or act in a very special way: *The scientist Albert Einstein was a **genius** who had great new ideas about light, energy, and the way things move at very high speeds.*

You have to be **gentle** if you touch a butterfly so you do not hurt its wings.

gentle ▲ • gentler, gentlest

If you are **gentle**, you act in a kind and careful way: *Sally was **gentle** when she picked up the baby kittens.*

geography • geographies

Geography is the study of all the different parts of Earth and what they are like: *Donna is studying the rivers of the United States in her class on **geography**.*

germ • germs

A **germ** is a living thing that is so tiny that you cannot see it without a microscope. Germs can make you sick: *You should wash your hands before you eat, to get rid of **germs**.*

get • got, got *or* gotten, getting

1. If you **get** something, you have something new or you earn something: *Mom wants to **get** a new car because our old one does not run very well.*

2. You also use **get** for when you come to a place: *Betty catches the bus to **get** home from school.*

ghost ▶ • ghosts

A **ghost** is a kind of make-believe person. Some people think that a ghost is a dead person who has come back to life: *I read a book about a strange old house that was full of **ghosts**.*

I got a statue of a **ghost** at the Halloween party.

giant ▼ • giants

1. A **giant** is a make-believe person who is very big and very strong: *In the story, the **giant** Paul Bunyan was so huge that when he walked, his feet made big holes in the ground.*

2. **Giant** means very big: *The **giant** pumpkin won a prize at the fair.*

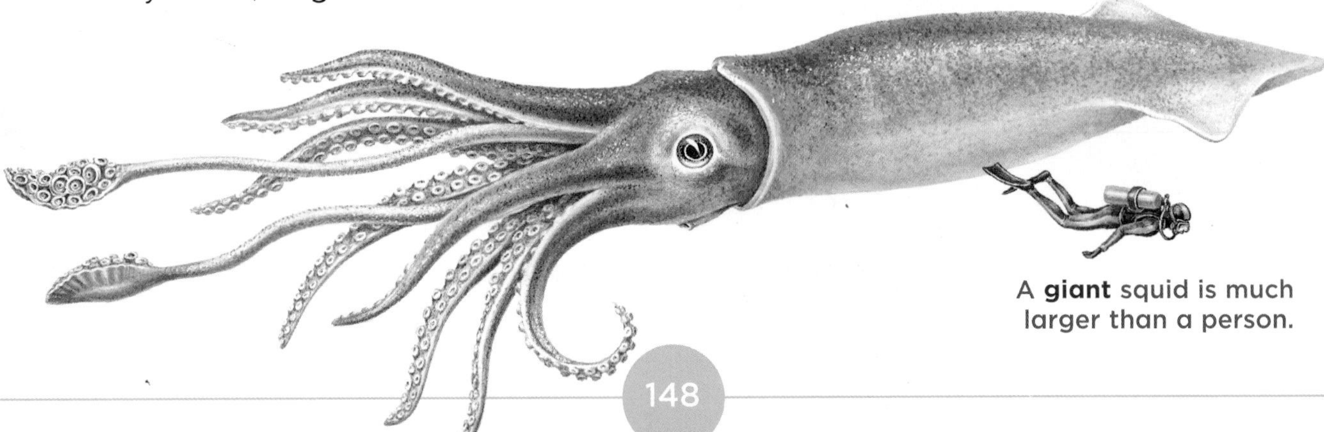

A **giant** squid is much larger than a person.

gift ▶ • **gifts**

A **gift** is something that you give to another person as a present: *We put all the **gifts** under the Christmas tree.*

There are so many **gifts,** I do not know which one to open first.

giraffe ▼ • **giraffes**

A **giraffe** is the tallest animal on Earth. It has long legs, a very long neck, and large, brown spots on its skin. Giraffes live in Africa: *The **giraffes** ate the leaves from the top of the trees.*

girl • **girls**

A **girl** is a female child.

give ▼ • **gave, given, giving**

Give means to hand or bring something to a person so they can have it or keep it: *Could you **give** me another piece of paper, please?*

glad • **gladder, gladdest**

When you feel **glad**, you feel good or happy about something: *Anne was **glad** to be going on a vacation at the beach.*

Michael **gives** flowers to his mom on Mother's Day.

giraffes

When a giraffe is born, it is six feet tall. That is the same height as some adult humans. Giraffes can grow to be 18 feet tall. They have to bend down a long way to drink. A giraffe grabs leaves with its long tongue and breaks branches from trees with its teeth.

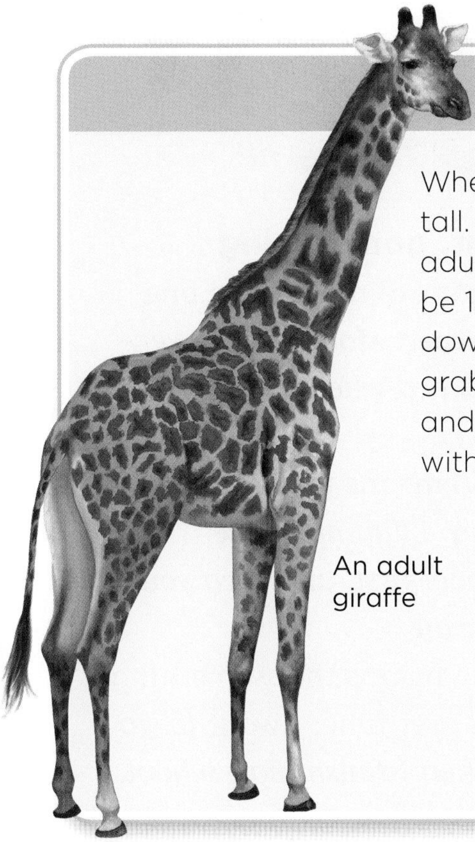

An adult giraffe

A giraffe eats leaves.

glass ▶ • glasses

1. Glass is a hard material that you can see through. You can break it easily. Things like windows and bottles are made out of glass. Some people wear special **glasses** to help them see better: *My grandfather accidentally sat on his reading **glasses** and broke them.*
2. A **glass** is a drinking container made of glass: *May I have a **glass** of orange juice please?*

You can find many countries on a **globe.**

globe ▶ • globes

A **globe** is a round ball with the map of the world on it: *The teacher showed us where America was on the **globe.***

glove ▼ • gloves

A **glove** covers your hand and has separate sections for each of the fingers and the thumb: *I put on my **gloves** before going out into the cold. Baseball players wear a **glove** to catch the ball.*

My brother let me borrow his baseball **glove.**

The bottles on the shelf are all made of **glass.**

glue • glues, glued, gluing

1. Glue is a thick liquid that is used to stick things together: *Isabelle used colored paper, silver stars, **glue**, and scissors to make a birthday card for her grandpa.*
2. To **glue** means to fix or stick together with this thick liquid: *Dad **glued** the handle onto the door.*

We **go** down the hill fast on our sled.

go ▲ • went, gone, going

1. To **go** means to move from one place to another: *Mom told us we had to **go** to bed when the TV show was over.*
2. To **go** also means to take part in something: *I'll jump in the swimming pool first, and then you can **go** after me.*
3. To **go** also means that something will happen over time: *I want to **go** to college when I finish high school.*

goal ▼ • goals

1. A **goal** is something that you want to do or have in the future: *When I get older, my **goal** is to buy my own car.*
2. When you are playing a sport, a **goal** is the net or space between posts where you have to hit, throw, or kick a ball to score: *The soccer player kicked the ball into the **goal**.*

gold ▶

1. Gold is a very valuable yellow metal that is used to make coins and jewelry: *Dad bought Mom a beautiful **gold** necklace for her birthday.*

The mask was made out of **gold** for a king.

2. Gold is also the bright yellow color of gold: *In fall, I rake up the orange, **gold**, and red leaves in the backyard. The **golden** leaves are my favorites to look at.*

goat ▶ • goats

A **goat** is an animal that looks a bit like a sheep, but with horns that curve backward and a short tail. Some goats have a little beard under their chin. Goats can live wild in the mountains, or they can be kept on a farm to give milk.

The wild **goat** has two long, curved horns.

God

People believe that **God** is the special being who made all of Earth and the Universe.

The player stops the ball from going into the **goal**.

The **geese** fly south for the winter.

golf ▼

Golf is a game played on grass where you use a special club to hit a small white ball into a hole: *Dad spends many Saturdays playing **golf** with his friends from work.*

gone

Gone is a form of the word GO: *By the time I got to the birthday party, all the food was **gone**.*

good • better, best

When something is **good**, it is nice or pleasing: *I think apple pie and ice cream tastes **good**.*

good-bye • good-byes

Good-bye is what you say when you are leaving somewhere or when someone else is leaving: *I called out **good-bye** to Mom after she dropped me off at school for the day.*

Good-bye is a shorter form of the old saying "God be with you." When someone said "good-bye" to a person, it was a way of asking God to watch over that person when they went away.

goose ▲ • geese

A **goose** is a bird that looks like a duck, but is bigger with a longer neck and more pointed beak: *We saw some **geese** swimming in the lake.*

Martha loves to play **golf** in her free time.

gorillas

Gorillas are the largest of all apes. They live in family groups. They eat leaves, fruits, and bark. In the day gorillas stay on the ground, but at night they sleep in trees.

gorilla ▲ • **gorillas**

A **gorilla** is a very large ape with big shoulders and long arms, short legs, and no tail. Gorillas live in rain forests in Africa.

Long ago, there were stories about a group of wild, hairy humans called the *Gorillas*. When people first saw real **gorillas**, the animals, they thought they were a kind of wild human being.

got

Got is a form of the word GET: *I* ***got*** *a new bicycle for my birthday.*

government • **governments**

The **government** is the group of people who are in charge of a country, state, or city: *The President is the leader of our* ***government****.*

governor • **governors**

A **governor** is a person who is the head of a state government: *The* ***governor*** *of Texas gave a speech about pollution.*

grab ▼ • **grabbed, grabbing**

To **grab** is to take hold of something suddenly: *I* ***grabbed*** *hold of the balloon before it floated away.*

The osprey **grabs** a fish with its claws.

grade • **grades**

1\. A **grade** is a class or year in school: *Claudia is in the fifth **grade**.*

2\. A **grade** is also a letter or number used to show how well you have done in school: *Patrick got a B **grade** for spelling.*

grand ▶ • **grander, grandest**

If something is **grand**, it is very large or important: *The rich man lived in a **grand** house by the ocean.*

grandchild • **grandchildren**

A **grandchild** is either a **grandson** or **granddaughter**: *My teacher showed everyone at school some cute pictures of her new **grandchild**.*

grandparent • **grandparents**

Your **grandparents** are the parents of your father or your mother. A grandparent is either a **grandfather** or **grandmother**: *We have dinner at my **grandparents'** house every Sunday evening.*

grape ▶ • **grapes**

A **grape** is a small, round, green or purple fruit that grows in a bunch: *Mom put a turkey sandwich and a bunch of **grapes** in my lunch box.*

Bunches of **grapes** grow on vines.

A king once lived in the **grand** castle.

grapefruit ▶ • **grapefruits**

A **grapefruit** is a large, round, yellow or pink fruit. It tastes a bit like an orange and a lemon mixed together.

My sister likes to eat **grapefruit** for breakfast.

grass • **grasses**

Grass is a green plant with narrow leaves that grows in lawns. Different kinds of grass grow all over the world: *Our dog likes to lie out on the **grass** all day.*

grasshopper ▶ • **grasshoppers**

A **grasshopper** is an insect with long back legs that jumps and flies. Grasshoppers eat many types of plants.

Koalas have **gray** fur.

gray ▸ • grayer, grayest

Gray is a color made by mixing black and white: *I saw some big **gray** elephants when I went to the zoo.*

great • greater, greatest

1. **Great** means large or lots of: *A **great** crowd of friends and family came to watch the school play.*
2. **Great** also means excellent or important: *The telephone was a **great** invention.*

green ▸ • greener, greenest

Green is the color of growing grass and living leaves. You can make this color by mixing yellow and blue together: *The traffic light turned from red to **green**, so it was OK to go.*

The dragonfly's body is **green.**

grew

Grew is a form of the word GROW: *The little seed **grew** into a tall plant.*

grocery ▾ • groceries

1. A **grocery** is a store that sells food and things that you use often: *Steven went to the **grocery** store to buy some milk, bread, and a new toothbrush.*
2. **Groceries** are the things that you buy in a grocery store: *Jemima walked home from the store with her bag of **groceries**.*

Mom put our **groceries** in a basket to carry around the store.

grasshoppers

Grasshoppers use their strong back legs to jump. Male grasshoppers also rub their back legs against parts of their wings to let the female grasshoppers know where they are.

Singing grasshopper

Jumping grasshopper

ground ▸ • grounds

The **ground** is the dry land that you stand on when you are outside: *I sat down on the **ground** outside my school and waited for Mom. In baseball, the batter is out if you catch a ball he hits before it touches the **ground**.*

group ▾ • groups

A **group** is a number of things or people that are together: *A **group** of my friends came to my home to sleep over for a night.*

grow • grew, growing

1. To **grow** means to get larger in size: *The kittens are **growing** bigger every day.*
2. To **grow** also means to come to life: *The tomato plant **grows** well in the sun.*

grown

Grown is a form of the word GROW: *Tim has **grown** into a very tall boy.*

The farmer uses a tractor to get the **ground** ready for planting.

grown-up • grown-ups

A **grown-up** is an adult or someone who is fully grown: *At our holiday dinner, the **grown-ups** sat at a different table from the children.*

guard • guards, guarded, guarding

1. To **guard** means to keep someone or something safe or protect them from being hurt: *His job is to **guard** the bank at night.*
2. A **guard** is someone who protects others from injury or danger: *The prison **guard** stopped the prisoner from escaping from jail.*

A large **group** of flamingos stands together in the water.

guess • **guesses, guessed, guessing**
1. To **guess** means to give an answer when you are not really sure if you are right: *Can you **guess** how old your teacher is?*
2. A **guess** is an answer that you give without being sure you are right: *I didn't know the answer to the last question on the test, so I just made a **guess**.*

guest • **guests**
A **guest** is a person who comes to visit you: *We cleaned the house because Mom said that she had a **guest** coming for dinner.*

She sings a song while she plays the **guitar**.

guilty • **guiltier, guiltiest**
When you feel **guilty**, you feel bad or ashamed because you have done something wrong: *At first no one knew who broke the window, but Robert felt **guilty** that he had done it and told his mother about it.*

guitar ▲ • **guitars**
A **guitar** is a musical instrument that usually has six or more strings. You play a guitar by pulling the strings.

gum[1] • **gums**
Your **gum** is the pink part of your mouth that your teeth grow out of: *The dentist says I should brush my teeth and **gums** in the morning and at night.*

I want to buy some **gum**.

gum[2] ▶ • **gums**
Gum is a sticky sweet that you chew, but do not swallow: *Sally got in trouble for chewing **gum** in class.*

gun • **guns**
A **gun** is a weapon that is used for shooting at something: *Dad keeps his **gun** locked up in a special box because guns are dangerous.*

gym ▼ • **gyms**
A **gym** is a room or building where you can play sports or do exercise: *We play basketball in the **gym** on Friday afternoons.* Gym is a short word for **gymnasium**.

My brother's team plays volleyball in the **gym** at school.

Hh

Lara's long **hair** flies up when she jumps.

had

Had is a form of the word HAVE: *I **had** bacon and eggs for breakfast this morning.*

hair ◀ • hairs

Hair is the thin threads that grow on your head. You also have hair on the rest of your body: *Felicity put a pink ribbon in her **hair**.*

habit • habits

A **habit** is something you do so often, you do it without thinking: *Louise has a **habit** of biting her nails when she's nervous.*

habitat ▼ • habitats

A **habitat** is the place where a plant or animal normally lives and grows: *Toucans live in a rain forest **habitat**.*

half • halves

If you divide something into two equal parts, each part is called a **half**: *Mom cut the apple into **halves** and gave one half to me, and one half to my brother. The first **half** of the soccer game is forty-five minutes long, then there is a fifteen-minute rest, then another half of forty-five minutes.*

Many kinds of animals live in the forest **habitat** where pine trees grow.

Trudy and Jill went trick or treating on **Halloween** and were given lots of candy.

hall • halls

A **hall** is a long, narrow room that leads to other rooms: *John walked down the **hall** and waited outside the school principal's office.*

Halloween ▲ • Halloweens

Halloween is a holiday celebrated on October 31, when people dress up in costumes and go from house to house asking for treats and playing tricks: *Nicholas dressed up as a scary ghost for **Halloween**.*

hamburger ▶ • hamburgers

A **hamburger** is tiny pieces of chopped beef put together in one flat, round shape and then cooked: *Dad cooked us **hamburgers** for dinner. I had mine with cheese.*

The **hamburger** gets its name from the German city of *Hamburg*. A hamburger was once called a "Hamburg steak." People from Hamburg were the first to serve this food in the United States.

hammer ▶ • hammers, hammered, hammering

1. A **hammer** is a tool with a heavy metal head on a long handle. It is used to hit nails: *Ben made a garden seat using some pieces of wood, a **hammer**, and some nails.*

The man aims his **hammer** to hit a nail.

2. To **hammer** is to hit something with a tool of this kind: *Josie **hammered** the nail into the wall and hung the picture from it.*

hamster ◀ • hamsters

The **hamster** eats seeds.

A **hamster** is a small, furry animal that looks something like a mouse. It has a short tail and is kept as a pet: *Thomas keeps his pet **hamster** in a cage.*

I like lettuce and tomato on my **hamburger**.

hand • hands, handed, handing

1. Your **hand** is the part of your body at the end of your arm below your wrist. Your hand has a thumb, four fingers, and a palm: *The teacher told us to put up our **hand** when we want to ask a question in class.*
2. A **hand** is also the thin piece on a watch or a clock that points to the numbers: *It's 2 o'clock, because the long **hand** is pointing to the "12," and the short hand is pointing to the "2."*
3. To **hand** something to someone is to give it to them: *I **handed** her a ten-dollar bill to pay for the movie ticket.*

handle ▼ • handles

A **handle** is a part put on an object to make it easier to pick up, hold, or open: *Patricia opened the door using the door **handle**.*

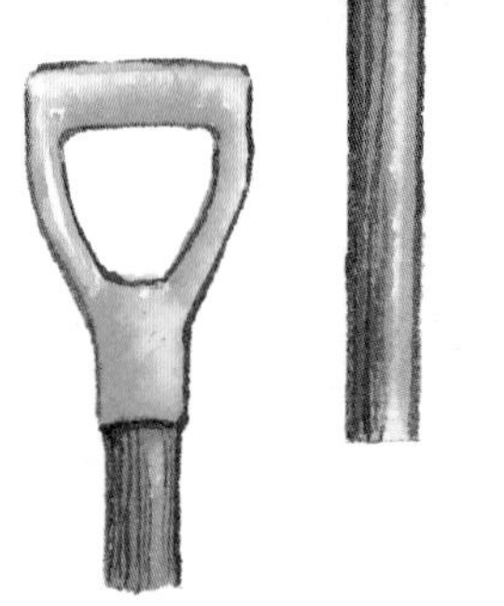

One **handle** is plastic, and the other is made of wood.

handsome

If we say a man or boy is **handsome**, this means he is good-looking: *He is so **handsome** he looks like a movie star.*

Some birds **hang** their nests on leaves.

hang ▲ • hung, hanging

To **hang** means to be attached from the top of something, but not at the bottom: *Carrie is going to **hang** the new curtains in the living room.*

Hanukkah ▼

Hanukkah is a Jewish holiday in December that is celebrated for eight days. People light a candle each night for eight nights. Hanukkah is sometimes spelled **Chanukah**.

Hanukkah

Hanukkah celebrates a miracle long ago when lamp oil in a temple burned for eight days. The oil should have lasted only one day. During Hanukkah, children are given chocolate coins and play games with a spinning top called a dreidel.

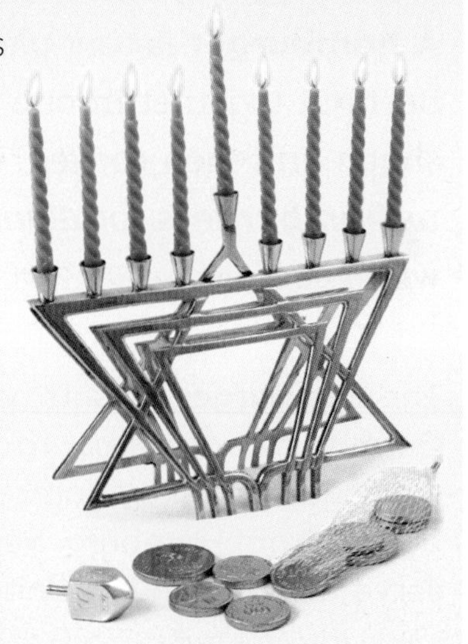

happen • happened, happening

To **happen** means to take place: *The first trip of Christopher Columbus to America **happened** in the year 1492. I read the last chapter of the book to find out what **happens** to the little girl in the end.*

happy • happier, happiest

When you are **happy**, you feel good and are full of joy: *Lucy was **happy** when she received lots of presents for her birthday.*

harbor ▲ • harbors

A **harbor** is an area of water near the coast where ships can stay, safe from rough seas: *The sailboat came into the **harbor** to stop for the night.*

hard • harder, hardest

1. **Hard** means not soft: *When we went camping, we slept outside on the **hard** ground.*
2. **Hard** also means not easy: *The math test today was **hard**—I think I got lots of answers wrong.*

hardware

Hardware is tools and equipment that you use to make or fix things: *Dad went to the **hardware** store to buy some more garden tools.*

has

Has is a form of the word HAVE: *Jessica **has** a new pair of pink sneakers.*

hat • hats

You wear a **hat** to cover your head. You can wear hats to protect you from the sun, to keep warm, or just for fun: *I always wear a **hat** when I'm at the beach.*

hatch ▼ • hatched, hatching

To **hatch** is to break out from an egg: *The baby ducklings **hatched** yesterday.*

Long ago, baby dinosaurs **hatched** from eggs.

hawks

Hawks are hunting birds with strong beaks. They have much better sight than people and can see small animals from a long distance.

African harrier hawk

Slate-colored hawk

Eurasian sparrowhawk

Rough-legged hawk

Eurasian sparrowhawk hunting

Pacific baza

hate • hated, hating

When you **hate** someone or something, you do not like them at all: *Claire **hates** going to the dentist.*

have • had, having

1. To **have** means to own something: *I **have** a red bicycle.*
2. To **have** also means to feel something: *I **have** a pain in my stomach from eating too much candy.*

hawk ▲ • hawks

A **hawk** is a bird with a short, hooked beak and sharp, curved claws. Hawks eat small animals, such as rabbits.

hay ▼

Hay is grass or other plants that are cut, dried, and used as food for animals: *The farmer fed the cows some **hay**.*

Farmers roll **hay** to put in the barn for winter.

Brent stands on his **head.**

he

He is used when you are talking about a boy or a man or a male animal: *My father said **he** wanted to take us out to dinner. **He'd** like us all to get to the restaurant early because **he's** got a surprise for us afterward. I think **he'll** also be taking us to the movies.*

head ▶ • heads

1. The **head** is the part of the body above the neck, where the nose, eyes, ears, and mouth are: *David has a big bump on his **head** from when he fell while ice-skating.*
2. The **head** is also the top or front part of something: *Aaron was at the **head** of the line in the store, in front of everyone else.*

heal • healed, healing

To **heal** means to get better or become well again: *The doctor gave me some special medicine to help **heal** the cut on my hand.*

health

Health is the way that your body feels, and whether or not you feel sick: *Angela's **health** has been poor since she got the flu last week. It will probably be a few more weeks before she feels better and is **healthy** again.*

hear • heard, hearing

To **hear** means to take in sound through the ears: *Their house is so close to the beach that you can **hear** the waves hitting the shore. I **heard** the neighbor's dog barking early this morning.*

hearing aid ▼

A **hearing aid** is something that you wear in or behind your ear to help you hear better: *Grandma takes her **hearing aid** off when she goes to sleep at night because she doesn't need it then.*

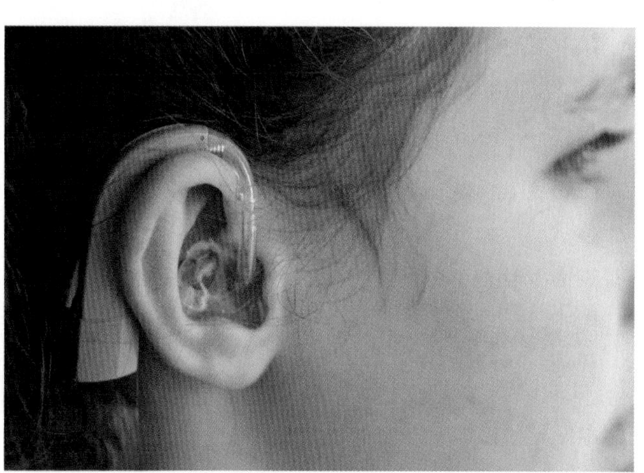

Karen wears a **hearing aid** so she can hear words and other sounds better.

heart • hearts

1. The **heart** is the part of the body inside your chest that pushes blood around the rest of your body. Animals and people have hearts.
2. A **heart** is also a shape that means love: *Jackie sent her friend a Valentine's Day card with a big red **heart** on the front.*

heat • heated, heating

1. **Heat** means being warm or hot: *We sat out on the beach in the **heat** of the sun.*
2. To **heat** something means to make it warm or hot: *Mom turned on the furnace to **heat** the room.*

heavy ▼ • heavier, heaviest

1. If something is **heavy**, it weighs a lot and is hard to carry: *The box was too **heavy** for me to lift by myself, so I asked Dad to help me.*
2. **Heavy** also means thick: *Charlie put on a **heavy** jacket before going out into the snowstorm.*

The men use a machine to lift the **heavy** fishing net.

heel ▼ • heels

1. The **heel** is the back part of your foot below your ankle: *I have a sore on my **heel** from wearing new shoes.*
2. The **heel** is also the bottom part of shoe that is raised: *Erica tripped over some stairs and broke the **heel** off her shoe.*

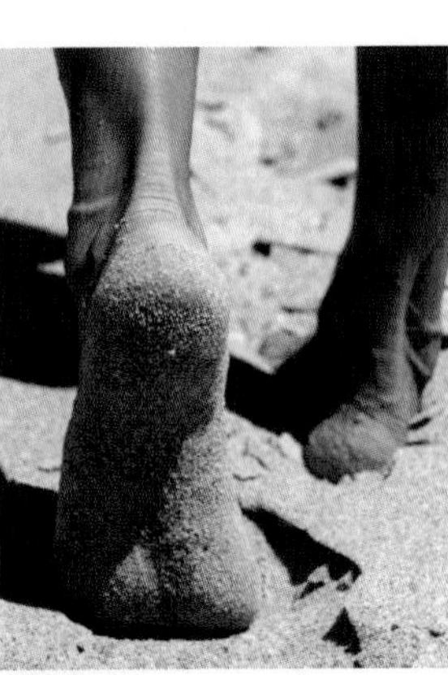

You lift your **heel** as you take a step.

Francesca's brother measures her **height**.

height ◀ • heights

The **height** of someone or something is how tall or high they are: *Roy's **height** is five feet nine inches.*

held

Held is a form of the word HOLD: *Max **held** on to his dad's hand to walk across the busy street.*

helicopter ▶ • helicopters

A **helicopter** is a machine without wings that flies in the air: *We went on a **helicopter** ride over the top of the Grand Canyon.*

hello • hellos

We say **hello** to people when we first see or speak to them: ***Hello** there, Sam! The principal answered her phone by saying, "**Hello**, Mrs. Randall speaking."*

helmet ▶ • helmets

A **helmet** is a hard hat that you wear to cover and protect your head: *Tanya wears a **helmet** when she rides her bicycle.*

Oscar always wears a **helmet** when he rides his skateboard.

helicopters

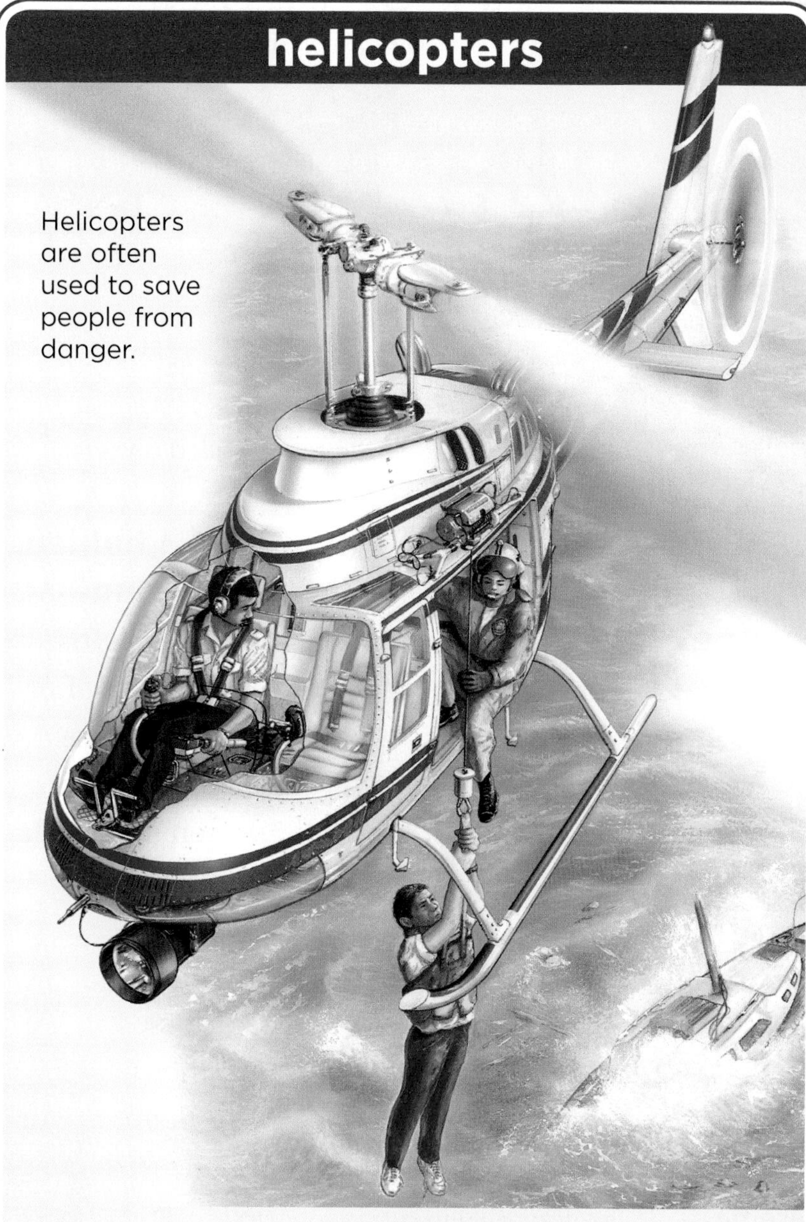

Helicopters are often used to save people from danger.

The turning blades on top of a helicopter are what keep it in the air. The blades on the tail keep the helicopter from spinning around. Helicopters can go straight up and down when they land and take off.

help ▸ • helped, helping

To **help** means to do something for someone else to make things easier for them: *I **helped** my mother set the table for our family's Thanksgiving dinner.*

hen ▾ • hens

A **hen** is a female chicken: *Penny collected the eggs that the **hens** had laid.*

My aunt keeps **hens** on her farm.

her

Her is used when you are talking about a female person or animal: *Gabrielle is my friend. I always have fun when I'm with **her**. She walked to the movies by **herself** to meet me. We bought ice cream—mine was chocolate, **hers** was vanilla.*

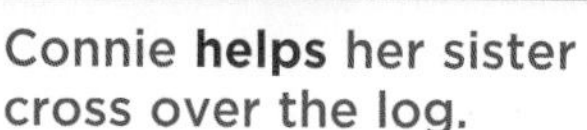

Connie **helps** her sister cross over the log.

The reindeer in the **herd** have large horns called antlers.

herd ▲ • herds

A **herd** is a large group of animals that move or stay together: *The farmer moved the **herd** of cattle into another field.*

here

Here means in or at this place right now: *Could everyone please stand over **here** so that I can take the picture? Put the box down **here** on the table.*

hero • heroes

A **hero** is a man or boy that people think is a very good person because he has done a brave or important thing: *The firefighter was called a **hero** for saving the boy in the burning house.*

heroine • heroines

A **heroine** is a woman or girl that people think is a very good person because she has done a brave or important thing: *The woman was a **heroine** for jumping in the lake to save the little girl.*

Janet **hides** from her brother behind a tree.

hide ◀ • hidden, hid, hiding

To **hide** means to put yourself or something else where it cannot be seen or found: *I am going to wrap Christmas presents and then **hide** them under my bed.*

high ▶ • higher, highest

1. High means far above the ground or tall: *That mountain is very **high**.*

2. High also means above the usual amount: *The police car drove at a **high** speed to catch the criminals.*

Taipei 101 is the **highest** building in the world.

hill ▼ • hills

A **hill** is a high, rounded area of land, not as high as a mountain: *It took us half an hour to walk to the top of the **hill**.*

The **hills** are covered with grass and trees.

him

Him is used when you are talking about a male person or animal: *I had to baby-sit my little brother yesterday. It's easy to take care of **him**, because he likes to sit by **himself** and play with his cars.*

hip • hips

Your **hip** is the large bone on either side of your body between the top of your leg and your waist: *The teacher always puts her hands on her **hips** when she gets mad.*

hippopotamus ▼ • hippopotamuses

A **hippopotamus** is a very large animal with a big head, a wide mouth, and thick gray skin. Hippopotamuses live in Africa and spend most of the time in water.

The word **hippopotamus** comes from two older words meaning "a river" and "horse." The hippopotamus lives in rivers and lakes in Africa. When people first saw it there, they thought it looked like a kind of large horse.

hippopotamuses

Hippopotamuses rest in the water for most of the day to stay cool. Their eyes and ears are on the top of their head, so they can still see and hear if they are mostly underwater. They eat only plants and use their two large bottom teeth to protect themselves from other animals.

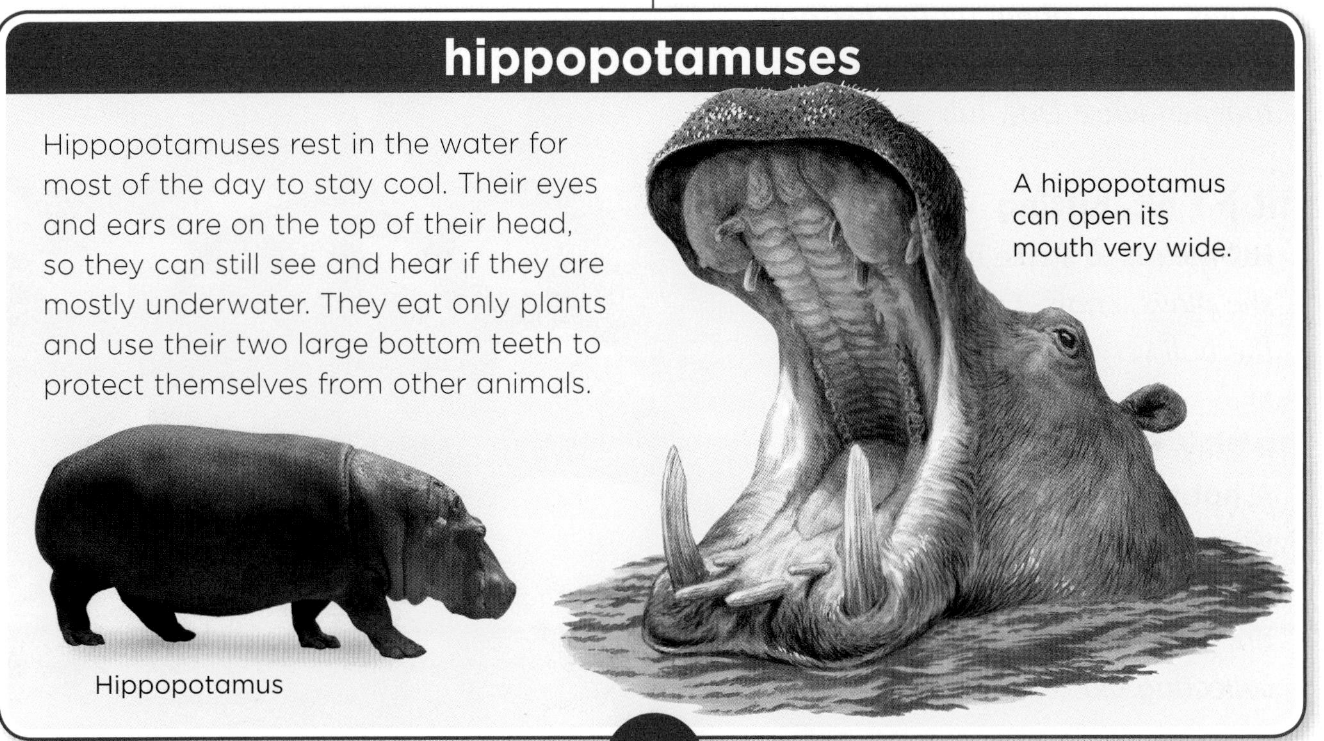

A hippopotamus can open its mouth very wide.

Hippopotamus

It was an important part of **history** when men walked on the Moon.

his

His means belonging to a male person or animal: *Giorgio lost **his** pencil, so I let him use mine.*

history ▲ • histories

History is the story of all the things that have happened in past times: *My older sister is reading a book about the **history** of the United States. It tells about all the **historic** things that have happened since Independence Day, July 4, 1776.*

hit ▶ • hit, hitting

Hit means to strike hard: *When she plays tennis, Denise **hits** the ball very hard.*

hobby • hobbies

A **hobby** is an activity that you do in your free time for fun: *Sarah's **hobbies** are playing softball and collecting old coins.*

The man tries to score a goal while playing ice **hockey.**

hockey ▲

1. **Hockey** is a sport played on ice between two teams of six players. The players use long sticks to hit a hard rubber disk into a goal: *When people play ice **hockey**, they wear ice skates on their feet.*
2. **Hockey** is also the name of a game played on a grass field between two teams of eleven players. The players use sticks to hit a ball into a goal: *The ball that is used in field **hockey** is small and round.*

The ball **hits** everything.

hog • hogs

A **hog** is a large, adult pig. Farmers raise hogs for their meat: *Steve's uncle has a farm where he keeps* ***hogs*** *in small areas called pens.*

The **hog** has a short, curly tail.

hold • held, holding

1. You **hold** something if you keep it up in your hands or arms: *Martha's mother asked her to* ***hold*** *the pan while she opened the oven door.*
2. **Hold** also means to have enough room for: *This large box will* ***hold*** *fifty oranges, but that smaller one will hold only twenty.*

hole • holes

A **hole** is an empty space or an opening in something solid: *A tree branch fell on our house and made a* ***hole*** *in the roof. Grandma dug a* ***hole*** *in her garden to plant the rose bush.*

Mimi puts her legs through the **hole** in the tire swing.

holiday • holidays

A **holiday** is a day when people stay home from work and school to celebrate something special that happened on that date: *Thanksgiving, in November, and Christmas, in December, are both* ***holidays*** *in the United States.*

hollow • hollower, hollowest

Something that is **hollow** is empty inside: *Water and gas come into our homes through long,* ***hollow*** *pipes.*

holy • holier, holiest

1. A person who is very religious and does good things is often called **holy**: *Christians believe that Jesus was a very* ***holy*** *person.*
2. A time or a place that is special for religious people is called **holy**: *Christmas is a* ***holy*** *time for Christians and Hanukkah is a holy time for Jewish people.*

Church windows show pictures of **holy** people.

home • homes

Home is where a person or animal lives: *Our* ***home*** *is a small house in Kansas City. Birds often make their* ***home*** *in trees.*

This dinosaur with three **horns** is called triceratops.

A B C D E F G H I J K L M N O P Q R S T U V W X Y Z

homework
Homework is work that a teacher gives students to do at home: *My sister's teacher gives her lots of math **homework**.*

honest
If someone is **honest**, it means that they tell the truth and that you can trust them: *Anita lost her purse yesterday, but an **honest** person found it and gave it back to her.*

honey ◀ • honeys
Honey is a sweet, thick liquid that bees make and that many people like to eat: *Jamie likes to eat **honey** on toast for breakfast.*

We keep a jar of **honey** on the table.

hop • hopped, hopping
When you **hop**, you move in small jumps up and down, or backward or forward, usually on only one leg: *In some games, children **hop** from one place to another.*

hope • hoped, hoping
When you **hope**, you wish very much that something will happen. You also believe that it may happen: *I **hope** our team wins the baseball game next week.*

horn ▲ • horns
1. A **horn** is something hard and hollow that grows on the head of some animals, such as cattle, sheep, and deer: *Male deer have long **horns** that bend in different directions.*
2. A **horn** is also something that you can push or squeeze to warn that you are getting close: *The truck driver sounded his **horn** to let the cars ahead know that he was coming up behind them.*
3. A **horn** is also a musical instrument that people blow into to make a sound: *Barbara plays the **horn** in the band.*

Alex trained her **horse** to do tricks.

horse ◀ • horses
A **horse** is a large, strong animal with four legs, a long neck, pointed ears, and a long tail: *People ride on **horses** and use them to pull carts and wagons.*

hospital ◀ • hospitals

A **hospital** is a place where people who are sick or have been injured are cared for by doctors and nurses: *When Andy fell out of a tree and broke his leg, an ambulance came and took him to the* ***hospital****.*

The sign points to the **hospital.**

In early times, a **hospital** was not a building where sick people were cared for. It was a place where people who were traveling could find a bed for the night and get food to eat.

hot • hotter, hottest

Hot means the opposite of cold. If you touch something hot it will burn you: *If you stand too near a fire, you will feel very* ***hot****.*

I like ketchup on my **hot dog,** but Ken likes mustard on his.

hot dog ▲

A **hot dog** is a thin, red kind of meat called a sausage, that is cooked and served in a piece of bread: *Dad always buys us* ***hot dogs*** *when we go to watch a baseball game.*

hour • hours

An **hour** is a certain time that lasts for sixty minutes. There are twenty-four hours in a day: *It took Jake a whole* ***hour*** *to do his homework yesterday, from 4 o'clock to 5 o'clock.*

house ▼ • houses

A **house** is a building that people live in. A house is separate from the houses next to it and has its own front door: *Our family lives in a small* ***house****, but my friend Jan's family lives in an apartment.*

how

1. How means the way to do something: *This cookbook will tell you* ***how*** *to make a pizza.*

2. We also use **how** when we ask a question about the amount of something, or what something is like: *I asked Garry* ***how*** *many dogs his family has and how they look after them all.*

however

However is a word we can use instead of but: *Our team lost the game yesterday.* ***However****, we hope to win the next one.*

The wooden **houses** are painted different colors.

Lisa and Hannah **hug** each other.

hug ▲ • hugs, hugged, hugging

1. When you **hug** someone or something, you put your arms around them and hold them close to your body: *I **hugged** my mother when she left to visit her friend.*

2. When you hold someone or something tight and close to your body, you give them a **hug**: *My little sister Miranda always gives her doll a big **hug** before she goes to bed.*

huge ▼ • huger, hugest

Something that is **huge** is very, very large: *Whales and elephants are **huge** animals.*

hum • hummed, humming

When you **hum**, you sing or make a long sound with your lips closed. You do not sing words when you hum: *Dad often **hums** quietly to himself while he drives the car.*

People look different from each other, but we are all **human.**

human ▲ • humans

1. Any person is a **human**: ***Humans** live in all the countries of the world.* A **human being** is another name we use for a person.

2. Human means anything to do with people: *Fear and joy are both **human** feelings.*

hungry • hungrier, hungriest

When you are **hungry**, you feel that you need to eat something: *I was **hungry** all afternoon because I did not have time to eat lunch.*

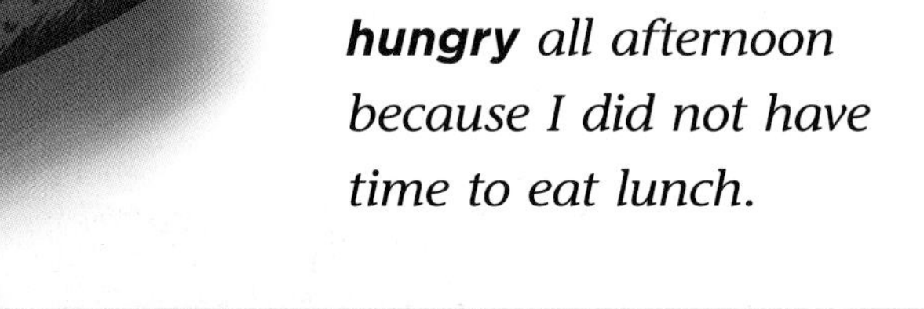

The **huge** stingray eats tiny animals and will not hurt the diver.

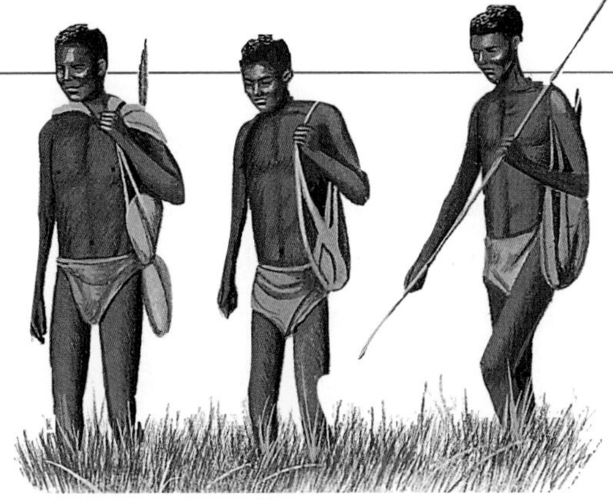
The **hunters** use spears to catch their food.

hunt ▲ • hunted, hunting
To **hunt** means to look for or chase something and try to catch it: *Many animals **hunt** other animals for their food.* A **hunter** is a human who hunts animals for sport or for food.

hurricane ▼ • hurricanes
A **hurricane** is a very big storm that brings strong wind and a lot of rain: *When the **hurricane** came, the rain flooded the town and the wind blew the roofs off many houses.*

hurry • hurried, hurrying
When you **hurry**, you move or do things more quickly than usual: *Sandra and Eugenia had to **hurry** to finish cleaning up their room before their mother came home.*

The dog **hurt** its paw.

The **hurricane** moves toward the coast of Florida.

hurt ▲ • hurt, hurting
1. If you **hurt** someone or something, you cause them to feel pain: *I **hurt** my ankle during the soccer game.*
2. **Hurt** also means to feel pain: *My fingers **hurt** because I caught my hand in the car door.*

husband • husbands
A man who is married is a **husband**: *My father is my mother's **husband**.*

Ii

When **ice** melts, it turns back into water.

I

I is the word you use when you mean yourself: ***I*** *have a new pair of shoes.* ***I'll*** *tell Dad that* ***I'd*** *like to go with him to the baseball game tomorrow.* ***I'm*** *very interested in baseball.* ***I've*** *seen lots of games.*

ice ▲

Ice is water that has frozen and become hard and solid: *In winter, the top of the pond is covered with* ***ice****.*

iceberg ▶ • icebergs

An **iceberg** is a very large piece of ice that floats and moves around in very cold parts of the ocean: ***Icebergs*** *are dangerous because ships can hit them and then sink to the bottom of the ocean.*

ice cream ▶

Ice cream is a sweet frozen food that is made with milk or cream, sugar, and other flavors: *Chocolate is my favorite flavor of* ***ice cream****.*

We often eat **ice cream** for dessert.

ice skate ▼

An **ice skate** is a special shoe with a thin piece of metal on the bottom that helps people move fast across ice: *On winter days Marianne and Francis put on their* ***ice skates****. Then they* ***ice-skate*** *for hours on the frozen pond.*

The man and woman perform tricks while wearing **ice skates**.

icebergs

Icebergs are large pieces that have broken off from a huge area of ice. Icebergs float in Earth's coldest oceans. They can be the size of a piano or be as high above the water as a very tall building. Only a small part of an iceberg can be seen above water.

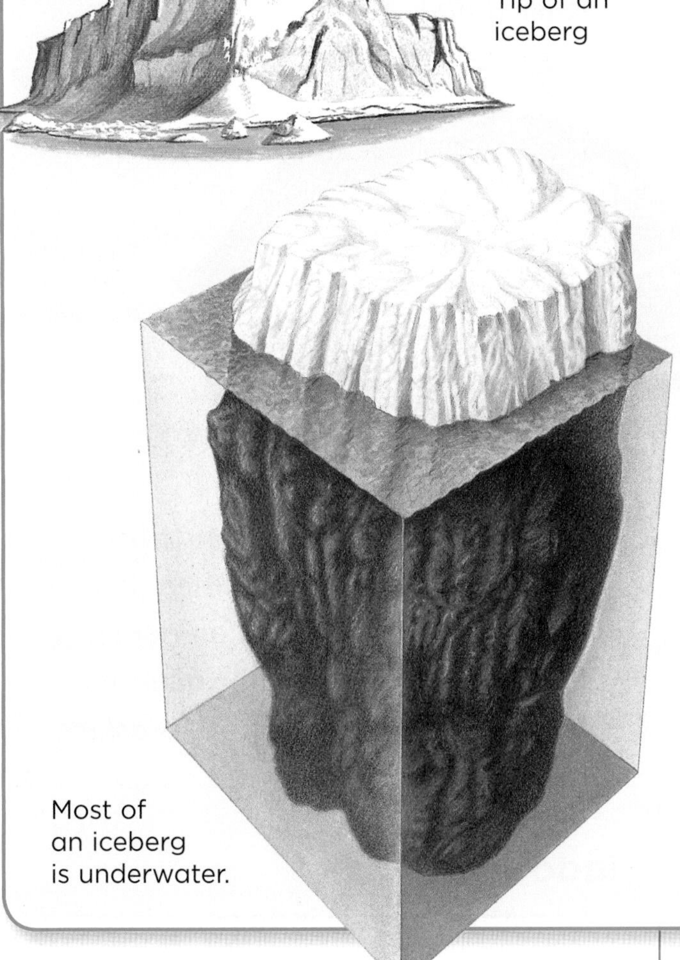

idea • ideas
An **idea** is something that you think, imagine, believe, or understand in your mind: *I have a good* ***idea*** *of what kind of job I want to do when I grow up. It was my sister's* ***idea*** *to name our dog "Mickey."*

if
We use the word **if** when we are not sure that something is true or that something will happen: ***If*** *it rains tomorrow, we won't be able to play our baseball game. Mom said I could watch the TV show,* ***if*** *I do my homework first.*

imagine • imagined, imagining
You **imagine** something when you have a picture or an idea of it in your mind: *I can* ***imagine*** *what our new house will look like, even though it has not been built yet. I can see it in my* ***imagination****, because Dad has told me about it.*

imitate ▼ • imitated, imitating
When you **imitate** something, you try to copy what it is doing, or what it sounds or looks like: *My friends all laughed when I* ***imitated*** *the way our teacher talks. They said I did a good* ***imitation*** *of her voice.*

Jake likes to **imitate** his dad, who is a rodeo clown.

Many **immigrants** arrived in the United States at Ellis Island in New York.

immediately

Immediately means right now, and not later: *If we don't leave **immediately**, we'll be late for school.*

immigrant ▲ • immigrants

An **immigrant** is someone who leaves one country and goes to live in another one: ***Immigrants** from many different countries have come to live in the United States.*

important

If something is **important**, it is something we should care about very much. It matters a lot: *It is **important** for all children to learn to read and write.*

impossible

If something is **impossible**, nobody can do it: *It is **impossible** to go all the way around the world in a plane in only one hour.*

in ▼

1. **In** means inside, or not outside, somewhere: *Our parents told us to stay **in** the house until they got back.*
2. **In** also means into a place: *Pete put the milk **in** the refrigerator.*
3. **In** can also mean during an amount of time or a period: ***In** summer, we can play outside after dinner, before it gets dark.*

The turtle hides **in** its shell.

include • included, including

You **include** something when you keep it with other things and do not keep it separate: *I hope Penny **includes** me in the list of people she is asking to her party.*

indoor ▼

Something that is **indoor** is placed or happens inside a building: *The big hotel where we stayed last winter had an **indoor** pool and there were lots of indoor sports you could play. In winter it is good to swim **indoors**.*

Tyler has to stay **indoors** because it is raining.

infant ▶ • infants

An **infant** is a baby or a very young child: *Parents take great care of* ***infants*** *to keep them from falling over or hurting themselves.*

The **infant** has just started to walk.

information

The **information** we have about something is everything that we know about it: *We need more* ***information*** *before we can decide what caused the fire in our kitchen.*

initial • initials

An **initial** is the first letter of a word. If you write your initials, you write only the first letter of each part of your name: *My name is Frank William Sorensen, and my* ***initials*** *are F.W.S.*

injure ▶ • injured, injuring

To **injure** means to hurt: *Layla* ***injured*** *herself when she fell over and cut her foot. She was lucky that her* ***injury*** *was not too bad, just a small cut.*

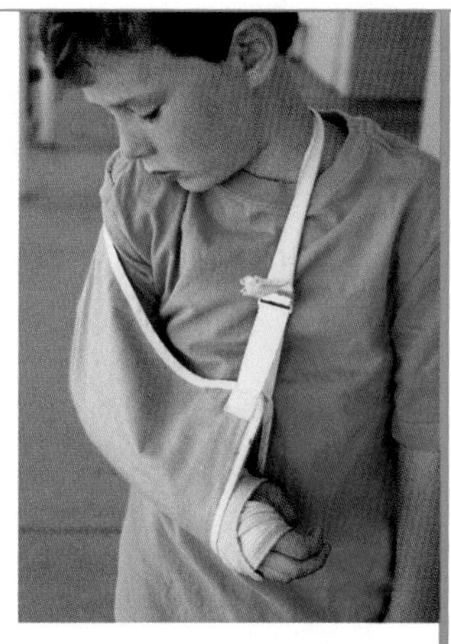

Donny **injured** his arm playing soccer.

ink ▼ • inks

Ink is a liquid that people use for writing or drawing. Ink can be black, blue, or red, or any other color: *Ken uses* ***inks*** *of different colors to draw pictures of animals and birds.*

The man uses a brush to write with **ink** on the sheet of paper.

A
B
C
D
E
F
G
H
I
J
K
L
M
N
O
P
Q
R
S
T
U
V
W
X
Y
Z

insects

There are more kinds of insects than all the other kinds of animals on Earth put together. Insects live in many different habitats, such as in deserts and streams. They feed on all sorts of things, such as wood, leaves, blood, other insects, and parts of flowers.

There are more than a million kinds of insects.

insect ◀ • insects

An **insect** is a very small animal with a body divided into three parts. All insects have six legs, and most have a pair of wings: *Ants, flies, mosquitoes, and beetles are different types of **insects**.*

inside ▶ • insides

1. The **inside** of something is the middle part of it, or the part that is not outside: *The **inside** of a refrigerator is cold.*
2. Inside means in or indoors: *Zach opened the front door and went **inside** the house.*

The smallest doll sits **inside** the other dolls.

instead

Instead means taking the place of something else or someone else: *We couldn't get tickets for the baseball game, so we bought tickets for the movies **instead**.*

instruction • instructions

When someone gives you an **instruction**, they tell you what to do or how to do something: *Our teacher gave us **instructions** about how to use a dictionary. My parents **instruct** me about lots of things, like how to eat the right food or how to study for school.*

instrument ▼ • instruments

1. An **instrument** is a tool that helps you do a job: *A hammer is an **instrument** that hits nails. A knife is an **instrument** that cuts things.*
2. An **instrument** is also something that makes music: *The piano is my favorite **instrument**.*

insurance • insurances

You take out **insurance** so that if something bad happens, you will get money to take care of it. Insurance can pay for your house to be fixed if it burns down, or for your car to be fixed if it is in a crash: *Mom took out **insurance** on her new car.*

intelligent

If you are **intelligent**, you are very smart: *Gina is the most **intelligent** girl in our class. She showed her **intelligence** by getting the best grades in math and spelling.*

The saxophone, violin, and double bass are different kinds of musical **instruments**.

interesting

Something is **interesting** if it makes you want to look at it or listen to it or know more about it: *It was such an **interesting** DVD about penguins, we watched it three times. Donald took a lot of **interest** in seeing how the baby penguins were born.*

international ▼

If something is **international**, it has to do with people from different countries: *He ran in an **international** race with runners from America, England, Japan, and Italy.*

Internet

You use the **Internet** when you send an e-mail, or look up information on a computer. The Internet is many different computers joined to each other from all over the world: *David looked on the **Internet** to find out more about electricity for his school report.*

into

1. **Into** means inside: *Judith put her book **into** her book bag.*
2. You can also use **into** to tell about a change in something: *The caterpillar turned **into** a moth.*

invent ▲ • invented, inventing

Invent means to make up something new that was not known before: *The jet airplane was **invented** about seventy years ago. The **invention** of the jet plane changed the way people travel around the world.*

invisible

If something is **invisible**, you cannot see it: *We read a story about a ghost that nobody could see because it was **invisible**.*

invitation • invitations

When you give an **invitation** to someone, you ask them to do something or go somewhere: *Pat gave me an **invitation** to her birthday party.*

invite • invited, inviting

Invite means to ask someone to do something or go somewhere: *Lauren **invited** me to go to the movies with her and her sisters.*

My **international** studies class made a picture showing people from all around the world.

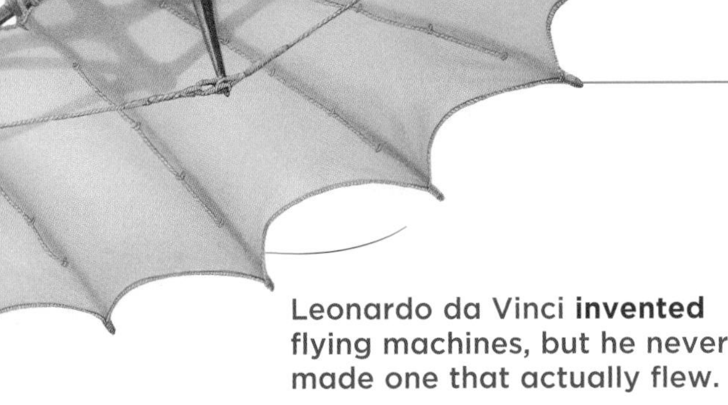

Leonardo da Vinci **invented** flying machines, but he never made one that actually flew.

iron ▼ • irons

1. **Iron** is a strong metal: ***Iron*** *can be used to make airplanes, cars and trucks, and many kinds of machines.*
2. You can use a hot **iron** as a tool that will make your clothes look neat and smooth.

The chair and table in our garden are made of **iron**.

is

Is is a form of the word BE: *Five plus five* ***is*** *ten. Alaska* ***is*** *the biggest state in the United States.*

island ▼ • islands

An **island** is some land with water all around it: *We took our boat to the* ***island*** *in the middle of the lake.*

There are no houses on the small **island**.

isn't

Isn't is a shorter way of saying "is not": *That book is mine. It* ***isn't*** *yours, so please give it back to me.*

it

It is a word that means the thing you are talking about: *You have to give the dog a bath, because* ***it*** *cannot wash itself the way people can.*

itch • itched, itching

When you **itch**, your skin tickles or stings. It feels as if you want to scratch it: *A flea bit me and now my arm* ***itches****.*

its ▼

Its means that something belongs to a person, animal, thing, or place: *The puppy has mud on* ***its*** *paws.*

The hermit crab is in **its** shell.

it's

1. **It's** is a shorter way of saying "it is": *Andrew's dog looks a bit mean, but* ***it's*** *really friendly.*
2. **It's** is also a shorter way of saying "it has": *We can't go outside to play, because* ***it's*** *been raining hard for the last two days.*

A
B
C
D
E
F
G
H
I
J
K
L
M
N
O
P
Q
R
S
T
U
V
W
X
Y
Z

Jj

Everyone wore **jeans** for the family photo.

jacket ▾ • jackets

A **jacket** is a short coat. It usually has long sleeves: *Mom told me to take my **jacket** with me in case it got cold.*

Ron got a special **jacket** because he made the school football team.

jail • jails

A **jail** is a place where people who have broken the law are kept locked up: *The robber was put in **jail** for two months.*

jar ▸ • jars

A **jar** is a container with a tight top. A jar is usually made out of glass: *We kept the insect in a **jar** for a day so we could study it, and then we let it go.*

jealous

If you are **jealous**, you want to have what someone else has: *Rachel was **jealous** because her friend Julie got a new bike for her birthday that is a lot nicer than the one she has.*

jeans ▴

Jeans are long pants that are made of strong cloth. They are usually a blue color.

Ruth filled lots of **jars** with fruits from her apricot trees.

jelly ▼

Jelly is a soft, sweet food made from fruit juice boiled with sugar until it is really thick. You can eat jelly on bread, toast, muffins, and other foods.

Strawberry **jelly** tastes delicious on toast.

jet ▶ • jets

A **jet** is a very fast stream of steam, liquid, or gas that shoots out hard from a small opening: *In the middle of the fountain, there was a big statue of a fish, which had a* ***jet*** *of water coming from its mouth.* A **jet plane** is an airplane with engines that move the plane forward when gases are pushed out of an opening at the back.

The word **jet** once meant "to throw hard." When hot gases shoot out from the back of a *jet plane*, or when a *jet* of water goes up high from a fountain, it looks like something is being thrown.

In 1947 this **jet plane** was the first to go faster than the speed of sound.

jewel ▼ • jewels

A **jewel** is a stone that is very expensive, such as a diamond: *Mary's grandmother has a ring with two* ***jewels*** *in it. She wears it when she goes out somewhere special. Sometimes she wears other* ***jewelry****, such as a necklace or a bracelet.*

People in ancient Egypt wore **jewelry** when they dressed up.

A B C D E F G H I J K L M N O P Q R S T U V W X Y Z

job ▶ • jobs

1. A **job** is work that you get paid to do: *My mom has a **job** making sandwiches at our town supermarket.*
2. A **job** is also any work that needs to be done: *I have to pull up the weeds in the garden, and it's a long, hard **job**.*

join ▼ • joined, joining

1. If you **join** things, you put them together so that they become one thing: *Thomas **joined** the pieces of wood to make a table.*
2. **Join** also means to become a member or a part of something: *Sarah **joined** the tennis club and now she plays tennis there every weekend.*

When you **join** a marching band, you have to wear your uniform when you play.

joke • jokes

1. A **joke** is something you say or do to make people laugh: *I love telling **jokes** to my best friend because she always laughs.*
2. A **joke** can also be a trick you play on someone: *I played a **joke** on my sister and put soap on the door handle.*

People earn money by doing many different kinds of **jobs.**

journal • journals

A **journal** is a book that you write in about things that have happened in your life, or things that you have thought about: *Jackson wrote in his **journal** every night when he was away at camp.*

The word **journal** comes from an older word meaning "a day." A person who keeps a journal usually writes something in it every day, or they may write in it once a day on different days.

joy • joys

If you feel **joy**, you feel very happy: *Amy felt **joy** when her dad told her she had a new baby brother.*

judge • judges

1. A **judge** is someone whose job is to decide things that have to do with the law: *The **judge** sent the man to jail for robbing the local store.*
2. A person who decides the winner of a contest is also called a **judge**: *Ruth was the **judge** for the best-looking baby contest at the school fair.*

juice ▼ • juices

Juice is the liquid from fruits or vegetables: *This orange has a lot of **juice**.*

Helen squeezed several grapefruits to make a glass of **juice** to drink.

jump ▼ • jumped, jumping

If you **jump**, you move up or through the air by pushing with your feet and legs: *Rowan had to **jump** to catch the basketball in the air.*

jungle ▶ • jungles

A **jungle** is a place where thick trees, vines, and other plants grow. Jungles are usually hot, and are very damp from a lot of rain.

A **jungle** is the home of many animals and birds.

just

1. If something is **just** right, it is exactly right, or perfect: *That dress is **just** what I have been looking for to wear to the dance.*

2. If something has **just** happened, it has happened a very short time ago: *I **just** got an e-mail from my friend, and I wrote back to him as soon as I got it.*

The women in the race all **jump** at the same time.

Stuart likes **ketchup** on his French fries.

kangaroo ▼ • kangaroos

A **kangaroo** is an animal with small front legs, a long tail, and big back legs. It moves by hopping: *Mother **kangaroos** have a soft bag of skin on their stomach called a pouch and they carry their babies in this.*

keep • kept, keeping

1. If you **keep** something, it means you still have it: *David says I can borrow his baseball glove for the game tomorrow, but I can't **keep** it.*
2. Keep also means to make something stay the same: *Please **keep** the door closed. The teacher asked us to **keep** quiet during the lesson.*

Kangaroos balance on their long tail when they stand up.

ketchup ▲

Ketchup is a red sauce made from tomatoes. People put ketchup on certain foods to make them taste better: *Do you want **ketchup** on your hamburger?*

I keep a set of **keys** in my bag.

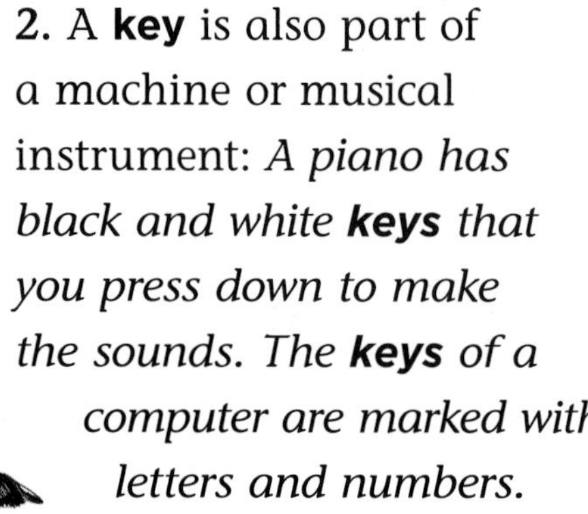

key ▶ • keys

1. A **key** is a small piece of metal that can open or close a lock: *He locked the door with his **key**.*
2. A **key** is also part of a machine or musical instrument: *A piano has black and white **keys** that you press down to make the sounds. The **keys** of a computer are marked with letters and numbers.*

keyboard ▶ • **keyboards**

A **keyboard** is a row or set of keys on a piano or computer.

kick ▼ • **kicked, kicking**

If you **kick** something, you hit it with your foot: *In soccer you score if you **kick** the ball into the other team's goal.*

kid • **kids**

1. A **kid** is a baby goat: *Nicole saw a goat and her **kid** on the farm.*
2. A **kid** is also a child: *All the other **kids** were allowed to play in the park, but I had to stay home because I was sick.*

A piano **keyboard** has black and white keys.

kill • **killed, killing**

To **kill** something means to make it die: *Our dog **killed** our pet hamster. Mom used a poisonous chemical to **kill** the weeds in the garden.*

killer whale

A **killer whale** is a black and white sea mammal that is a kind of dolphin. Killer whales have a tall fin on the top of their body. They eat mainly fish, and sometimes seals, too. Killer whales are also called **orcas**.

The zebra **kicks** the hyena to stop it from attacking.

A B C D E F G H I J K L M N O P Q R S T U V W X Y Z

kind[1] • kinder, kindest

If you are **kind**, you are nice and give help: *My aunt is very* ***kind*** *to our family and always does things to help us.*

kind[2] • kinds

Kind means a group of things that are like each other: *Swans are a* ***kind*** *of bird.*

Frank has a collection of different **kinds** of hats.

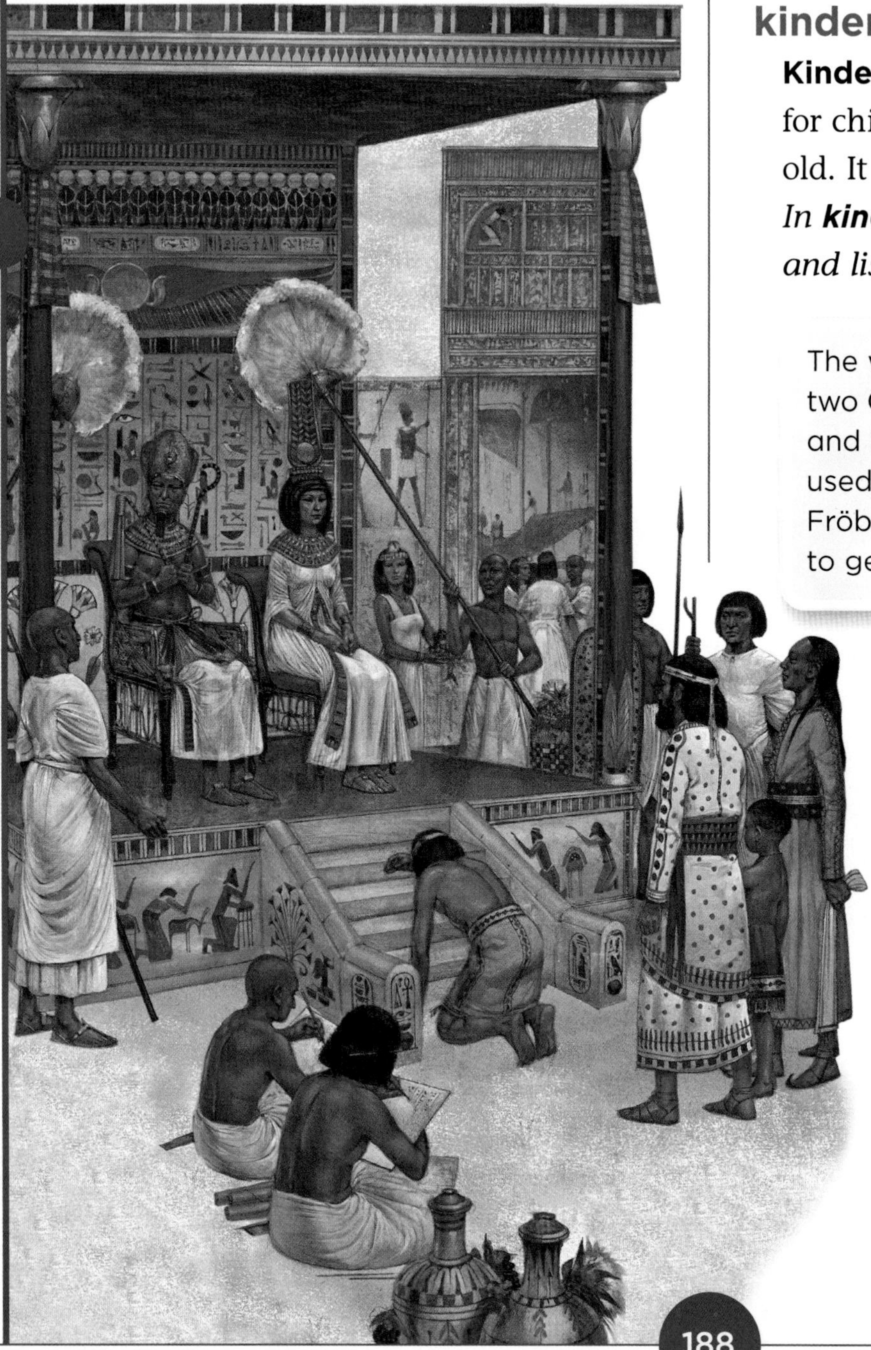

kindergarten • kindergartens

Kindergarten is a grade in school for children from four to six years old. It comes before first grade: *In* ***kindergarten****, we paint, play, and listen to stories.*

The word **kindergarten** comes from two German words meaning "children" and "a garden." The name was first used by a German teacher, Friedrich Fröbel, who taught young children to get them ready for regular school.

king • kings

A **king** is a man who rules a country: *In past times many countries had a* ***king*** *as the head of the country. If the king died, then his oldest son would become the new king.* A country ruled by a king or queen is called a **kingdom**.

The **king** of Egypt sits on his throne with the queen.

kiss ▼ • kissed, kissing
If you **kiss** someone, you touch them with your lips to show that you love them: *Mom and Dad **kiss** me before I go to bed at night.*

Fiona and Luke **kiss** their grandmother.

kit ▼ • kits
A **kit** is a set of things that you use to do something: *We used the bike **kit** to fix my flat tire.*

The first aid **kit** has a supply of bandages and medicine.

kitchen • kitchens
A **kitchen** is a room where you make food. Most kitchens have a sink, a stove, a refrigerator, and a table to eat at: *We eat breakfast in our **kitchen**.*

Harry flies his **kite** on the windy beach.

kite ▲ • kites
A **kite** is something that you fly on the end of a long string. A kite is made of strong pieces of wood or plastic that are covered in paper, cloth, or soft plastic: *It's a nice, windy day—let's go fly our **kite**.*

kitten ▼ • kittens
A **kitten** is a baby cat: *My sister got a **kitten** for her birthday.*

The little **kittens** play together in the basket.

A B C D E F G H I J K L M N O P Q R S T U V W X Y Z

knights

In old times, knights were an important part of a ruler's army. The most valuable things that a knight owned were his armor, his weapons, and his horse. A knight had men to look after the horses and to help him get dressed in his armor. These people were called pages and squires, and they trained to become knights themselves.

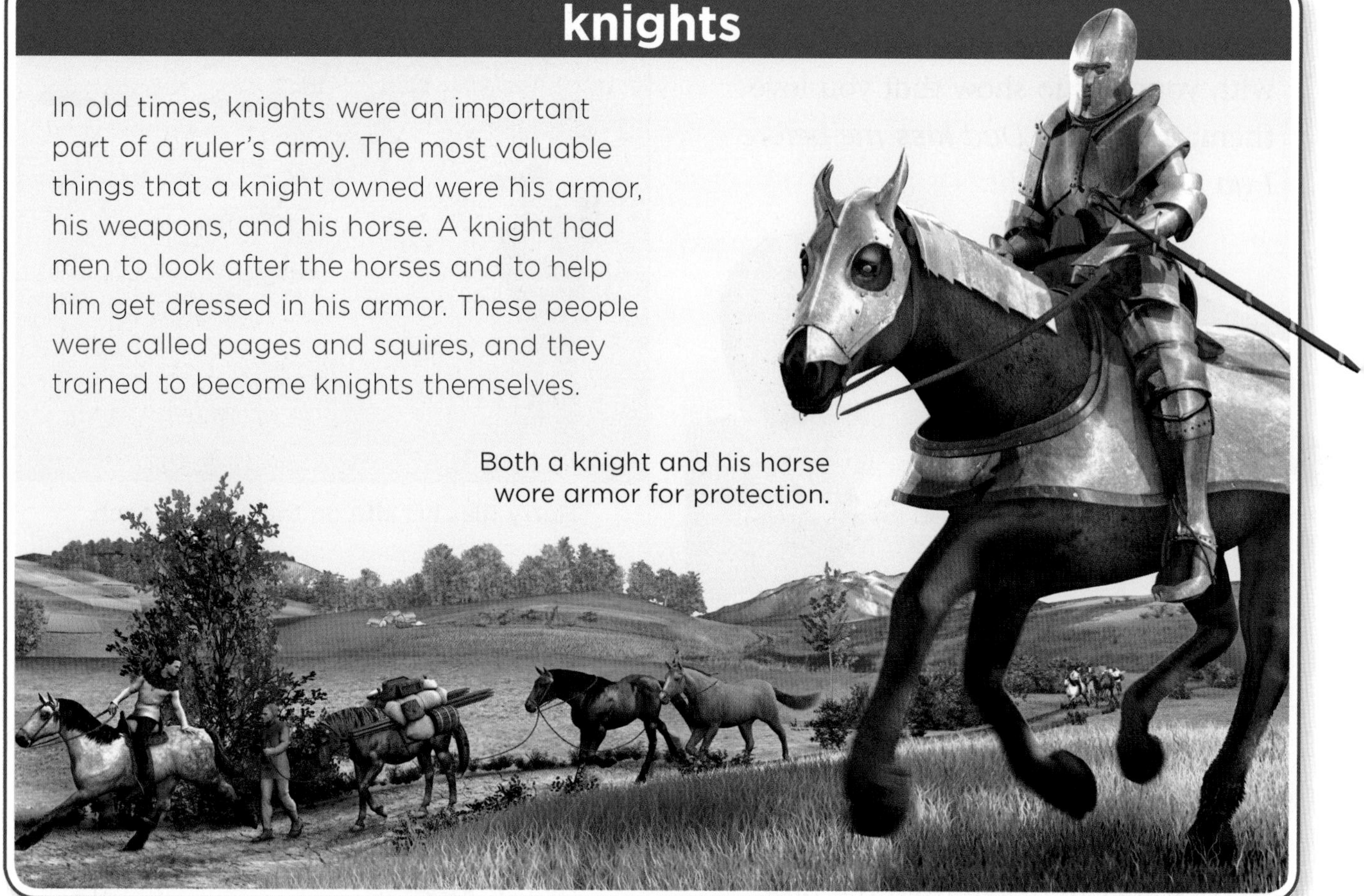

Both a knight and his horse wore armor for protection.

knee ▸ • knees

Your **knee** is in the middle of your leg. It is the part where your leg bends: *I cut my **knee**. Now it hurts when I **kneel** on it for too long.*

Trish protects her **knees** when she plays volleyball.

knew

Knew is a form of the word KNOW: *I wish I **knew** how to play the piano.*

knife ▾ • knives

A **knife** is used for cutting. It has a sharp blade on the end of a handle: *I cut the apple into pieces with a **knife**.*

Dad set the table with a **knife,** a fork, and a spoon.

knight ◀ • **knights**
A **knight** is a soldier from past times. A knight fought for a king or queen. Knights wore heavy metal called armor and rode horses: *The teacher read us a story about a **knight** who killed a dragon.*

knit ▼ • **knitted, knitting**
When you **knit**, you use long needles and wool to make a sweater, scarf, or other clothes: *Mom **knitted** me a warm hat for winter.*

I am **knitting** a scarf to wear when I go skiing.

knob ▶ • **knobs**
A **knob** is a small, round handle for opening a door or drawer. Some radios and televisions also have knobs: *I turned the **knob** and the door opened. Juanita turned the **knob** on the radio to make the sound louder.*

All the **knobs** on the furniture in my bedroom are orange.

Sam **knocks** on the door to see if his friend is home.

knock ◀ • **knocked, knocking**
1. To **knock** something means to bang or hit it: ***Knock** on the door to see if anyone is home at Erin's house.*
2. To **knock** also means to bump against something so that it falls: *Jessie **knocked** her glass of milk over with her elbow.*

knot • **knots**
A **knot** is where a piece of string, rope, or thread is tied up: *To make sure the string around the package wouldn't come loose, Jay tied it with a **knot**.*

know • **knew, known, knowing**
If you **know** something, you understand it and are sure about it: *I **know** that Los Angeles is the biggest city in California. Paul **knows** he has to brush his teeth every night before he goes to bed.*

A
B
C
D
E
F
G
H
I
J
K
L
M
N
O
P
Q
R
S
T
U
V
W
X
Y
Z

The **lamb** has soft, white wool.

ladder ▶ • ladders

A **ladder** is a piece of equipment that helps you climb. Ladders can be moved from place to place. They have bars or flat steps to put your feet on as you go up or down: *Jerry climbed up the **ladder** into the attic.*

lady • ladies

Lady is a polite word for a woman: *I was not sure where the music store was, so I asked a **lady** for directions.*

lake ▼ • lakes

A **lake** is a large area of water with land all around it: *Instead of walking around the **lake**, Mike took a boat across it.*

There is an island in the middle of the **lake**.

lamb ◀ • lambs

A **lamb** is a young sheep: *The little **lamb** ran across the field behind its mother.*

lamp • lamps

A **lamp** is a light that can be moved from place to place: *Mom put the **lamp** on the table beside the bed so she could see to read her book.*

The man on the **ladder** picks berries off the tree.

land • lands, landed, landing

1. **Land** is any place in the world that is not covered by water: *Our house is built on the high **land** that looks over the ocean.*
2. To **land** means to come down to the ground from the air: *The seagull **landed** on the rock.*

You can look up a word in another **language** in a foreign dictionary.

language ◀ • languages

Language is the words that people use to speak and write to each other: *Luis can speak two **languages**, Spanish and English.*

The word **language** goes back to a Latin word meaning "the tongue." Many of the words in English and other modern languages come from Latin.

lap ▶ • laps

When you sit down, your **lap** is the top part of your legs above your knees: *Charlotte sat on her dad's **lap** and he read her a story.*

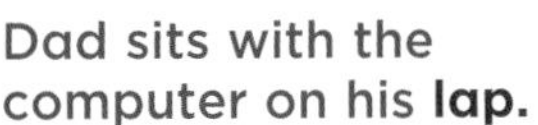

Dad sits with the computer on his **lap**.

large ▶ • larger, largest

If something is **large**, it is big: *When they moved, they used a **large** truck to take all their things to the new house.*

last[1]

1. If something is **last**, it comes after everything else: *On the **last** day of school we had a big party.*
2. **Last** also means the time before now: ***Last** week Gail had a cold, but this week she feels better.*

last[2] • lasted, lasting

If something **lasts**, it goes on the way it already is: *The snow did not **last** long on the ground because it got very warm the next day.*

late • later, latest

1. If you are **late**, you do something after the time you are supposed to: *Carla was **late** getting home because her bike got a flat tire.*
2. **Late** also means the time at night near the end of the day: *Saturday night we got to stay up **late** to watch a special movie.*

laugh • laughs, laughed, laughing

1. When you **laugh**, you use your voice to make a sound that shows you are happy, or think something is funny: *The TV show was so funny that Ray could not stop **laughing**.*
2. A **laugh** is the sound you make when you are laughing: *The baby gave a **laugh** when her father tickled her.*

The dog with spots is **larger** than the puppy.

Rockets are used to **launch** spacecraft.

launch ▲ • launched, launching

If you **launch** something, you start it up and send it off: *Chris turned on his toy boat and **launched** it across the pond.*

laundry • laundries

Laundry is clothes and things like sheets that are dirty and need washing, or that have just been washed: *John put the dirty **laundry** in the washing machine.*

law • laws

A **law** is a rule made by a government that its people must obey: *It is against the **law** to drive a car through a red light.* Someone whose job is to study laws and know a lot about them is called a **lawyer**.

lawn ▶ • lawns

A **lawn** is an area of grass that is usually close to a house or other building: *The **lawn** was growing long, so Todd had to cut it.*

lay[1] • laid, laying

1. To **lay** means to put something down carefully: *James **laid** his cards on the table to show that he had won the game.*
2. To **lay** also means to make an egg: *Ostriches **lay** white eggs that are six inches long.*

lay[2]

Lay is a form of the word LIE[1]: *Grandpa **lay** down on the couch and had a nap.*

layer • layers

A **layer** of something is a covering or coating of it: *Joel's birthday cake had a thick **layer** of cream on the top and eight candles.*

lazy • lazier, laziest

If you are **lazy**, you do not feel like working hard or doing a lot: *Gabrielle was feeling **lazy** and didn't want to clean her room.*

Marjorie cuts the **lawn** with a lawn mower.

The dog that is the **leader** knows which way to go.

lead[1] ▶ • led, leading

When the word **lead** rhymes with "feed," it means to go in front or show the way: *Anita will **lead** the way in our parade. She will be our **leader**.*

lead[2] • leads

When the word **lead** rhymes with "fed," it is the thin black part of a pencil that makes marks: *I had to sharpen my pencil because the **lead** was broken.*

Different trees have **leaves** with different shapes and colors.

leaf ▲ • leaves

A **leaf** is a flat, thin part of a plant. Leaves are usually green and grow from stems or twigs: *The caterpillar ate a **leaf** from the lemon tree.*

league • leagues

A **league** is a group of people, countries, or groups that join together for a reason. A sports league is a group of clubs that play games against each other: *Dad's favorite team in Major **League** Baseball is the Chicago Cubs.*

leak ▼ • leaked, leaking

If something **leaks**, it lets out part of what it is holding through a small hole: *Water was **leaking** out of the bucket through a hole in the bottom.*

lean • leaned, leaning

If something bends or curves toward something, it **leans**: *The fence needs to be fixed because it is **leaning** over.*

Water is **leaking** through a hole.

leap • **leaped** *or* **leapt, leaping**

If you **leap**, you jump or move quickly: *Jason* ***leaped*** *up into the air to catch the football.*

learn ▸ • **learned, learning**

If you **learn** something, you find out about it and understand it: *In class today, I* ***learned*** *all about how to choose and eat healthy food.*

Jim's father helps him **learn** to ride a bike.

leash ▾ • **leashes**

A **leash** is a long rope or chain that you join to an animal's collar to hold or control it: *Doris put a* ***leash*** *on her dog and took him for a walk.*

least

Least means the smallest amount of something: *Most of the food at the party was gone by the time Thomas arrived, so he had the* ***least*** *to eat of anyone there.*

The dog carries the **leash** in its mouth.

leather ▸ • **leathers**

Leather is material that is made from animal skin: *My shoes are strong because they are made of* ***leather****.*

The bag is made of brown **leather.**

leave ▾ • **left, leaving**

1. If you **leave**, you go away from a place: *Please shut the door behind you when you* ***leave*** *the house.*

2. If you **leave** something, you let it stay where it is: *I decided to* ***leave*** *my umbrella at home because I didn't think it was going to rain.*

The turtle is **leaving** its den.

led

Led is a form of the word LEAD[1] that means "went in front" or "showed the way": *The mother duck* ***led*** *her ducklings over the hill and down to the lake.*

left[1] ▶

When you say something is to the **left**, you mean it is on the same side as the left side of your body. The opposite side is the right side: *Mom wears her watch on her **left** wrist. Turn **left** at the end of the street and you will come to the post office.*

The arrow points to the **left.**

left[2]

Left is a form of the word LEAVE: *Michael was in a hurry to get to school and **left** his pencil case at home.*

leg • legs

Your **leg** is one of the long parts of your body that you use for standing and walking. Your feet are joined to the bottom of your legs: *People have two **legs**, dogs have four, and beetles have six. When Millie was swimming, she kicked her **legs** to help her move through the water.*

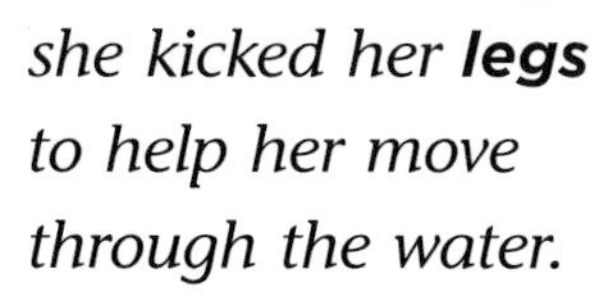

lemon ◀ • lemons

A **lemon** is a fruit with yellow skin that tastes sour: *The juice from a **lemon** tastes good with fish.*

This tree has many **lemons** growing on it.

lend • lent, lending

If you **lend** something, you let someone use it for a while: *Would you please **lend** me your eraser? Thank you for the **loan** of your eraser.*

length • lengths

Something's **length** is how long it is from one end to the other: *From the tip of its nose to the end of its tail, the **length** of the blue whale was ninety feet.*

A **leopard's** claws help it climb trees.

leopard ▲ • leopards

A **leopard** is a large wild cat that has yellow fur with black spots: *The **leopard** rested in the tree after it had gone hunting.*

> The word **leopard** was made up by putting together two other words for large animals in the cat family. The word *leo* was used for the lion, and the word *pard* meant a panther.

less

If you have **less** of something, it means you do not have as much of it: *Mary's cup is smaller than Kirsty's, so it holds **less** milk.*

Catherine writes a **letter** to Santa Claus to ask for a guitar for Christmas.

lesson ▼ • lessons

A **lesson** is anything that you learn or is taught to you: *Travis is taking* ***lessons*** *to learn how to play the piano. When I pulled my dog's tail and he bit me, I learned my* ***lesson*** *and never did it again.*

let • let, letting

To **let** means to permit or allow someone to do something: *Deborah* ***let*** *Jake have a turn playing her computer game. The coach* ***let*** *us go home early from practice today.*

let's

Let's is a shorter way of saying "let us": ***Let's*** *go inside and get out of the rain.*

During her swimming **lesson**, Shirley practices kicking.

letter ◀ • letters

1. A **letter** is a sign that you write to show a sound. There are twenty-six letters in the alphabet: *Samantha's name starts with the* ***letter*** *"S."*
2. A **letter** is also a message that you write and send to another person: *When Dominick went on vacation to Hawaii, he sent a* ***letter*** *to his friend back home.*

lettuce ▶

A **lettuce** is a vegetable with large, thin, green leaves that grow in a ball shape: *The salad had tomatoes, carrots, and fresh* ***lettuce*** *in it.*

Dad grows **lettuce** in our garden.

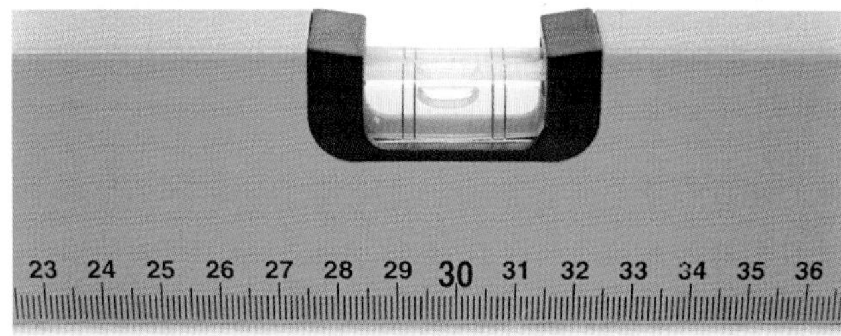

The tool is **level** when the bubble is between the lines.

level ▲ • levels

1. When something is **level**, it is flat and even: *Lucas practiced using his roller skates on the* ***level*** *ground, so he wouldn't be as likely to fall over.*
2. When something has reached a **level**, it is at a certain height or place: *The water got so high during the flood that it reached the* ***level*** *of the roofs of the houses.*

library ▸ • libraries

A **library** is a place where books are kept. You cannot buy the books, but you can read them at the library or borrow them to take home: *Earl went to the* ***library*** *to look for some books about airplanes for his project. The* ***librarian*** *helped him a lot. She found lots of books on airplanes for Earl to borrow.*

The word **library** comes from a very old word meaning "the bark of a tree." Paper is made from different plants, especially from trees. The first paper for books came from the bark of certain trees.

license • licenses

A **license** is a card or a piece of paper that shows you are allowed to do something: *It is against the law to drive a car unless you have passed your driver's test and been given a driver's* ***license****.*

lick ▾ • licked, licking

If you **lick** something, you touch it with your tongue: *Josh* ***licked*** *the last bit of ice cream off his spoon.*

The tiger **licks** its fur to clean it.

I went to the **library** to find books for my class project.

lie[1] ▾ • lay, lain, lying

If you **lie**, your body is resting flat: *If you* ***lie*** *down on this comfortable bed, I'm sure you'll soon be able to go to sleep.*

Warren **lies** on the grass to rest after playing tag.

lie[2] • lies, lied, lying

1. A **lie** is something you say that you know is not true: *Ellen said she didn't take the last cookie, but I saw her do it, so I know she was telling a* ***lie****.*
2. You **lie** when you say something that you know is not true: *Shane* ***lied*** *when he said he was too sick to go to school—he just didn't want to go.*

life • lives

1. If something has **life**, it can grow and keep changing: *People, plants, and animals have **life**, but rocks and cars do not.*
2. The time between when you are born and when you die is called your **life**: *In class I read about the **life** of Abraham Lincoln. Some giant redwood trees have had a **life** of over three thousand years.*

lift ▶ • lifted, lifting

If you **lift** something, you pick it up: *Mom asked me to **lift** my toys off the floor so she could clean it.*

light[1] • lights, lighter, lightest, lighted *or* lit, lighting

1. **Light** is a form of energy that comes from things like the Sun, a flame, or an electric light bulb. Light makes us able to see things: *It was dark out, but the flashlight gave off enough **light** for Harriet to see where she was going.*
2. A **light** is also something that gives off light to help us see: *Dad turned on the **light** over the kitchen table and we sat down to eat our dinner.*
3. A color that is pale is **light**: *Steven added white to the blue paint to make **light** blue for the sky in his picture.*
4. If you **light** something, you start it burning or make it give off light: *I helped Mom **light** the candles on the birthday cake.*

light[2] • lighter, lightest

Something is **light** if it does not weigh much: *My schoolbag is **light** today because there are not many books in it.*

The man uses a machine to **lift** the heavy box.

lightning ▼

Lightning is a flash of light in the sky that happens during thunderstorms. Lightning is made by electricity that moves between clouds or between clouds and the ground: *We ran inside when it started to rain and there was **lightning** and thunder.*

lightning

Lightning usually strikes the highest place, such as the top of a building or a tall tree. Standing next to a tree in a thunderstorm is dangerous. If you cannot go inside a building, you will be safer in a car than being outside.

lions

Lions live in big family groups. There can be as many as 10 female lions with their cubs and one or more males in the group. The females do most of the hunting. The male lion protects the group from other animals.

A group of lions is called a pride.

The children stand in a **line** to get on the bus.

like[1]

If one thing is **like** another thing, it is the same in some way: *Pauline has a pair of gloves that are red, just* ***like*** *Eliza's. People always say that I look a lot* ***like*** *my older brother.*

like[2] • liked, liking

When you **like** something, you feel good about it or enjoy doing it: *Jeff* ***likes*** *playing basketball.*

lime ▶ • limes

A **lime** is a round fruit that looks like a small, green lemon. It has a sour taste: *You can make a drink with* ***limes****, water, and sugar.*

line ◀ • lines

1. A **line** is a straight, thin mark on a piece of paper or other surface: *The pages in my notebook have* ***lines*** *for me to write on.*
2. A **line** is also a group of people or things side by side or one behind the other: *There was a long* ***line*** *of people waiting to buy movie tickets.*

lion ▲ • lions

A **lion** is a type of large wild cat that lives in Africa. Lions have a strong body and light brown fur: *The male* ***lion*** *has long fur around its face and neck and makes a loud sound like a roar.*

We picked fresh **limes** from our tree.

lip • lips

A **lip** is one of the two soft edges on the outside of your mouth in front of your teeth: *The teacher put a finger on his* ***lips*** *to show us that we must not talk.*

The paints in the jars are **liquids.**

liquid ◀ • liquids

A **liquid** is anything that can be poured. A liquid is wet when you touch it: *Milk, water, and juice are* ***liquids***.

list • lists

A **list** is a group of things written down one after the other: *Dad made a* ***list*** *of all the things we needed to buy at the store.*

listen ▼ • listened, listening

When you **listen**, you try in a careful way to hear something: *My sister asked me to* ***listen*** *to a new song that she really likes.*

If you ***listen****, you can sometimes hear the sound of the ocean from my room.*

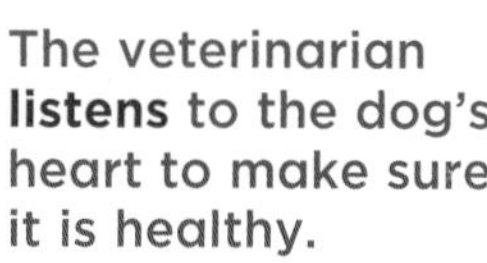

The veterinarian **listens** to the dog's heart to make sure it is healthy.

literature

Literature is writing that people think is good and special and that will be read for a long time: *Poems, plays, and stories are* ***literature***. *The most famous author in English* ***literature*** *is William Shakespeare.*

little ▼ • littler, littlest

1. If something is **little**, it is small in size: *A mouse is a* ***little*** *animal.*

2. **Little** also means not much: *Our team lost, so we had* ***little*** *reason to feel happy after the game. Kyle needs a* ***little*** *more paint to finish painting the gate.*

The **littlest** tortoise is on top of the other two.

live[1] • lived, living

1. When the word **live** rhymes with "give," it means to be alive: *People, animals, and plants* ***live***.

2. We use the same word to mean that if you **live** somewhere, you have your home there: *My aunt* ***lives*** *in Seattle, Washington. Fish* ***live*** *in water.*

live[2]

When the word **live** rhymes with "dive," it means something is alive and not dead: *Albert found a* ***live*** *snake in his house.*

Lobsters turn bright red when you cook them.

lizard • lizards

A **lizard** is an animal with a long, thin body and four short legs: *Some **lizards** live in hot places and eat insects.*

load • loads

A **load** is something that is carried: *The truck has a big **load** of bricks.*

loaf • loaves

A **loaf** is bread baked in one large piece: *Mom cut the **loaf** into smaller pieces so she could make sandwiches.*

lobster • lobsters

A **lobster** is an animal with a hard shell that lives in the sea. A lobster has a long tail and large claws on its front legs: *People cook **lobsters** and eat the meat under the shell.*

local

If something is **local**, it belongs to a place, like your city or town: *I go to the **local** park because it is close to home.*

lizards

Lizards usually live in warm places, but some live where it is cold. Many of them eat insects, but some eat fruits and leaves. Some very big lizards eat large animals, such as goats and chickens.

lock • **locks, locked, locking**

1. A **lock** is an object that keeps something closed. You open most locks with a key: *There is a **lock** on our front window. Will has a **lock** on his bicycle.*
2. When you **lock** something, you close it using this kind of object: *Don't forget to **lock** the door when you leave.*

log ▼ • **logs**

A **log** is a large piece of wood from a tree: *These **logs** are too thick to burn in our fireplace.*

The giant **log** came from a very old tree.

lonely • **lonelier, loneliest**

If you are **lonely**, you are not happy because you are alone and you are missing other people: *José felt **lonely** when his best friend went on vacation. Another friend came to visit him, so he wasn't **lonesome** for long.*

long • **longer, longest**

1. Something is **long** if one end is far away from the other end: *Gina's **long** hair goes down to her waist. It is a **long** drive from New York to Florida.*
2. Long also means taking a lot of time: *The movie was so **long** that my little brother fell asleep before the end.*

look ▼ • **looked, looking**

1. When you **look**, you use your eyes to see something: *The teacher asked us to **look** at the picture.*
2. Look also means how you seem to other people when they see you: *Josh **looked** tired after helping his uncle work on the farm all day.*

loose • **looser, loosest**

If something is **loose**, it is not tight the way it should be: *Tina has a **loose** tooth and it will fall out soon.*

lose • **lost, losing**

1. When you **lose** something, you do not have it and you cannot find it: *Don't **lose** this ticket or you won't be able to get into the movie.*
2. Lose also means not being able to keep something: *The coach told me if I'm late for the game I will **lose** my place on the starting team.*
3. Lose also means to not win: *Michael's team **lost** the game. They were all sad about the **loss**.*

People **look** at the whales swimming in the water.

The anteater's head is **low** as it collects ants with its tongue.

lost

Lost is a form of the word LOSE: *The hikers were **lost** in the woods.*

lot • lots

If there are a **lot** of people or things, it means there are large numbers of them: *There are a **lot** of children at our school. This rose bush has **lots** of flowers.*

loud • louder, loudest

If something is **loud**, it makes a lot of sound: *The airplane made a **loud** noise as flew up into the sky.*

loudspeaker • loudspeakers

A **loudspeaker** is something that makes sounds louder: ***Loudspeakers** are used in radios and in some telephones.*

love • loved, loving

When you **love** someone or something you have a strong feeling of liking them very much: *Grandma **loves** all her grandchildren.*

low ◀ • lower, lowest

1. If something is **low**, it is close to the ground: *Our dog can easily jump over our **low** fence.*

2. Low also means below the usual amount: *Cars have to drive at a **low** speed when they go by the school.*

luck ▼

Luck is something that happens to you in a way that has not been planned. Luck is mostly something good, but you can have bad luck too: *Eddie had the good **luck** to win the contest. It wasn't Sally's fault that the towel blew into the water—it was just bad **luck**.*

Some people think four-leaf clovers bring good **luck**.

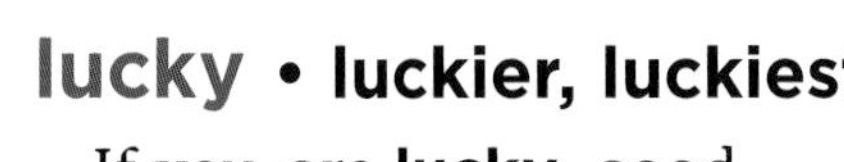

lucky • luckier, luckiest

If you are **lucky**, good things happen to you: *Ellen was **lucky** to get the last two tickets for the concert.*

lumber

Lumber is logs that have been cut into boards for building things: *Joe bought some new **lumber** to fix up his house.*

lunch ▼ • lunches

Lunch is the meal you eat in the middle of the day, between breakfast and dinner: *At school, Anna gets her **lunch** in the cafeteria.*

Becky eats a healthy **lunch** every day.

Mm

A lawn mower is a **machine** that cuts grass.

machine ▲ • machines

A **machine** is something we use to do work. A machine has a lot of parts that work together to do something that can help people: *Televisions, car engines, and air conditioners are **machines**.*

mad ▶ • madder, maddest

If someone is **mad**, they feel very angry about something: *Mom sometimes gets **mad** when we don't clean up our room the way we're supposed to.*

My neighbor is **mad** because I kicked a ball into her yard.

made

Made is a form of the word MAKE: *Carlo **made** a toy boat from a drink carton.*

Katie cut pictures out of **magazines** to use in her project for school.

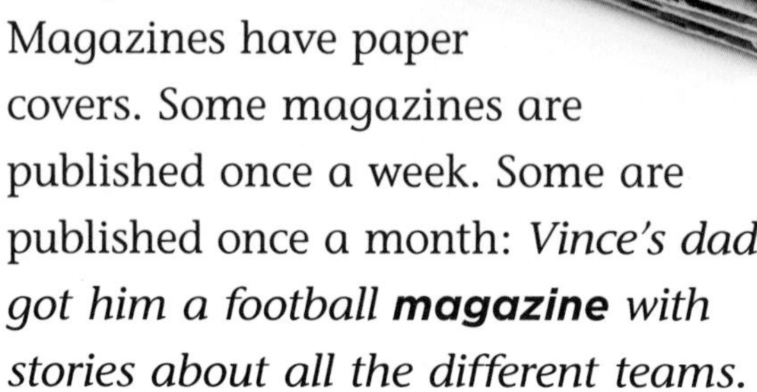

magazine ▶ • magazines

A **magazine** is a collection of printed stories and pictures. Magazines have paper covers. Some magazines are published once a week. Some are published once a month: *Vince's dad got him a football **magazine** with stories about all the different teams.*

magic

Magic is using special powers to make things happen that are not usually possible. Magic looks real, but it is not: *The book was about a witch who used **magic** to turn a prince into a frog. The witch's **magical** spell was broken when a princess kissed the frog and turned it back into a prince again.*

magician ▶ • magicians

A **magician** is someone who uses magic to do tricks: *The **magician** said three special words and then pulled a white rabbit out of his hat.*

Dan dressed up as a **magician** and did magic tricks.

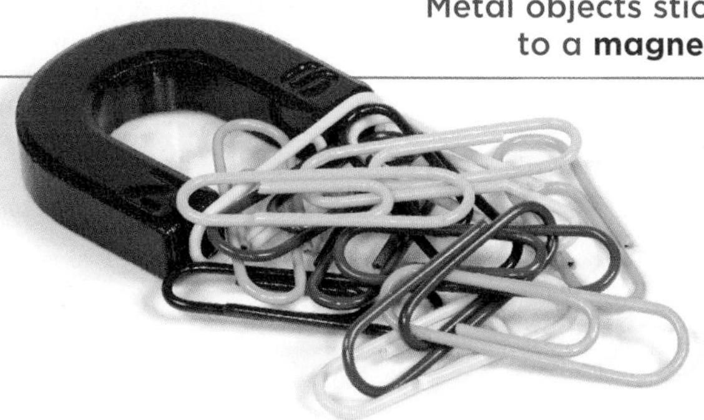
Metal objects stick to a **magnet**.

magnet ▲ • magnets

A **magnet** is a piece of metal that can pull things made of metal toward it: *Mom uses a **magnet** to stick notes onto the refrigerator door. This piece of metal is **magnetic**, so you can use it to pick up pins.*

The word **magnet** comes from the ancient city of *Magnesia*. People saw that rocks near this city had the power to pull other things toward them, and they named them "Magnesian stones."

magnify ▼ • magnified, magnifying

If you **magnify** something, you make it look larger than it really is: *Grandad's reading glasses **magnify** the letters on a page so he can read more easily. When I look at my finger with a **magnifying glass**, I can see the tiny curved lines that make my fingerprint.*

The **magnifying glass** makes Alison's eye look bigger.

mail ▼ • mailed, mailing

1. The letters, cards, and packages that you get or send are **mail**: *I got a birthday card from my aunt and uncle in today's **mail**.*

2. When you send someone a letter or card, you **mail** it: *You'll have to **mail** the present to Rosie today, so it gets to her by her birthday.*

Troy collects the **mail**.

main ▼

The **main** thing is the most important or biggest thing: *The **main** reason we went to the zoo was to see the baby rhinoceros that was born last month.*

The **main** part of the airport is always busy.

major

If something is **major**, it is bigger or more important than other things: *Traffic on the highway was stopped for an hour by a **major** accident.*

a b c d e f g h i j k l m n o p q r s t u v w x y z

make ▼ • made, making

1. When you **make** something, you put things together to create a new thing: *Toni helped Sam* ***make*** *some cookies.*

2. **Make** also means to cause something to happen: *The teacher* ***made*** *us finish our homework at lunchtime.*

The woman **makes** a rug out of pieces of cloth.

make-believe

When something is **make-believe**, it is not real: *In the movie, the children stepped through a door into a* ***make-believe*** *world where animals could talk.*

male ▶ • males

A **male** is a person or animal that cannot lay eggs or give birth to babies. A male is the opposite of a female: *Men and boys are* ***males.***

There are stores on every floor of the **mall.**

mall ▲ • malls

A **mall** is a place where people shop to buy clothes and many other things. A mall has a lot of different stores in one place: *Nicky and Maria went to the* ***mall*** *to buy a shirt for their dad for Father's Day.*

mammal ▶ • mammals

A **mammal** is an animal whose babies feed on their mother's milk. Humans, cats, horses, bears, and whales are all mammals.

The lion with long fur around its face is a **male,** and the other lion is a female.

mammals

There are nearly 4,000 kinds of mammals. Most of them have hair or fur. Mammals live in forests, deserts, on high mountains, and in the sea. The echidna and the platypus are the only mammals that lay eggs.

Lucinda looks at the **map** of the United States.

man • men

A **man** is a grown-up male person: *Grandpa is the oldest **man** in his swimming club.*

manage • managed, managing

If you **manage** something, it is your job to look after it and make sure it runs in the right way: *My father will **manage** the store while his boss is on vacation. Mom thinks that he will be a good **manager**.*

manners

When you have good **manners**, you act in the right way and you are polite to other people: *He has good **manners** and always says "please" and "thank you."*

mansion ▼ • mansions

A **mansion** is a very large, grand house that would cost a lot of money to buy: *The rich family lived in a **mansion** with a tall stone fence all around it and a big swimming pool in the backyard.*

We can pay to go inside the old **mansion** to look around.

many • more, most

Many means a large number of people or things: *There are **many** books in our school library.*

map ◀ • maps

A **map** is a picture or plan of a place that shows where different things are. Maps show roads, railroad lines, rivers, and mountains. They show where towns and cities are: *A **map** of the whole world shows where all the different countries are, and what shape they are.*

Each **marble** has different colors inside it.

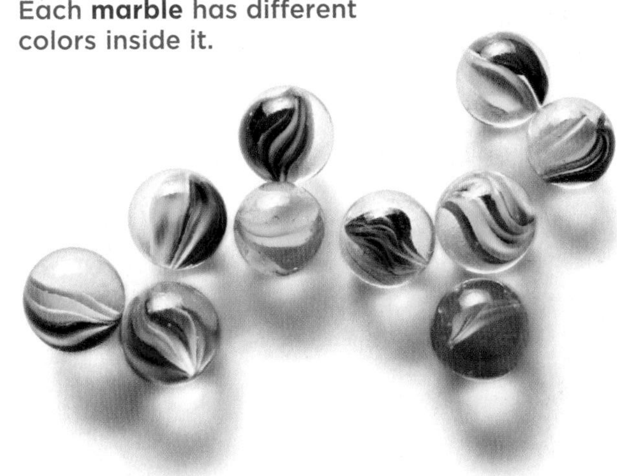

marble ▲ • marbles

1. **Marble** is a type of smooth, hard stone: *People use **marble** in buildings and to make statues.*
2. A **marble** is also a small ball made of glass that is used in games: *John won a yellow **marble** from Sam by knocking Sam's marble out of the circle. John is very good at playing **marbles**.*

The children **march** in a line.

march ▲ • marched, marching

When people **march**, they walk like soldiers. They all take steps at the same time, and swing their arms at the same time: *The band **marched** down the street at the Fourth of July parade.*

mark ▶ • marks, marked, marking

Elliot got a **mark** of A+ on his math homework.

1. A **mark** is a spot, stain, line, or scratch made by one thing on another: *The pen in Adam's shirt pocket leaked and left a blue **mark**.*
2. A **mark** is also the number or letter put on a person's work to show how good it is: *The teacher gave Marcia a **mark** of 77 out of 100 for her assignment.*
3. If you **mark** something, you make a spot, stain, line, or scratch on it: *Kevin got into trouble for **marking** the wall with a pencil.*

market ▼ • markets

A **market** is a place where food and other things are sold: *My aunt got fresh corn, some oranges, and a big bunch of flowers at the Saturday farmers' **market**. Dad bought crabs at the fish **market**.*

marry • married, marrying

When you **marry** someone, you take that person as your husband or wife: *My big sister is getting **married** this Saturday. Mom and Dad are very happy about her **marriage**.*

People in the **market** buy food to eat.

People wear **masks** at carnivals.

mask ▲ • **masks**

A **mask** is a cover that you wear over your face to protect or hide it: *We wore monster **masks** for Halloween.*

match[1] ▶ • **matched, matching**

Things **match** when they are like each other: *This skirt and T-shirt **match** because they are the same orange color.*

match[2] • **matches**

A **match** is a short stick of wood or paper with a chemical on the tip. Matches make a flame when you rub them against something: *Dad used **matches** to light the candles on my birthday cake.*

Rose and Beatrice wear shirts that **match.**

material ▼ • **materials**

Material is what something is made of: *Wood is a **material** often used to build houses. This coat is very warm because it is made of a heavy wool **material**.*

Men look at the **material** they want to buy.

mathematics ▼

Mathematics is the study of numbers, amounts, measurements, and shapes: *When I add up how much pocket money I have, I am doing **mathematics**.* A short word for mathematics is **math**: *We have **math** class in school every day.*

In **math** class, the teacher writes numbers on the chalkboard.

matter • mattered, mattering

1. **Matter** is anything that takes up space and that you can see, touch, smell, or taste. All things are made up of matter: *A glass of water, a human body, and the air you breathe are all different kinds of **matter**.*
2. **Matter** also means to be important: *It doesn't **matter** if it rains because I have my umbrella with me.*

Oliver jumped up and down on his **mattress**.

mattress ▲ • mattresses

A **mattress** is the thick, soft part of your bed that you lie on: *Mom pulled the sheets up over the **mattress**.*

may • might

1. You say **may** when you ask for something or ask to do something: ***May** I leave the table now, Mom?*
2. You also use **may** if there is a chance that something will happen, but you are not sure: *There **may** still be fish in this pond, but we haven't seen any in a while.*

maybe

Maybe means that something could be: ***Maybe** I'll get a new bicycle for my birthday. I can't find my book and I think **maybe** I left it at school.*

I had a **meal** of fish and vegtables.

me

You say **me** when you talk about yourself: *Can you help **me** lift this box? José sent **me** a letter and I wrote back to him.*

meal ▲ • meals

A **meal** is the food that you eat at one time. Breakfast, lunch, and dinner are the three meals that you have every day: *Danielle's favorite **meal** is spaghetti and meatballs.*

mean[1] • meant, meaning

1. You use **mean** to show that two things are the same: *Tiny **means** very small.* The words "tiny" and "very small" have the same **meaning**.
2. You also use **mean** to show what you are thinking or planning: *Karen's brother didn't **mean** to step on her toe—it was an accident.*

mean[2] • meaner, meanest

If you are **mean**, you are not nice to other people. You are not friendly or kind: *Don't be **mean**, let your little brother play the game too.*

measure ▼ • measured, measuring

When you **measure** something, you find out its size or amount: *Joseph used a ruler to **measure** how tall his friend Tony was. The **measurement** was four feet two inches.*

meat • meats

Meat is the part of an animal that we eat: *Hamburger and steak are my two favorite kinds of **meat**.*

The man **measures** spices to sell at the market.

My grandfather has a collection of **medals** from when he fought in the war.

medal ▲ • medals

A **medal** is a piece of metal that looks like a coin. It often has writing on it, and hangs on a ribbon or chain. Medals are given to people when they do something brave or important, or if they win in sports: *Katie got a **medal** for winning the swimming race.*

medicine • medicines

Medicine is something that you take when you are sick to help you get better: *The doctor gave me some **medicine** when I had a bad cold. Jessica had to study hard at **medical** school to become a doctor.*

Tom shakes Al's hand when they **meet**.

meet ▶ • met, meeting

When you **meet** someone, you see them and come together with them: *Let's **meet** at the basketball court after school today. Dad couldn't watch my game, because he had to go to a **meeting** at work.*

melon ▼ • melons

A **melon** is a large, juicy fruit that grows on a vine: *Watermelon is a kind of **melon** that I like to eat in the summer.*

Melons have seeds that you do not eat.

melt ▶ • melted, melting

Melt means to change something from being hard and solid to being soft or liquid by heating it: *When the sun came out, it soon **melted** the snow.*

member ▼ • members

A **member** is a person or thing that belongs to a group or a club: *Marco is a **member** of the school's chess club. Coyotes and wolves are **members** of the dog family.*

All the **members** of my soccer team wear blue shirts.

memory • memories

1. **Memory** is being able to remember things: *Rosa has a very good **memory** for phone numbers.*

2. A **memory** is also a thing or a person that you remember: *One of my happiest **memories** is when our family went to Disneyland.*

The snowman **melts** because it is a warm day.

men

You say **men** for more than one MAN: *In baseball there are nine **men** on a team and in football there are eleven men.*

mess ▶ • messes

A **mess** is something that is dirty or not neat and as it should be: *The neighbor's dog made a **mess** when she dug up the garden. Now their yard looks very **messy**.*

The paint made a **mess**.

message • messages

A **message** is information that one person sends to another person: *Sue left a **message** on the phone saying that she was at her friend's house.*

met

Met is a form of the word MEET: *We **met** the new neighbors for the first time yesterday.*

metal ▼ • metals

Metal is a shiny material that can be melted. Some different kinds of metals are steel, iron, silver, and gold: *A car, a knife, and a coin are all made of **metal**.*

The pans are made of **metal** with plastic handles.

meter • meters

A **meter** is a machine that shows how much time has passed or how much of something has been used: *Grandma put four dollars in the parking **meter**. We have a **meter** on the side of our house to show how much electricity we use.*

mice

You say **mice** for more than one MOUSE: *Our cat caught four **mice** in the barn.*

Two of the singers use **microphones** to make their voices sound louder.

microphone ▲ • microphones

You use a **microphone** to make sounds louder or to record sounds: *The teacher spoke into the **microphone** at the school sports fair.*

microscope ▼ • microscopes

A **microscope** is a tool that makes very tiny things look much bigger when you look into it: *The scientist used a **microscope** to see the germs.*

microwave • microwaves

A **microwave** is a type of electric oven that cooks food very quickly: *Grandma warmed up her dinner in the **microwave**.*

Randy uses a **microscope** in science class.

middle ▼

The **middle** is the point half of the way between two ends or things: *In the word "lunch," the **middle** letter is "n." Iowa is a state in the **middle** of the United States.*

midnight

Midnight is 12 o'clock at night. It is the middle of the night: *We stayed up until **midnight** on New Year's Eve to watch the fireworks.*

At the start of the game, the ball is in the **middle** of the table.

might

Might is a form of the word MAY: *Don't touch that spider—it **might** be dangerous.*

milk

Milk is a white drink that comes from cows, goats, and sheep. Milk is used to make cheese: *Sarah wants a glass of **milk** because she's thirsty.*

mind

• **minds**

The part of you that thinks, knows, decides, and feels is your **mind**: *When the teacher asked what I wanted to do during summer vacation, I just said the first thing that came into my **mind**, which was that I want to visit my cousins.*

mine[1]

When something belongs to me, it is **mine**: *The pink bicycle is my sister's and the blue one is **mine**.*

mine[2] ▲ • mines

A **mine** is a deep hole that people dig into the earth to take out coal, diamonds, and other things that people can use: *The workers dug for gold at the **mine**.*

mineral ▼ • **minerals**

A **mineral** is a thing in the world of nature that is not a plant or an animal. Most rocks are made up of more than one mineral: *Salt, coal, iron, and gold are all **minerals**.*

minus ▶ • **minuses**

You use **minus** when you take one number away from another number: *Twelve **minus** eight is four.* Sometimes we use a **minus sign** (-) instead: *12 - 8 is 4.*

minute • **minutes**

A **minute** is sixty seconds of time. There are sixty minutes in one hour: *Hurry up—the bus will be here in five **minutes**!*

mirror • **mirrors**

A **mirror** is a piece of special glass that you can see yourself in. Some mirrors hang on the wall, while others are for you to hold in your hand: *She looked at herself in the **mirror** to make sure that her hair was neat.*

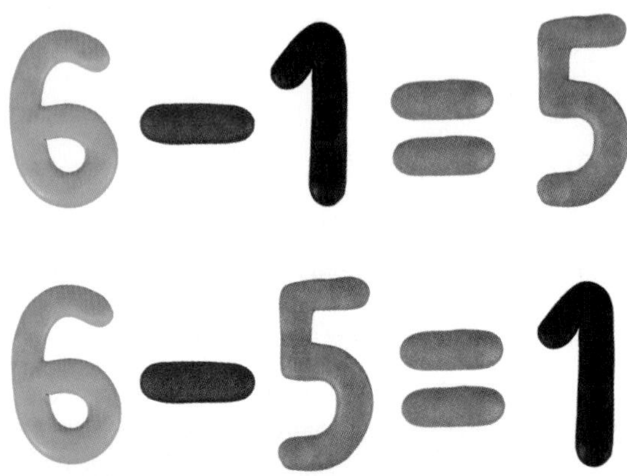

A **minus** sign tells you to subtract one number from another number.

miss • **missed, missing**

1. **Miss** means to not do something that you were planning to do: *We got there late, so we **missed** the train. Steven tried to hit the ball, but he **missed**.*
2. **Miss** also means to be sad because someone or something is not there: *I **miss** my best friend since she moved away.*
3. **Miss** also means to not have something: *The puzzle is **missing** an important piece.*

The students look at rocks made of different **minerals**.

There are five pairs of **mittens**, hanging in a row.

Miss • Misses

You say **Miss** before the name of a girl or woman who is not married: *My teacher's name is **Miss** Lopez.*

I got rid of my spelling **mistake** with an eraser.

mistake ▲ • mistakes

When you make a **mistake**, you do something wrong: *I made two **mistakes** on the math test. It was a **mistake** to get on that train because it didn't stop at our station.*

mitten ▲ • mittens

A **mitten** is a type of glove that has one part for your thumb and one part for your four fingers. You wear mittens to keep your hands warm: *Dave put his **mittens** on before he went out to play in the snow.*

mix ▼ • mixed, mixing

Mix means to put different things together: *In that soccer league, they **mix** the boys with the girls on each team. Ellie **mixed** blue paint and yellow paint to make green paint.*

The recipe says to **mix** butter and brown sugar together in a bowl.

model ▶ • models

A **model** is a small copy of something: *Ben built a **model** of a racing car and painted it red.*

modern ▼

If something is **modern**, it is new or recent: *Our new car is very **modern**—you can watch DVDs in it. One hundred years ago it took weeks to travel from New York to California, but in **modern** times you can do it in a few hours.*

This hotel is a **modern** building.

Mom ▼ • Moms

Mom is a name you use for your mother: *I love my **mom**. I used to call her **Mommy** when I was little.*

When Estelle gets tired, her **mom** picks her up and carries her.

money ▼ • moneys

Money is the coins and paper bills that people use to buy things: *I asked my dad if I could have some **money** to buy an ice cream.*

I save **money** to buy things that I want.

monkey ▶ • monkeys

A **monkey** is a small, furry animal with long arms, long legs, and a long tail. Most monkeys live in forests in hot countries: ***Monkeys** swing from tree to tree, looking for fruits to eat.*

monkeys

There are almost 150 kinds of monkeys. They eat plants, fruits, and insects. Most monkeys in Central and South America have a tail that can grab branches. Monkeys in Africa and Asia cannot grab branches with their tail.

A full **Moon** looks bright in the night sky.

monster ▼ • **monsters**
A **monster** is a make-believe creature that is big, strange, and scary: *At the end of the movie, the hairy, one-eyed* ***monsters*** *went back to their own planet.*

month • **months**
A **month** is one of the twelve parts of the year. The twelve months are January, February, March, April, May, June, July, August, September, October, November, and December: *Our summer vacation starts in the* ***month*** *of June.*

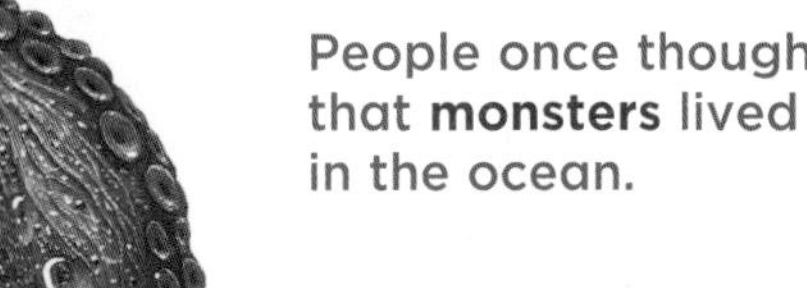

People once thought that **monsters** lived in the ocean.

Moon ◀ • **Moons**
The **Moon** moves in a circle around Earth. It shines in the sky at night: *The* ***Moon*** *is full about once a month, and then you see all of it.*

more ▶
More means a bigger number or a bigger size: *Nine is one* ***more*** *than eight. My brother knows* ***more*** *about dinosaurs than I do because he's read a lot of books about them.*

The glass on the right has **more** orange juice than the other glass.

morning ▸ • mornings

Morning is the part of the day from sunrise until noon: *Gabrielle has band practice in the* ***morning*** *before school starts.*

mosquito ▾ • mosquitoes *or* mosquitos

A **mosquito** is a small flying insect that bites your skin and makes it itchy. Some kinds of mosquitoes can make people very sick when they bite them.

Mosquitoes lay their eggs in water.

most

Most means the biggest in number or amount: *California has the* ***most*** *people of any state in the United States. In the game "Monopoly," the player who has the* ***most*** *money at the end wins the game.*

mother • mothers

Your **mother** is your female parent: *My* ***mother*** *sometimes reads me a story at bedtime before I go to sleep.*

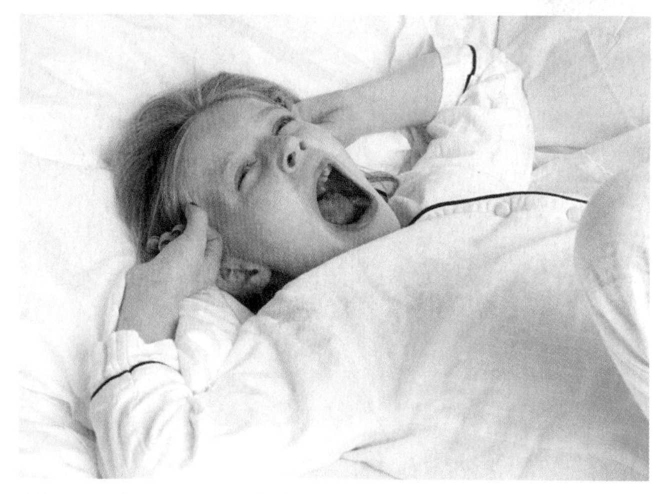

Alex wakes up early in the **morning** and yawns.

motor • motors

A **motor** is the part of a machine that makes it work: *The air conditioner has a* ***motor*** *in it that makes it run to cool off the room.*

motorcycle ▾ • motorcycles

A **motorcycle** is a fast, heavy vehicle with two wheels and an engine. It looks something like a bicycle: ***Motorcycles*** *can move in and out of traffic a lot faster than cars can.*

You must wear a helmet when you ride a **motorcycle**.

The man stops to rest while climbing the tall **mountain.**

mountain ▲ • **mountains**
A **mountain** is a high area of land, much higher than a hill: *The tallest **mountain** in the world is Mount Everest. It is about 29,000 feet high.*

mouse ▶ • **mice**
A **mouse** is a small furry animal with a long, thin tail, a pointed nose, and sharp teeth: *Mom screamed when she saw a **mouse** run across the kitchen floor.*

The **mouse** sleeps in a small nest.

mouth ▶ • **mouths**
Your **mouth** is the opening in your face that you use to talk and eat. On the outside of your mouth are your lips, and on the inside are your tongue and teeth: *Paul opened his **mouth** wide so that the dentist could check his teeth.*

move • **moved, moving**
To **move** means to go from one place to somewhere else: *My grandparents are going to **move** to Florida next year.*

movie ▶ • **movies**
A **movie** is made up of moving pictures that are shown on a screen: *Do you want to go see that new pirate **movie** this weekend?*

Mr.
Mr. is put before a man's name: ***Mr.** Davis is our next-door neighbor.*

Mrs.
Mrs. is put before a married woman's name: ***Mrs.** Parker works with her husband at Foodland Supermarket.*

Ms.
Ms. is put before a woman's name: ***Ms.** Wheeler is my favorite teacher at school.*

The turtle tries to catch a fish in its **mouth.**

We saw a **movie** last weekend about traveling in space.

much • more, most

Much means a lot of something: *Emma can't watch TV tonight because she has too **much** homework to do. I liked the second "Space Fish" movie, but the first one was **much** better.*

mud

Mud is dirt that is wet: *My sneakers were covered with **mud** after we played soccer in the rain.*

muffin ▸ • muffins

A **muffin** is a small, sweet bread that is shaped like a small cake: *Emily had a banana **muffin** and a glass of milk for breakfast.*

multiply • multiplied, multiplying

To **multiply** means to add a number to itself a number of times: *If you **multiply** six by two you get twelve. I learned how to do **multiplication** in math class at school.*

murder • murdered, murdering

To **murder** means to kill someone on purpose: *The criminal spent fifty years in prison for **murdering** another man.*

Michelle baked **muffins** to sell at the school fair.

You can see the **muscles** working under your skin.

muscle ▲ • muscles

Your **muscle** is a part of your body that helps to make it move about: *Dad has strong **muscles** in his arms, which means he can lift heavy things.*

museum ▼ • museums

A **museum** is a building where important and interesting things are kept and shown to people: *My class went on a trip to visit the **museum** to see the show on dinosaurs.*

We went to the **museum** to see the ancient mummies from Egypt.

mushroom ▶ • mushrooms

A **mushroom** is type of plant that grows in damp places and looks like a small, fat umbrella. Some mushrooms can be eaten, but others are poisonous.

music ◀

Music is the nice sound made by people singing or instruments playing: *Tina loves listening to **music**. When she had to learn a **musical** instrument, she chose the guitar. Her teacher said that Tina was a very good **musician** and should try out for the school band.*

Rob plays **music** on his guitar.

must ▼

If you **must** do something, it means that you have to do it: *The teacher says that we **must** hand in our science projects on Friday morning.*

Mom says we **must** wash our hands before we eat.

Several kinds of **mushrooms** grow in the woods behind my house.

mustache ▼ • mustaches

A mustache is a line of hair that grows above a man's lip: *The man's **mustache** was so long that it curled at the ends.*

mustard ▶

Mustard is a thick, yellow liquid with a hot taste made from the seeds of the mustard plant. You add mustard to food to give it flavor: *When I eat a hot dog, I always put **mustard** on it.*

Each of the men has a **mustache** and a beard.

my

My means that something belongs to me: *I packed **my** lunch box into my schoolbag and walked by **myself** to school.*

I like **mustard** on my hot dog.

mystery • mysteries

A **mystery** is something strange or puzzling that you cannot explain: *The police said that how the robbers got into the house was a **mystery** to them. They said that it was very **mysterious** that the robbers hadn't broken any windows or doors to get in.*

Lewis wears a **napkin** to keep his shirt clean.

Nn

napkin ◀ • **napkins**

A **napkin** is a piece of cloth or paper that you use while you are eating to clean off your mouth and fingers, and to protect your clothes in case you spill your food: *Mom always makes us put **napkins** on our laps when we eat dinner.*

nail ▶ • **nails, nailed, nailing**

1. A **nail** is the hard, flat part at the end of your fingers and toes: *Sarah painted her **nails** a bright red color.*
2. A **nail** is also a thin piece of metal with one end sharp and pointed and the other end flat. You can hammer a nail into two pieces of wood to join them together.
3. To **nail** means to join together with a nail: *Dad **nailed** a board over the hole in the back fence so the dog could not get out that way.*

I used **nails** to repair my wooden toy.

narrow • **narrower, narrowest**

When something is **narrow**, it is not wide: *The road was too **narrow** for the bus to be able to drive through.*

nation • **nations**

A **nation** is a group of people living in a country that is ruled by one government: *Mexico, the United States, and Canada are the three **nations** of North America. The **national** flag of Mexico is green, white, and red.*

name • **names, named, naming**

1. A **name** is the word that you know a person, place, or thing by: *The **name** of our street is Glenview Road.*
2. When you **name** something or someone, you choose a name to call them by: *We **named** our dog Buster.*

nap ▶ • **naps**

A **nap** is a short sleep during the daytime: *Grandpa likes to take a **nap** every afternoon at 3 o'clock.*

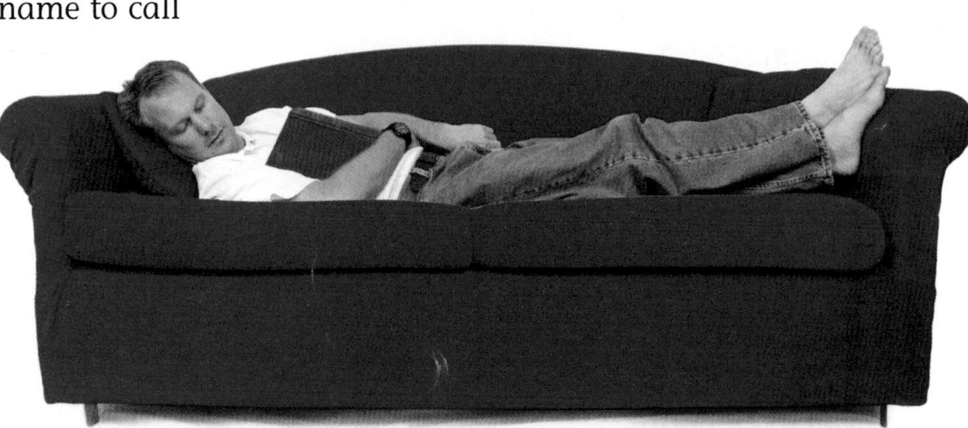

Dad is taking a **nap** on the couch.

Many different plants and animals are found in **nature**.

natural

If something is **natural**, it means it is formed by nature and not made by people: *Hurricanes, floods, and earthquakes are all* ***natural*** *happenings.*

nature ▲ • natures

Nature is everything in the world that is not made by people. Plants, animals, rocks, and the ocean are all part of nature: *I like walking in the mountains because I love being out in* ***nature****.*

Although **nature** is everywhere and has always been part of the world, it is a fairly new English word. Only after cities were built did people think of *nature* as a different place away from cities.

navy • navies

The **navy** is a large group of people who are trained to fight for their country at sea in a war: *My father was in the United States* ***Navy*** *in the Gulf War.*

near ▼ • nearer, nearest

If something is **near**, it is close by: *Jamie can walk to his school because it is quite* ***near*** *where he lives. Louise can't walk to her high school, because it's* ***nearly*** *five miles from her house.*

The golf ball landed **near** the hole, but it did not go in.

Eliza put her pencils in a **neat** line.

neat ▶ • **neater, neatest**

Neat means clean and in good order: *I keep my bedroom **neat**, but my sister's bedroom is always messy.*

neck ▼ • **necks**

Your **neck** is the part of your body that joins your head to your shoulders: *Debbie tied a thick woolen scarf around her **neck** to keep warm. A giraffe has the longest **neck** of any animal.*

The tortoise on the left stretches its **neck** to reach the cactus.

necklace ▼ • **necklaces**

A **necklace** is jewelry that you wear around your neck: *Dad bought Mom a beautiful gold **necklace** for their anniversary.*

The **necklace** is made out of candy.

necktie • **neckties**

A **necktie** is a long, thin piece of cloth that you wear around your neck under the collar of a shirt, with a special knot at the top: *Dad always wears a **necktie** to work. Mom bought him a new striped **tie** to wear with his suit.*

need • **needed, needing**

If you **need** something, you have to have it: *I **need** new shoes because my old ones have holes in them. Those flowers **need** a lot of water, or else they won't grow well.*

needle ▲ • needles

1. A **needle** is a small, thin piece of metal that you use when you sew. It has a sharp point at one end and a little hole at the other end for the thread: *Susan used a **needle** and thread to sew up a hole in her socks.*
2. A **needle** is also a thin hollow tube that a doctor or nurse uses to give you medicine.

The girls are **neighbors,** and they play together a lot.

neighbor ▲ • neighbors

A **neighbor** is someone who lives close by: *We had new **neighbors** move into the house next door. They said that they were happy to be moving to a **neighborhood** with lots of trees and places for children to play.*

neither

Neither means not one or the other: ***Neither** the cat nor the dog is allowed to sleep in the house at night.*

nephew • nephews

Your **nephew** is the son of your brother or sister: *Sometimes Alice baby-sits for her **nephew**, so that her brother and his wife can go out to dinner by themselves.*

nerve • nerves

A **nerve** is a part of your body that carries messages to and from your brain: *Dad hurt the **nerves** in his back muscle when he fell off the ladder. When you try to catch a ball, the **nerves** send a message from your brain to the muscles of your hand and arm.* You have many different nerves in your body that make up your **nervous system**.

nervous ▼

If you are **nervous**, you are excited or a bit afraid about something: *Felicity was **nervous** about singing in the school musical.*

Jack is **nervous** because it is his turn next.

nest ▼ • nests

A **nest** is a home built by birds to lay their eggs in. Birds build nests using grass, sticks, mud, and other things: *The bird used some twigs and dry grass to make a **nest** for her eggs.*

net ▶ • nets

A **net** is a kind of material made from thread, string, or rope that has holes in it. Nets can be used in sports, like a tennis net or a basketball net. Nets can also be used to catch things, such as fish or butterflies.

nests

Birds make many kinds of nests to keep their eggs and babies safe. Kingfishers make tunnels in the dirt. Stilts make nests from piles of sticks. Other birds, such as weavers, make nests that hang. Cuckoos do not look after their own eggs or babies. They lay their eggs in other birds' nests.

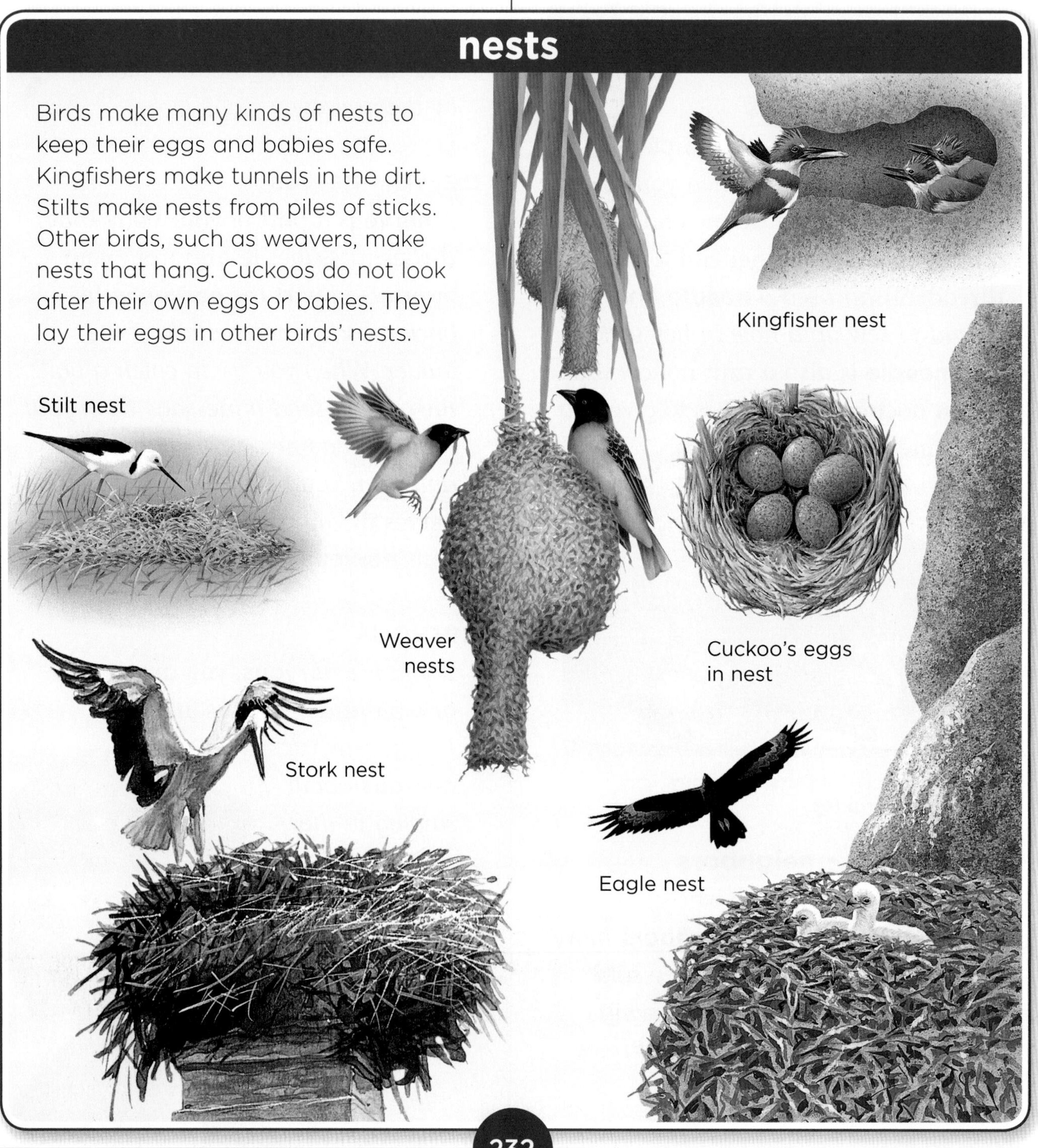

The fisherman puts a **net** into the water to catch fish.

network • networks

1. A **network** is a large group of parts that are joined: *There is a **network** of highways that cross all over the United States. The ABC television **network** has TV stations in many American cities.*
2. A **network** is also a group of computers that are joined to other computers: *At the school library, all the computers are part of the same **network**.*
3. A **network** can be a large group of people who know each other: *Mom has a **network** of friends that she met at the golf club.*

never

Never means not even once: *Sarah was excited about her trip to Texas because she had **never** been on an airplane before.*

new ▶ • newer, newest

1. When something is **new**, it has not been used before: *Paul got a **new** red bicycle for his birthday.*
2. You say that something is **new** if it is just beginning: *My favorite actor is in a **new** movie that is starting this week.*

The **new** plant has only two leaves.

news

News is information or a story of something that has just happened. We get news from the radio or television, in newspapers, and on the Internet: *Did you see the **news** story in today's paper about a firefighter who saved a little girl?*

newspaper ▼ • newspapers

A **newspaper** is a collection of news stories that are printed on paper, often with photos that go with the stories. Newspapers have stories about famous people, sports, movies, wars, and lots of other things that happen in the world.

We put our **newspapers** in a pile for recycling.

next

1. **Next** means coming right after someone or something: ***Next** Saturday is my friend's birthday party.*
2. **Next** also means close to or beside: *I think my uncle's office is on the block **next** to the library.*

A B C D E F G H I J K L M N O P Q R S T U V W X Y Z

nice • **nicer, nicest**
If something is **nice**, it is enjoyable or pleasant: *We had a **nice** time on our trip to the mountains.*

nickname • **nicknames**
A **nickname** is a name you use instead of someone's real name: *My **nickname** is "Ginger" because I have red hair.*

niece • **nieces**
Your **niece** is the daughter of your brother or sister: *My aunt says that I am her favorite **niece**.*

You can see the Moon at **night**.

night ◀ • **nights**
Night is the time between sunset and dawn. At night it is dark outside and you can see the Moon and the stars: *I usually go to sleep at 9 o'clock at **night**.*

nightmare • **nightmares**
A **nightmare** is a bad or scary dream: *I had a **nightmare** that a giant spider was chasing me.*

The word **nightmare** comes from stories about an evil being called a "nightmare." This strange being would sneak up on people while they slept and scare them.

You cannot park here because the sign says **no** parking.

no ◀
1. When you say **no**, it means that you do not agree with someone or something. No is the opposite of yes: ***No** thank you, I do not want fried beans for dinner.*
2. No also means not any or none: *The teacher said that there would be **no** homework for the weekend.*

nobody ▼ • **nobodies**
Nobody means no person: ***Nobody** is allowed to take food into the school library. **No one** tries to bring it in because they are too scared of getting into trouble.*

nod • **nodded, nodding**
When you **nod**, you move your head up and down as a way of saying yes: *Beverly **nodded** her head when the teacher asked if she had finished her homework.*

All the chairs are set up, but **nobody** has arrived yet.

Sophie covers her ears so she cannot hear the loud **noise.**

noise ▸ • noises

A **noise** is a sound that is loud or bothers you: *There's so much **noise** from the traffic outside that I have to close my window when I go to bed.*

none

None means not one person or thing: *Cameron reached into the cookie jar for a cookie, but there were **none** left.*

nonsense

Something is **nonsense** if it is silly and does not make sense: *The teacher told Mark that he was talking **nonsense** when he told the class that he had built a time machine.*

noodle ◂ • noodles

A **noodle** is a kind of food that is a long, flat strip of pasta. Noodles are made of eggs, flour, and water. The strips are dried, then cooked in boiling water.

Mom will cook **noodles** for dinner tonight.

noon ▸

Noon is 12 o'clock in the day: *The lunch bell rings at **noon** each day.*

When it is **noon,** both hands on the clock point to twelve.

nor

Nor means and not. You can use the word "nor" together with the word "neither": *Neither my brother **nor** I like washing the dishes.*

normal

Something that is **normal** is usual or ordinary: *The **normal** temperature of a healthy person is 98.6 degrees. It's **normal** for the school bus to be a bit late on rainy mornings.*

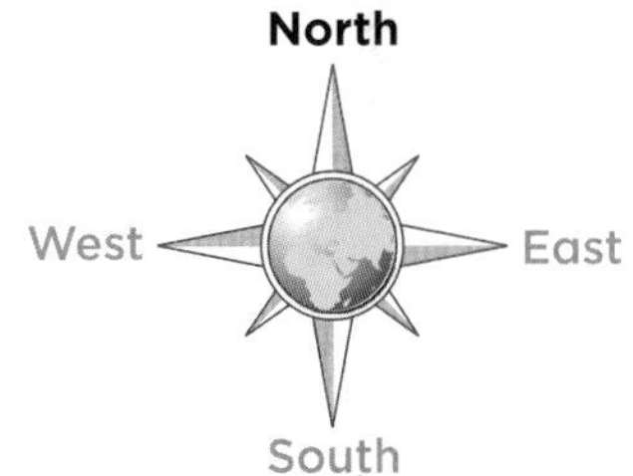

The compass shows the direction for **north.**

north ▸

North is a direction. If you look at the sun when it rises in the morning, north is on your left side. North, south, east, and west are the four main directions. The opposite of north is south: *We went to the Grand Canyon in Arizona, then we drove **north** to visit Salt Lake City. Salt Lake City is in the **northern** part of Utah.*

Charles puts his **nose** close to the flower to smell it.

nose ▲ • noses

Your **nose** is the part of your face that you use for smelling and breathing: *Michelle wiped her **nose** with a tissue.*

not

Not means no way or at no time: *I did **not** finish my homework last night, so I had to do it this morning.*

note ▼ • notes

A **note** is a short message or letter written on paper: *The teacher wrote a **note** for me to take home to my parents. The author had a **notebook** where he wrote down notes for stories he wanted to write.*

Mom left me a **note** to help me remember to clean my room.

nothing ▼

Nothing means not anything: *The dog ate all the food in its bowl until there was **nothing** left.*

There is **nothing** left to eat on the plate.

notice • notices, noticed, noticing

1. To **notice** means to see something or pay attention to it: *Kieryn was about to leave the house when she **noticed** that she had put on two different colored socks.*

2. A **notice** is a sign or message giving information about something: *There was a **notice** in the store window to say that the store was closed for the day.*

noun

A **noun** is a word that is the name of something. The words *popcorn, tree, teacher,* and *book* are all nouns. Sometimes you use a **pronoun**, such as *it, they, we, her,* and *him* instead of a noun. In the sentence *She took the chocolate and put it in her mouth,* "chocolate" and "mouth" are nouns, and "She," "it," and "her" are pronouns.

now

Now means at this moment: *If we don't leave **now**, we'll miss the bus.*

nowhere

Nowhere means not anywhere: *Frank looked all over the house, but his shoes were **nowhere** to be found.*

The **numbers** in the squares show the the order in which you have to hop.

number ▲ • numbers

1. A **number** tells you how many there are of people or things: *The **number** of children in our family is four.*
2. A **number** is also used to tell one thing different from another: *Each basketball player has his own **number** on the back of his shirt. I have the **numeral** "3" on my shirt.*

My grandmother is getting better because the **nurse** is looking after her.

nurse ▲ • nurses

A **nurse** is a person whose job it is to work to take care of sick people. Nurses often work with doctors: *In the hospital, the **nurse** showed the little girl how to put a bandage on her sore arm.*

nut ▼ • nuts

A **nut** is a dry seed or fruit that has a hard shell. Inside the hard shell is the part that you can eat.

There are many kinds of **nuts** that people eat.

Acorns are the nuts of an **oak.**

oak ▲ • **oaks**

An **oak** is a large tree that has fruits called acorns. The wood from oak trees is hard and is used to build furniture, boats, or houses.

obey • **obeyed, obeying**

To **obey** means to do what somebody tells you to do: *Connor **obeyed** the teacher and put all the books in a neat pile on the table.*

object ▶ • **objects**

An **object** is something that you can see or touch, but that is not alive: *Rosario's desk was covered with books, pens, pencils, erasers, and lots of other **objects**.*

I am taking these **objects** to the beach.

ocean ▼ • **oceans**

The **ocean** is the large area of salt water that covers most of Earth. Many different animals, such as fish and whales, live in the ocean.

oceans

There are five oceans around the world. Nearly three-quarters of Earth is covered by oceans. Plants can grow only where light from the Sun reaches them. Some animals are able to live in the deepest water, without any light from the Sun.

Fish, plants, and animals of many different sizes live in the ocean.

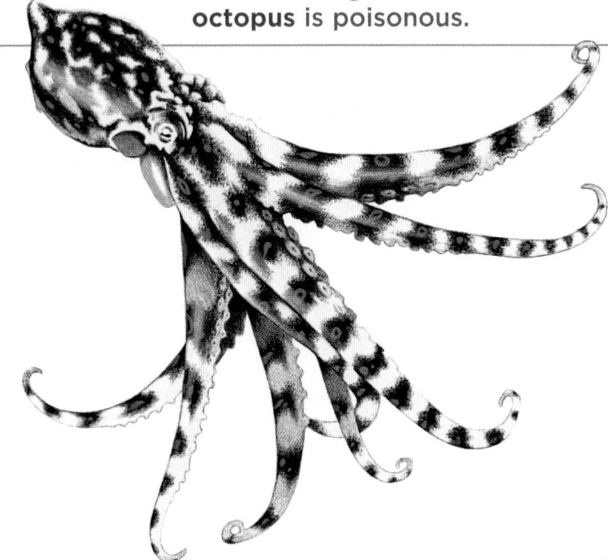

The blue-ringed **octopus** is poisonous.

o'clock

You use the word **o'clock** when you are talking about what time it says on a clock: *We finish school at 3* ***o'clock****.*

octopus ▲ • octopuses *or* octopi

An **octopus** is a sea animal with a soft body and eight long arms. The octopus uses special parts called suckers on its arms to help it move about and catch food.

The **octopus** gets its name from *octo*, the word for "eight" in the ancient Latin language. The octopus is known for having eight long arms.

odd • odder, oddest

1. **Odd** means unusual or strange: *It's* ***odd*** *that the school bus didn't come this morning—that's never happened before.*
2. Also, you say a number is **odd** if it cannot be divided by two. Numbers like one, three, five, seven, and nine are odd numbers, while two, four, six, and eight are even numbers.

of

1. You use **of** to tell what something is made from, or what it has in it: *I had a glass* ***of*** *orange juice and a bowl of cereal for breakfast this morning.*
2. You also use **of** to show what something belongs to or has to do with: *January is the first month* ***of*** *the year.*

off ▼

1. You use **off** when you mean away or down from something: *The plate fell* ***off*** *the kitchen table and broke into pieces on the floor.*
2. **Off** also means not on: *I took* ***off*** *my shoes and socks so I could put my bare feet in the water.*

office • offices

An **office** is a place where people work or do business: *Mom and I went to Dad's* ***office*** *to pick him up after work.*

The penguin dives **off** the ice.

Jeff makes the **OK** sign with his fingers.

A B C D E F G H I J K L M N

P Q R S T U V W X Y Z

officer • officers

1. An **officer** is a person who is in charge of others in the army, navy, or air force.
2. An **officer** is also someone who works for the police department: *The police **officer** chased the robber down the street.*

often

Often means many times: *We **often** go to the beach during the summer.*

oil ▼ • oils

1. Oil is a liquid that comes from vegetables, plants, and animals. You can use oil in cooking: *Dad poured some **oil** into the pan to cook some eggs for breakfast.*
2. A different kind of **oil** comes from under the ground. This oil is thick and black and is used for gasoline to make cars run. It is also used for heating and making machines run properly: *The car mechanic put some **oil** in the car engine.*

Workers drill for **oil** in the ground under the ocean.

OK ◀

OK means that something is all right: *Carla asked if she could use my pencil, and I said, "**OK**, you can." I hurt my knee but I think it will be **OK** by tomorrow.* This word is sometimes spelled **okay**.

People use **OK** often, but no one knows for sure how this word came into the English language. One idea is that it is short for "Oll Korrect," another way to spell "All Correct."

The stone bridge over the river is **old**, but it is still strong.

old ▲ • older, oldest

1. You are **old** if you have lived for a long time: *My grandma is very **old** and has white hair.*
2. Things that have been used a lot and are not new are also called **old**: *I threw my **old** sneakers out because they had holes in them.*
3. You also use the word **old** when you talk about the age of someone or something: *My little brother Jack is three years **old**.*

The police officer rides **on** a horse.

on

1. **On** means above something and touching it: *Rosie put her hat **on** her head.*
2. **On** also means the time when something happens: *Our next soccer game is **on** Saturday. She was born **on** March 8, 1997.*
3. **On** can also mean covering something: *Jane put some socks **on** her feet to keep them warm.*
4. **On** can also mean to be in use: *Susan put the radio **on** while she was washing the dishes.*

once

1. **Once** means one time and no more: *Our mail is delivered to our house **once** a day.*
2. **Once** also means as soon as: ***Once** the movie starts, everyone will have to stop talking.*

one • ones

1. **One** is the first and smallest number. The number one is written "1."
2. You say **one** when you are talking about a single person or thing: *I take **one** apple to school each day to have after my sandwich.*

onion • onions

An **onion** is a small, round vegetable with white, brown, or purple skin. Onions grow underground and have a strong smell and sharp taste: *Mom cut up the **onion** to put in the vegetable soup.*

Onions have a strong flavor.

The dancer stands on **only** one hand.

only

Only means just one: *Hawaii is the **only** U.S. state that is a group of islands. We scored **only** one run, but it was enough to win the game 1–0.*

open • opened, opening

1. **Open** means not shut or closed. If something is open, you can go through it: *The door was **open** and the dog ran out into the yard. Then it went into the street through an **opening** in the fence.*
2. To **open** something means to cause it to be no longer closed: *Please **open** that window, so that the fresh air can come in.*
3. To **open** also means to start or begin: *The new adventure movie **opened** in town last week. There were lots of people at the **opening**.*

The book lies **open** on the table.

opossum ▶ • opossums

An **opossum** is a small American animal that lives in trees and has gray fur and a long tail. Female opossums carry their babies in a pocket on their stomach: *Most **opossums** sleep during the day and feed at night on small animals, insects, and fruits.*

The players are at **opposite** ends of the table.

opposite ▲ • opposites

1. If someone is **opposite** you, they are on the other side of something and facing toward you: *Marion sat **opposite** me at the dinner table.*
2. If two things are the **opposite** of each other, they are as different as they can be: *Hot is the **opposite** of cold.*

The musicians in the **orchestra** sit in the front of the theater.

The shy **opossum** looks out from behind the leaves.

or

1. We use the word **or** when we want to show a choice between different things: *Would you like an apple **or** an orange with your lunch?*
2. We also use **or** to mean if not: *You had better leave now, **or** you will be late for the movies.*

orange ▶ • oranges

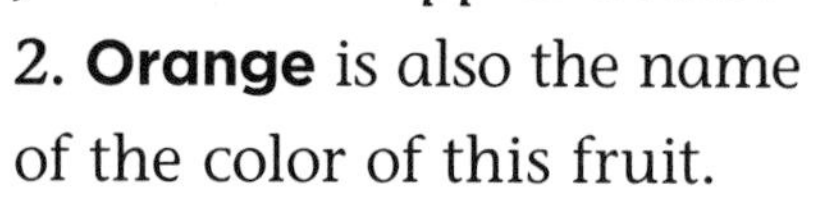

Oranges grow on trees.

1. An **orange** is a small, round fruit with a thick skin. Oranges have sweet juice: ***Oranges** are my favorite fruits, but my friend Jacinta likes apples better.*
2. **Orange** is also the name of the color of this fruit. You can make this color by mixing yellow and red together.

orchestra ◀ • orchestras

An **orchestra** is a group of musicians who play together on different kinds of instruments. There are usually more players in an orchestra than in a band: *Marcel is learning the violin because he wants to play in the school **orchestra**.*

order • orders

1. An **order** is an instruction to do something: *He obeyed the police officer's **order** to pull his car over to the side of the road.*
2. When things are in **order**, they are where they should be, or in the correct place: *Dylan's mom said that he had to put his room in **order** before he could go out and play.*

organization • organizations

An **organization** is a group of people who work together to get things done: *Tom's dad works for an **organization** called the Red Cross that helps people all around the world.*

ostrich ▶ • ostriches

An **ostrich** is a large bird from Africa that cannot fly, but can run very fast on its long legs. The ostrich is the largest of all the world's birds.

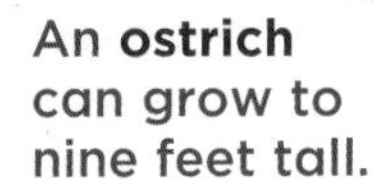

An **ostrich** can grow to nine feet tall.

other

1. When we use **other**, we mean different from, or separate from, something we have talked about: *Leonie was walking toward the gate, but then she turned around and walked the **other** way.*
2. **Other** also means extra or more: *There was one car on the street in front of the house, and two **other** cars in the garage.*

The killer whale leaps **out** of the water to hit the ball.

our

We use **our** when we mean something that belongs to us: *These are **our** toys. They are **ours** because we bought them **ourselves** from the store.*

out ▲

1. **Out** means away from the inside or center of something: *Edward carried the garbage **out** of the house and threw it away.*
2. **Out** also means outside or away from where you are or you were: *Nancy just went **out**, but she will be back soon.*
3. We can also use **out** to mean through, from inside to outside: *When she left the house, Alexandra went **out** the front door.*

We went to an **outdoor** restaurant for breakfast.

outdoor

If something is **outdoor**, it is in the open air and not inside a building: *We sat at an **outdoor** table to have our lunch. We like eating **outdoors** when the weather is good.*

outside • outsides

1. The **outside** of something is the part of it that is out, or not inside: *There's a black mark on the **outside** of this apple.*
2. Outside means out of a building, or not in a place: *When Oliver came in from the garden, he left his muddy shoes **outside** on the steps.*

oven • ovens

An **oven** is a part of a stove with a door that you can open and close. You put food in an oven to cook it or heat it up: *Mom baked a cake in the **oven**.*

over

1. Over means above or on top of: *When it started to rain, Gerry held an umbrella **over** his head.*
2. Over also means above and from one side to the other: *Helena jumped **over** the fence.*
3. When something is finished, we can say it is **over**: *The tennis game was **over** in less than half an hour.*
4. You can also say **over** to mean once more or a few times more: *Harry's paper had a lot of mistakes, so the teacher asked him to do it **over**.*
5. Another meaning of **over** is down or on to one side: *Our cat jumped on the table and knocked **over** a bowl of soup.*

Jody's horse jumps **over** the bar.

owls

Most owls hunt at night. That is when the animals they eat come out. Owls can see and hear well in the dark. They have special wing feathers that help them fly quietly to sneak up and catch animals.

A great horned owl feeds its chicks.

Little owl

Snowy owl

Barred owl chicks

Barn owl

Spotted owl

owe • **owed, owing**

If you **owe** something to someone, you have to give it to them: *Sharon* ***owes*** *Stephen a dollar for the cookies he bought for her.*

owl ▲ • **owls**

An **owl** is a bird with very big eyes and a curved beak. Owls hunt for mice, frogs, snakes, and insects: *You don't see* ***owls*** *very often because they usually fly around at night.*

own ▼ • **owned, owning**

1. If something belongs to you, you **own** it: *Kenny* ***owns*** *a skateboard, and his sister Monica owns two pairs of roller skates.*

2. You use **own** to describe something that belongs to you: *Karen rides her* ***own*** *bike to school every day. Her father is the* ***owner*** *of a big red car.*

Our dog has its **own** house to sleep in.

A
B
C
D
E
F
G
H
I
J
K
L
M
N
O
P
Q
R
S
T
U
V
W
X
Y
Z

Pp

Nathan **packs** his books into his backpack.

pack ▲ • packed, packing

1. When you **pack** things, you put them into a container, or you wrap them together so that you can carry them or put them away: *When she was moving to a new house, Norma **packed** all her toys into a big box.*

2. You also **pack** something when you put things in it or fill it up: *Mom and Dad **packed** our suitcases before we left for our vacation.*

package ▼ • packages

You make a **package** when you put some things into a container, or wrap them together to take or send somewhere: *Our school library got a big **package** of new books this morning.*

Maya wrapped the **package** and tied string around it.

pad • pads

A **pad** contains a number of pieces of paper that are held together along one edge: *José wrote down the answers to the questions on a page of his note **pad**.*

page • pages

A **page** is one side of a piece of paper in a book, magazine, newspaper, pad, or letter: *The teacher asked the pupils to turn to the next **page** of their books and look at the picture there.*

pail ▼ • pails

A **pail** is a round container with a flat bottom that is open at the top and has a handle: *Tania took the **pail** to the faucet and filled it with water.*

The shells fall out of the **pail**.

pain • pains

A **pain** is the feeling you have when something is hurting you or when a part of your body feels sore: *Joel's grandmother sometimes has a bad **pain** in her back.*

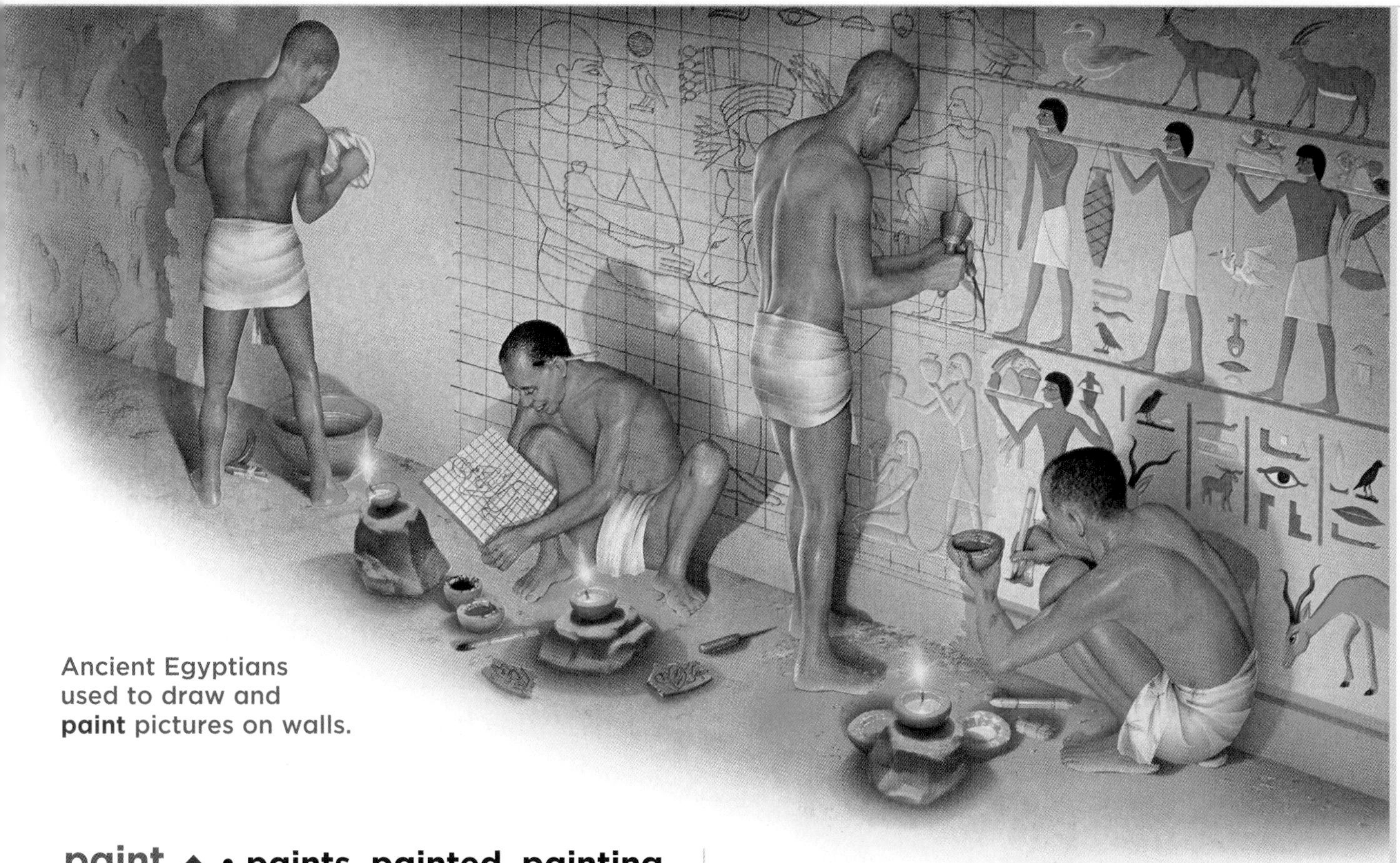

Ancient Egyptians used to draw and **paint** pictures on walls.

paint ▲ • paints, painted, painting

1. **Paint** is a liquid that you put on something to add color to it or to change its color: *Dad said he would use red **paint** for the door and white paint for the walls of my room.*

2. When you put this kind of liquid on something, you **paint** it: *Steve helped his dad **paint** the back fence.*

3. You also **paint** something when you use this liquid to make a picture of it: *Glenda used green and brown colors to **paint** a picture of a tree. She is a very good **painter**.*

painting • paintings

A **painting** is a picture that someone makes by using paints: *My big sister Shirley made a beautiful **painting** of our garden.*

pair ▼ • pairs *or* pair

1. A **pair** means two things of the same kind that belong together: *Rhonda is wearing a red **pair** of sneakers today.*

2. A **pair** is also something with two parts that are joined together: *Tim's father bought him a new **pair** of pants.*

I hung a **pair** of striped socks on the line.

pajamas

Pajamas are clothes that you wear when you go to bed. Pajamas are usually loose and comfortable and are in two parts: *My favorite **pajamas** have red pants and a blue top.*

palace ▸ • palaces

A **palace** is a very large, grand building. A palace is the home of a king, queen, prince, princess, or other such person: *Queen Elizabeth of Great Britain lives in a famous old building in London called Buckingham **Palace**.*

This **palace** was built in Guatemala for the president of that country.

pan ▾ • pans

A **pan** is a container that is used for cooking or baking. Most pans are made of metal and have a handle but no cover: *We often cook hamburgers in a wide, flat **pan**.*

Mom used a **pan** to cook an egg.

panda ▸ • pandas

A **panda** is a large kind of animal with black and white fur that lives in western China and eats plants. It is also called a giant panda: *I have seen a **panda** on TV, but pandas do not live in America except in zoos.*

panther • panthers

A **panther** is a large animal of the cat family that lives in Africa and Asia. It is a kind of leopard, but it has fur that is almost black in color instead of spots: *Most **panthers** hunt at night for their food.*

pants

Pants are clothes that you wear around your waist and over all or part of your legs. Pants have a separate part for each of your legs: *I wear short **pants** when I play sports, and long pants when I go to school.*

pandas

Pandas live in forests in China where a kind of plant called bamboo grows. A mother panda takes care of the cubs. Pandas live alone most of the time. There are only about 1,600 pandas still living in the wild. About 200 pandas live in zoos around the world.

Pandas eat bamboo.

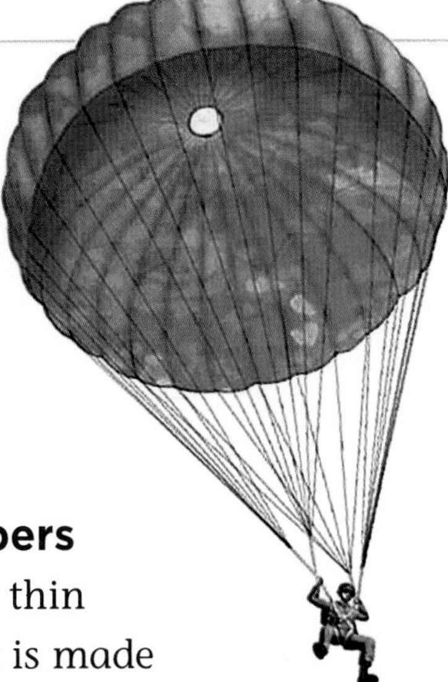

A **parachute** falls slowly to the ground.

paper • papers

1. Paper is a thin material that is made from wood, straw, rags, or other things. People use paper to write or print on, to wrap things in, and for many other purposes: *The pages of this dictionary are made of white **paper**. We used green, blue, and red **paper** to wrap the birthday presents.*

2. Paper is also a short word for NEWSPAPER: *I read all about last night's baseball game in the **paper** this morning.*

The word **paper** comes from *papyrus*. Papyrus is a tall plant that grows in the Nile River area of Egypt. In ancient times paper was made from this plant.

parachute ▲ • parachutes

A **parachute** is a wide, round piece of cloth with ropes attached to it that opens out like a large umbrella. If a person is held up by a parachute, they can fall slowly from high in the air without hitting the ground very hard: *Some people jump out of airplanes with **parachutes** just for fun.*

parade ▼ • parades

A **parade** happens when many people, vehicles, or animals move together in a line along a street or some other public place: *Every year at Halloween there is a big **parade** of people through the main street of our town.*

Men playing instruments called bagpipes march in the St. Patrick's Day **parade**.

paragraph • paragraphs

A **paragraph** is part of a story or something else that you write. A paragraph has a group of sentences about the same subject or idea: *In the first **paragraph** of my story about our vacation, I told how we traveled to Florida; in the second paragraph I said what we did there; and in the last paragraph, I told about our trip back to Boston.*

parakeet • parakeets

A **parakeet** is a small bird that lives in warm countries. Parakeets have a long tail, and many kinds of parakeets have feathers with bright colors: ***Parakeets** usually travel together in large groups.*

parrots

Most parrots live in the southern half of the world. They are found in forests, on grassy plains, and in deserts. Many parrots, such as rosellas, eat the seeds of grasses and other plants. Some, such as Pesquet's parrots, eat fruits and parts of flowers.

Black-capped lory

Red-fan parrot

Eastern rosella

Pesquet's parrot

Scarlet macaw

Night parrot

Gray parrot

Ground parrot

parent • parents

A **parent** is a mother or a father: *My **parents** never leave me alone at home when they go out.*

park ▼ • parks, parked, parking

1. A **park** is an area of land that usually has no large buildings and that has grass, trees, and other plants. Many parks have playgrounds in them: *Ducks swim in the big pond in the **park** near our house.*

2. When you leave a car, bike, or other vehicle somewhere for some time, you **park** it: *When Mom takes us to visit our aunt and uncle, she **parks** the car in the street outside their house.*

There is a large **park** named Central Park in New York City.

parrot ▲ • parrots

A **parrot** is a type of bird. Parrots have a curved beak and long tail, and can hold food in their claws. Some parrots have feathers of different colors: *Francesca has taught her pet **parrot**, Polly, to say, "Polly is pretty."*

part • parts

A **part** is a bit or a section of something, but not all of it: *A branch is one **part** of a tree. I am almost finished with the book, but I still have to read the last **part**.*

The time when people used telephones like this one is long **past.**

party • parties

A **party** happens when a lot of people get together to celebrate something, or to eat and drink and have fun together. People often play games at parties: *I am going to Gina's birthday* ***party*** *tomorrow.*

pass ▼ • passed, passing

1. To **pass** means to move in front of or behind something and then go farther on: *The bus to school* ***passes*** *my grandmother's house.*
2. **Pass** also means to hand or give something to someone: *Dad asked me to* ***pass*** *him the ketchup.*
3. **Pass** also means to do well enough on a test: *I* ***passed*** *the math test because I got most of the answers right.*

Michelle **passes** a note to Roger during class.

Passover

Passover is a Jewish holiday that celebrates the time, many years ago, when the Jews came out of the country called Egypt: *Every year in spring, Benjamin's family has a special meal to celebrate* ***Passover.***

past ◀

1. If something is **past**, it has already happened, or it is finished: *When Christmas Day comes, both Halloween and Thanksgiving are already* ***past****, because they are earlier in the year.*
2. You go **past** something when you pass it or go by it: *We walk* ***past*** *the baseball field on our way to school.*

Vivian likes to eat **pasta** with butter.

pasta ▲

Pasta is a type of food that is made from a special kind of wheat. You boil pasta in water before you eat it, and it is usually mixed with other kinds of food to give it flavor. Spaghetti is one kind of pasta.

paste • pastes, pasted, pasting

1. **Paste** is a mixture of flour and water that people use to glue things together, especially paper: *I used* ***paste*** *to stick pictures of animals in my book.*
2. To **paste** something means to use this mixture to glue things together: *The teacher told us to* ***paste*** *our drawings on to large cards and hang them on the wall.*

Peaches grow on trees.

pat • patted, patting

Pat means to tap something or someone softly with the hand: *Eugene **patted** the tiny puppy on the head.*

path • paths

A **path** is a narrow kind of road that you walk along. You can ride a bike or a horse along some paths: *If you follow this **path** through the woods, you will come to a big lake.*

pattern • patterns

A **pattern** is the way that shapes, colors, lines, or pictures are placed on something to create its appearance: *A leopard's fur has a **pattern** of spots on it.*

paw ▶ • paws

A **paw** is an animal's foot that has nails or claws. Dogs, cats, bears, and raccoons have paws: *Our kitten has soft **paws**, but they have very sharp claws in them.*

pay • paid, paying

When you **pay**, you give someone money for something that you get from them, or something they do for you: *Mr. Burke **pays** Justin five dollars each Saturday for helping him in the garden.*

pea • peas

A **pea** is a small, round, green vegetable that grows in a long, narrow shell called a pod: *For dinner we often have **peas** with meat and other vegetables.*

peace

There is **peace** when people or countries are not fighting each other. Peace is the opposite of war: *For many years the two countries were at war, but now there is **peace** between them.*

peach ▲ • peaches

A **peach** is a round, soft fruit with sweet juice, yellow and pink skin, and a large, hard seed in the middle: *When we have fruit salad, we put **peaches**, apples, pears, and oranges in it.*

The sea otter holds a sea urchin with its **paws**.

These mountain **peaks** have snow on them, and there are no plants growing there.

peak ▶ • **peaks**

A **peak** is the narrow, sharp top of a mountain or a hill: *Charlotte could not see the mountain **peak** because it was covered by clouds.*

peanut • **peanuts**

A **peanut** is a small, round, light brown nut that grows under the ground in a soft shell: *Jason sometimes eats **peanuts** while he watches TV. His sister Genevieve likes to have **peanut butter** on toast for breakfast.*

pear ▼ • **pears**

A **pear** is a fruit with a sweet taste. It has a shape like a bell and a thin, light green or brown skin: *Apples are my favorite fruits, but I like **pears** almost as much.*

Pears have small seeds in the middle of them.

pebble • **pebbles**

A **pebble** is a small, smooth stone that is usually almost round in shape: *Lots of beaches are covered with sand, but some beaches have **pebbles** instead.*

peek ▼ • **peeked, peeking**

Peek means to take a quick look at something without being seen: *Josie **peeked** in the teacher's book to see what mark she got on the test.*

Chris **peeks** out of the play house.

peel • **peeled, peeling**

Peel means to take the skin off a fruit or a vegetable: *I helped Mom **peel** the potatoes for dinner.*

pen • **pens**

A **pen** is a long, thin tool that you write with. A pen has ink in it: *Write your name on the first line with this blue **pen**.*

pencil • **pencils**

A **pencil** is a tool that you write or color with. A pencil is a stick of wood with lead in it: *James colored the picture of the boat with his **pencils**.*

penguins

Penguins are found only in the southern half of the world. They eat fish and other sea animals. The largest penguin is the emperor penguin.

King penguin

Chinstrap penguin

Yellow-eyed penguin

Emperor penguin

Fjordland penguin

Rockhopper penguin

Magellanic penguin

Fairy penguin

Penguins are very good swimmers.

penguin ▲ • penguins

A **penguin** is a black and white sea bird that lives in southern ocean areas. Penguins cannot fly, but they can use their wings to swim: *Many **penguins** live in very cold places.*

people ▼ • people

People means men, women, and children: *There are five **people** living in our house—my mom and dad, my two sisters, and me.*

There are many **people** on the bus.

pepper • peppers

1. You use **pepper** to make food taste spicy. Pepper is the dried berry of a tree. **2.** A **pepper** is also a red, green, or yellow vegetable: *Dad chopped the red **pepper** for the salad.*

perfect

If something is **perfect**, it means nothing is wrong with it: *If you get all twenty questions right on a test, you get a **perfect** score of 100. The teacher said my coloring of the picture was **perfect**—none of it was outside the lines.*

Rex is Tracy's only **pet**.

perhaps

Perhaps means maybe: *I'm not sure where my notebook is—**perhaps** I left it at school.*

period • periods

1. A **period** is a dot (.) that is used at the end of a sentence: *Most sentences end with a **period** just like this one does.*
2. A **period** also means a length of time: *Because of his broken leg, Ken could not play sports for a **period** of six months.*

permit • permits, permitted, permitting

1. **Permit** means to let someone do something: *My parents **permit** me to go the mall with my friends.*
2. A **permit** is a special piece of paper that shows you are allowed to do something: *My dad has a **permit** that lets him park his car in the city.*

person • persons

A **person** is a man, woman, or child: *The **person** in charge of a library is called a librarian.*

pet ◀ • pets

A **pet** is an animal that you keep in your home and take care of: *Angela has four **pets**—a dog, a cat, and two fish.*

pharmacy • pharmacies

A **pharmacy** is a store where you buy drugs that are used as medicines: *Maria went to the **pharmacy** to buy some pills for her headache.* A pharmacy is sometimes called a **drugstore**.

phone • phones, phoned, phoning

1. A **phone** is a short word for TELEPHONE: *I picked up the **phone** and called Grandma.*
2. If you **phone** someone, you use a telephone to call them: *Every year I **phone** my friend in Chicago to wish her "happy birthday."*

photo ▶ • photos

A **photo** is a picture taken with a camera: *Matt showed us **photos** of his trip to New York City.* Photo is a short word for **photograph**.

My parents have a **photo** of me when I was a baby.

Photograph comes from two words meaning "light" and "writing." The idea is that a photograph takes a picture with light and then "writes" it on film.

piano • pianos

A **piano** is an instrument that you can play music on. You press the black and white keys on a piano to make the music: *My brother plays the **piano** and I play the drums.*

pick • picked, picking

Pick means to choose something: *The teacher let me **pick** a story to read to the class.*

picnic • picnics

When you go on a **picnic**, you take food to eat outdoors: *We took bread and cheese and fruits for a **picnic** in the park.*

picture • pictures

A **picture** is a drawing or painting. You can also take a picture with a camera: *She painted a **picture** of her dad for his birthday.*

pie • pies

A **pie** is something that you eat. Pies can be filled with meat, fruits, or other things: *My favorite dessert is apple **pie** with ice cream. Francis ate a meat **pie** for lunch today.*

The family has a **picnic** in the country.

Rebecca makes a picture with **pieces** of colored glass.

piece • pieces

1. A **piece** is one part of a whole thing: *Emma cut a **piece** of the chocolate cake for her brother and another piece for herself.*
2. A **piece** also means one bit of a group of many things: *Finn thought he had lost a **piece** of the puzzle, but he found it under the couch.*

pig • pigs

A **pig** is an animal with a round body, short legs, and a small, curled tail. People often use the meat of a pig for food. This can be called pork or ham.

The **pig** digs to find food.

pile • piles, piled, piling

1. A **pile** is a lot of things on top of each other: *My sister left a **pile** of dirty clothes on the floor.*
2. When you put things on top of each other, you **pile** them: *Richard's school books are **piled** on his desk.*

pill • pills

A **pill** is a small, hard kind of medicine. You take a pill when you are sick: *When Marcia had the flu, she took a **pill** and went to bed to rest.*

pillow • pillows

A **pillow** is a cloth bag filled with feathers or a soft material: *He put his head on the **pillow** and went to sleep.*

A B C D E F G H I J K L M N O P Q R S T U V W X Y Z

pilot • pilots

A **pilot** is someone who flies an aircraft or spacecraft: *The **pilot** landed the plane safely in the heavy rain.*

pin • pins, pinned, pinning

1. A **pin** is a short, thin piece of metal with a point at one end. Pins hold or join things together: *Samantha used a **pin** to keep the flower on her hat.*
2. When you use a pin to join things together, you **pin** them: *Mom **pinned** the two small pieces of material to make one large one.*

pine • pines

A **pine** is a tree with cones and leaves that look like needles. The needles stay on the tree all year: *My bed is made of wood from a **pine**.*

pink • pinker, pinkest

Pink is a light red color. You can make pink if you mix red and white.

pipe • pipes

A **pipe** is a long tube that liquid or gas can go through. Water comes to your home through a pipe: *The **pipe** broke and water went all over the kitchen.*

pirate ▼ • pirates

A **pirate** is a person who robs ships at sea: *In the story, the **pirates** jumped onto the other ship to steal all their gold.*

pitch • pitched, pitching

Pitch means to toss or throw something: *Josh **pitched** the ball across the field.* A **pitcher** is a baseball player who throws the ball to another player who tries to hit it with a bat.

pizza • pizzas

Pizza is a type of pie made from a kind of bread. It is usually flat and round with tomato and cheese on top. Some pizzas also have things like meat and vegetables on top.

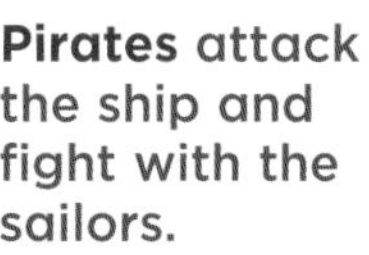

Pirates attack the ship and fight with the sailors.

Mecca is a holy **place** for Muslims.

place • places

1. Place means where something is: *This looks like a good **place** to plant the tree. We found a **place** to park the car right near the store.* **2. Place** also means someone's home: *Would you like to come to our **place** for lunch tomorrow?* **3. Place** can also mean a seat or space for someone: *Will you save me a **place** in the line?*

plaid • plaids

A **plaid** is a pattern with lines of different colors that cross over each other. This pattern is often used in cloth: *Mom has a green and red **plaid** skirt.*

plain • plainer, plainest

Plain means easy to understand, see, or hear: *Joe's foot was bleeding, so it was **plain** to see where the glass had cut it. Mom made it **plain** that it was time for us to leave.*

plan • plans, planned, planning

1. If you **plan** something, you work out how to do it before you do it: *They **planned** a surprise party for Tom.* 2. A **plan** is the way you work out doing something before you do it: *Dad's **plan** was to have dinner first and then go to the game.*

plane • planes

Plane is a short word for AIRPLANE: *We flew in a **plane** from New York to Chicago to see my uncle.*

planet • planets

A **planet** moves around a star. The planet that we live on is Earth. It moves around the Sun: *The eight **planets** that travel around the Sun are Mercury, Venus, Earth, Mars, Jupiter, Saturn, Uranus, and Neptune.*

plant • plants, planted, planting

1. A **plant** is something that grows in the ground. Trees, grass, and flowers are plants: *Our garden is full of **plants**.* 2. When you put a plant in the ground to grow, you **plant** it: *Carly **planted** daisies in her back garden.*

Many kinds of **plants** grow in different habitats.

planets

The four closest planets to the Sun, Mercury, Venus, Earth, and Mars, are made of rock. The next two planets, Jupiter and Saturn, are mostly gas. The two planets farthest from the Sun, Uranus and Neptune, are mostly ice.

The plates and cups we take on picnics are made of **plastic.**

plastic ▲ • plastics

Plastic is a material that is used to make things. Plastic is pushed into a shape when it is soft, then it becomes hard: *This soda bottle is made of **plastic**.*

plate • plates

A **plate** is a dish: *Please put your **plate** in the sink after dinner.*

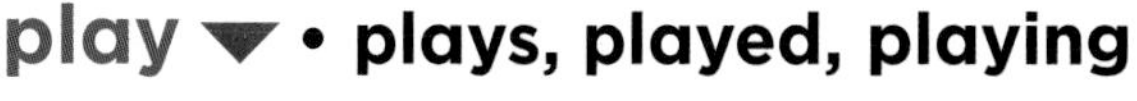

play ▼ • plays, played, playing

1. When you **play**, you do something for fun: *The children **played** in the park after school.*
2. You **play** a sport or game if you take part in it: *Jeremy **plays** soccer every winter. He is the team's best **player**.*
3. **Play** also means to use an instrument to make music: *Gerard **plays** the piano and Andrew plays the guitar. Andrew is a better guitar **player** than Gerard.*
4. To **play** also means to act in a show: *Julian **played** the part of an old man in the school play.*
5. A **play** is a story that you act out: *The **play** was about a girl and three bears.*

Three of the musicians in the band **play** the drums.

playground ▸ • playgrounds

A **playground** is a place outside where you go to play: *We went to the **playground** to play on the slides and swings.*

please

Please is a word you use to ask for something in a nice way: ***Please** pass me the cookies.*

plenty ▾

Plenty means lots of something: *There are **plenty** of fish in that lake.*

plural • plurals

Plural means more than one. You use the plural when you want to talk about more than one person or thing. The plural of the word "dog" is "dogs." The plural of the word "man" is "men."

There are lots of things to climb on at the **playground**.

plus • pluses

You use **plus** when you add one number to another number: *Three **plus** two is five.* Sometimes we use a **plus sign** (**+**) instead: *3 **+** 2 is 5.*

pocket ▸ • pockets

A **pocket** is like a small bag that holds things. Your clothes often have pockets in them: *Max found a dollar in his shirt **pocket**.*

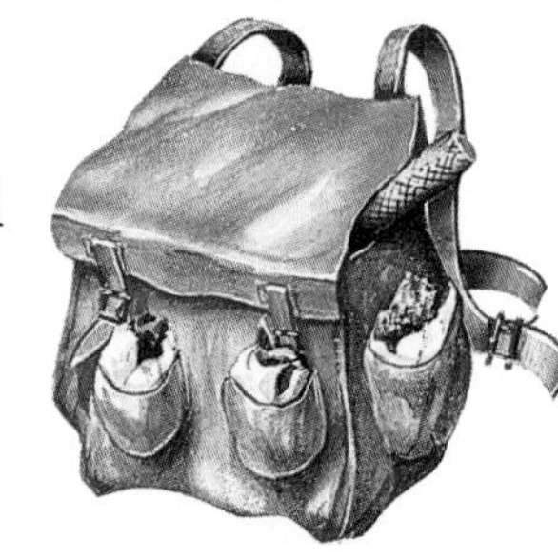

The bag has **pockets** to put small things in.

The boat has **plenty** of men to row it.

polar bears

Polar bears are the largest kind of bear. They live mostly on floating ice. Their white fur makes it hard to see them against snow and ice. They have thick fur on the bottom of their paws to protect them from cold.

A polar bear mother looks after her cubs for about three years.

poem • poems

A **poem** is a kind of writing. Poems sometimes have short lines and words that rhyme. Another word for a poem or a group of poems is **poetry**. A person who writes poetry is a **poet**.

point ▼ • points, pointed, pointing

1. A **point** is the sharp end of something. Pens, pencils, and needles have points: *Robin used the **point** of the needle to make a hole in the cloth.*

2. When you **point**, you use your finger or another thing to show where something is: *Trudy **pointed** the way to town. The coach **pointed** to me to show it was my turn to bat.*

A marlin's nose has a long **point** to attack the fish it eats.

poison ▶ • poisons, poisoned, poisoning

1. **Poison** is something that hurts or kills things: *Some spiders use **poison** to catch insects to eat. Some plants can be **poisonous**, too.*

This frog has skin that is **poisonous** to touch.

2. When you **poison** something, you use poison to kill it: *Dad **poisoned** the weeds in the garden.*

polar bear ▲

A **polar bear** is a big, white animal that lives near the North Pole. Polar bears have thick fur to keep them warm. They have sharp claws and are very good swimmers. Polar bears eat fish and seals.

The **police** protect the people in our town.

pole • poles

A **pole** is a long piece of wood or other material: *My uncle has the American flag on a **pole** in front of his house.*

police ▲

The **police** are a group of people who work for the government to protect us and keep us safe. Police make sure everyone obeys the laws: *The **police** ran after the bank robbers and stopped them before they could get away.*

polite • politer, politest

If you are **polite**, you have good manners. You act in a nice way and you are careful about other people's feelings: *It is **polite** to say "thank you" and "please."*

politics

Politics means the things that have to do with controlling or managing a country, state, or city. The people who decide how to manage the country are called **politicians**. The President, Senators, and Governors are all politicians.

pollution ▼ • pollutions

Pollution means that something dirty is in the ground, water, or air: ***Pollution** from the factory got into the river and killed the fish. The factory got into trouble for **polluting** the river.*

Pollution in the air comes from power stations, factories, and vehicles.

We have a **pond** with a fountain in our garden.

pond ▲ • **ponds**

A **pond** is a small area of water with land around it: *Evette and her dad built a **pond** in the garden for her pet fish.*

We saw a **pony** at the state fair.

pony ▶ • **ponies**

A **pony** is a small horse: *The children had a riding lesson on **ponies**.*

pool ▼ • **pools**

A **pool** is a small area of water usually for swimming in. Some pools are built outdoors, and some are built indoors: *Jason dived into the swimming **pool** to get ready for the race.*

Kimberly swims in the **pool** at the hotel.

poor • **poorer, poorest**

1. If you are **poor**, you do not have much money or many things: *The **poor** man did not have enough money to buy his children new shoes.*

2. Also, something that is not as good as it could be is **poor**: *He did not study for the test at all and got a **poor** mark of four questions right out of ten.*

I like to eat **popcorn** while watching TV.

pop • **popped, popping**

To **pop** means to make a short, loud, breaking sound: *Leo's bag of candies **popped** when it broke, and they spilled everywhere.*

popcorn ▲

Popcorn is a snack made by heating the seeds of corn until they pop open: *Lily made some **popcorn** in a pan and put butter on it.*

popular

If something is **popular**, a lot of people know about it and like it: *Monica is very **popular** in our school because she is so friendly and kind.*

A **porcupine** raises the spines on its back when it is scared.

porcupine ▲ • porcupines

A **porcupine** is a wild animal that is covered with long, sharp, pointed parts called spines: *We watched the **porcupine** climb into the tree and chew some bark.*

Porcupine comes from an old word meaning "a pig." People used to think a porcupine looked like a pig, although it has long, sharp spines on its body.

position • positions

1. Your **position** is the place where you are: *When we played hide-and-seek, I could see Eric searching for me from my **position** under the bed. In baseball, the **position** Dwayne plays is catcher.*
2. Your **position** is also the way you are standing, sitting, or lying: *Elise could not get into a comfortable **position** on the hard wooden bench.*

possible

When something is **possible**, it could happen or could be done: *It is **possible** to throw a baseball ninety miles per hour, but not possible to throw a baseball nine hundred miles per hour. I can't find my sunglasses anywhere—it's **possible** I lost them at the beach.*

post office

A **post office** is a place where you buy stamps and mail letters or packages: *Billy and Mom went to the **post office** to mail a birthday card to Grandpa.*

pot ▼ • pots

A **pot** is a container that is round and deep. Pots are used to store things, for cooking, or to grow plants in: *Mom cooked soup in a big **pot** on the stove. Julian planted some flowers in a clay **pot**.*

The men make **pots** and then paint pictures on them.

potato ▶ • potatoes

A **potato** is a vegetable. You eat the round, white root part of the plant, not the leaves: *We had **potatoes** with our fried chicken for dinner.*

The **potatoes** are washed and ready to cook.

powder • powders

Powder is something made of lots of tiny, dry pieces: *Ted put the laundry **powder** into the washing machine with the clothes, then he turned it on to wash them.*

pound[1] • pounds

A **pound** is a measurement that tells you how much something weighs: *My baby sister weighed seven **pounds** when she was born. Mike bought a **pound** of beef to put into the stew for dinner.*

These wind machines make **power** that people can use.

pound[2] ▼ • pounded, pounding

To **pound** is to hit something hard again and again: *Anthea stood outside and **pounded** on the door until someone came to answer it.*

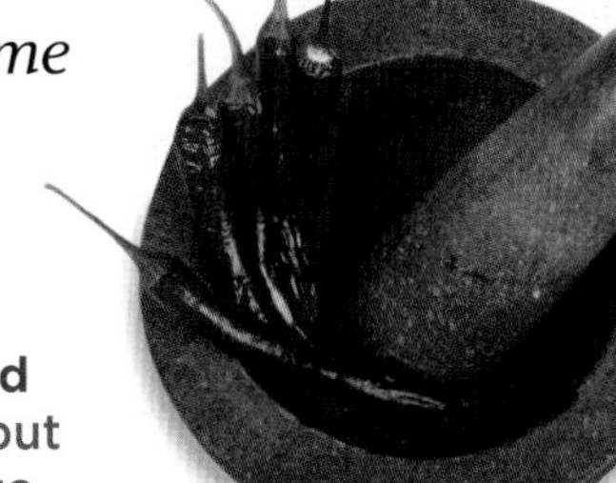

You can **pound** peppers and put them in food to make it taste hot.

power ▲ • powers

To have **power** means to be able to do something or make something happen: *The engines of a jet plane have to use a lot of **power** to get the plane off the ground. In the story, the magic bird had the **power** to let the boy make three wishes that would come true.*

pour ▶ • poured, pouring

1. To **pour** means to make something that is liquid go from one thing into another: *Gary **poured** me a glass of apple juice from the bottle.*

2. Also, when water flows or falls quickly, it is said to **pour**: *During the big storm, the rain was **pouring** down.*

Roberto **pours** water into the bucket.

practice • practices, practiced, practicing

1. When you **practice** something, you do it over and over to get better at it: *Ken* ***practiced*** *singing the song until he knew all the words.*

2. A **practice** is when you do something lots of times so that you get better at it: *We have soccer* ***practice*** *every Tuesday and Friday and then we play our games on Saturday.*

The Muslim man kneels on a small rug to **pray**.

pray ▲ • prayed, praying

When you **pray**, you talk to God: *In church, the people* ***prayed*** *that the war would end. They hoped their* ***prayer*** *would be heard.*

present[1] • presents

A **present** is something given as a gift to someone else: *Judy knitted a scarf as a birthday* ***present*** *for her aunt.*

present[2]

The **present** is also the time that is now: *The story Max wrote is about the way children dress in the* ***present****, not the way they dressed many years ago.*

The faces of four American **presidents** are carved into Mount Rushmore.

president ▲ • presidents

A **president** is the leader of a group or business, or a country: *David won the election for* ***president*** *of our club by six votes. The* ***President*** *of the United States gave a speech after he was elected.*

press • pressed, pressing

1. If you **press** something, you push it: *I* ***pressed*** *the button to turn on the radio. The* ***pressure*** *of my finger pushed the button in.*

2. To **press** is also to use an iron to make clothes smooth: *Greg will have to* ***press*** *his shirt before he goes out.*

pretend ▼ • pretended, pretending

To **pretend** means to act as if something is true when it is not: *Ralph and Kayla played a game where they* ***pretended*** *to be wild horses.*

Hank **pretends** to be a detective in the high school play.

pretty • prettier, prettiest

Something that is **pretty** is nice to look at or listen to: *Natalie looks **pretty** with a ribbon in her hair. The music Simon played on his guitar was very **pretty**.*

pretzel ▼ • pretzels

A **pretzel** is a snack food that is baked in the shape of a knot or stick. It has salt on it: *Olivia likes hot **pretzels**, but Sophie likes to eat them cold.*

We eat **pretzels** as a snack after school.

price ▼ • prices

The amount of money that something costs is its **price**: *The **price** of the new car was much more than the price of the older one.*

The **price** of the corn is written on the sign.

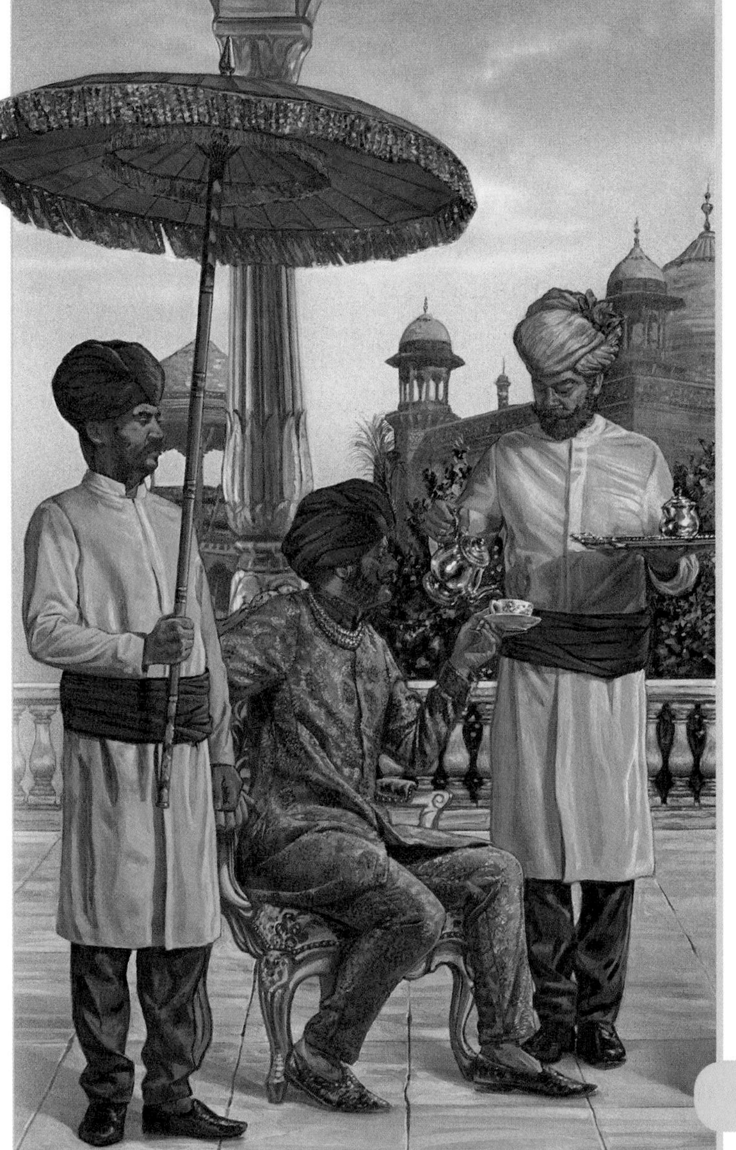

A man pours a cup of tea for the Indian **prince**.

prince ▲ • princes

A **prince** is a son of a king or queen.

princess • princesses

A **princess** is a daughter of a king or queen, or the wife of a prince.

principal • principals

A **principal** is the person in charge of a school: *The teacher sent Janey to take a note to the school **principal**.*

print ▼ • printed, printing

1. To **print** means to write with letters that are not joined together: *Claire **printed** her name on her pencil box to make it easier to read.*

2. To **print** also means to make writing or pictures on paper using a machine with ink: *Jerry wrote his story on a computer, then **printed** it to take to school the next day.*

printer • printers

A **printer** is a machine that is joined to a computer. It is used to print out on paper the words or pictures stored on the computer: *Before I could print the photos I had taken, I had to put more ink in the **printer**.*

This machine was used to **print** books more than 550 years ago.

Mandy has to write the answer to the math **problem** on the chalkboard.

prison • prisons

A **prison** is a building where people who have broken the law are locked up: *The man who robbed the bank was sent to **prison**. Now he is a **prisoner**.*

private

A thing that is **private** is something that you do not want to share with other people: *Ryan writes his **private** thoughts in his journal.*

prize • prizes

A **prize** is something that you win in a contest or a game: *Barbara won second **prize** in the singing contest. Her **prize** was a new CD player.*

probably

If something will **probably** happen, it is likely to happen but you are not quite sure: *Look at those dark clouds—I think it is **probably** going to rain.*

problem ◀ • **problems**

1. A **problem** is a question that needs to be answered: *Linda worked out all the math **problems** the teacher gave her.*
2. A **problem** is also something that is wrong that needs to be fixed: *The car would not go because there was a **problem** with the engine.*

produce ▼ • **produced, producing**

If you **produce** something, you make it: *The people who work in that factory **produce** cars. The **products** they make are sold all over the country.*

The Native American woman **produces** blankets.

program ▼ • **programs**

1. A **program** is a television or radio show: *Laura likes to watch cooking **programs** on TV and try out the recipes she sees on them.*
2. A **program** is also a set of instructions that tells a computer what to do: *At school Ben used a special computer **program** to draw a map.*

Betsy listens to a **program** on her radio.

project ▼ • **projects**

If you do a **project**, you do a special piece of work: *Mrs. Nelson gave the class two weeks to do a **project** on the country of Japan. This summer, our family **project** is to paint the outside of the house.*

Nancy and her friends are working on a class **project** together.

promise • **promised, promising**

To **promise** is to tell someone you will be sure to do something: *Mark **promised** to clean his room on the weekend. Rowena and Maggie **promised** not to argue anymore.*

pronounce • **pronounced, pronouncing**

To **pronounce** a letter is to say it in a certain way: *You **pronounce** the letters "ph" in Sophie's name as an "f." The **pronunciation** of "p" and "h" together in many words is the same as "f."*

protect ▼ • **protected, protecting**
If you **protect** something or someone, you keep it safe from being hurt: *Vernon put on his hat to* ***protect*** *his skin from the sun. He needed this* ***protection*** *because it was such a hot, sunny day.*

proud • **prouder, proudest**
If you are **proud**, it means you are pleased about something you or someone else has done: *Janet's parents were* ***proud*** *when she got a good report card. It filled them with* ***pride*** *when she got a prize for being such a good student.*

Mom made banana **pudding** for dessert.

prove • **proved, proving**
If you **prove** something, you show it is true: *Melissa* ***proved*** *she could read by reading the book out loud to me. The police say they have* ***proof*** *that he is the one who stole the money.*

public
When something is **public,** it is open to everybody: *Anyone who lives in this town can use the* ***public*** *library. This is a* ***public*** *beach and you don't have to pay money to swim here.*

publish • **published, publishing**
To **publish** means to print and try to sell a newspaper, book, magazine, or something else that is written: *That magazine about cars is* ***published*** *once every month.*

The crocodile **protects** its nest.

pudding ◀ • puddings

A **pudding** is a sweet dessert that is soft. It is mainly made from eggs, sugar, and milk: *Kathryn had ice cream with her chocolate **pudding**.*

Carol jumps in the muddy **puddle** in her boots.

puddle ▲ • puddles

A **puddle** is a small pool of water on the ground or floor: *After the snow began to melt, there were **puddles** on the ground.*

pull ▶ • pulled, pulling

To **pull** something means to hold it and move it toward you, or to drag it behind you: *Ray **pulled** the book off the shelf. The car **pulled** the trailer.*

pumpkin ▼ • pumpkins

A **pumpkin** is a large, round, orange vegetable that grows on a vine on the ground: *It was hard work cutting up the **pumpkin** to cook it to put in the pie.*

We will carve a face into the **pumpkin** for Halloween.

punch • punched, punching

If you **punch** something, you hit it hard with your fist: *Riley got into trouble for getting angry and **punching** Ian in the stomach.*

punish • punished, punishing

You **punish** someone if they have done something wrong: *Our teacher decided to **punish** us for talking in class. Our **punishment** was to clean up the classroom after school.*

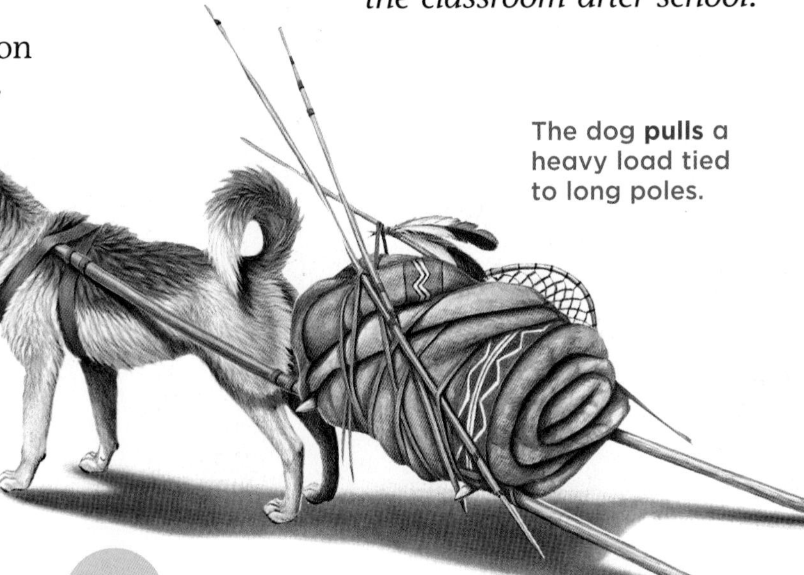

The dog **pulls** a heavy load tied to long poles.

A B C D E F G H I J K L M N O P Q R S T U V W X Y Z

We made **puppets** out of old socks.

pupil • pupils

A **pupil** is someone who is taught in school: *Mrs. Collins has thirty* ***pupils*** *in her class.* Another word for pupil is STUDENT.

puppet ▲ • puppets

A **puppet** is a doll that you can move to make it look alive. One type of puppet fits on your hand like a glove and you move your fingers to make it move. Another type has strings joined onto it that you pull to make it move.

puppy ▶ • puppies

A young dog is called a **puppy**: *When my dog's* ***puppies*** *were very small, they kept their eyes closed and slept most of the day.*

Our **puppy** is only ten weeks old.

purchase • purchased, purchasing

When you **purchase** something, you buy it: *Austin used the money he had saved up to* ***purchase*** *a baseball glove.*

The mask is **purple** and gold.

pure • purer, purest

Something that is **pure** has nothing mixed in with it: *Dad bought* ***pure*** *apple juice with no water or sugar added to it.*

purple ▲

Purple is the color made by mixing red and blue together.

Alicia **puts** a star on the top of the Christmas tree.

purpose

If you do something on **purpose**, you mean to do it: *Max thinks that I bumped into him on **purpose**, but it was an accident.*

purse ▼ • purses

A **purse** is a small bag for carrying money and other small things: *Ginny put the shopping list in her **purse.***

Meryl bought a red **purse** to match her shoes.

push • pushed, pushing

When you **push** something, you press hard against it to make it move: *When the car broke down, they had to **push** it to the side of the road.*

put ◀ • put, putting

When you **put** something in a place, you move it to that place: *Sally **put** the plate of tomatoes on the table.*

puzzle ▼ • puzzles

1. A **puzzle** is something that is hard to understand: *Mom says that it is a **puzzle** to her how my room always gets so messy.*
2. A **puzzle** is also a toy or game that is fun because it gives you an interesting problem to work out or find the answer to: *When Toby put the pieces of the **puzzle** together, it made a picture of a tiger.*

Casey is doing a **puzzle** of the Three Little Pigs.

A B C D E F G H I J K L M N O P **Q** R S T U V W X Y Z

The teacher put a **question mark** on my test because she didn't understand my answer.

quarter ▼ • **quarters**

If you divide something into four equal parts, each one of the parts is a **quarter**: *We each had a **quarter** of an orange when our soccer game was over.*

The orange is cut into **quarters.**

question ▲ • **questions**

When you want to find out something, you ask a **question**: *When the teacher asked a **question** about what horses eat, Alice put up her hand because she knew the answer.* When you write a question, you finish the sentence with a sign (**?**), which is called a **question mark**.

The man gives the **queen** a necklace.

queen ▶ • **queens**

A **queen** is a woman who rules a country: *The **queen** wore a crown with a large diamond in the center.*

Josie is on a bicycle, so Sasha will have to be **quick** to catch her.

quick ▲ • **quicker, quickest**

When something is **quick**, it moves fast or is done in a very short time: *Eddie had a **quick** drink of juice and then rushed out the door for school. He walked **quickly** because he was late.*

The teacher asks us to be **quiet** in class.

quiet ▲ • **quieter, quietest**

1. When something is **quiet**, it does not make much noise or sound: *Molly was so **quiet** that we didn't hear her come into the room. She took off her shoes so she could walk **quietly**.*

2. If you are somewhere **quiet**, it means that there is no sound around you: *Grandad found a **quiet** place in the park where he could sit and rest.*

quilt • **quilts**

A **quilt** is a cover for a bed. It is made of two pieces of cloth with feathers or soft material between them: *In winter, Stanley has a **quilt** on his bed to keep him warm.*

quit • **quit** *or* **quitted, quitting**

If you **quit** doing something, you stop doing it: *Amy **quit** reading and turned out her light. My uncle Doug is going to **quit** his job and take a new job in a different city.*

quite

Quite means more than usual or very: *You don't need to wear a coat, it's **quite** warm this morning.*

quiz ▼ • **quizzes**

A **quiz** is a short test: *We had a **quiz** in math class today at school.*

The word **quiz** comes from an old word meaning "what." A quiz will often have questions that start with "What," such as "*What* is six times two?" or "*What* is another word for 'sad'?"

Angela takes a **quiz** so her teacher can see how much she has learned.

Rr

The **raccoon** climbs along a branch.

rabbit • rabbits

A **rabbit** is a small animal with soft fur, long ears, and a short tail. Rabbits can run very fast. They eat grass and other plants, and they usually live in holes they dig in the ground.

raccoon ▲ • raccoons

A **raccoon** is a small furry animal with black marks on its face and black rings on its long tail. Raccoons live in trees in the woods. They come out at night to look for food.

race ▶ • races, raced, racing

1. A **race** is a contest to see who is the fastest: *The Kentucky Derby is a famous horse **race**. Dad took us to see the car **races** on Friday night.*
2. To **race** means to move very quickly: *Amy had to **race** to catch the bus.*

radar ▶

Radar is a machine that can follow things like ships, airplanes, and storms. Radar can show where things are and how fast they are moving: *Planes use **radar** to see where things are when they fly through the air. The **radar** at the weather station showed that the hurricane was heading toward the coast of Florida.*

radio • radios

A **radio** is a machine that you turn on to hear news, music, or other programs: *Jon listens to a sports program on the **radio** as he drives home from work.*

raft • rafts

A **raft** is a kind of flat boat. Rafts are mostly made of logs or boards that are joined together. Some rafts are made of rubber or plastic and filled with air: *The boys floated down the river on a **raft**.*

The red car is winning the **race**.

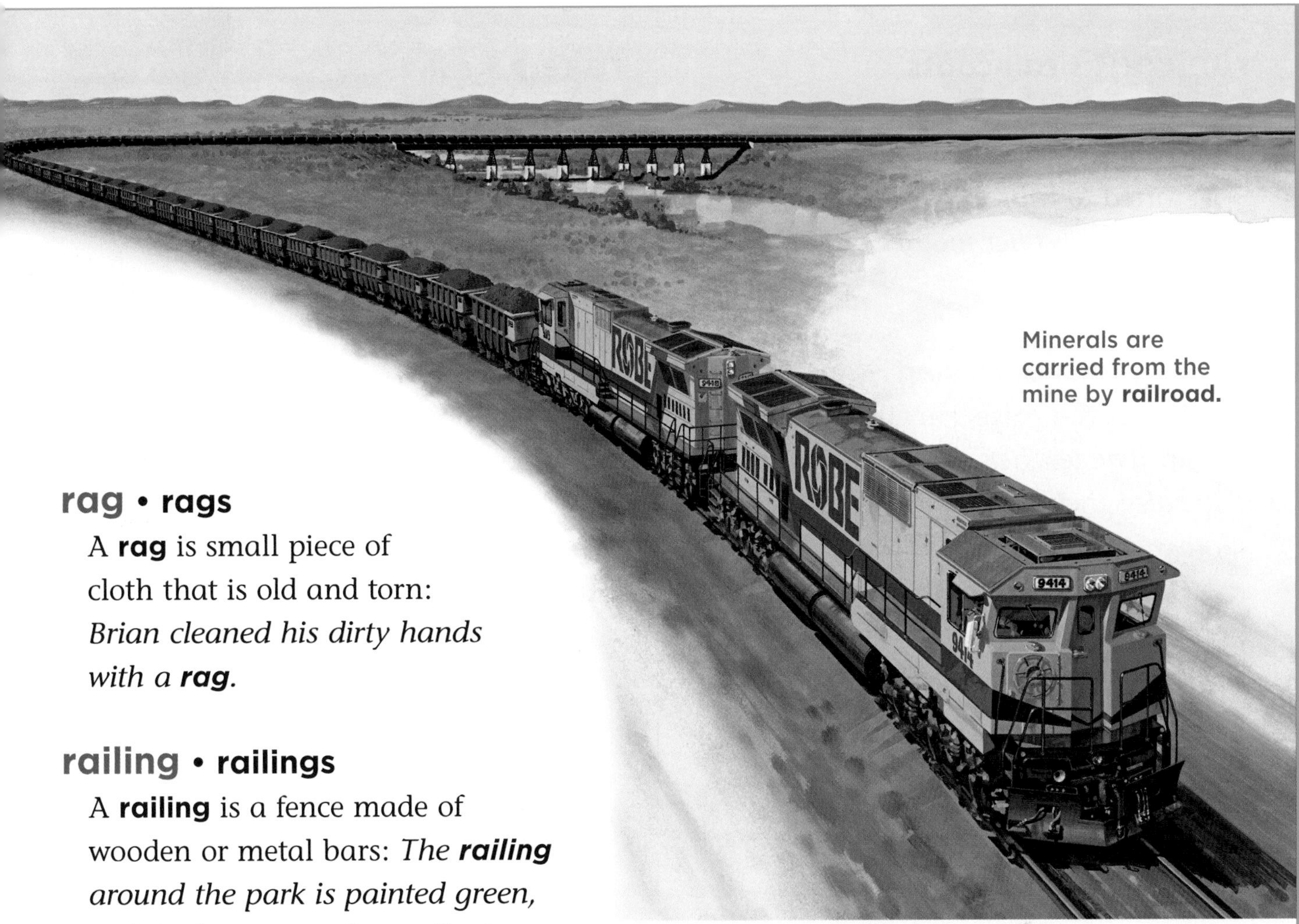

Minerals are carried from the mine by **railroad.**

rag • rags

A **rag** is small piece of cloth that is old and torn: *Brian cleaned his dirty hands with a* ***rag****.*

railing • railings

A **railing** is a fence made of wooden or metal bars: *The* ***railing*** *around the park is painted green, so it is the same color as the trees.*

railroad ▲ • railroads

A **railroad** is a way of traveling from one town to another. A railroad includes tracks, trains, and stations: *Talia's dad takes the* ***railroad*** *to get to his job in New York City.*

rain • rains, rained, raining

1. Rain is drops of water that fall from the clouds down to the ground: *Farmers need* ***rain*** *when the corn is growing.*

2. To **rain** means to fall as drops of water from the clouds: *It* ***rained*** *all day and we couldn't play outside.*

rainbow ▼ • rainbows

A **rainbow** is the curved line of colors that you sometimes see in the sky after it rains. Rainbows are made when light from the sun shines through drops of water in the air: *One end of the* ***rainbow*** *went behind the hills and the other end went into the sea.*

Jess saw a **rainbow** in the sky after the storm.

a b c d e f g h i j k l m n o p q r s t u v w x y z

raincoat • raincoats

A **raincoat** is a coat that you wear to keep you dry in the rain: *When it started to rain, Shelly put on her **raincoat** and her mother put up an umbrella.*

raise • raised, raising

1. When you **raise** something, you lift it up: *The teacher asked the students to **raise** their hand if they knew the answer to the question.*
2. Raise also means to take care of something while it is growing: *Tony's aunt **raises** ducks on her farm.*

Long ago, people used **ramps** to carry stones to the tops of buildings.

rake ▶ • rakes, raked, raking

1. A **rake** is a tool that you use in the garden to gather up leaves, grass, or hay, or to move dirt. A rake has a long wooden or metal handle and pointed parts at the end: *Pete used a **rake** to clear away the grass after Dad cut the lawn.*
2. To **rake** means to gather things up with a tool like this: *Ellie **raked** the leaves that had fallen in her yard.*

The man uses a **rake** to keep things neat.

ramp ◀ • ramps

A **ramp** is a kind of road or sidewalk that goes from one place to another: *Joanne went down the **ramp** in her wheelchair.*

ran

Ran is a form of the word RUN: *The dog **ran** up to the gate and barked.*

A cowboy uses a rope to catch horses on his **ranch**.

ranch ▲ • **ranches**

A **ranch** is a large farm that has cattle, sheep, or horses on it: *Amy's uncle works as a cowboy on a **ranch**.*

ranger • **rangers**

A **ranger** is a person whose job is to watch over and take care of a forest or park: *The **ranger** said that we could camp beside the lake.*

rat ▼ • **rats**

A **rat** is an animal that looks like a large mouse. A rat has a long nose and a long, thin tail. Rats have big front teeth that are strong enough to bite through hard things such as rope or wire.

The **rat** comes out at night to eat seeds.

rate

The **rate** of something is the speed that it takes to happen: *The bean plants grew at the **rate** of about two inches a week.*

rather

If you would **rather** do something, you want to do it more than something else: *I would **rather** go to the baseball game today than go see a movie.*

raw ◀

Raw means not cooked: *Our dog eats **raw** meat.*

Meredith served **raw** vegetables at the party.

reach ▼ • **reached, reaching**

1. If you can **reach** something, you can put your arm or hand out to touch it: *Miranda **reached** up to pick an apple from the tree.*

2. Reach also means to get to a place: *Karl shouted with joy when he **reached** the finish line ahead of all the other people in the race.*

read ▶ • **read, reading**

To **read** is to look at words and understand what they mean: *When children go to school, they learn to **read** and write. They do **reading** in class every day.*

The boy **reaches** the duck that is trying to fly away.

Maggie **reads** in bed with a flashlight.

ready • **readier, readiest**

If you are **ready**, you can do something right away: *Are you **ready** to leave for school?*

real

When something is **real**, it is true: *The story in this book is **real**, and not made up. Dragons are not **real** animals.*

really

1. Really means actually or truly: *Did Charlie **really** run all the way up the hill?*

2. Really also means very: *Tammie was **really** excited about winning the prize.*

reason • **reasons**

A **reason** is the thing that makes something happen or explains why it has happened: *Billy's **reason** for missing class was that he was sick.*

receive • **received, receiving**

If you **receive** something, you are given it: *Jim **received** a camera as a present for his birthday.*

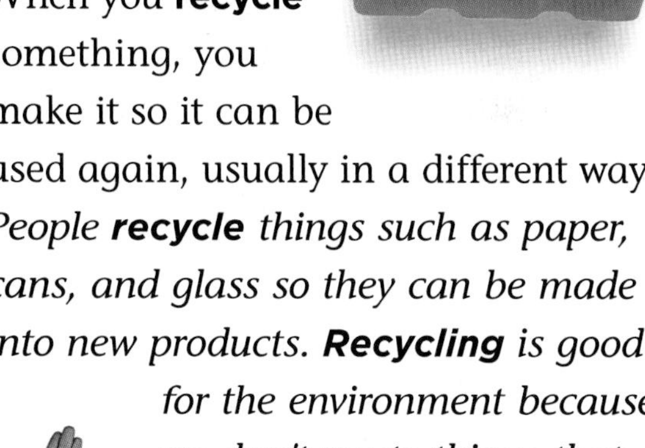

Larry takes the empty containers to be **recycled**.

recent

If something is **recent**, it happened or was made not long ago: *Mrs. Davis showed us a* ***recent*** *photo of her grandson. We could tell the photo was taken* ***recently****, because he was wearing his Halloween costume.*

recess • recesses

A **recess** is a short time when you stop working: *At school we have a snack at* ***recess****.*

recipe • recipes

A **recipe** gives you a list of the things you need to make something to eat, and tells you how to make it: *We should read the* ***recipe*** *first, to make sure we have everything we need to make the cake.*

record • records

1. A **record** is the highest score that any person has had for something: *Shelly broke the school* ***record*** *in the long jump.*
2. A **record** is also a flat disk made of plastic. It has music and other sounds on it: *Terry's uncle likes listening to old* ***records****.*

The football **referee** makes the signal for a touchdown.

rectangle • rectangles

A **rectangle** is a flat shape with four straight sides and four corners: *The top of my desk has the shape of a* ***rectangle****.*

recycle ▶ • recycled, recycling

When you **recycle** something, you make it so it can be used again, usually in a different way: *People* ***recycle*** *things such as paper, cans, and glass so they can be made into new products.* ***Recycling*** *is good for the environment because we don't waste things that can be used again.*

This ladybug is mostly **red** with black spots.

red ▶ • reds

Red is a bright color like the color of blood: *Ripe tomatoes and most kinds of apples are* ***red****.*

referee ◀ • referees

A **referee** is a person in charge of a sports game who makes sure that the players follow the rules: *The* ***referee*** *blew her whistle to start the soccer game.*

Mom loves to **relax** when we go on vacation.

refrigerator • **refrigerators**

A **refrigerator** is a large machine that keeps food and drinks cold: *Sue put the carton of milk in the* ***refrigerator***.

regular

If something is **regular**, it is normal or usual: *Larissa asked for a* ***regular*** *size drink, and Jo asked for an extra large one.*

relative ▶ • **relatives**

A **relative** is someone who is part of your family: *Katrina invited her grandmother, her aunt and uncle, her cousins, and other* ***relatives*** *to her wedding.*

relax ◀ • **relaxed, relaxing**

When you **relax**, you rest and feel comfortable: *Hannah likes to* ***relax*** *by listening to music.*

religion ▶ • **religions**

Religion is what people believe about God or gods. There are many different kinds of religions in the world: *The* ***religions*** *that have the most members in the world are the Christian, Muslim, Hindu, and Buddhist religions. In the* ***religion*** *of ancient Greece, Neptune was the god of the sea.*

A **religious** person is someone who strongly believes in God or a religion.

remember • **remembered, remembering**

When you **remember** something, you bring it back into your mind: *Rory couldn't find his house key and then he* ***remembered*** *he left it on the table.*

My uncle took a photo of all our **relatives** at the family picnic.

In some **religions**, people believe in many different gods.

remind • reminded, reminding

Remind means to help someone remember: *Ruth called to **remind** us that it was her brother Sam's birthday this weekend.*

rent • rents

Rent is money you pay to use something that belongs to someone else: *My sister and her friends share the **rent** on an apartment.*

repair ▶ • repaired, repairing

When you **repair** something that is broken, you make it good again: *Dad helped me to **repair** the cup that I broke.*

repeat • repeated, repeating

Repeat means that you do or say something again: *Please **repeat** the question—I didn't hear it the first time.*

report • reports

A **report** is news or information about something: *There was a **report** on TV last night about a forest fire in the mountains. Billy wrote a book **report** on "Charlotte's Web," by E.B. White.*

report card

A **report card** is the information that your teacher writes to your parents about how good your school work is: *My parents were very proud of me when they read my **report card**.*

Dad helps Adam **repair** his bicycle.

reptiles

Reptiles have skin covered in scales, and most lay eggs. Some reptiles, such as turtles and tortoises, also have a hard shell. To keep their body from getting too cold, reptiles need to be in the sun or next to something warm.

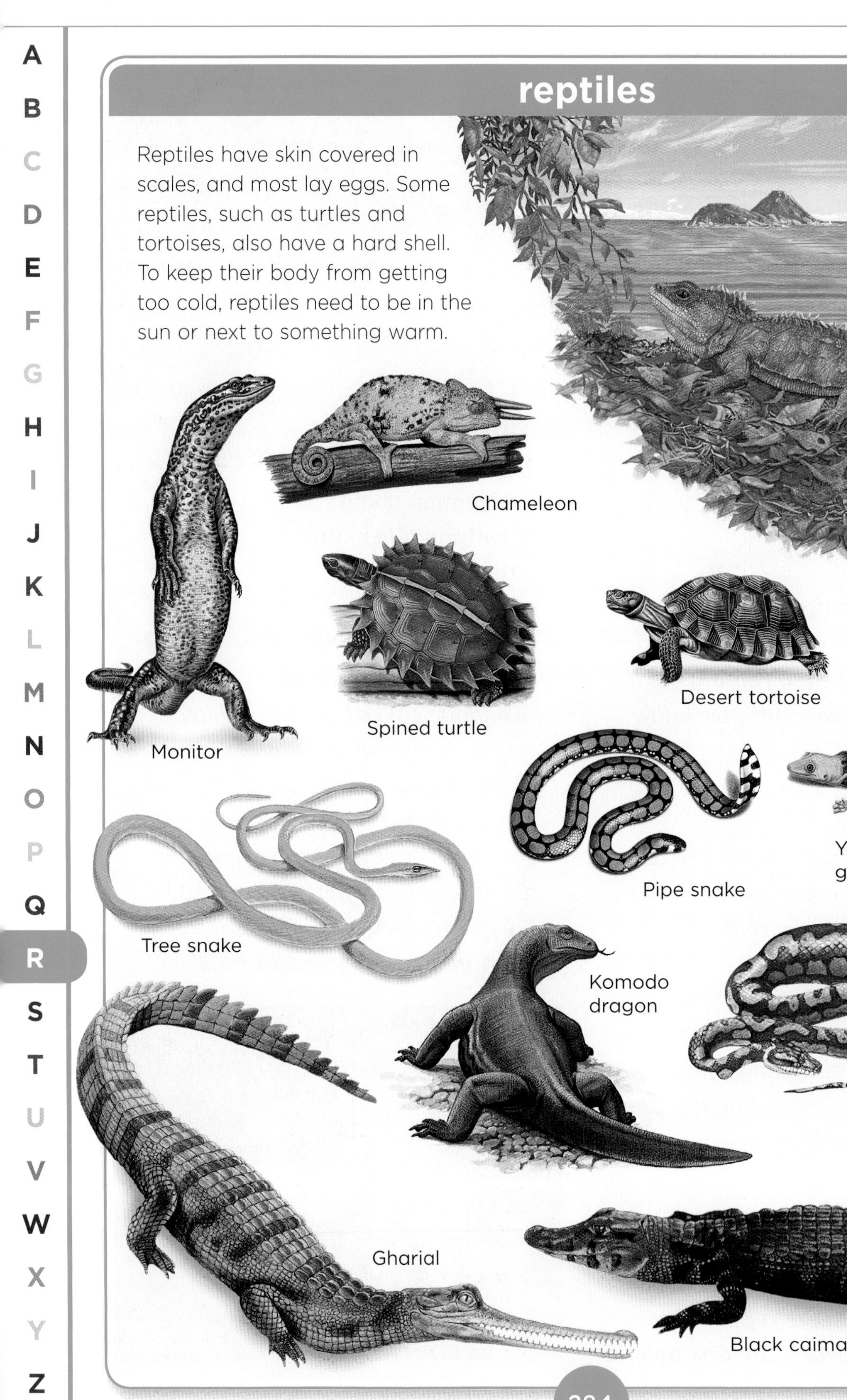

reptile • reptiles

A **reptile** is an animal that crawls on its stomach or on very short legs. Lizards, snakes, turtles, and alligators are all reptiles. Most reptiles lay eggs: ***Reptiles*** *lie in the sun to warm up before they move around.*

rest[1] • rests, rested, resting

1. **Rest** means to stop what you are doing because you are tired and sleepy, or to be still and quiet for a while: *The doctor told Ellie to* ***rest*** *in bed for two days so she'd get better.*
2. A **rest** is the time when you are resting: *Grandpa always lies down for a* ***rest*** *after lunch.*

After riding their bikes around the park, Alex and Shirley **rest** on a bench.

rest[2]

Rest means the part that is left after everyone or everything else has gone: *I've done most of my homework, and I'll finish the* ***rest*** *later.*

We will save the **rest** of the cake to eat later.

restaurant • restaurants

A **restaurant** is a place to eat away from home. You order what you would like to eat, someone brings you the food, then you eat it and pay for it: *We went to a Chinese* ***restaurant*** *for Dad's birthday last night.*

return • returned, returning

1. When you **return**, you go back or come back: *Jess will* ***return*** *from camp on Sunday.*
2. Also, when you **return** something, you give it back: *I* ***returned*** *the book to the library.*

reward • rewards

You may give a **reward** to someone if they find something important that belongs to you: *Our neighbor gave Tom a* ***reward*** *of ten dollars for finding her lost purse.*

There is a **reward** for finding the lost cat.

rhinoceros ▼ • **rhinoceroses**

A **rhinoceros** is a very big, strong animal with one or two horns on its nose. Rhinoceroses have very thick skin and short legs: *Some* ***rhinoceroses*** *eat grass, and others eat the leaves of plants.*

The **rhinoceros** gets its name from a word for "nose." The most unusual things about a rhinoceros are its large nose and the horns attached to it.

rhyme • **rhymed, rhyming**

Words **rhyme** when they sound like each other: *The words "hat," "cat," and "mat"* ***rhyme****.*

rhythm • **rhythms**

A **rhythm** is a pattern of sounds or movements: *The soldiers marched in time to the* ***rhythm*** *of the music.*

rhinoceroses

There are five kinds of rhinoceroses alive today, and all are in danger of dying out. Rhinoceroses eat grass or leaves. All kinds have thick skin, but only the Sumatran rhinoceros has thick hair. They roll in mud to keep cool.

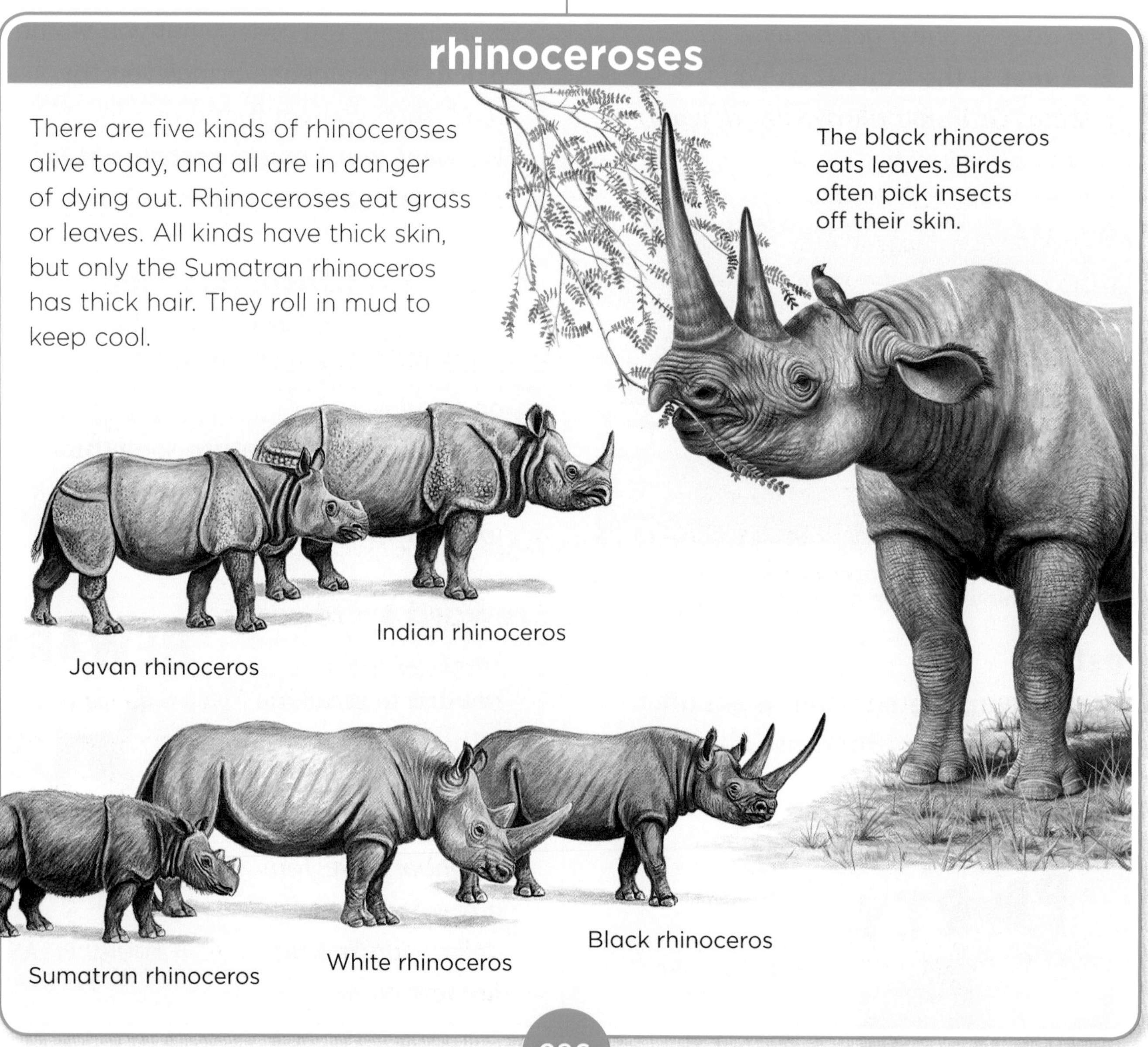

The black rhinoceros eats leaves. Birds often pick insects off their skin.

Javan rhinoceros

Indian rhinoceros

Sumatran rhinoceros

White rhinoceros

Black rhinoceros

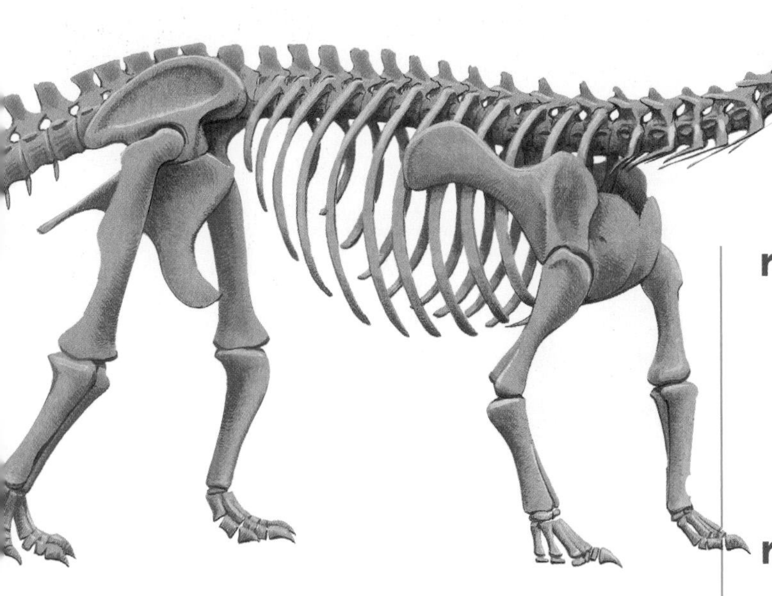

These bones show that the dinosaur had large **ribs** between its two sets of legs.

rib ▲ • ribs

A **rib** is one of the curved bones in your chest: *Your **ribs** protect your heart.*

ribbon ▼ • ribbons

A **ribbon** is a thin strip of material that you use to tie things up or to make them look nice: *Peyton tied two red **ribbons** in her hair.*

rice

Rice is the white or brown seeds of a plant. You cook and eat rice: *Mom made fried **rice** for dinner.*

Lisa has a collection of **ribbons**.

rich • richer, richest

If you are **rich**, you have a lot of money or land: *In the story that Vanessa was reading, the **rich** king counted his piles of gold all day.*

riddle • riddles

A **riddle** is a clever question or problem that is hard to answer: *Here is a **riddle**: What has a head and a tail but no body? Answer: A coin.*

The man **rides** an elephant during the festival.

ride ▲ • rides, rode, ridden, riding

1. When you **ride** something, you sit on it or in it and move along: *Daphne **rides** her bicycle to school.*

2. A **ride** is a short trip on or in something: *We took a taxi **ride** to the airport.*

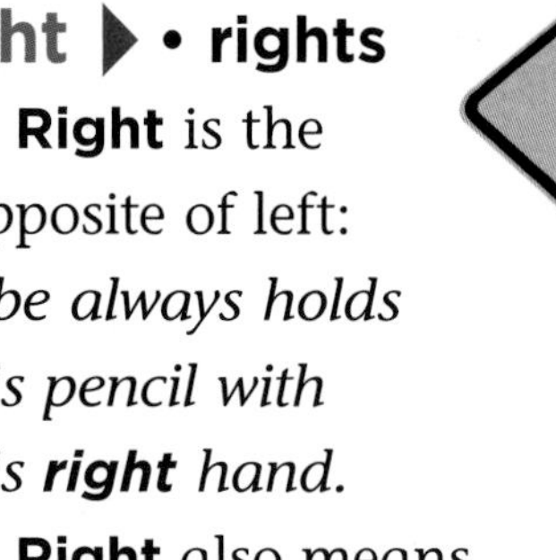

The arrow curves to the **right**.

right ▶ • **rights**

1. **Right** is the opposite of left: *Abe always holds his pencil with his **right** hand.*
2. **Right** also means that something is correct: *In the spelling test, I got nine words **right** and one wrong.*
3. You can also use **right** to mean immediately: *Dad said you've got to come home **right** after school finishes.*

ring[1] ▼ • **rings**

A **ring** is something in the shape of a circle: *The children stood in a **ring** around the pole and waited for the principal to raise the flag. Mrs. Jackson wears a diamond **ring** on her finger.*

ring[2] • **rang, rung, ringing**

To **ring** means to make a sound like a bell: *When the bell **rings**, school is finished for the day. Someone **rang** the bell at our front door.*

A dolphin leaps through a **ring**.

In winter, we like to go skating at the **rink** in the city.

rink ▲ • **rinks**

You can ice-skate or roller-skate at a **rink**: *Aleesha and Jade went to the roller-skating **rink** on Sunday.*

rip • **ripped, ripping**

If you **rip** something, you tear it: *Tony **ripped** a hole in his jeans when he fell in the playground.*

Cherries turn red when they are **ripe**.

ripe ◀ • **riper, ripest**

When something is **ripe**, it has finished growing and is ready to eat: *When the strawberries in our garden turn red, they are **ripe** and we can pick them to eat.*

rise ▶ • **rose, risen, rising**

Rise means to go up or to get up: *I saw the sun **rise** at 6 o'clock this morning.*

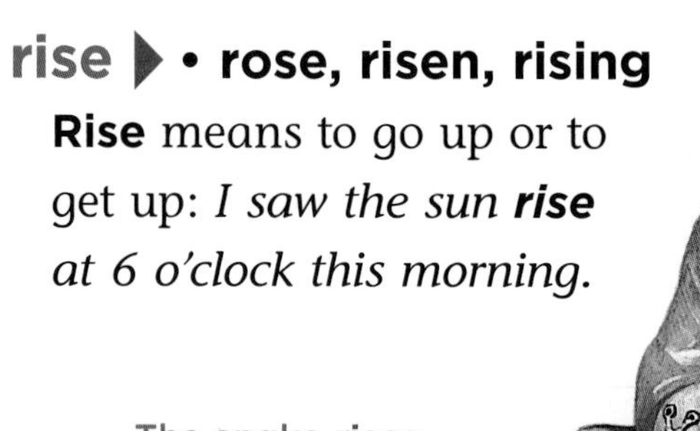

The snake **rises** from the basket.

The girls **roast** marshmallows on sticks over the fire.

river ▼ • **rivers**

A **river** is a large stream of moving water. Rivers run from higher ground to lower and finish at a lake, ocean, or another river: *The Amazon River is the longest **river** in South America.*

road • **roads**

A **road** is a wide path that cars and other vehicles travel on: *Jeff crossed the **road** at the traffic light.*

roar • **roared, roaring**

Roar means to make a loud, deep sound: *Lions and bears **roar**. The crowd **roared** when the home team won the game.*

Over many years, the **river** has cut a canyon through the rock.

roast ◀ • **roasted, roasting**

When you **roast** something, you cook it for a long time in an oven or over a fire: *Mom always **roasts** the turkey for our Thanksgiving dinner.*

rob • **robbed, robbing**

Rob means to take something that is not yours: *A man **robbed** the house next door last Tuesday. The **robber** stole a TV and some jewelry. The **robbery** happened in the afternoon, when no one was home.*

The **robin** has caught an insect.

robin ◀ • **robins**

A **robin** is a small bird with a red or orange chest and a gray or black head, back, and tail: *The **robin** built a nest and laid three blue eggs in it.*

robot ▶ • **robots**

A **robot** is a machine. Robots can move about and do some of the work that people do: ***Robots** help to make cars at the car factory.*

This **robot** looks like a person.

rocks

Most rocks are made up of more than one mineral. Some rocks come from deep inside Earth, and some are formed from sand and small rocks that have been pressed together. Rocks called meteorites sometimes fall to Earth from space.

Some people collect the rocks that they find.

Rocks in space

rock[1] ▲ • **rocks**

A **rock** is a piece of stone: *The boy threw a* ***rock*** *at the window and broke it.*

rock[2] • **rocked, rocking**

To **rock** means to move backward and forward or from side to side in a gentle way: *Dad* ***rocked*** *the baby to sleep in his arms.*

rocket ▼ • **rockets**

A **rocket** is a type of vehicle that flies up into the air very quickly: *The* ***rocket*** *flew to the planet Mars and took photos of it.*

rode

Rode is a form of the word RIDE: *Amelia* ***rode*** *on the roller coaster at the fair.*

Flames shoot out as the **rocket** takes off into space.

rodeo ▼ • **rodeos**

A **rodeo** is a show with contests where cowboys and cowgirls ride horses, rope bulls, and do other tricks.

At the **rodeo,** the cowboy tries to stay on the horse as long as he can.

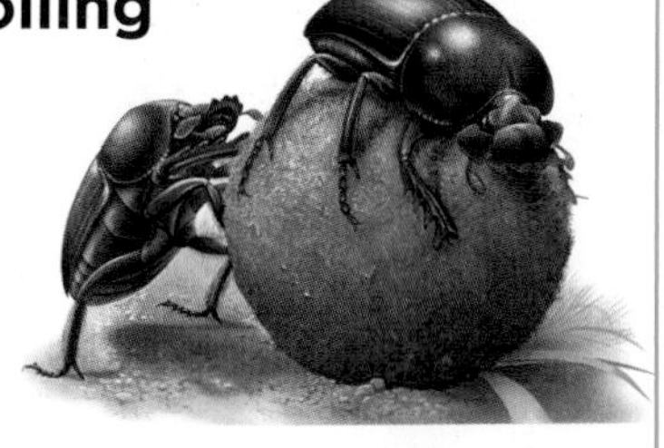

Two beetles **roll** a ball along the ground.

roll ▶ • **rolled, rolling**

1. **Roll** means to move along by turning over and over: *Deborah tried to **roll** up her towel so it would fit into her bag.*
2. **Roll** also means to move on wheels: *The train **rolled** along the railroad track.*

roller skate

A **roller skate** is a skate with four wheels on the bottom: *Linda got a pair of **roller skates** for her birthday. Now she wants to **roller-skate** after school every day.*

roof ▼ • **roofs**

A **roof** is something that covers the top of a building and protects it: *The builders are putting the **roof** on our new house today.*

room • **rooms**

1. A **room** is a part of a house or building. It has walls around it: *Their house has six **rooms**.*
2. If you have **room**, that means you have space: *If you move over on the seat, there will be **room** for me to sit down too.*

rooster ▶ • **roosters**

A **rooster** is a male chicken: *The **rooster** next door wakes us up every morning with its loud cry.*

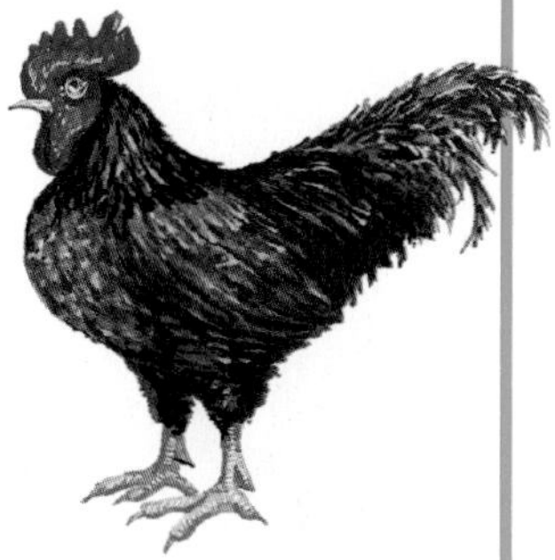

The **rooster** has long tail feathers.

root • **roots**

A **root** is the part of a plant that grows under the ground. Roots take water and food to the plant: *Geoff pulled the weeds out by their **roots** so they wouldn't grow again.*

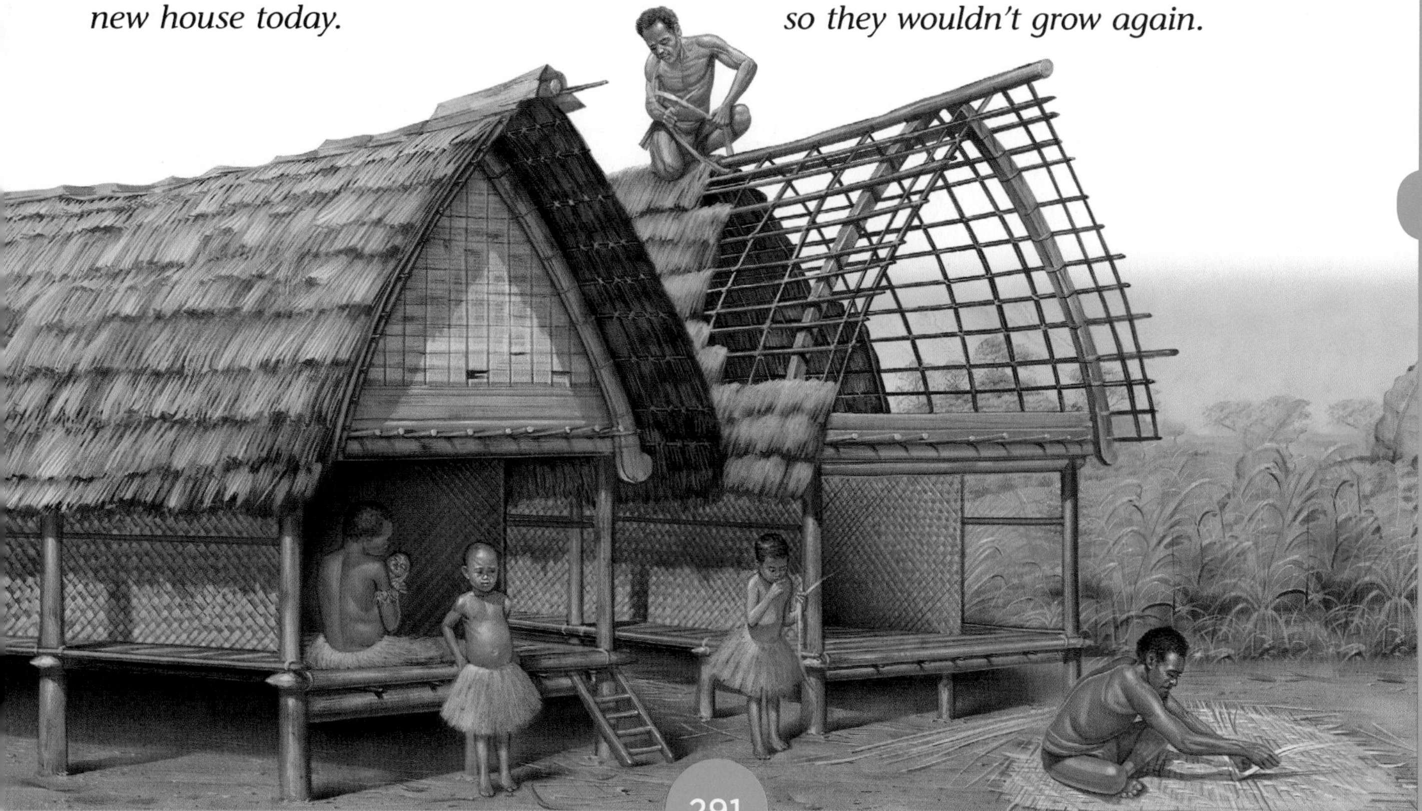

The men are making a new **roof** from wood and grass.

rope ▶ • **ropes**
A **rope** is a strong, thick string. Ropes are used for lifting, pulling, or hanging things, or for holding them in place: *Dad tied our bikes onto the car roof with* ***rope****.*

Roses have a sweet smell.

rose ◀ • **roses**
A **rose** is a pretty flower that may be red, pink, white, yellow, or other colors. Roses grow on a bush: *Sandy took his aunt a bunch of* ***roses*** *when he visited her in the hospital.*

rough • **rougher, roughest**
1. If something is **rough**, it feels hard and bumpy and not smooth or even: *The car bounced along the* ***rough*** *road.*
2. Rough also means wild or not gentle: *Paul could not go sailing because the ocean was too* ***rough****. If you're* ***rough*** *when you play with the kitten, you might hurt it.*

round ▶ • **rounder, roundest**
If something is **round**, it is shaped like a circle or a ball: *A basketball is* ***round****. A gold ring is* ***round****.*

The base and the top of the ride at the fair are **round**.

A cowboy swings a **rope** through the air.

row • **rows**
A **row** is a line of things or people that are side by side: *Rachel planted a* ***row*** *of flowers along the path. We sat in the back* ***row*** *at the movies.*

rub • **rubbed, rubbing**
Rub means to move something backward and forward against something else: *Jake* ***rubbed*** *at the dirty mark on his face with the washcloth.*

rubber • **rubbers**
Rubber is a material that stretches without breaking. Rubber keeps water out. Tires and some balls are made of rubber: *Mom wears* ***rubber*** *gloves when she washes the dishes.*

rude • **ruder, rudest**
If you are **rude**, you are not polite to someone: *It was* ***rude*** *of Mike to talk in class while the teacher was giving the lesson.*

rug • **rugs**
A **rug** is a piece of heavy cloth that covers part of the floor: *I tripped on the* ***rug*** *in the middle of the living room floor.*

One dinosaur is **running** away from the other one that is chasing it.

ruin • **ruined, ruining**

You **ruin** something if you cause it to be so bad that it has no use or value: *He **ruined** the picture when he spilled water on it and the paint got all wet. I left the pie in the oven much too long, and it was **ruined**.*

rule • **rules, ruled, ruling**

1. A **rule** is an instruction that tells you what you can and cannot do: *At my school it is against the **rules** to drop paper on the ground.*
2. To **rule** means to be in charge: *The king **ruled** his country for twenty years.*

ruler ▼ • **rulers**

1. A **ruler** is a long, straight strip of wood or plastic. Rulers have inches marked along the side to measure how long something is: *Ronny used his **ruler** to draw four straight lines that were each six inches long.*
2. A **ruler** is also a person who leads a country: *The queen was a good and kind **ruler**.*

run ◀ • **ran, run, running**

1. When you **run**, you move your legs quickly to go fast: *A cheetah is an animal that can **run** very fast. We all **ran** in the race and Patty won.*
2. **Run** also means that something works without any problems: *Sam fixed the engine and now it **runs** really well.*

rush • **rushed, rushing**

Rush means to move quickly: *Water **rushed** in through the hole in the boat. We **rushed** to catch the bus on time.*

The **ruler** is carried to his palace on a chair.

Ss

Early Americans **sailed** from England on a ship called the Mayflower.

Joan is **sad** because she dropped her ice cream.

sad ◀ • sadder, saddest

You are **sad** when you feel unhappy. Sometimes you cry when you are feeling sad: *We were all **sad** when our team lost the final game.*

safe ▼ • safer, safest

When you are **safe**, you are free from danger. Nothing bad can happen to you when you are safe: *It is **safe** to cross the road at this traffic light. Jim checked that the light for walking had turned green, then he crossed the road **safely**. We are learning about road **safety** at school.*

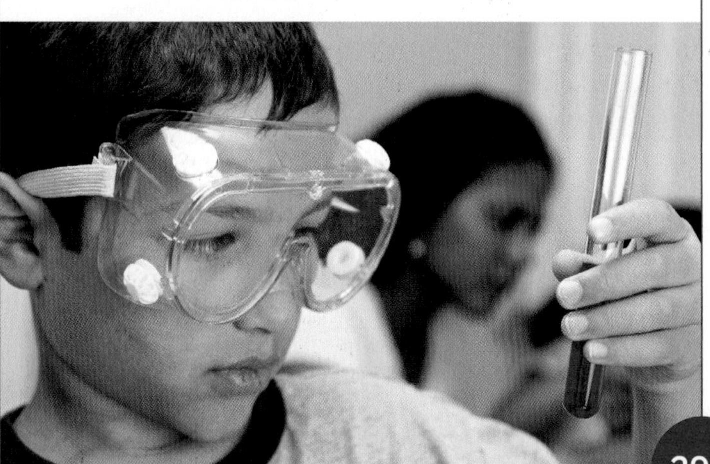

Lionel wears glasses to keep his eyes **safe**.

said

Said is a form of the word SAY: *The teacher **said**, "Put your hand up if you have finished all the math questions."*

sail ◀ • sails, sailed, sailing

1. A **sail** is a piece of strong material on a boat that catches the wind and moves the boat through the water.
2. To **sail** means to travel across water: *I go **sailing** on the river in my uncle's **sailboat** every Sunday. He says that I am becoming a good **sailor**.*

A **salad** made with different raw vegetables can be a healthy meal.

salad ▲ • salads

Salad is a cold dish of different vegetables, such as lettuce and tomato. Salads can be also be made with small pieces of meat, cheese, or fruits: *Daniel ordered a steak for dinner and asked for a **salad** of lettuce and tomato on the side.*

sale • sales

A **sale** is the selling of something, usually for less than it would have normally cost: *The store is having a big **sale** on summer clothes—they are all half price.*

salt

Salt is a white powder that is used in cooking to add flavor. Salt is found in the ground as well as in sea water: *Mom put some **salt** on the potatoes.*

These puppies are all the **same** kind of dog.

same ▲

When something is the **same**, it is not different. It is just like something else in every way, or it does not change: *I have the **same** kind of soccer shoes as my friend Jack. Both my favorite TV shows are on the **same** night, Tuesday.*

sand

Sand is tiny pieces of rock that you find on beaches and in the desert: *I shook the **sand** from my shoes after my walk on the beach.*

sandwich ▶ • sandwiches

A **sandwich** is two pieces of bread with some other food between them: *I had a ham **sandwich** for lunch.*

My **sandwich** is made with brown bread.

The Earl of *Sandwich* lived in England many years ago. He liked to play cards, so he invented the **sandwich** to have something to eat while he played.

satellite ▼ • satellites

1. A **satellite** is something in space, such as the Moon, that goes around and around a bigger thing, like another planet.
2. A **satellite** is also a spacecraft that is sent out into space to go around and around something bigger, like Earth. Satellites gather information about things like the weather, and they can also be used to send TV programs around the world.

This **satellite** collects information and sends it back to Earth.

People try to **save** the whales that swam onto the beach.

save ▲ • saved, saving

1. To **save** means to keep someone or something safe from harm: *The woman dived into the pool to **save** the little boy from drowning.*
2. To **save** also means to keep something to use later: *I'm going to **save** as much money as I can each week to buy a new bicycle.*

saw[1]

Saw is a form of the word SEE: *I **saw** a really exciting adventure movie with my friends last night.*

Brad used a **saw** to cut wood for his project.

saw[2] **▲ • saws**

A **saw** is a tool or machine with a blade that has sharp metal teeth. You move the blade backward and forward across something to cut it: *Dad used the **saw** to cut the branch off the tree.*

say • said, saying

If you **say** something, you speak words: *Every day, the teacher **says** "good morning" to the class.*

scale ▼ • scales

1. A **scale** is a machine for weighing things to see how heavy they are: *Uncle Mike stood on the **scale** and it said he weighs two hundred pounds.*
2. **Scales** are also the thin, flat, hard pieces of skin that cover fish, snakes, and other animals.

The **scales** measure the difference in weight between the two objects.

We stuffed clothes with hay to **scare** the birds.

scare ▸ • scared, scaring

To **scare** means to frighten or become frightened: *The movie really* ***scared*** *me. It had lots of giant spiders and other* ***scary*** *things in it.*

Hillary wraps a **scarf** around her face to keep warm.

scarf ◂ • scarves *or* scarfs

A **scarf** is a piece of material you wear around your neck or head to keep warm: *I wrapped a woolen* ***scarf*** *around my neck and put on gloves before I went outside.*

schedule • schedules

A **schedule** is a list of times that shows when things are planned to happen: *George read the bus* ***schedule*** *to see what time the next bus would get there.*

school • schools

School is a place where you go to learn things, like how to read and write and do math: *My favorite thing to do at* ***school*** *is going to the library to get a good book to read.*

science • sciences

Science is the way we learn about the world around us. When you study science, you learn all about Earth, space, plants, and animals.

scientist ▾ • scientists

A **scientist** is someone who works in a certain part of science: *Anders Celsius was a famous* ***scientist*** *who invented a way to measure temperature.*

scissors

Scissors are a tool made with two sharp blades that are held together in the middle. You use scissors to cut things like paper: *Jane used the* ***scissors*** *to cut out some photos from a magazine.*

The **scientists** look through microscopes.

I **scored** when the ball went into the basket.

score ▶ • **scores, scored, scoring**

1. A **score** is the number of points or correct answers that you get in a game or a test: *Liz got a **score** of 9 out of 10 for her spelling test. The **score** of the baseball game was Cubs 4, Dodgers 2.*
2. To **score** means to get points in a game, or on a test: *Our team **scored** three goals during the game.*

The donkey **scratches** behind its ear.

scratch ▲ • **scratched, scratching**

1. To **scratch** means to cut with something sharp: *The cat **scratched** Jackie with her claws.*
2. To **scratch** also means to rub your skin with your nails or something else to stop it from itching: *Nick **scratched** at the mosquito bite on his arm.*

scream • **screamed, screaming**

To **scream** means to cry out with a loud sound. People scream when they are excited or angry, or if they get badly hurt or scared: *Natasha **screamed** when she saw a mouse running across the kitchen floor.*

screen • **screens**

1. A **screen** is a frame that holds a wire net: *Dad put **screens** on all our windows to stop the bugs from getting inside.*
2. A **screen** is also the part of a computer or television where you can see the picture.

sea ▼ • **seas**

The **sea** is the salt water that covers most of Earth: *We are staying in a house by the **sea** during our vacation.* Another word for sea is OCEAN.

Many kinds of animals live in the **sea**.

seals and sea lions

There are two kinds of seals. Some seals, such as sea lions and fur seals, have small ears and they can turn their back flippers around to walk on land. Others, such as leopard and harp seals, do not have ears that stick out and they cannot turn their flippers to walk.

Sea lions live in big groups called colonies.

seal[1] ▲ • seals
A **seal** is a fish-eating sea animal with a smooth, furry body and big, flat feet called flippers. A **sea lion** is a type of seal.

seal[2] • sealed, sealing
To **seal** means to close something tightly so that nothing can leak out of it: *Medicine bottles are **sealed** with special tops so that children cannot open them.*

search ▼ • searched, searching
To **search** means to try to find someone or something: *Belinda **searched** all over the house for her watch, but she still couldn't find it.*

Owen pretends he is in Africa, **searching** for wild animals.

As the **seasons** change from spring to winter, a tree and its leaves look very different.

Summer Fall Spring Winter

season ▶ • **seasons**
A **season** is one of the four parts of the year: spring, summer, fall, or winter: *I love the **season** of winter because we get to play in the snow.*

seat ▼ • **seats**
A **seat** is a piece of furniture that you use to sit on, like a chair or bench: *On the airplane my **seat** was number 32A, and Mom had seat 32B. We all had to be **seated** while the plane was landing.*

seatbelt • **seatbelts**
A **seatbelt** is a special belt in a car, bus, truck, or airplane that holds you in your seat. You wear a seatbelt in case there is an accident and you get bumped out of your seat. It is also called a **safety belt**.

The Chinese prince sits on a special **seat** called a throne.

second[1]
Second means being the next one that comes after the first: *Annie won the running race and Helen got **second** place.*

second[2] • **seconds**
A **second** is one part of a minute. There are sixty seconds in one minute: *The teacher told the children that they had thirty **seconds** to put away all their books.*

secret ▶ • **secrets**
A **secret** is something that only a few people know about, and others are not supposed to know: *We are planning a party for Tanya, but don't tell her— it's a **secret**.*

Kate's book has a lock, so no one can read her **secrets**.

secretary • **secretaries**
A **secretary** is someone whose job is to write letters, send e-mails, and answer the phone for another person or group of people, as in a business office: *The **secretary** at school types letters for the principal and plans meetings for him.*

section • sections

A **section** is a part of something: *Zoe looked in the biography **section** of the library to find a book about President John F. Kennedy.*

see • saw, seen, seeing

1. To **see** means to use your eyes to look at something: *I can **see** some dark clouds in the sky, so I think it's going to rain.*

2. To **see** also means to find out or discover: *Ted heard a knock at the front door, so he went to **see** who it was.*

seed ▶ • seeds

A **seed** is a very small, hard part of a plant. If you put a seed in the ground, it can grow into a new plant: *We planted the **seeds** in the spring so that the flowers would bloom in the summer.*

Seeds fall from the pine cone.

seem • seemed, seeming

To **seem** means to look or be a certain way: *The new girl in our class **seems** to be quite shy.*

seesaw ▶ • seesaws

A **seesaw** is a piece of children's play equipment. It is a long plank of wood with seats at both ends so that when you sit on one end, the person on the other end goes up in the air.

Ravi carefully **selects** a cricket bat to play with.

select ▲ • selected, selecting

To **select** means to choose something or someone carefully: *The teacher **selected** the best drawings and put them up on the wall. Frank was really pleased, because his drawing was included in her **selection**.*

selfish

If someone is **selfish**, it means that they care only about themselves and not about other people: *Rhonda is very **selfish**—she never shares any of her toys with her little sister.*

The girls play on the **seesaw** in the park.

A B C D E F G H I J K L M N O P Q R S T U V W X Y Z

sell • sold, selling

To **sell** means to give something to someone for an amount of money: *My brother wants to **sell** his old car for a price of one thousand dollars.*

Lynette **sends** a message with her phone.

send ◀ • sent, sending

To **send** means to have something go from one place to another: *Dad always **sends** Grandma flowers on her birthday. I'm going to **send** an e-mail to my friend to tell her about a movie I just saw.*

sense • senses

A **sense** is one of the five special powers that your body has to know about the things around you. The senses are taste, touch, hearing, sight, and smell: *Robin has a cold today, so her **sense** of smell isn't very good.*

sentence • sentences

A **sentence** is a group of words that form a whole idea. Sentences start with a capital letter and usually end with a period.

separate • separated, separating

To **separate** means to keep apart or divide: *The teacher **separated** the class into two groups, boys on one side of the room and girls on the other.*

Shane looks **serious** while he listens to the teacher.

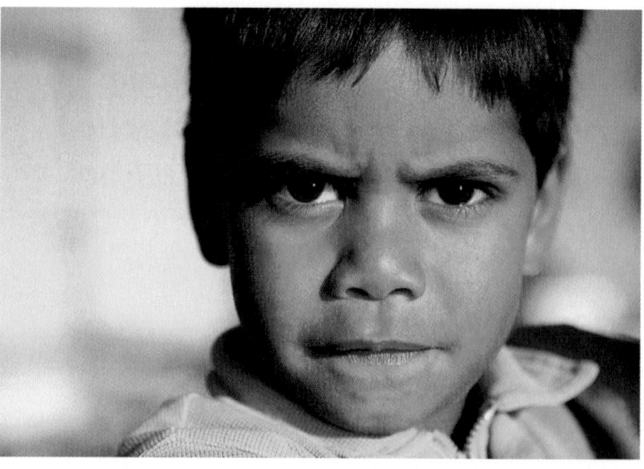

serious ▲

When you are being **serious**, you are thinking carefully about something and not making any jokes: *The school principal looked very **serious** when he called me into his office.*

serve • served, serving

To **serve** means to give food or drink to someone: *The restaurant **served** us some drinks while we were waiting for our dinner.*

There are twelve colors in this **set** of paints.

set ▲ • sets, set, setting

1. To **set** means to put something somewhere on purpose: *I **set** my knife and fork down on my plate after I had finished eating dinner.*

2. A **set** is a group of things that belong together: *I bought Dad a new hammer to add to his tool **set**.*

several ▼

Several means more than two but not a lot: ***Several*** *of my friends play on the same softball team that I do.*

There are **several** trees outside my mom's office building.

sew • sewed, sewed *or* sewn, sewing

To **sew** means to join together using a needle and thread: *My mother sewed the button back onto my shirt for me.*

shade • shades

1. **Shade** is a place away from the sun's light: *It was too hot to sit out in the sun, so we looked for a place in the* ***shade****. We found a nice* ***shady*** *spot under a big oak tree.*

2. A **shade** is also something used to block out light: *I have a* ***shade*** *over my window so that the sun doesn't shine in early in the morning.*

shadow ▶ • shadows

A **shadow** is a dark area of shade made when someone or something stands in the way of the sun or a light: *The huge tree made a long* ***shadow*** *across our whole backyard.*

shake • shook, shaken, shaking

To **shake** means to move backward and forward or up and down really quickly: *William was* ***shaking*** *the branch of the apple tree so hard that three apples fell off.*

shall

Shall means the same as WILL: *The rules of this game say that the person with the most cards at the end* ***shall*** *be the winner.*

In the late afternoon, the wolves make big **shadows**.

shampoo • shampoos, shampooed, shampooing

1. To **shampoo** means to wash your hair with a special liquid soap: *I **shampoo** my hair every morning to keep it clean and shiny.*
2. A **shampoo** is what you call the liquid soap that you wash your hair with: *Mom bought some new **shampoo** that makes my hair smell like strawberries.*

shape ▼ • shapes

The **shape** of something is the form of it: *Mom made my birthday cake in the **shape** of a football.*

We are going to make cookies in the **shapes** of people, stars, and trees.

share ▶ • shared, sharing

1. To **share** means to divide up something of yours and give some to someone else: *Pat **shared** her bag of candy with her two best friends.*
2. To **share** also means to use something together with others: *My sister and I **share** the same bedroom.*

shark ▶ • sharks

A **shark** is a large fish that lives in the ocean. Sharks have very sharp teeth, tough skin, and a fin that sticks out of their back. They get food by eating other fish and they sometimes attack people.

sharp ▼ • sharper, sharpest

1. If something is **sharp**, it is able to cut things easily: *Dad used a **sharp** knife to carve the roast turkey.*
2. You call something **sharp** if it has a pointed end: *I like to write with a **sharp** pencil.*

The cactus has **sharp** parts growing on it.

she

She is used when you are talking about a girl or a woman, or any female animal: *My mom said **she** wants to buy a kitten and that **she'll** be going to the pet store tomorrow. **She'd** like me come with her because **she's** letting me choose which kitten to buy.*

Paula **shares** a picture she took on vacation with her friends.

sharks

There are about 340 kinds of sharks. They can be as big as a school bus or as small as your hand. Some sharks hunt other sea animals, while others are not dangerous and eat only tiny sea creatures and plants.

a b c d e f g h i j k l m n o p q r s t u v w x y z

sheep ▶ • sheep

A **sheep** is a farm animal with a thick, heavy coat of wool. Sheep eat grass and are used for their wool and their meat.

sheet • sheets

A **sheet** is a large piece of cloth that you put on your bed to sleep on: *Mom put some clean **sheets** on the bed in the guest room, because Grandpa was coming to stay a while.*

shelf • shelves

A **shelf** is a flat, thin piece of board that you put things on. Shelves can be inside furniture, like a closet, or attached to a wall: *Georgia put her new books on the **shelf** next to her bed.*

shell ▼ • shells

A **shell** is the hard part that covers and protects something. Eggs and nuts have shells, and so do some animals like turtles and crabs.

shine • shone *or* shined, shining

1. To **shine** means to give out light: *We had a great time at the beach—the water was clean, and the sun was **shining** all day.*

2. To **shine** also means to make bright: *Mom **shined** her silver dish until it was bright and sparkling.*

The big **ship** carries lots of people.

ship ▲ • ships, shipped, shipping

1. A **ship** is a large boat that sails on the ocean. Ships can carry people or things from place to place: *Mom and Dad had a vacation on a cruise **ship** to Mexico.*

2. To **ship** means to send something to somewhere: *Grandma had her furniture **shipped** to her new home when she moved to Florida.*

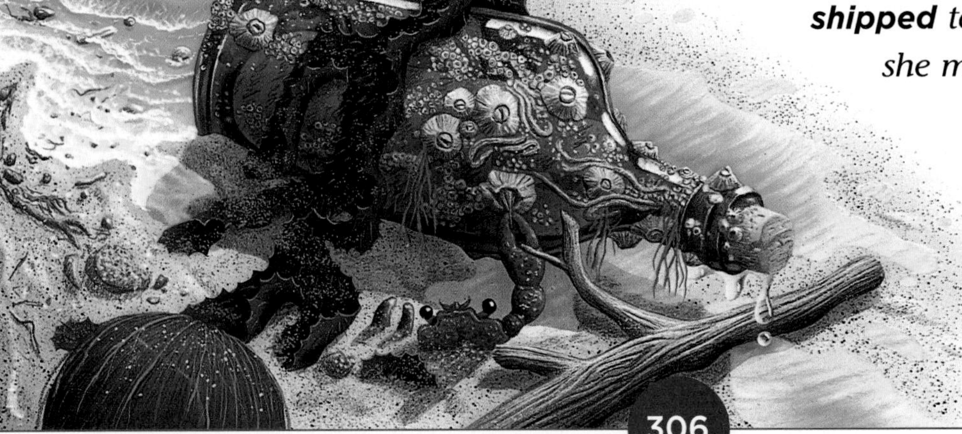

There are **shells** growing on the old bottle.

Matt wears a red and orange **shirt**.

shirt ◀ • **shirts**
A **shirt** is a piece of clothing that you wear on the top half of your body. Some shirts have collars or buttons or pockets on them: *Mom ironed my new* ***shirt*** *and pants for me to wear on the first day of school.*

shoe ▼ • **shoes**
A **shoe** is something that you wear on your foot to cover and protect it: *Josh put on his* ***shoes*** *before he went outside to play.*

My new **shoes** are soft and comfortable.

shoot • **shot, shooting**
1. To **shoot** means to make a bullet or arrow fly out from a weapon: *The farmer had to* ***shoot*** *his gun to scare off the wolf that was trying to eat his sheep.*
2. To **shoot** also means to try to get a goal in games such as soccer, hockey, and basketball: *When Matthew got the ball in front of the goal, the other boys on the team yelled "****Shoot!****"*
3. To **shoot** also means to come up or past quickly: *The race car came* ***shooting*** *past us as it went around the track.*

The ship got stuck in the sand near the **shore** many years ago.

shop • **shops, shopped, shopping**
1. A **shop** is a place where you can buy things that you need: *Debbie went to the grocery* ***shop*** *to buy some sugar.*
2. To **shop** means to go to stores to buy things: *I went* ***shopping*** *all day with Mom, but we couldn't find a dress we both liked.*

shore ▲ • **shores**
The **shore** is the land along the edge of the ocean, a lake, or a river: *We stood on the* ***shore*** *of the lake and waved at Dad on his sailboat.*

short • **shorter, shortest**
Short means not long or tall: *I am the* ***shortest*** *person in my family, and even my younger brother is taller than me.*

shot • **shot** *or* **shots**
1. The shooting of a gun or other weapon is called a **shot**: *First we heard the sound of* ***shots****, and then we heard the police cars coming.*
2. If you receive a **shot,** you receive medicine through a needle: *The doctor gave Ella a* ***shot*** *to stop her getting the flu this winter.*

should

Should means that you must do something: *You **should** phone me for a ride if you miss the bus—you **shouldn't** walk home by yourself.*

shoulder ▼ • shoulders

Your **shoulder** is the part of the body between your neck and your arm: *Mom carries her purse on her **shoulder**.*

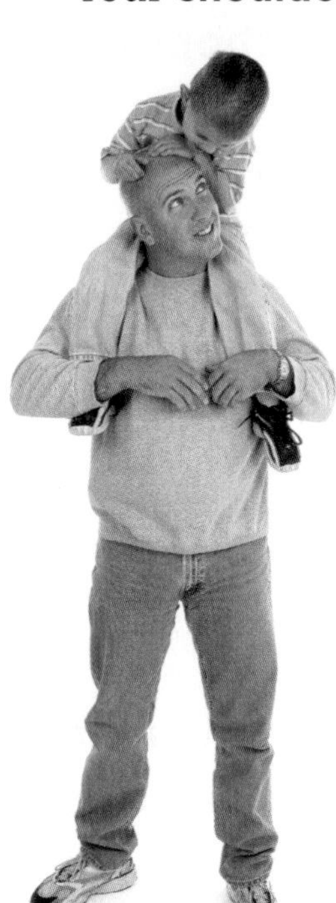

Dylan is on his dad's **shoulders**.

shout ▼ • shouted, shouting

To **shout** means to speak loudly: *I **shouted** out to my friend over the back fence to see if he wanted to come over and play.*

shovel • shovels, shoveled, shoveling

1. A **shovel** is a garden tool with a long handle. It is used for digging: *Dad used the **shovel** to dig some holes in the ground for the new plants.*
2. To **shovel** means to use a shovel to dig: *We spent two hours **shoveling** snow off the front steps of our house.*

The man **shows** some pieces of animal fur to people who might buy them.

show ▲ • shows, showed *or* shown, showing

1. To **show** means to let someone see something: *Xavier **showed** me the photos of his vacation in New York.*
2. A **show** is a program on television or radio, or something that you watch on stage: *Sabrina is singing in the school talent **show** this year.*

shower ▶ • showers

1. A **shower** is where you wash yourself. You stand under water that falls down on you: *Leanne likes to take a **shower** in the mornings before she goes to school.*
2. A **shower** is also a short fall of rain: *By the time I got my umbrella, the **shower** had already finished.*

To scare his enemies, the man **shouts** and carries a weapon.

shut • **shut, shutting**
To **shut** means to close something: *I **shut** the window because I was getting cold.*

shy • **shyer** *or* **shier, shyest** *or* **shiest**
When you are **shy**, you are not relaxed and may be a bit frightened when other people are around: *The new boy was too **shy** to come and play with us at recess.*

sick • **sicker, sickest**
When you are **sick**, you do not feel well: *I was **sick** with a cold and cough and stayed in bed the whole day.*

side • **sides**
1. A **side** is one part of something: *In this country cars drive on the right **side** of the road, but in England they drive on the left **side**.*
2. A **side** is also the edge or outside part of something: *Mom planted some tomatoes and beans in a garden on the **side** of our house.*

Our eyes have a power called **sight** that we use to look at things.

sidewalk • **sidewalks**
A **sidewalk** is a path for people to walk on the side of a road: *I don't like riding my bicycle on the road, so I ride on the **sidewalk** instead.*

sight ▲
1. **Sight** is your special power to see things: *Grandma's **sight** is not as good as it used to be when she was younger.*
2. **Sight** is also the area that you can see: *The police officers were hiding out of **sight** to surprise the robber.*

Almost everyone put up an umbrella when the **shower** started.

The **sign** warns people that there are bears in the area.

sign ▲ • signs, signed, signing

1. A **sign** is a special word or picture that tells you something important. Signs are used to tell us what something is, or where to go, or what to do: *There was a road **sign** to show us where we could cross the road safely.*

2. To **sign** means to write your own name on something: *I **signed** the letter to my friend and drew a smiling face under my name.*

signal • signals

A **signal** is something that tells you what to do. A signal can be a sound, a light, or an action: *The coach blew a whistle as a **signal** to start the game.*

silly ▶ • sillier, silliest

When you are being **silly**, you are being funny and foolish: *Dad looked **silly** dressed up in his Halloween costume.*

Gina makes us laugh when she is **silly**.

silver 

Silver is a shiny, pale gray metal that is valuable. Silver can be used to make jewelry, coins, knives and forks, and other things.

The tea pot is made of **silver**.

similar

People or things are **similar** if they are like each other in some way. They are not like each other in every way: *Rhona's dress was **similar** to Gail's, but Rhona's had a blue belt and Gail's had a red one.*

simple • simpler, simplest

If something is **simple**, it is easy to understand or use: *I finished my math homework quickly because it was so **simple**.*

since

1. **Since** means from a while ago until now: *I've had a bandage on my foot **since** I hurt it last week.*

2. **Since** can also mean because: *Frank didn't want to watch that movie, **since** he had already seen it twice before.*

sing • sang *or* sung, singing

To **sing** means to use your voice to make musical sounds: *I will be **singing** "Happy Birthday" at Grandma's seventieth birthday party. Everyone says that I'm a good **singer**.*

The woman **sits** in front of the man.

single

Single means only one: *There was a **single** piece of chocolate cake left, so I shared it with my sister.*

sink • sinks, sank *or* sunk, sunk *or* sunken

1. A **sink** is a bowl fixed to a wall in the kitchen, bathroom, or laundry area that you can wash things in. Sinks have faucets that are used to fill them with water, and a hole to let the water out when you are finished.
2. To **sink** means to fall slowly down into water: *The wind blew the toy boat over and we watched it **sink** to the bottom of the lake.*

sister • sisters

Your **sister** is a girl who has the same parents as you do: *I sometimes share my toys with my little **sister**.*

sit ▲ • sat, sitting

To **sit** means to rest with the bottom part of your body on something: *Dad was **sitting** down on the chair, watching the football game on TV.*

size ▼ • sizes

The **size** of something is how big or small it is: *I can't wear my mom's shoes because her feet are a bigger **size** than mine.*

skate • skates, skated, skating

1. A **skate** is a special shoe. Some skates have a metal blade on the bottom so that you can move on ice. They are called ice skates. Other skates have wheels on them so that you can move on the ground. They are called roller skates.
2. To **skate** means to move on skates: *We spent the whole afternoon **skating** on the frozen lake.*

skateboard • skateboards

A **skateboard** is a low, flat board with four wheels on the bottom. You can ride a skateboard by standing on it and pushing with one foot.

The buildings are different **sizes**.

ski • skis, skied, skiing

1. A **ski** is one of a pair of long, thin strips of wood or plastic that you attach to special boots when you want to move over snow or water: *We packed our **skis**, boots, and warm jackets for our ski trip.*
2. To **ski** means to move on skis: *Kylie **skied** all the way down the mountain without falling over in the snow. She practiced all day because she wants to become a better **skier**.*

skin • skins

Skin is what covers the outside of the bodies of humans and animals. Fruits and vegetables also have skin around them: *Some apples have red **skin**, and some have green skin.*

skip • skipped, skipping

1. When you **skip**, you move along by making small hops on one foot and then the other: *Karl **skipped** down the street all the way to the store.*
2. **Skip** also means to jump up and down over a rope that is turning over and over: *My sisters turned the rope while I **skipped** up and down.*

Steve likes to go **skiing** every winter.

skirt • skirts

A **skirt** is a type of clothing that women and girls wear and that hangs down from the waist. The bottom part of a dress is also called a skirt: *When she goes out at night, Mom sometimes wears a long **skirt** that reaches almost to the ground.*

skunk • skunks

A **skunk** is an animal with black fur, white stripes, and a bushy tail. Skunks make a very bad smell when they are frightened or angry: *My cousin Bruce has never seen a **skunk**, because he lives in Australia and skunks live only in America.*

sky • skies

The **sky** is what you see above you when you look up from the ground: *When the weather is nice, the **sky** looks blue, but when it rains, the sky looks gray.*

A snake's old **skin** peels off, and there is new skin under it.

sled ▶ • **sleds**

A **sled** is something made of wood or metal that has long, thin pieces of metal under it. You sit or stand on a sled to move across snow or ice: *In some places, big dogs pull **sleds** across the snow.*

Horses pull the **sled** across the frozen lake.

sleep ▼ • **slept, sleeping**

When you **sleep**, you are asleep. People usually are lying down and have their eyes closed when they sleep: *Most people **sleep** at night, but many kinds of animals sleep in the day and are awake at night.*

The puppy **sleeps** on the floor.

sleeve • **sleeves**

A **sleeve** is the part of clothing that covers your arms: *Mom told me to wear my blue shirt that has long **sleeves**, because I might get cold later.*

slide • **slides, slid, sliding**

1. When you **slide**, you move along or across something that is smooth or slippery: *The sled was **sliding** quickly down the hillside covered with snow.*
2. A **slide** is something children play on. They move from the top to the bottom along a slippery piece of metal or plastic: *There are two **slides** and three swings in the playground in the park.*

slip • **slips, slipped, slipping**

1. If you **slip**, you slide, but not on purpose. Sometimes if you slip, you fall down: *Penelope **slipped** and fell on the wet floor.*
2. A **slip** means a small piece of something: *Jerome wrote a note to his brother on a **slip** of paper.*

slipper • **slippers**

A **slipper** is a soft, flat kind of shoe that people sometimes wear indoors: *Dad wears **slippers** when he watches TV, because he says they are more comfortable than his work shoes.*

slippery

Something that is **slippery** is smooth and easy to slip on or slide on: *Don't walk on that **slippery** wet floor.*

slow • **slower, slowest**

Slow means not quick or fast. If you do something in a slow way, you do not hurry: *We went for a **slow** walk through the park yesterday. We walked **slowly** so that we could enjoy being outdoors for longer.*

small ▼ • smaller, smallest
Small means the opposite of large. If something is small, it does not take up very much space: *An elephant is a very large animal, but a mouse is a very **small** one.*

smart • smarter, smartest
Smart means being able to use your mind well. A smart person is able to understand things quickly or to think quickly: *She is a **smart** girl and gets good grades in all her classes. Our dog Trixie is very **smart** because she understands us when we speak to her.*

smell • smells, smelled, smelling
1. When you **smell** something, you feel it or have a sense of it through your nose: *We knew there was a fire down the street, because we could **smell** the smoke.*
2. A **smell** is something you feel or sense through your nose: *Many people love the **smell** of roses.*

Small birds pick insects off the rhinoceros.

smile ▼ • smiles, smiled, smiling
1. You **smile** when you turn up the corners of your lips and have a happy look on your face: *Peggy **smiled** when she saw her dog running to meet her.*
2. A **smile** means the way your face looks when you smile: *When Julie saw Charlie's friendly **smile**, she smiled back at him.*

The button has a big **smile** on it.

smoke
Smoke is the white, gray, or black gas that you can see or smell in the air when something is burning: *People in the city could see and smell the **smoke** from the fires in the forest.*

smooth • smoother, smoothest
Something that is **smooth** does not feel rough when you touch it. It feels even and without bumps: *Simone skated over the **smooth** ice on the frozen lake.*

snack • snacks
A **snack** is a small amount of food that you eat between one meal and the next: *Sometimes after school I have a small **snack** of crackers and honey.*

snake ▶ • snakes
A **snake** is a reptile that has a long body and no arms or legs. Snakes move by sliding along the ground: *Some **snakes** will bite you if they are angry or frightened.*

snakes

There are nearly 2,400 kinds of snakes. Some snakes grow to only 8 inches long, but others can grow as long as 33 feet. Many snakes have a poisonous bite that they use to kill the animals they eat.

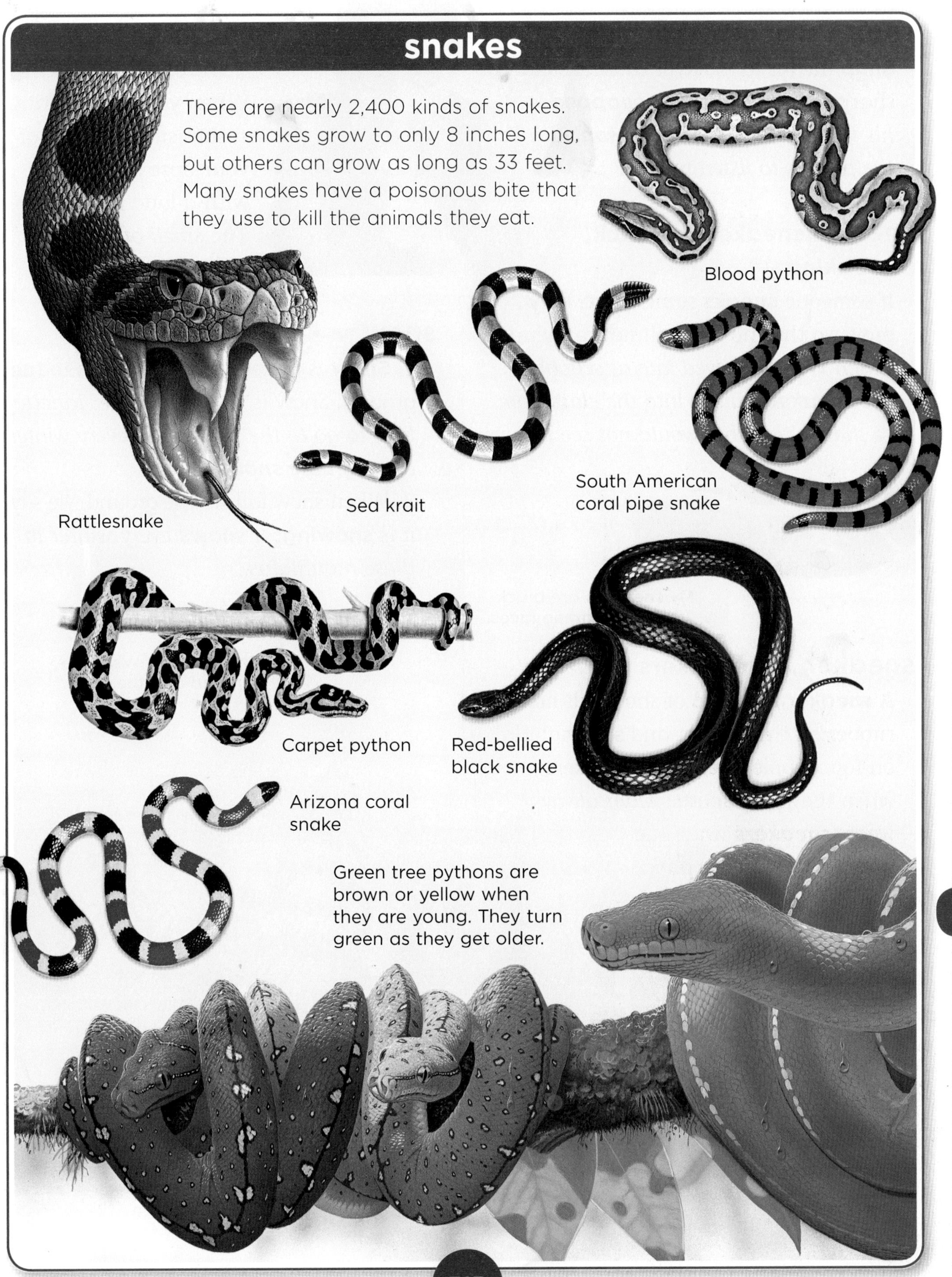

Green tree pythons are brown or yellow when they are young. They turn green as they get older.

You should cover your nose and mouth when you **sneeze**.

snap • **snapped, snapping**
Snap means to make or cause a sudden, sharp sound: *The coach* ***snapped*** *his fingers loudly when he wanted the players to listen to him.*

sneak • **sneaked** *or* **snuck, sneaking**
If someone **sneaks** somewhere, they move so that no one will notice them: *When Wendy arrived late at school, she* ***sneaked*** *quietly into the classroom so that the teacher would not see her.*

My **sneakers** are black with bright green laces.

sneaker ▲ • **sneakers**
A **sneaker** is a kind of shoe that has rubber on the bottom and soft material on top. People often wear sneakers when they play sports: *Mom always wears* ***sneakers*** *when she goes walking in the park.*

sneeze ◀ • **sneezed, sneezing**
When you **sneeze**, air rushes suddenly out of your nose and mouth with a loud noise: *The smell of pepper can make me* ***sneeze****.*

snow ▼ • **snowed, snowing**
1. **Snow** is frozen water that falls to the ground. Snow is soft and white: *Janette likes to go to the mountains every winter to ski on the* ***snow****.*
2. When snow falls to the ground, we say it is **snowing**: *It* ***snows*** *every winter in these mountains.*

Thick **snow** covers the ground and the trees.

snowman • snowmen

A **snowman** is a kind of figure that you make out of snow and that has the shape of a person: *When it snowed, Larry and Sonia made a big* ***snowman*** *in their backyard.*

so

1. **So** is another way of saying very, or a lot: *I am* ***so*** *happy that we are going on vacation tomorrow.*
2. You can also use **so** to show how much you feel something or are something: *I was* ***so*** *tired that I went to bed very early last night.*
3. **So** also means for that reason: *George was feeling cold,* ***so*** *he put on his sweater.*
4. Another meaning of **so** is also: *Eunice went to the game, and* ***so*** *did her brother.*

soap ▶ • soaps

Soap is something you use with water to wash yourself, your clothes, and lots of other things. Sometimes soap is in solid bars and sometimes it is a liquid: *I will need to use a lot of* ***soap*** *to wash all this dirt off my hands.*

Mary uses **soap** and water to wash her mom's car.

The men playing **soccer** run to get to the ball first.

soccer ◀

Soccer is a game played on a grass field between two teams of eleven players. The players use their feet, head, and any part of their body except their hands and arms to kick or strike a round ball into a goal.

Everyone is wearing striped **socks** with toes.

sock ▲ • socks

A **sock** is a piece of clothing that you wear under your shoe. If socks are short, they cover just your foot and ankle. Long socks can stretch almost up to your knees: *Henrietta wore bright red* ***socks*** *and shoes and a light green dress to the party.*

soda ▶ • sodas

Soda is a drink made with water that has bubbles in it and that has some kind of flavor added to it: *Gus likes* ***soda*** *with orange flavor.*

Lydia likes to drink her **soda** with a straw.

soft • softer, softest

1. Something that is **soft** is not hard. It is easy to bend it and change its shape: *The cushions on this chair are very **soft** and comfortable to sit on.*
2. We also use **soft** to describe something that is smooth and that feels nice to touch: *This woolen sweater feels **soft** when you touch it.*
3. Soft also means gentle or not loud or bright: *Sandra's voice is so **soft** that it is hard to hear what she is saying. The light from this lamp is very **soft**.*

Celeste has several **soft** teddy bears.

soldier • soldiers

A **soldier** is a person who is a member of an army. Soldiers sometimes fight in wars: *My grandfather was a **soldier** who joined the U.S. Army in 1965.*

The Greek **soldier** has weapons and wears armor for protection.

solid

If something is **solid**, it is hard and has a shape. It is not a liquid or a gas: *A brick is **solid**, but water is a liquid and is not solid.*

software

Software means the programs you use to control the way a computer works: *The **software** that we got with our new computer includes some great computer games.*

solar system

The Sun, Earth, the planets, the moons, and other things in space that move around the Sun make up the **solar system**: *Earth is one of the eight planets in the **solar system**.*

sold

Sold is a form of the word SELL: *Dan **sold** his old car and bought a new one.*

some

1. Some means a part or a section of something, or of a number of things: *Laura ate **some** of the cookies that she baked today and saved the rest for tomorrow.*
2. Some also means a number of things or an amount of something. Some does not tell you exactly how many or how much: *Beth's father gave her **some** money to buy her lunch.*

You use a ball to play **some** kinds of sports.

Bob and Karla have one **son**, whose name is Paul.

someone

When you say **someone**, you mean some person, but you do not say who that person is: ***Someone*** *forgot to shut the gate. Will* ***somebody*** *please go and shut it now?*

somersault ▼ • somersaults

When you do a **somersault**, you roll your body right over in a backward or forward direction. As you turn over, you bring your feet over your head: *We do* ***somersaults*** *when we go to the gym.*

Marlene does a **somersault** on the soft sand.

something

When you use the word **something**, you mean one thing, but you do not say what that thing is: *Holly is going to give Anna* ***something*** *for her birthday, but she won't tell us what it is yet.*

sometimes

Sometimes means some of the time, but not always: ***Sometimes*** *Arthur walks to school, but sometimes he rides his bike.*

somewhere

When you say **somewhere**, you mean in some place, but you do not say exactly where: *I lost my hat* ***somewhere*** *in the park.*

son ▲ • sons

A **son** is a male child of a mother or father: *Alberto Hernandez is the* ***son*** *of Mr. and Mrs. Hernandez.*

song ▼ • songs

A **song** is a piece of music with words that people can sing: *Joel is a very good singer and he knows a lot of* ***songs****.*

soon

Soon means before long, or in a short time: *Lunch will be ready* ***soon****.*

The words to the **song** are written under the music.

The man kneels and says **sorry** to the judge for doing something wrong.

sore • **sorer, sorest**
If something is **sore**, it hurts or causes pain: *Ben fell over when he was playing hockey and now he has a **sore** arm.*

sorry ▲ • **sorrier, sorriest**
1. If you feel **sorry** about something, you feel sad about it: *I was **sorry** that Luke was sick and couldn't come to my birthday party.*
2. **Sorry** is also what you feel or say when you feel bad about something you did wrong: *Hayley said she was **sorry** for being rude to her teacher.*

Kristin **sorted** the beads by color and shape.

sort ▲ • **sorted, sorting**
When you **sort** things, you put them into groups or into correct order: *I **sorted** my pencils by putting the red ones in one box and the blue ones in another.*

sound ▼ • **sounds**
1. A **sound** is a noise, or anything that you can hear: *I like the **sound** of rain falling on the roof.*
2. A **sound** is also one of the noises that you make when you talk: *The word "shore" starts with a "sh" **sound** and ends with an "or" sound.*

Perrin tries to hear the **sound** of Tom's voice with the string telephone.

soup ▼ • soups

Soup is a liquid food made by boiling vegetables, meat, or fish in water. You eat most soups when they are hot: *Chicken **soup** is my favorite kind, but Jeremy likes vegetable soup better.*

Tomato **soup** is thick and red.

sour • sourer, sourest

Something that is **sour** has a bitter, sharp taste or smell. Things that are sour often taste or smell bad: *Apples that are not ripe have a **sour** taste, and milk that has gone bad has a sour smell.*

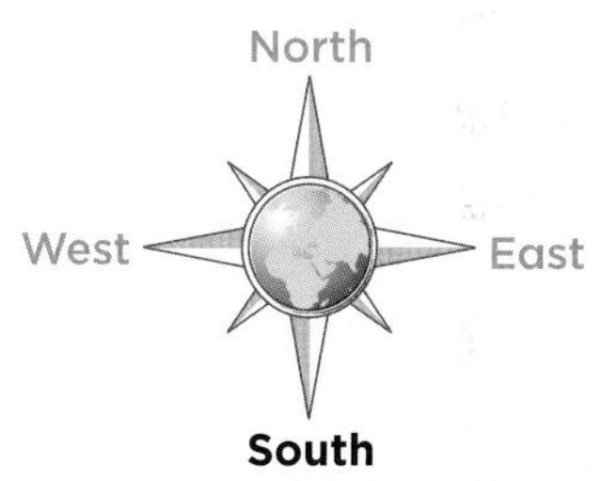

The compass shows the direction for **south.**

south ◀

South is a direction. If you look at the sun when it rises in the morning, south is on your right side. North, south, east, and west are the four main directions. The opposite of south is north: *If you look at a map, you will see that Florida is **south** of Georgia. It is one of the **southern** states of the United States.*

space ▼ • spaces

1. A **space** is an empty place or area that you can use in some way: *There is a **space** on the shelf where you can put that book.*
2. **Space** is also the huge area where everything in the Universe is: *There are huge numbers of stars in **space**.*
3. Sometimes we say **space** when we mean all of the Universe that is away from Earth: *You can use a telescope to look into **space** and see other planets.*

There are many stars in **space,** as well as clouds of gas.

a b c d e f g h i j k l m n o p q r s t u v w x y z

spacecraft ▼ • spacecraft

A **spacecraft** is a vehicle like an airplane that carries astronauts and their equipment into space: ***Spacecraft*** *travel through space at very great speed.*

spaghetti

Spaghetti is a kind of pasta that is made in long, thin strips. People often eat spaghetti with a liquid that has a tomato or meat flavor.

speak • spoke, spoken, speaking

Speak means to talk. You use your voice and you say words when you speak: *When I talk to my grandmother, I have to* ***speak*** *loudly so that she can hear me.*

There is something **special** for Taylor inside the package.

special ◀

If something is **special**, it is not normal and is different from other things: *As a* ***special*** *treat, Dad took me to see a baseball game last week.*

speech • speeches

1. Speech means the sounds you make and the words you use when you speak: *Our teacher said that people use* ***speech*** *to tell things to other people.*

2. If someone makes a **speech**, they talk about a subject, usually in front of an audience: *Jamie made a* ***speech*** *today at school about what he did during his last vacation.*

A satellite separates from the **spacecraft** as it flies above Earth.

The man on the sled is moving at a fast speed.

speed ▶ • speeds, sped *or* speeded, speeding

1. If you do something with **speed**, you move or act quickly: *Airplanes travel at great **speed**.*

2. The **speed** of something also means how fast it is moving or going: *The jet plane was flying at a **speed** of more than five hundred miles an hour.*

3. To **speed** means to move or to act fast: *The ambulance was **speeding** to the place where the accident happened.*

spell ▼ • spelled *or* spelt, spelling

When you **spell**, you put letters together to make a word: *My little sister can **spell** her name. With the letters "d," "o," and "g," I can **spell** the words "dog" and "god."*

The letters on the blocks **spell** the word "educate."

spelling • spellings

1. **Spelling** is the way that letters are put together to make a word: *"Cathy" and "Kathy" are two different **spellings** of the same name.*

2. **Spelling** is also a subject that you study in school to learn the right way to put letters together to make words.

spend • spent, spending

When you **spend**, you pay money to buy something: *My big brother is going to **spend** all the money he has saved to get a new car.*

spice ▼ • spices

A **spice** is something used to add flavor to food. Spices come from plants. Pepper is a kind of spice.

Each jar has a different kind of **spice** in it.

spiders

There are 35,000 kinds of spiders. A spider's body has two main parts. They have eight legs and many eyes. A spider's bite can be poisonous, but only 30 kinds of spiders are dangerous to people. Spiders hunt and eat small animals, especially insects. Many spiders trap insects in webs.

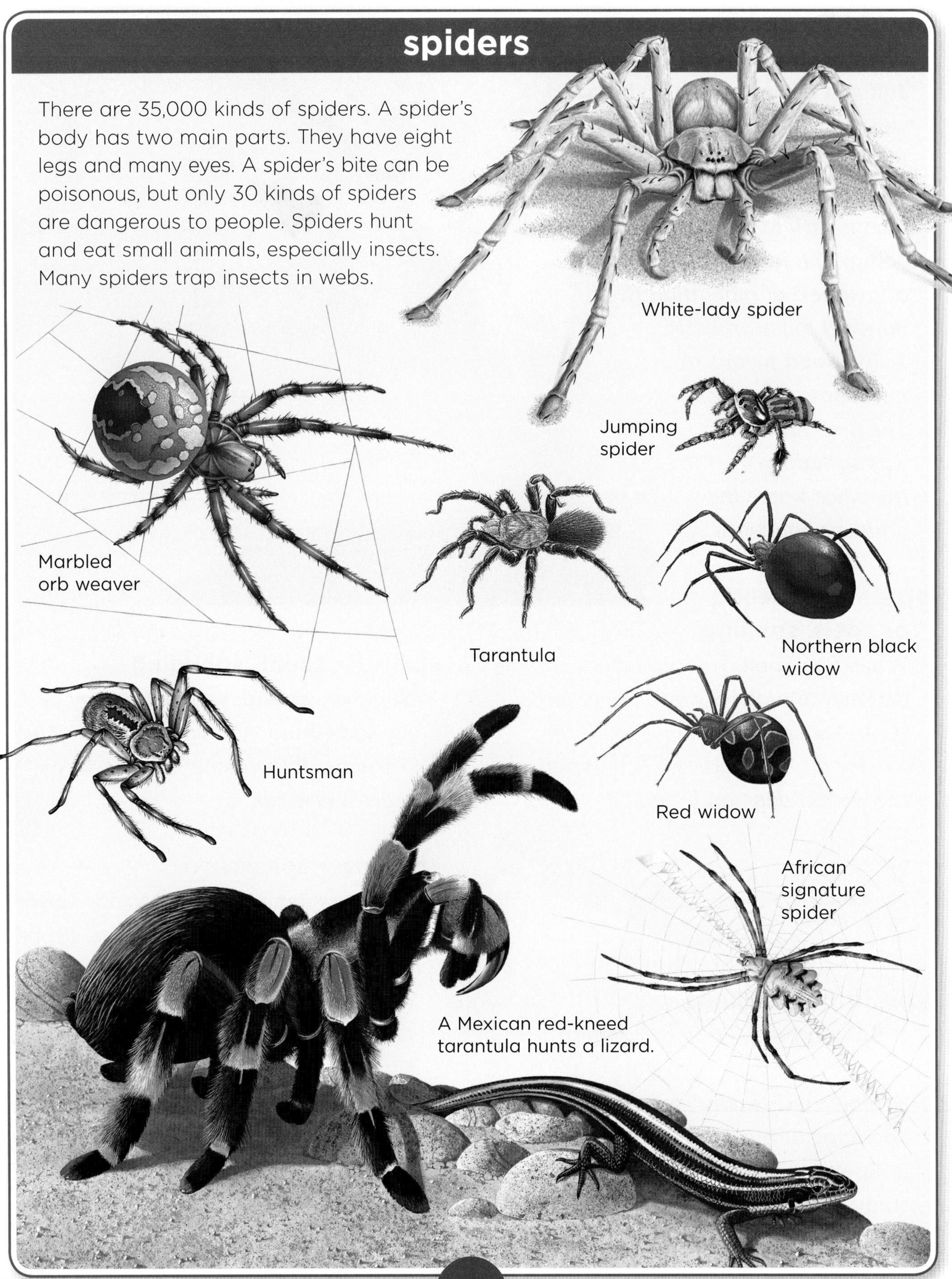

A Mexican red-kneed tarantula hunts a lizard.

spider ◀ • **spiders**
A **spider** is a small bug with eight legs: *A big **spider** made a web in the tree outside our front door.*

spill • **spilled** *or* **spilt, spilling**
When you **spill** something, you let it fall out: *I **spilled** the drink from my cup onto Grandma's new rug.*

spin ▶ • **spun, spinning**
When you **spin** something, you make it go around in a circle: *My brother can **spin** a basketball on his finger.*

splash ▼ • **splashed, splashing**
Splash means to make a liquid move around: *After Charlotte **splashed** paint onto the floor, the teacher helped her clean up the mess.*

The rockets on the toy **spin** around.

A snow leopard has **spots** on its fur.

spoon • **spoons**
A **spoon** is something you use to lift food to your mouth. A spoon is also used to stir food. A spoon has a handle with a small bowl at one end: *The restaurant gave us **spoons** to eat our ice cream.*

sport • **sports**
A **sport** is a game with rules. Baseball, hockey, basketball, and football are sports.

spot ▲ • **spots**
A **spot** is a small mark: *The clown had a red **spot** on each cheek.*

Dolphins **splash** as they leap out of the water.

During **spring,** peach trees have pink blossoms.

spring ▲ • springs

Spring is the time of year after winter and before summer: *In **spring**, the air gets warmer, the snow melts, and plants start to grow again.*

square ▶ • squares

A **square** is a shape that has four sides and four corners. The sides of a square are all the same.

If you put the little **squares** next to each other, you can make a big square.

squeeze ▶

• squeezed, squeezing

When you **squeeze**, you press hard on the sides of something:

*I **squeezed** the last bit of toothpaste from the tube onto my toothbrush.*

Jade **squeezes** her new toy dog.

squirrel ▶ • squirrels

A **squirrel** is a small animal with reddish-brown or gray fur and a big, bushy tail. Squirrels live in trees and usually eat nuts: *There are lots of **squirrels** in the park near our house.*

We watch the band play on the **stage.**

stage ▲ • stages

A **stage** is a place where people act, dance, sing, and make speeches in front of an audience: *Ethan was worried about having to walk out onto the **stage** for our school play.*

squirrels

Squirrels are common in North America. They eat nuts, fruits, seeds, insects, and leaves. They move about during the day. Flying squirrels have large areas of skin between their front and back legs that help them float from tree to tree.

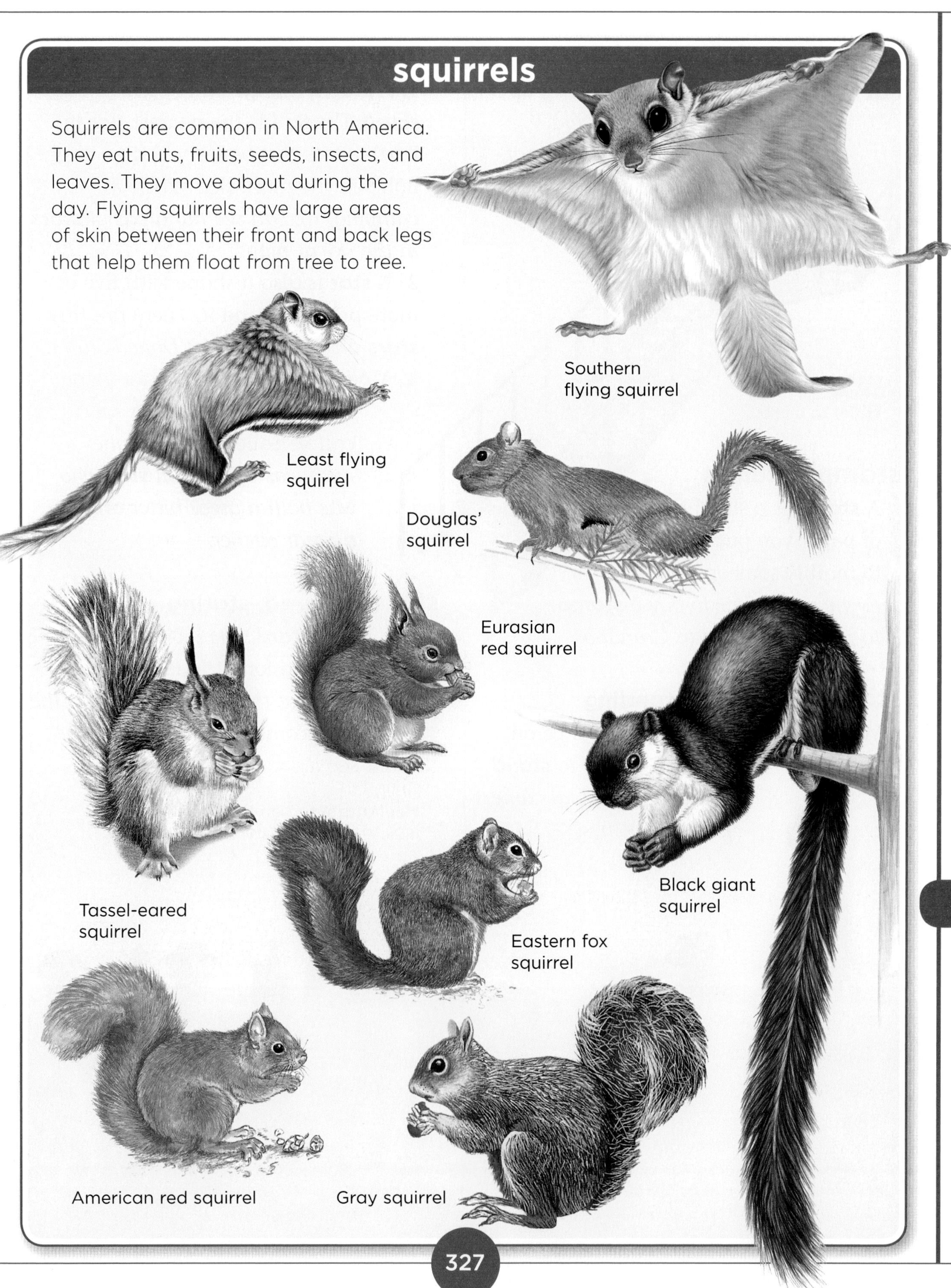

stair ▼ • stairs
A **stair** is one of many steps going up or down: *There are **stairs** in our house that go down to the basement.*

There are many **stairs** to climb.

stamp • stamps
A **stamp** is a small piece of paper you put on a letter to mail to someone: *We went to the post office to buy a **stamp** to put on our card to Grandpa.*

stand ▼ • stood, standing
When you **stand**, you get up to be on your feet: *The teacher asked us to **stand** when the principal came into the room.*

star • stars
1. A **star** is a huge ball of gas in outer space. The Sun is the nearest star to Earth. Stars can be seen as tiny, bright lights in the night sky: *When we go camping, we can see hundreds of **stars** in the sky at night.*
2. A **star** is also a shape with five or more points around it: *There are fifty **stars** on the flag of the United States.*
3. A person who is famous for being in movies or playing a sport can be called a **star**: *Babe Ruth was a baseball **star** who was both a great hitter and a great pitcher.*

stare • stared, staring
When you **stare**, you look at something carefully for a long time: *Oliver sat and **stared** at the tree, hoping that the bird would come out of its nest so he could see it.*

Meerkats **stand** on their back legs to watch for danger.

start • **started, starting**

1. When you **start**, you begin to do something: *Kate has **started** to learn to play the guitar. She had her first lesson last week.*

2. **Start** also means to make something happen: *Richard **started** the car by turning the key.*

state • **states**

A **state** is one certain area in a country: *Hawaii is one of the smallest **states** of the United States.*

station ▲ • **stations**

A **station** is a place used for one kind of work. People get on and off trains at the train station. Fire trucks are kept at fire stations. Television programs are made at a television station.

statue ▶ • **statues**

A **statue** is a piece of art in the shape of a human or animal. A statue is often made out of metal, stone, or clay: *In Washington, D.C., there is a famous **statue** of President Abraham Lincoln that is almost twenty feet high.*

stay ▼ • **stayed, staying**

1. When you **stay**, you do not leave somewhere for a while: *We **stayed** inside until the rain stopped.*

2. **Stay** also means that something goes on in the same way: *The store usually closes at 6 o'clock, but on Friday night they **stay** open until 9 o'clock.*

Bryce teaches his dog to **stay** in place.

steak • **steaks**

A **steak** is a thick, flat piece of meat or fish: *Dad cooked **steaks** on the barbecue for dinner.*

steal • **stole, stolen, stealing**

When you **steal**, you take something that belongs to someone else: *Steven always keeps a big lock on his bike because he is afraid someone might **steal** it. The man was sent to prison for **stealing** a car.*

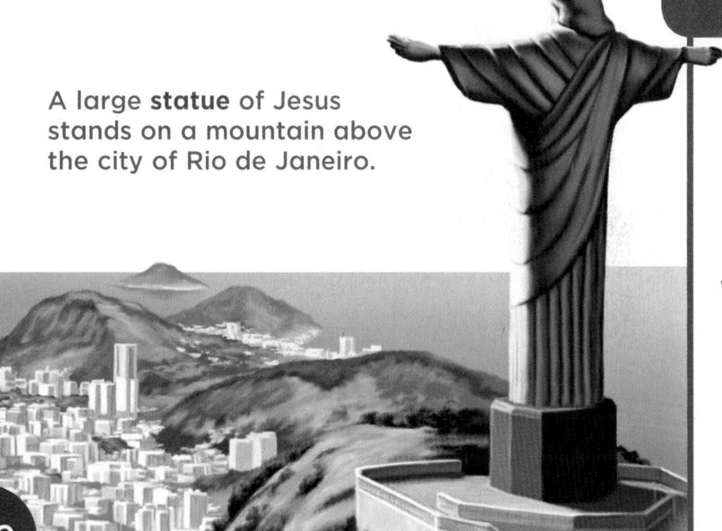

A large **statue** of Jesus stands on a mountain above the city of Rio de Janeiro.

Steam comes out of the train engine used in the Harry Potter movies.

steam ▲

Steam is made when water gets very hot and starts to boil: ***Steam*** *came from the pot when we cooked the noodles.*

steel

Steel is a strong, very hard metal: ***Steel*** *is used to make machines, cars and other vehicles, buildings, and bridges.*

steer • steered, steering

If you **steer** something, you make it go in the direction you want: *Dad* ***steered*** *the car over to the side of the road and then stopped it.*

stem ▲ • stems

A **stem** is the long, thin part of a plant that grows up from the roots. The stem of a plant holds the leaves, flowers, and fruits.

step • steps, stepped, stepping

1. When you **step**, you pick your foot up and put it down in another place: *Lucy slowly* ***stepped*** *over her dog to get out of the room.*
2. A **step** means a place to put your foot when you are going up or down: *There are four* ***steps*** *from our house down to our garage.*

stew • stews

A **stew** is a hot meal made by cooking meat or fish and vegetables together in a pot for a long time: *Mom always makes us lamb* ***stew*** *in winter.*

stick[1] ▼ • sticks

A **stick** is a thin piece of wood or a small broken branch from a tree: *Hugh gathered* ***sticks*** *to make the campfire.*

The flower has a long **stem**, so I can put it in a vase.

Fergus carries a **stick** in his mouth.

Some bees can **sting** people and hurt them.

stick[2] • stuck, sticking

1. **Stick** means to push a sharp thing into something else: *Joe kept **sticking** his fork into the meat to try to pick it up.*
2. **Stick** also means to make a thing stay on something else: *The teacher asked the class to **stick** the pictures they cut out of the magazines into their book.* If something sticks to things by itself, we say it is **sticky**.

still • stiller, stillest

1. **Still** means not moving: *We jumped into the **still** water of the lake.*
2. If a thing is **still** happening, it goes on and has not stopped: *Matt fell asleep last night with the TV on, and it was **still** on when he woke up in the morning.*

sting ▲ • stings, stung, stinging

1. A **sting** means a tiny cut made by an insect: *The pain of the bee **sting** made Jill cry.*
2. If an insect **stings** you, it makes a tiny cut on your skin.

stir ▶ • stirred, stirring

Stir means to mix by moving a spoon or stick around in something: *Mom **stirred** the soup in the pot.*

stomach • stomachs

Your **stomach** is a bag in your body where food goes after you swallow it: *My **stomach** is full of candy and soda.*

stone ▶ • stones

Stone means a rock or a small piece of rock: *We walked up the **stone** steps to the front door. Brad picked up a **stone** and threw it at the fence.*

The smallest **stone** sits on top of the others.

stool • stools

A **stool** is a seat with no back or arms: *The farmer sat on a low **stool** so that he could get the milk from the cow.*

Anna **stirs** the paint before she helps to paint the wall.

A B C D E F G H I J K L M N O P Q R S T U V W X Y Z

stop • stopped, stopping

When you **stop**, you no longer go or do something: *When the light turns red, the cars have to **stop**. The teacher told us to **stop** running inside the school building.*

store ▼ • stores, stored, storing

1. A **store** is a place to buy things: *Mom went to the **store** to buy some flour to make a cake.*
2. To **store** means to put away something to use later: *The squirrel **stored** nuts to have some to eat in winter.*

We **store** our photos in a box.

storm • storms

In a **storm**, it rains or snows. Sometimes in a storm, the wind blows hard and there is also thunder and lightning. When there are lots of storms, we say it is **stormy** weather.

story ▶ • stories

When you tell a **story**, you tell about something that has happened. A story can be true or it can be make-believe: *"Cinderella" is a famous **story** about a poor girl who marries a handsome prince. Ray told an exciting **story** about how his dad saw some men robbing the bank.*

stove • stoves

A **stove** is something that you use to cook food on or to make a room hot. Stoves use gas, electricity, or wood to make them hot: *Mom cooked soup on the **stove**.*

straight ▼ • straighter, straightest

If something is **straight**, it goes in one direction and does not bend or turn: *Use a ruler to draw a **straight** line. The teacher told us to sit up **straight**.*

The ships travel in a **straight** line.

Nanette reads her favorite **story.**

strange ▼ • stranger, strangest

Strange means odd or unusual. If something is strange, it is very different from what you expect: *In old stories, a centaur was a **strange** creature with the head of a man and the body of a horse. I thought it was **strange** that my friend walked right by without saying hello to us.* If you do not know someone and have not seen them before, that person is a **stranger** to you.

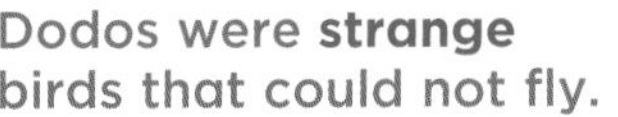

Dodos were **strange** birds that could not fly.

straw • straws

1. A **straw** is a thin tube for drinking a liquid: *Eve drank her apple juice with a **straw**.*
2. Straw also means the dry stems of some plants: *When the kittens were born, Liam made them a bed out of **straw** next to their mother.*

strawberry • strawberries

A **strawberry** is a sweet, juicy, red fruit: *We had **strawberries** and ice cream for dessert.*

stream • streams

A **stream** is water that is moving over the ground: *The boys spent hours looking for fish in the **stream**.*

street ▼ • streets

A **street** is a road in a town or city with buildings on both sides. Streets often have sidewalks.

People sell pictures along our **street** on Saturdays.

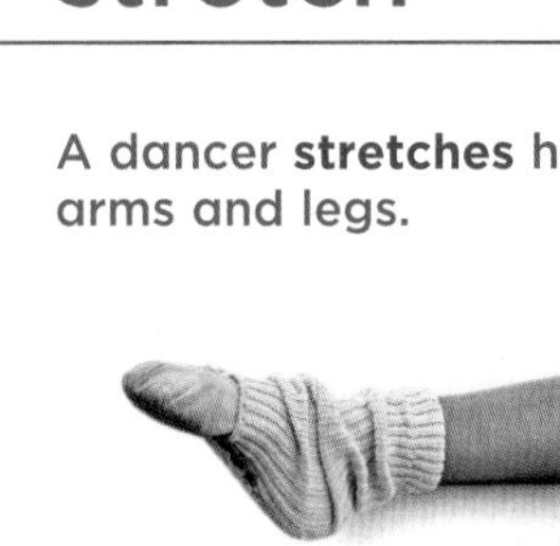

A dancer **stretches** her arms and legs.

stretch ▲ • stretched, stretching
When you **stretch** something, you make it longer: *My socks can **stretch** up to my knees.*

strike • struck, striking
If you **strike** something, you hit it: *I showed him how to **strike** the golf ball with the club.*

string • strings
1. **String** is a thin piece of rope: *I tied up the box with **string**.*
2. **String** also means a long, thin piece of other material. You use the strings to make music on instruments such as a guitar or violin.

strip • strips
A **strip** is a long, narrow piece of something: *Rowan used **strips** of colored paper to make a pattern.*

stripe ▼ • stripes
A **stripe** is a long band of color that looks different from the one next to it: *The American flag has seven red **stripes** and six white ones.*

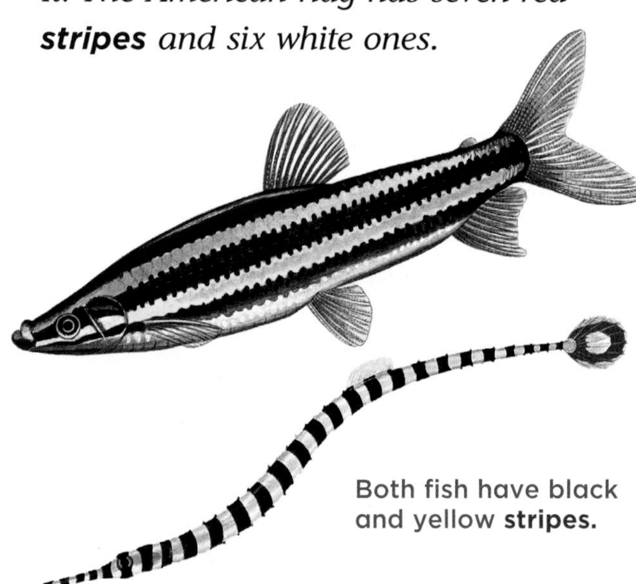

Both fish have black and yellow **stripes**.

strong ▼ • stronger, strongest
If you are **strong**, you have the power to lift or move heavy things: *Two **strong** men moved all our furniture into our new house.*

The **strong** elephants move heavy logs with their trunk.

stuck

Stuck is a form of the word STICK: *My foot got **stuck** on the bike pedal.*

student ▶ • students

A **student** is someone who learns things at school: *How many **students** does this school have?* Another word for student is PUPIL.

Wesley is a good **student** who likes to read books.

study • studied, studying

To **study** is to spend time learning about something or looking closely at it: *Michael **studies** the piano every day after school. My aunt is **studying** to become a doctor.*

stuff ▼ • stuffed, stuffing

1. **Stuff** is any kind of thing: *There is so much **stuff** in my room, it's hard to see the floor.*
2. To **stuff** means to put things into something until it is very full: *Malcolm **stuffed** all his socks into one drawer, but then he couldn't close it.*

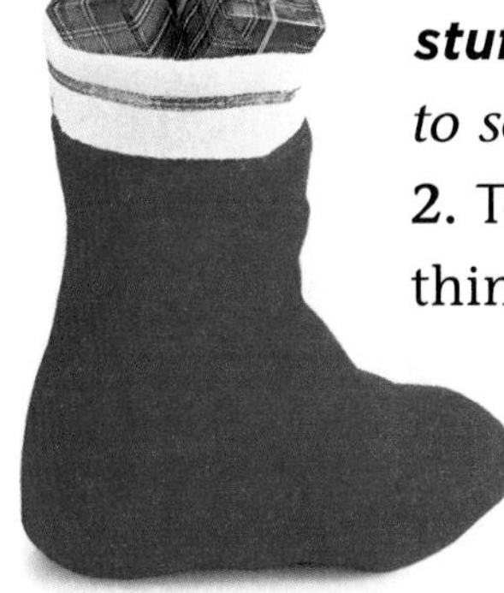

The stocking is **stuffed** with gifts.

subject • subjects

A **subject** is something that you are talking, writing, or learning about: *The **subject** of the song, "My Favorite Things" is things that make you happy. The **subject** Mr. James teaches us is* Computer Science.

submarine ▼ • submarines

A **submarine** is a type of boat that can travel under water as well as on top of it: *The sailors went below the deck of the **submarine** when it was about to dive under the water.*

The **submarine** comes up to the surface.

subtract • subtracted, subtracting

To **subtract** a number you take it away from another number: *If you **subtract** seven from ten, you get three. That kind of **subtraction** is not very hard.*

The **subway** train leaves the station.

subway ▲ • subways

A **subway** is a railroad powered by electricity that runs under the ground: *Mom and I went down to the **subway** station to catch the train.*

such

Such means very much: *That was **such** a funny TV show.*

sudden

Something that is **sudden** happens quickly and when you do not expect it: *A **sudden** bang upstairs made Sarah jump. Her brother **suddenly** ran in and told her he had thrown a ball through the window.*

We pushed on the **suitcase** to close it.

Some people put **sugar** on strawberries.

sugar ▶ • sugars

Sugar is a thing that is added to food or drink to make it taste sweet. Sugar comes from plants. It can be white or brown: *Patrick put some **sugar** in his coffee to make it sweeter.*

suggest • suggested, suggesting

To **suggest** is to give someone an idea to think about: *It was raining outside, so Grandpa **suggested** we play a board game. We liked his **suggestion** and we all played Scrabble together.*

suit • suits

A **suit** is a set of clothes with two parts that go together. A suit is usually made up of a jacket that goes with pants or a skirt: *Mom bought a new blue **suit** when she got her new job.*

suitcase ◀ • suitcases

A **suitcase** is a flat bag that is used to carry clothes and other things when you travel: *Leo packed his clothes in his **suitcase** for his plane trip to California.*

sum • sums

The **sum** is the number you get by adding numbers together: *The **sum** of five and five is ten. You can also write this as 5 + 5 = 10.*

summer ▼ • summers

Summer is the season of the year that comes after spring and before fall: *When we had our **summer** vacation at the beach, the weather was hot.*

Sun • Suns

The **Sun** is the closest star to Earth. It gives its heat and light to us. We can see it shining in the sky during the daytime: *Earth travels around the Sun.* This word is often spelled **sun**: *Yesterday there were lots of clouds and we could not see the **sun**. Today there are no clouds and it is **sunny**.*

In **summer,** Kim and her brothers like to go to the beach to swim and look at fish.

sunrise • sunrises

Sunrise is the time when the Sun can first be seen at the beginning of the day: *Jason got up just before **sunrise** to go on his trip and it was still dark.*

sunset ▶ • sunsets

Sunset is the time when the Sun goes down at the end of the day: *This evening at **sunset** the clouds in the sky looked pink with golden edges.*

Tanya buys vegetables at the **supermarket.**

supermarket ▲ • supermarkets

A **supermarket** is a large store where people take what they want from the shelves and pay for everything as they leave: *Dad and I went to the **supermarket** and bought food, fruit juice, and toothbrushes.*

supper • suppers

Supper is a meal at the end of the day. If you eat a big meal in the middle of the day and then have a lighter meal at night, that could be called supper instead of dinner.

Jen watched a beautiful **sunset** from the deck.

A B C D E F G H I J K L M N O P Q R S T U V W X Y Z

suppose • supposed, supposing

1. If you **suppose** something is true, you think it is true without knowing for sure: *I* ***suppose*** *Mom will let me have a party for my birthday.*

2. To be **supposed** to do something means you are expected to do it: *Graham is* ***supposed*** *to feed his pet hamster every morning, but sometimes he forgets.*

sure • surer, surest

If you are **sure** of something, you know it is right: *Peta was* ***sure*** *her father would like the picture she drew for him. He would* ***surely*** *put it up on the wall.*

surprise ▶ • surprises, surprised, surprising

1. A **surprise** is something that happens that you did not expect: *Mandy got a* ***surprise*** *when Jim jumped out from behind the curtain and said, "Boo."*

2. If you **surprise** someone, you do something they did not expect: *Phil* ***surprised*** *his mom by cleaning up without being asked.*

Tom **surprises** his cousin.

swallow • swallowed, swallowing

When you **swallow** food or drink, it goes down your throat to your stomach: *Henry had to* ***swallow*** *some medicine for his cold and he did not like the taste at all.*

When it flies, a **swan** steers with its tail.

swamp • swamps

A **swamp** is an area of low ground that is very wet: *I saw some birds standing in the mud looking for worms in the* ***swamp****.*

swan ▲ • swans

A **swan** is a large type of water bird that looks like a duck with a long, thin neck: *Two* ***swans*** *built their nest in the water on the edge of the lake.*

sweater • sweaters

A **sweater** is a piece of clothing you wear on the top part of your body to keep warm: *Karl wears a woolen* ***sweater*** *when it's really cold. He likes to wear his cotton* ***sweatshirt*** *when it's not as cold.*

sweep • swept, sweeping

To **sweep** is to clean the ground or a floor with a broom or brush: *Linda spent all morning* ***sweeping*** *the leaves off the path.*

sweet ▼ • **sweeter, sweetest**
Something is **sweet** if it tastes like sugar: *The strawberries I picked in the garden taste **sweet**.*

Fruits and fruit juice taste **sweet.**

swim • **swam, swum, swimming**
To **swim** is to move through water: *Rick watched his goldfish **swim** around its fish tank. Kerri kicked her legs and moved her arms to **swim** across the river. She is a good **swimmer**.*

swing ▶ • **swings, swung, swinging**
1. A **swing** is a hanging seat that you can swing backward and forward on: *Sumiko went as high as she could on the **swing** at the park.*
2. If you **swing** something, you move it backward and forward while you hold it at one end: *Roger was **swinging** his bat at the ball, but he kept missing it.*

synagogue • **synagogues**
A **synagogue** is a building where Jewish people gather together to pray: *Dena and Joel go to the **synagogue** every Saturday to pray and sing.*

synonym • **synonyms**
A **synonym** is a word that means the same or nearly the same thing as another word: *I didn't want to use the word "big" twice in my story about the lion, so I used the **synonym** "large" the second time.* An **antonym** is a word that means the opposite or nearly the opposite thing as another word: *The mouse in the story was "tiny," which is an **antonym** of "huge."*

system • **systems**
1. A **system** is a group of things that work together: *In our city's subway **system**, the trains usually come at the right time.*
2. A **system** is also a way of doing something that is organized: *Books in the library are put on the shelves using a **system**, so that they are easy to find.*

Caden pushes his sister on the **swing** to make her go higher.

table ▼ • **tables**

A **table** is a piece of furniture with legs that hold up a flat top: *Mitchell put the cereal and bowls on the* ***table*** *for breakfast.*

Eva sits on top of the **table** while playing chess.

tag

Tag is a game where a person who is "it" chases the other players. When the person who is "it" catches another player, that player becomes "it": *I couldn't catch Fred when we played* ***tag*** *because he is a fast runner.*

tail ▶ • **tails**

An animal's **tail** is a part of its body at the end of its back: *The pony moved its long* ***tail*** *from side to side to keep the flies away.*

William **takes** some candy without asking.

take ▲ • **took, taken, taking**

1. If you **take** something, you carry or bring it with you when you go somewhere: *It looks like it will rain, so* ***take*** *your umbrella when you go for a walk.*

2. Also, if you **take** something, it means you get hold of it: *I saw Gary* ***take*** *the last cookie from the jar.*

3. To **take** also means to have or use something: *After Tim got dirty, his dad told him to* ***take*** *a bath. Diane and her grandma are going to* ***take*** *a train to the city.*

4. Also, if you **take** something, you learn it or do it: *Karen* ***takes*** *dancing classes. John* ***took*** *a photo of a bird he saw in the yard.*

The whales raise their **tail** above the water.

tale ▶ • tales

A **tale** is a story: *Grandpa tells us **tales** about his life growing up on a farm.*

talk • talked, talking

When you **talk**, you use words and speak: *David is **talking** with his friend on the telephone.*

tall ▼ • taller, tallest

How high something is from the ground up is how **tall** it is: *Mom measured me and found I have grown to four feet and one inch **tall**.*

tame • tamer, tamest

A **tame** animal is quiet and not scared around people. Some tame animals have been trained to do as people say: *The **tame** birds flew down from the trees and ate seed from Evan's hand.*

tan • tanner, tannest

Tan is the yellowish-brown color some people's skin will have after they have been out in the sun for a long time: *After Nell went to the beach on vacation, her skin was **tan**.*

The children listen as their father tells them a **tale** about seeing a bear.

tap • tapped, tapping

If you **tap** something, you hit it in a gentle way: *Freya **tapped** her feet to the music.*

tape • tapes

1. **Tape** is a long, flat, narrow strip of cloth, paper, or plastic that is sticky on one side: *Nola used **tape** to stick the card to the present she wrapped for Janet.*

2. **Tape** is also a long, flat, narrow plastic strip that records sound and pictures: *Ted and Bill listened to a story **tape** in the car so they wouldn't notice the long trip.*

The giraffe is much **taller** than the two men.

a b c d e f g h i j k l m n o p q r s t u v w x y z

The woman aims at the **target** with her bow and arrow.

target ▲ • targets
A **target** is something that you try to hit: *In the story, Robin Hood hit the center of the* ***target*** *every time he shot an arrow at it.*

taste • tastes, tasted, tasting
1. The **taste** of something is its flavor: *That soup has a very spicy* ***taste****.*
2. If you **taste** a food or drink, you put a small amount of it in your mouth to find out what its flavor is like: *After Roland* ***tasted*** *the pie, he found he liked it, so he ate it all.*

tax • taxes
A **tax** is an amount of money that people pay to the government of their country, state, or city so that it will have money to do things for people: *The* ***taxes*** *people pay help the government build roads and hospitals.*

taxi • taxis
A **taxi** is a car with a driver that you pay to take you where you want to go: *Dad called a* ***taxi*** *to take us to the train station. When we got there, Dad paid the* ***taxicab*** *driver.*

tea • teas
Tea is a drink you make by pouring boiling water onto the dried leaves of a certain plant: *Polly poured the* ***tea*** *into Mandy's cup.*

teach ▼ • taught, teaching
When you **teach** someone, you help them learn how to do something: *Naomi's grandma is* ***teaching*** *her to knit a sweater.*

teacher • teachers
A **teacher** is a person who helps someone else learn something: *Our* ***teacher*** *helps us practice our writing every day. Cory's art* ***teacher*** *taught him how to make a clay pot.*

Long ago in Egypt, children were **taught** to write with a brush and ink.

Players on both **teams** jump up to try to catch the ball.

team ▲ • teams

A **team** is a group of people who play together on one side in a game: *Everyone on our **team** played their best in the basketball game.*

tear[1] • tears, tore, torn, tearing

When the word **tear** rhymes with "hair," it means you pull something apart: ***Tear** a piece of paper out of your notebook and I will write my address on it. When Judith fell over, she got a **tear** in her skirt.*

tear[2] • tears

When the word **tear** rhymes with "dear," it is a drop of salty water that comes out of the corner of your eye: *When Avril was listening to the sad story, **tears** came to her eyes. Wanda laughed so much at the clown, she had **tears** falling down her cheeks.*

tease • teased, teasing

To **tease** people means to upset them by making fun of them: *Everyone **teased** Roslyn when her shoe fell off in the race.*

teenager ▼ • teenagers

A **teenager** is a person who is between thirteen and nineteen years old: *When Jonathan turned thirteen last week he became a **teenager**.*

My sister is a **teenager,** and she is learning to drive a car.

teeth ▸

You say **teeth** for more than one TOOTH: *Omar is going to the dentist to have his **teeth** checked.*

telephone • telephones

A **telephone** is something you use to speak with someone who is a long way away. The sound of the voices travels between telephones by electric wires or by signals that go through the air: *Joshua's aunt lives in another city, so he called her on the **telephone** to wish her "happy birthday."*

telescope ▾ • telescopes

A **telescope** is something you use to look at things that are a long way off. It makes them look closer and bigger: *We set up the **telescope** in the backyard so we could see the planet Jupiter.*

Spencer looks at the sky through the **telescope**.

teeth

Different animals have teeth of different shapes. Most sharks have rows of sharp teeth to tear meat, and they are always growing new teeth. Horses and mice have pointed front teeth to cut through plants and flat back teeth for chewing.

Mouse

Horse

Shark

television • televisions

A **television** is something you watch and listen to programs on: *Gus watched his favorite cartoon show on **television**.* It is called a **TV** for short: *At 6 o'clock Dad asked him to turn the **TV** off and come eat dinner.*

The word part *tele-* means "far away" and *vision* means "seeing." **Television** allows us to see things that are far away from us. Another word like this is *telephone* ("sound from far away").

Greta **tells** Joy a secret.

tell ▸ • told, telling

1. To **tell** means to use words to give someone information: *Hank always **tells** his mom where he's going before he goes out.*
2. To **tell** also means to know and understand something: *I can **tell** Viola is happy because she is smiling.*

temperature • temperatures

The **temperature** of something is a measure of how hot or cold it is: *Today's **temperature** is cold and I don't think the snow will melt. Marty felt very hot, so his dad took his **temperature** with a thermometer.*

tennis

Tennis is a game that two or four people can play. The players score points by hitting a ball to each other over a net: *When Doug and Chen play **tennis,** they hit the ball hard and make it go fast.*

tent • tents

A **tent** is a place to live that is made of cloth held up by poles. Tents can be folded up and carried: *When we went camping, Ethan put up the **tent**.*

terrible ▾

1. Something **terrible** makes you afraid: *Bryce was scared by that book because it is about a **terrible** monster.*
2. Also, something **terrible** is very bad: *Elsa had a **terrible** pain in her ear so she went to the doctor.*

terrorist • terrorists

A **terrorist** is someone who kills or hurts other people, or has a secret plan to kill or hurt other people, as a way of fighting against a country or group that they hate: *The man who put the bomb in the shopping mall was a **terrorist**. He was caught and sent to jail for **terrorism**.*

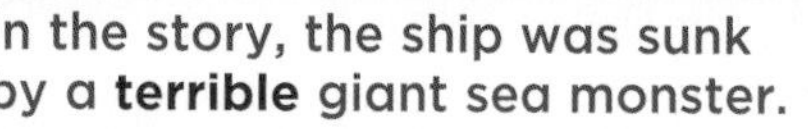
In the story, the ship was sunk by a **terrible** giant sea monster.

The girl points to the whale bones and says, "**That** whale was a huge animal."

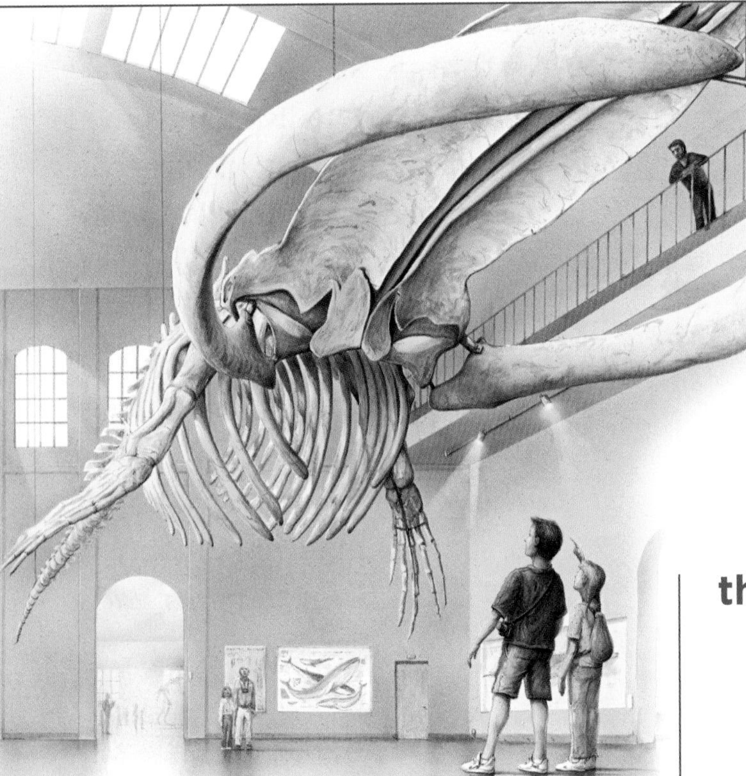

Thanksgiving

• Thanksgivings

Thanksgiving is a holiday in the United States. It is held on the fourth Thursday in November. On Thanksgiving, people give thanks for everything they have: *We had dinner for* ***Thanksgiving*** *at my grandparents' house.*

test ▼ • tests

When you do a **test,** you show how much you know by answering questions or problems: *Della got only one question wrong in her math* ***test***.

than

You use the word **than** when you talk about how things are different from each other: *Abraham can run faster* ***than*** *Neil.*

thank • thanked, thanking

When you **thank** someone, you tell them you are happy about something they have done for you: *Rick* ***thanked*** *his big brother for helping him with his homework.*

that ◀ • those

1. You use **that** when you are talking about one certain person or thing: *Mary likes* ***that*** *doll you gave her for her birthday.* ***That*** *dog across the street barks a lot.*
2. Also, **that** is used to talk about something farther away than another thing: *I don't want to read this book here—I want* ***that*** *one on the shelf.*
3. Also, **that** is used to tell why something is so: *The thunder was so loud* ***that*** *it woke me up.*
4. **That** is also used to begin something someone has said: *Mom said* ***that*** *I had to put away my toys.*

the

You use the word **the** when you talk about a certain thing, person, or group: *Nikki threw* ***the*** *ball to Sal.* ***The*** *children went to class when the bell rang.*

Millie and Edward are taking a history **test.**

theater ▼ • theaters

A **theater** is a building where you go to watch plays, movies, or other shows: *Betty's grandma took her to the **theater** to see the ballet.* This word is sometimes spelled **theatre**.

their

The word **their** is used to show that something belongs to some people or animals or things: *Jacob and Miles took **their** shoes off when they went inside. Our cats eat **their** dinner outside. That food bowl is **theirs**.*

them

You use the word **them** if you talk about more than one person or thing: *Tad picked up his toys and put **them** in the box. I wrote an invitation to Candice and Joe to ask **them** to come to my party. They said they would come by **themselves**.*

then

1. You use the word **then** to talk about something that happens after something else: *Will finished his homework, **then** he went outside to play ball.*
2. You also use **then** to talk about something that can happen instead of something else: *If you don't water the flowers, **then** they won't grow very well.*

there

1. You use the word **there** to talk about something in a particular place: *I left my wet umbrella over **there** by the door.*
2. Also, **there** is sometimes used to start a sentence: ***There** are twenty children in our class.*

Long ago, famous author William Shakespeare put on his plays in the Globe **Theater** in England.

A B C D E F G H I J K L M N O P Q R S T U V W X Y Z

thermometer ▼ • thermometers

You use a **thermometer** to measure how hot or cold something is. Some thermometers are made from a glass tube with numbers written along the side. Liquid inside the tube rises as it gets hotter and falls as it gets cooler: *The doctor used a **thermometer** to take Mason's temperature to check if he had a fever. The **thermometer** in our backyard said ninety-three degrees, which is very hot.*

Dad took my temperature with a **thermometer.**

these ▼

1. **These** is a form of the word THIS and is used when you are talking about people or things that are closer than something else: *Those red chips are worth five cents each in the game, and **these** blue ones here are worth ten cents.*
2. **These** is also used when you are talking about things that are here: ***These** girls in the picture are my sisters, Carmen and Ronnie.*

These books are very heavy.

they

You use the word **they** when you talk about more than one person, animal, or thing: *Megan and Hunter were arguing because **they** both wanted to play a game on the computer. Their mom said **they'd** have to finish their dinner before they could play. Our cousins Julian and Stella are coming to visit. **They'll** be arriving at 10 o'clock in the morning. **They're** staying with us for a week. **They've** been traveling for the last two days.*

Our dog has **thick** fur around its face.

thick ▲ • thicker, thickest

1. If something is **thick,** it is a long way from one side of it to the other: *This telephone book is **thick** because it has lots of pages.*
2. A **thick** liquid does not move easily and is hard to pour: *The honey was so **thick**, Jason had to use a spoon to get it out of the jar.*

thief • thieves

A **thief** is someone who steals things: *The **thief** was caught stealing jewelry from the queen's room.*

thin ▼ • **thinner, thinnest**
1. If something is **thin**, it is not far from one side of it to the other: *This shirt is made from **thin** cloth, so it is cool to wear in summer.* 2. A person or animal who is **thin** is not fat: *The pants Jackie tried on in the store were too big for her because she is **thin**.*

This house has many windows and several small towers on its roof.

thirsty • **thirstier, thirstiest**
If you are **thirsty**, you feel that you need something to drink: *When Archie went bike riding, he put a bottle of water in his backpack in case he got **thirsty**.*

thing • **things**
A **thing** is whatever you can talk about, think of, or do: *All the clothes and other **things** in the closet fell out onto the floor. To get the water to go on, you push down on this **thing** here. **Things** are much better for Grandma now that she is not sick anymore.*

think • **thought, thinking**
1. When you **think**, you use your mind to work something out: *It didn't take me long to **think** of the answer to the math problem.*
2. To **think** is also to have an idea in your mind about something or someone: *Do you **think** Stan will want to play ball with us? I **think** we should make a pie, not a cake.*

this ▲ • **these**
1. You use the word **this** to talk about something that is closer to you than something else: *I drew **this** picture, and my sister did that one on the wall over there.*
2. You also use **this** to talk about someone or something that is here: ***This** little girl is lost, so we should help her find her way home.*

those
1. **Those** is a form of the word THAT and is used when you talk about certain people or things: ***Those** woolen socks Mom bought me make my feet itchy. The teacher said that the trip is for fourth graders, and only **those** children will get to go.*
2. Also, **those** is used to talk about things that are farther away than other things: *I don't like these brown shoes—I like **those** black ones I saw in the other store.*

The flamingo has long, **thin** legs.

a b c d e f g h i j k l m n o p q r s t u v w x y z

The road goes **through** the large rock.

though

The word **though** means in another way or but: *Rita forgot her lunch money,* ***though*** *her mom had told her twice to take it. That puzzle was fun to do,* ***though*** *it was really hard.*

thought • thoughts

1. **Thought** is a form of the word THINK: *I* ***thought*** *I had left the door open, so I went back to check.*
2. A **thought** is an idea: *Andy told me his* ***thoughts*** *about what we could do for the school play.*

thread • threads

A **thread** is very thin string that you use when you sew: *Wayne sewed a button on his shirt with a needle and* ***thread****.*

throat • throats

Your **throat** is the front part of your neck. Food, drink, and air go into your body down the tubes inside your throat: *Shelby has a sore* ***throat*** *and finds it hard to swallow.*

through ◀

1. To go **through** something means to go from one end or one side to the other: *The sharp nail went right* ***through*** *the bottom of Gloria's shoe. The train went* ***through*** *the tunnel.*
2. When you are **through** doing something, you are finished: *I am* ***through*** *cleaning my room, so may I watch TV now?*

throw ▼ • threw, thrown, throwing

When you **throw** something, you use your hand and arm to make it go through the air: *In football, one way to score is to* ***throw*** *the ball to another player who takes it over the goal line.*

The girl wants to **throw** the ball to another player on her team.

During the game, Dan and Bonnie **tied** their cousin to the chair.

thumb ▼ • thumbs

Your **thumb** is the short, thick finger on the inside of your hand. It helps you pick things up.

thunder

Thunder is the deep, loud noise that you hear during a storm: *Looking out his window, Juan saw a flash of lightning and then he heard the sound of **thunder**.*

ticket • tickets

A **ticket** is a piece of card or paper that shows you have already paid for something: *Lyle and his mom bought **tickets** to ride on the bus.*

tickle • tickled, tickling

To **tickle** is to touch someone's skin lightly to make them laugh: *Molly couldn't stop laughing when Heidi **tickled** her toes.*

Freddy points his **thumbs** up to show that he is having fun.

tie ◀ • tied, tying

To **tie** is to hold or join something together with a string, rope, or ribbon: *Shelly **tied** her shoes. While we played ball, we used a rope to **tie** the dog to the fence so he wouldn't run away.*

tiger ▼ • tigers

A **tiger** is a large, wild cat. Most tigers have orange fur with dark brown or black stripes: *Carla learned that **tigers** hunt at night from watching a TV program.*

A **tiger** uses its claws and teeth to catch the animals it eats.

tight • tighter, tightest

1. Something that is **tight** is hard to move or make loose: *Hold on **tight** to the string of your balloon so it doesn't fly away.*
2. Clothing that is **tight** fits close to your body: *Peggy needs new shoes because her old ones are too **tight**.*

time • times

1. When you talk about **time**, you are talking about when something happens. Time is measured in seconds, minutes, hours, days, weeks, months, and years: *Davy looked at his watch and saw that the **time** was 6 o'clock.*
2. Time is also how long something takes to happen: *There isn't much **time** left before the show starts.*
3. Also, **time** is something that has happened to you: *Keiko had a good **time** when she went horse riding.*
4. Time is also how often something happens: *This is the second **time** I told him not to bother me. She took the driving test three **times** before she finally passed it.* When you multiply a number, you use the word **times**: *Five **times** two is ten.* Sometimes we use a **times sign** (**x**) instead: *5 **x** 2 = 10.*

tiny • tinier, tiniest

Something that is **tiny** is very small: *The baby has **tiny** fingers and toes.*

The **tips** of all the pencils are sharp.

tip ▲ • tips

The **tip** of a thing is its pointed end: *The **tip** of Toby's pencil broke off just before he finished drawing his picture.*

This truck has huge **tires** that make it tall.

tire ▲ • tires

A **tire** is a rubber ring that fits around the wheel of a car, bicycle, or truck: *When Elise's bike got a flat **tire**, she had to fill it with air again.*

tired ▼

If you are **tired**, you need to rest or sleep: *After Michelle helped her dad in the garden all day, she felt **tired**.*

tissue • tissues

A **tissue** is a piece of soft, thin paper that you use to wipe your nose: *Travis used a whole box of **tissues** when he had a bad cold.*

title • titles

A **title** is the name of a book, movie, song, or piece of music or art: *The **title** of Will's favorite movie is "Star Wars."*

Martin is too **tired** to finish his school work.

to

1. You use the word **to** when you are saying where something is going: *Max is going **to** the supermarket.*
2. You also use the word **to** when you are talking about something that you do: *I like **to** play drums in the school band.*
3. Also, **to** is used to mean on or against: *The honey stuck **to** Arlene's fingers. The leaves came off the tree and fell **to** the ground.*

toad ▼ • toads

A **toad** is a small animal that looks a lot like a frog. Toads spend more time on land than frogs do. Toads have rough, dry skin.

A leopard **toad** has brown spots on its skin.

toast

You make **toast** by cooking a piece of bread to make it brown: *I like warm **toast** with butter and strawberry jam for breakfast. I make my toast in the electric **toaster**.*

today

Today means this day: *I worked on my project all day yesterday because I have to hand it in **today**. We have a soccer game after school **today**.*

toe • toes

Your **toe** is one of five separate parts at the end of your foot: *Ned hurt his big **toe** when he was running. When I want to walk quietly, I walk on my **toes**.*

Paul and his dad build some shelves **together.**

together ▲

When things are **together**, they are with each other: *Grace and Libby went for a bike ride **together**. To make a cake, you mix **together** milk, eggs, sugar, and flour.*

tomato ▼ • tomatoes

A **tomato** is a soft, juicy, red fruit: *Ken cut up a **tomato** to put in the salad.*

The word **tomato** comes from a Native American name for this plant. They were the first to grow the plant, and other people learned about it from them.

There are tiny seeds inside **tomatoes.**

tomorrow

Tomorrow means the day after today: *Hannah is excited because **tomorrow** is her birthday.*

A B C D E F G H I J K L M N O P Q R S T U V W X Y Z

The chameleon catches an insect with its long **tongue**.

tongue ▲ • tongues

Your **tongue** is a part of your body that is in your mouth. It can move, and it helps you to taste, swallow, and talk: *Rodney licked his ice-cream cone with his **tongue**.*

tonight

Tonight is the night at the end of today: *I can't stay up late **tonight** because tomorrow is a school day.*

too

1. Too means also or as well as: *John liked the movie and Stuart did **too**.*
2. Also, **too** means something is more than you want or need: *It was **too** cold to go outside, so Jackie played inside. Raul had **too** many books to fit into his backpack, so he left some at home.*

tool ▼ • tools

A **tool** is something you use to help you do a job: *Mom got the hammer and some other **tools** to fix the closet door. Walt keeps the rake, shovel, and other garden **tools** in his garage.*

These are old building **tools**.

tooth ▼ • teeth

1. A **tooth** is one of the hard, white parts in your mouth. You use your teeth to bite and chew food: *My front **tooth** was very loose. It fell out when I was brushing my teeth with my **toothbrush**.*
2. A **tooth** is also one of a row of sharp parts on a comb, rake, or saw: *When Martha combs her hair, the knots get caught on the **teeth** of the comb.*

Heather cleans her **teeth** with a toothbrush.

top • tops

1. You are at the **top** of something when you reach its highest point: *There is snow on **top** of the mountain. We had to take the elevator to get to the **top** floor of the tall building.*
2. A **top** is also a cover: *I put the **top** back on the bottle of tomato juice.*

torn

Torn is a form of the word TEAR[1]: *Dean's pants were **torn** when he climbed over the fence.*

tornado▼ • tornadoes *or* **tornados**

A **tornado** is a storm with very strong winds that form a dark, spinning cloud shaped like a circle. A tornado moves over the land and can knock down or blow away anything in its way: *The **tornado** blew the roof off the house.*

toss • tossed, tossing

If you **toss** something, you throw it, but not very fast or hard: *Jamie **tossed** the empty box into the garbage can.*

touch • touched, touching

Touch means to put your hand lightly on something: *I **touched** the frog to feel how slippery its skin was.*

tow▼ • towed, towing

Tow means to pull something along behind you: *Their car got stuck in the mud, and a truck had to **tow** it out.*

The truck **tows** the car that broke down.

toward

If you go **toward** something, you go in the direction of it: *Dave ran **toward** the player with the ball to try to get it away from him. The teacher told everyone to move **toward** the front of the room.* This word is sometimes spelled **towards**.

tornadoes

Tornadoes are the strongest winds on Earth. These storms also have heavy rain, and lots of thunder and lightning. Tornadoes can travel up to 60 miles in one hour. Some states, such as Kansas, Missouri, Oklahoma, and Texas, have many tornadoes each year.

Tornadoes are strong enough to break apart buildings, rip trees from the ground, and carry heavy objects long distances.

Peter's favorite **toy** is a robot that walks when you turn the key.

towel • towels

A **towel** is a piece of soft cloth or paper that you use to dry wet things: *Maria washed her hands, then dried them with the **towel**.*

tower • towers

A **tower** is a tall, narrow part of a building, such as a church or a castle: *The queen's flag flew from the **tower** at the top of the castle.*

town ▼ • towns

A **town** is a place with lots of buildings where many people live and work. A town is smaller than a city: *Mandy's cousins live in a little **town** in Maine.*

toy ◀ • toys

A **toy** is a thing that children or animals play with: *Dolls, balls, puzzles, and bikes are all **toys**.*

trace • traced, tracing

To **trace** means to copy a picture. First you cover the picture with a piece of thin paper, then you follow the lines of the picture with a pencil. You can trace maps too: *We **traced** a map of Africa in geography class.*

track • tracks

1. A **track** is one of the long pieces of metal that the wheels of a train run on.
2. A **track** is also a mark left by an animal's foot: *The wolves left very clear **tracks** in the snow.*

This **town** by the sea has many interesting old buildings.

tractor • tractors

A **tractor** is a machine with big back wheels and a strong engine. Tractors are used for farm work or to pull heavy loads: *The farmer digs up the fields with his **tractor** before he plants the corn.*

trade • traded, trading

If you **trade** with someone, you give them something of yours and take back something of theirs: *Do you want to **trade** my baseball card of Barry Bonds for your Derek Jeter card?*

traffic

Traffic is all the cars, buses, and trucks that go along a road: *There was a lot of **traffic** on the road to the beach, so it took us over an hour to get there.*

trail • trails

1. A **trail** is a path through wild country: *The walking **trail** went a long way into the forest and crossed a river.*
2. A **trail** is also the marks, smell, or other signs left by an animal or person: *The hunters followed the **trail** left by the deer.*

trailer • trailers

A **trailer** is a vehicle that is pulled by a car or truck. It has wheels, but no engine. Some trailers are for people to live in, and some are for carrying things: *The car was pulling a **trailer** with a small boat on it.*

train ▼ • trains, trained, training

1. A **train** is an engine and a line of railroad cars that go along a railroad track. Trains carry people or things from one place to another: *Our teacher uses a **train** to get to school.*
2. To **train** means to teach a person or animal how to do something: *Mimi is **training** the dance group for the concert. My grandpa **trained** his parrot to say "That's all, folks."*

An electric **train** goes very fast.

trap • traps, trapped, trapping

1. A **trap** is something that is used to catch an animal or person: *We put cheese in the **trap**, but it didn't catch the mouse.*
2. When you **trap** something, you catch it in a trap: *The hunters **trapped** two raccoons in the woods.*

trash

Trash is all the things people throw away that they do not want any more, like food waste and old papers: *Dad puts the **trash** out on Monday night, and a truck from the city picks it up and takes it away on Tuesday.*

Crocodiles **travel** through water with only the top of their head above the surface.

travel ▲ • traveled, traveling

Travel means to go from one place to another: *Christina **traveled** to Mexico by airplane.*

treasure ▼ • treasures

Treasure is money, gold, jewels, or other things that are valuable: *The pirates buried their **treasure** on a desert island.*

treat • treats

A **treat** is something special that makes you happy: *We are going to the zoo as a **treat** for my birthday.*

tree • trees

A **tree** is a tall plant that has a trunk, branches, and leaves: *Marcie climbed up into the **tree** to hide from her brother.*

The old chest is full of **treasure.**

triangle • triangles

1. A **triangle** is a flat shape with three straight sides: *The roof of a house often looks like the shape of a **triangle**.*
2. A **triangle** is also a small musical instrument with three sides. It is made of metal, and it sounds like a bell when you hit it with a metal stick.

trick • tricks

1. A **trick** is something that you do to pretend or to make people think you have done something else: *I didn't really leave my sister behind at the park—I was only hiding from her to play a **trick** on her.*
2. A **trick** is also a special act that an animal or person must practice a lot to be able to do well: *The dolphin balances a ball on its nose and does other **tricks** too. The magician showed Jason how to do a card **trick**.*

tricycle • tricycles

A **tricycle** is like a bicycle, but it is easier to ride. It has two wheels at the back and one at the front: *Lizzie likes to ride her **tricycle** around the yard.*

trip • trips, tripped, tripping

1. A **trip** is when you travel from one place to another: *Mom has to take a **trip** to Chicago for her work.*
2. To **trip** means to fall over something: *Dave **tripped** over the dog and fell flat on his face.*

Nicholas is learning to play the **trumpet**.

trophy • trophies

A **trophy** is an award such as a cup or small statue. It is given to someone for winning a contest or game, or for doing something special: *Our team got a **trophy** for having the best team in our town's Little League.*

The **truck** is taking food to the supermarket to be sold.

trouble • troubles

1. **Trouble** is something that causes a problem. It can mean that something is hard to do, or that it is dangerous: *Grandma had to go to the hospital because she had heart **trouble**. The bus driver had **trouble** driving on the icy roads.*
2. You get in **trouble** when you have done something wrong and someone is angry or upset: *Mary got into **trouble** with her dad after she came home late.*

truck ▲ • trucks

A **truck** is a large motor vehicle. It is bigger and heavier than a car, and it is used to carry heavy things: *The **truck** delivered the load of bricks to our house.*

Elephants sometimes use their **trunk** to spray water over themselves.

true • truer, truest

If something is **true**, it is correct or it really happened. It is not false: *It is not **true** that the Moon is made of green cheese. Dad says the story in the newspaper is **true**, because he was there and saw what happened.*

trumpet ▲ • trumpets

A **trumpet** is a musical instrument made of metal. You blow into the long tube and sound comes out the other end: *Some people in the marching band play the **trumpet**.*

trunk ▼ • trunks

1. A **trunk** is the main or middle part of a tree that branches grow out from.
2. A **trunk** is also the long nose of an elephant that it uses to breathe and to pick things up with.

trust • trusted, trusting

Trust means to believe that someone is honest or that they will help you if you need them to: *Miguel let his friend borrow some money because he **trusts** him to pay it back.*

truth • truths

Truth is something that is true and that really happened. It is the opposite of a lie: *My parents taught me to always tell the **truth**.*

I used a test **tube** for the science experiment.

try • tried, trying
Try means to see if you can do something: *Sandra **tried** to open the door, but she couldn't because it was locked.*

tube ▲ • tubes
A **tube** is a long, hollow piece of glass, metal, rubber, or plastic. It is used to carry liquids or gases: *The science teacher filled the glass **tube** with water.*

tulip ▶ • tulips
A **tulip** is a flower that grows from a bulb. It is shaped like a cup: *Our garden is full of red **tulips** in spring.*

Turkeys fan out their feathers.

tuna • tuna *or* tunas
A **tuna** is a large fish that lives in the ocean. People eat tuna: *Dan ate a **tuna** sandwich for lunch.*

turkey ◀ • turkeys
A **turkey** is a large bird with a red neck and black and brown feathers. People eat turkey meat: *We are having **turkey** for Thanksgiving dinner.*

The **turkey** is a North American bird, but it gets its name from the country of Turkey. Perhaps turkeys from America were taken to Turkey to be sold, and people thought they came from there.

turn • turns, turned, turning
1. **Turn** means to move in a circle or in part of a circle: *To get to the park you **turn** right at the next corner. Jessie **turned** the handle to open the door.*
2. **Turn** also means to make something work, or to stop it working: *Mrs. Miller **turned** on the lights in the classroom in the morning. Please **turn** the TV off.*
3. A **turn** is a person's chance or time to do something: *It was Dave's **turn** to use the computer.*

Mom cut **tulips** from the garden and put them in a glass container.

turtle ▶ • turtles
A **turtle** is a reptile with a hard shell that covers its soft body. Some turtles live in water and some live on land: *A **turtle** pulls its head and legs inside its shell to protect itself from danger.*

twice
Twice means two times: *We rang the doorbell **twice** to make really sure that there was no one home.*

twig • twigs
A **twig** is a small, thin stick from a tree: *The bird made its nest from small **twigs**.*

turtles

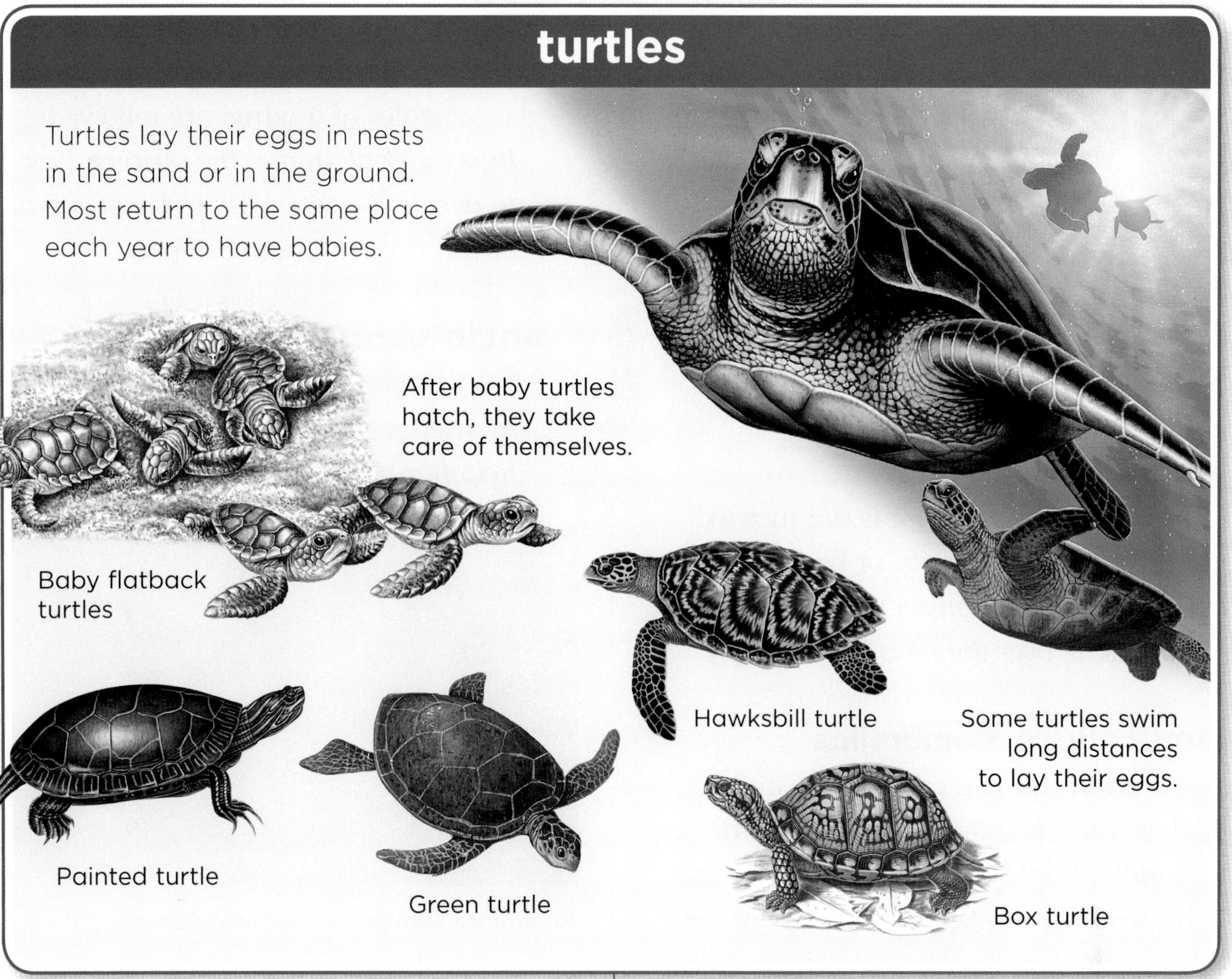

Turtles lay their eggs in nests in the sand or in the ground. Most return to the same place each year to have babies.

After baby turtles hatch, they take care of themselves.

Baby flatback turtles

Hawksbill turtle

Some turtles swim long distances to lay their eggs.

Painted turtle

Green turtle

Box turtle

twin • twins

A **twin** is one of two children who are born at the same time to the same mother. Some twins look the same, and some do not: *My two sisters have the same birthday and they're the same age because they are **twins**.*

type ▼ • types

A **type** of thing is a kind or sort of thing: *An eagle is a **type** of bird. What **type** of movie do you want to go see?*

People from different countries wear different **types** of clothes.

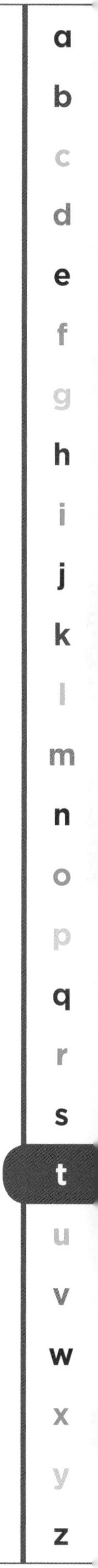

Jeremy's **umbrella** has several colors.

ugly • uglier, ugliest

If something is **ugly**, it is not nice to look at. It is not pretty or beautiful at all: *The green monster's mask with black bumps all over the nose is really **ugly**.*

umbrella ▲ • umbrellas

An **umbrella** is a circle of plastic or cloth on a frame with a stick in the middle. It folds up and down. You use an umbrella to keep off rain or protect yourself from the Sun: *Nearly everyone on the sidewalk put **umbrellas** up when it started to rain. Jackie sat in the shade under the beach **umbrella**.*

Umbrella is from *umbra*, an old word for "shade." The first umbrellas were used in hot weather to give shade from the Sun, and it was not until later that people used them to keep off the rain.

umpire ▼ • umpires

An **umpire** makes sure that the rules of a game are followed: *In a baseball game, the **umpire** has to decide if a pitch is a strike or a ball, or if a runner is safe or out.*

uncle • uncles

Your **uncle** is the brother of your mother or father: *Billy's **uncle** let Billy help him fix the car.*

An **umpire** stands behind the catcher.

under ▼

Under means in a place below something: *James looked for his shoes **under** the bed. Linda wore a blue shirt **under** her sweater.*

The pelican puts its head **under** the water to catch fish.

Mr. Jacobs helps Ralph **understand** the difficult math problem.

underline • underlined, underlining

Underline means to draw a line under words: *The teacher told us to **underline** the name of the story that we wrote.*

understand ▲ • understood, understanding

If you **understand** something, you know what it means: *The teacher explained the lesson twice to make sure we all could **understand** it. When I tell my dog "sit!" or "get down!" she **understands** what I am saying.*

uniform ▼

A **uniform** is a set of special clothes that you wear to show the job you do, the school you go to, or the team you play for: *My mom wears her nurse's **uniform** to work at the hospital.*

The marching guards are dressed in their **uniforms**.

Universe ▼ • Universes

The **Universe** is the whole of space. It includes the stars, Earth, planets, and everything else that is in it: *Scientists called astronomers study the **Universe** by looking through huge telescopes.*

Universe

The Universe has many galaxies, which are what big groups of stars are called. Our solar system, which includes the Sun, Earth, and seven other planets, is in a galaxy called the Milky Way. Astronomers take pictures of other parts of the Universe with special telescopes.

Solar system

Our solar system is a tiny part of the Milky Way galaxy.

The Milky Way

Galaxies

university • universities

A **university** is a place where you can learn after you leave high school: *You can study at a **university** to become a doctor, a lawyer, or a teacher.*

unless

Unless means except if something happens: *The game will be played at 2 o'clock today, **unless** it rains. I'll take you to the park, **unless** you don't want to go.*

until

Until means up to the time of something: *I can't have dessert **until** I eat all my vegetables. Jenny can't wait **until** her summer vacation starts.*

Hal cannot write his report **until** he collects the data he needs.

unusual

If something is **unusual**, it is not usual or common. It is different from what you expect: *This warm weather in March is very **unusual**.*

The motorcycle is **unusual** because it is covered in cloth that looks like fur.

This **university** in England was started about 800 years ago.

up

1. When you go **up**, you move from one place to a higher one. Up is the opposite of down: *The cat climbed **up** to the top of the fence.*

2. Up also means in, on, or at somewhere higher: *When Katarina looked **up** from the computer, she saw a spider on the wall.*

3. Sometimes, **up** means no longer in bed or not yet in bed: *I stayed **up** until 10 o'clock last night and now I have been up since 6 o'clock this morning.*

upon

Upon means on or on top of: *Patrick placed a book **upon** his head and walked slowly around the room.*

upset • upset, upsetting

1. If you **upset** something, you knock it over: *Charlie accidentally **upset** the bottle of juice and it spilled all over the floor.*

2. If someone is **upset**, they are nervous, unhappy, or worried: *Rachel was **upset** because she lost the bracelet her mother gave her.*

upside-down ▼

If something is **upside-down**, the top of it is where the bottom usually is, and the bottom is where the top usually is: *The picture on the wall of our classroom looks funny, because someone turned it **upside-down**.*

upstairs

Upstairs means on or to a higher floor of a building: *All the bedrooms in our house are **upstairs**.*

us

Us is one of the words we use when we mean ourselves: *We wanted to go to the beach, but Dad asked **us** to help him work in the garden.*

use • used, using

When you **use** something, you make it help you to do something: *Brian **used** a brush to paint his picture.*

When the sky is clear at night, we **usually** can see lots of stars.

usually ▲

If something **usually** happens, it happens most of the time: *It **usually** snows here at Christmas. Last Christmas the weather was warmer than **usual**, and there was no snow.*

People scream when they are **upside-down** on the ride.

Vv

vacation • vacations

A **vacation** is a time when people do not go to work or to school. When you are on vacation, you can go away from home to relax and enjoy yourself: *I think summer is the best time for a **vacation**.*

My family likes to go to the beach on **vacation**.

I got a **valentine,** but I do not know who sent it.

valentine • valentines

A **valentine** is a card with a message that a person sends to someone they love: *On February 14, my big sister Donna was surprised when she received a **valentine** from her special friend Shane. She had forgotten that it was **Valentine's Day**.*

valley • valleys

A **valley** is a low area that has mountains or hills around it: *When we walked through the **valley**, we looked up at the high mountains all around us.*

value • valued, valuing

1. If you **value** something, you like it very much and think that it is important: *We really **value** the time we spend visiting our grandparents.*
2. If something has **value**, it is important, or it costs a lot of money to buy: *Mom says that her jewelry has great **value**. Her diamond ring is especially **valuable**.*

The rivers from the mountains flow down into the **valley**.

van • vans

A **van** is a large or small truck that is usually covered at the back and that people use to move furniture, animals, or other things. Sometimes a van can have seats and windows and can carry people from one place to another: *When we moved to a new house, a large **van** came to take our furniture.*

vanilla

Vanilla comes from the seeds of a plant that grows in hot places. It is used to add flavor to some kinds of food: *I like ice cream with a **vanilla** flavor.*

They sell **vegetables** at the market.

VCR • VCRs

A **VCR** is a machine that you can use to watch a video or to make a copy of a television program onto a kind of tape that you put into the machine: *We made a copy of the football game that was on TV, and then we watched it later on our **VCR**.*

vegetable ▲ • vegetables

A **vegetable** is the part of a plant that is used as food. Beans, carrots, potatoes, and lettuce are vegetables.

Many **vehicles** are traveling on the road.

vehicle ▲ • vehicles

A **vehicle** is a machine that carries and moves people and things. Cars, trucks, and buses are vehicles.

verb • verbs

A **verb** is a word that tells you what a person, animal, or thing is doing or feeling. The words *run, see, jump, think,* and *play* are verbs.

very

Very means a lot of something: *I was happy to come in second in my race, but I would have been **very** happy if I had won.*

veterinarian ▼ • veterinarians

A **veterinarian** is a doctor for animals: *When a car hit our neighbor's cat, they took her to a **veterinarian**.* A short word for veterinarian is **vet**.

The **veterinarians** care for the dog.

A B C D E F G H I J K L M N O P Q R S T U V W X Y Z

vice president

A **vice president** of a club or an organization is a person who does the president's job when the president is away. The **Vice President** of the United States takes the place of the President when the President is very sick or cannot work.

video ▸ • videos

A **video** is moving pictures. You can watch videos on computers and televisions: *Dad made a **video** of our school play. When it was raining outside, we played **video games** on our computer.*

Jim films a **video** with his camera.

village ▾ • villages

A **village** is a small town: *We take a train from the city to the **village** where my grandparents live. Their village has only four stores.*

There are fields around the **village** in the mountains.

Orangutans can move through the forest by grabbing onto **vines** and branches.

vine ▸ • vines

A **vine** is a climbing plant with a very thin, long stem. Vines can grow on fences, walls, and trees: *Some fruits and vegetables grow on **vines**, such as melons, grapes, and pumpkins.*

violin • violins

A **violin** is a musical instrument. Violins are made of wood and have four strings. A violin makes music when you rub a long, thin piece of wood called a bow over the strings.

virus • viruses

A **virus** is a very tiny living thing that grows inside humans and animals and can make them sick: *Colds and flu are caused by **viruses**.*

visit • visited, visiting

When you **visit**, you go to see someone or something: *Rebecca and I **visit** our grandma every week. Grandma says we are her favorite **visitors**.*

vitamin • vitamins

A **vitamin** is something inside good foods that helps keep you from getting sick. People need vitamins so that their body will be healthy and will work in the right way: *Fruits and vegetables have lots of **vitamins**.*

volcanoes

Before volcanoes explode, they often give a warning by letting out a small amount of smoke or hot melted rocks, called lava. When there is a big explosion, a large area of land around the volcano can be covered with lava.

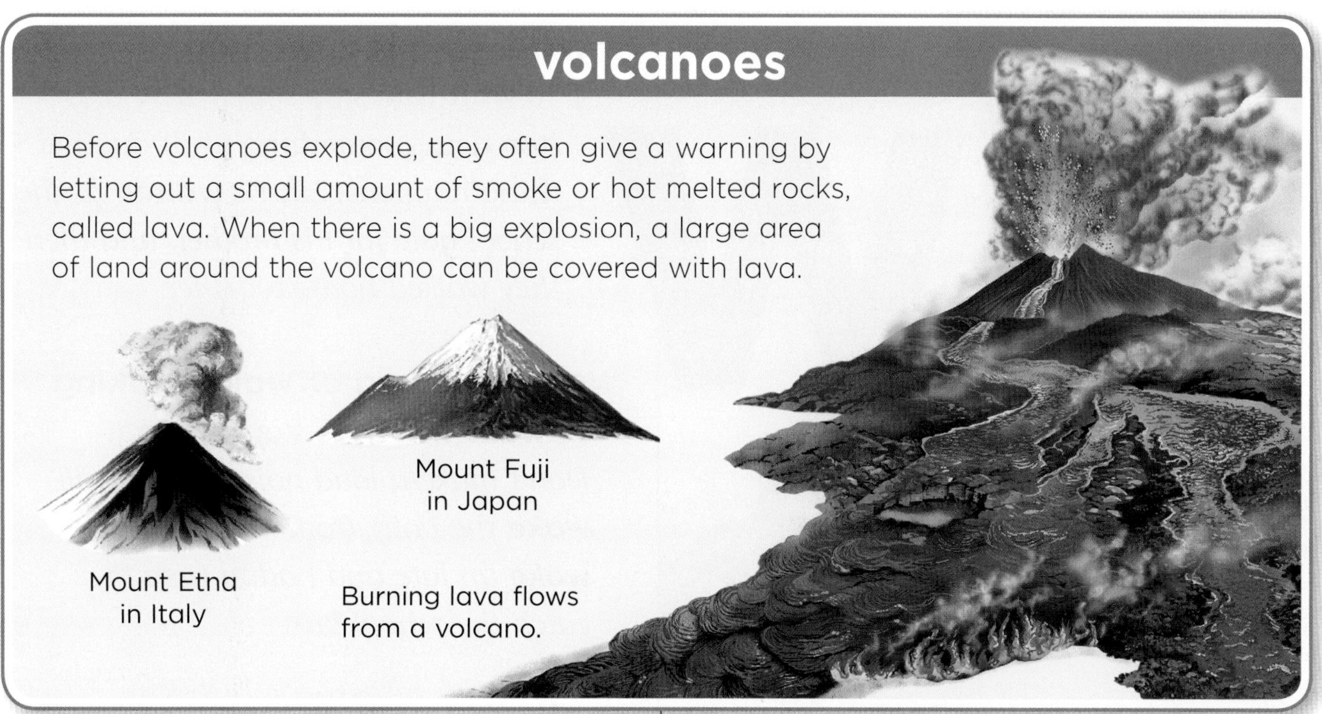

Mount Etna in Italy

Mount Fuji in Japan

Burning lava flows from a volcano.

vocabulary • **vocabularies**

Your **vocabulary** is all the words you know: *My teacher gives us a new word each day to add to our* ***vocabulary****.*

voice • **voices**

Your **voice** is the sound you make when you talk or sing: *When I had a cold, my* ***voice*** *sounded funny.*

volcano ▲ • **volcanoes** *or* **volcanos**

A **volcano** is a mountain with a hole at the top. Sometimes hot gas and melted rocks from inside Earth go up into the air from this hole: *Before the* ***volcano*** *exploded, all the people living near it moved away.*

The word **volcano** comes from the name *Vulcan*. He was the god of fire in the religion of the people in ancient Rome.

vote ▼ • **voted, voting**

When you **vote**, you choose which person or idea you agree with: *People all over the United States* ***vote*** *to pick the person who will be President for the next four years. In 1860 and 1864 the* ***voters*** *chose Abraham Lincoln to be President.*

Mom checked the box marked "yes" when she **voted.**

vowel • **vowels**

A **vowel** is a letter that is not a CONSONANT. The vowels in the English alphabet are *a, e, i, o, u,* and sometimes *y.*

Ww

In the past, Americans traveled in **wagons** across the country.

wagon ▲ • wagons

A **wagon** is a type of vehicle with sides and four wheels. Wagons are used to carry things: *Maggie put her toy dog in her little **wagon** and pulled it down the hall.*

waist ▶ • waists

1. Your **waist** is the narrow part of your body between your hips and your ribs: *Leanne pretended to be a pirate and tied a belt made of red material around her **waist**.*
2. Also, the **waist** of a piece of clothing is the part that covers the waist of your body: *The **waist** on these pants is too loose.*

Fran spins a hula hoop around her **waist**.

wait • waited, waiting

To **wait** is to stop somewhere or to stop doing something until another thing happens: *Harris **waited** at the school gate for his brother, and then they walked home together.*

wake • waked *or* woke, waking

To **wake** means to stop sleeping: *Don't make a loud noise, or you will **wake** the baby from his nap. Eric **woke** up late and had to rush to catch the school bus.*

walk ▼ • walked, walking

To **walk** is to move by putting one foot on the ground in front of the other foot: Alison and *Myra **walked** through the woods looking at flowers.*

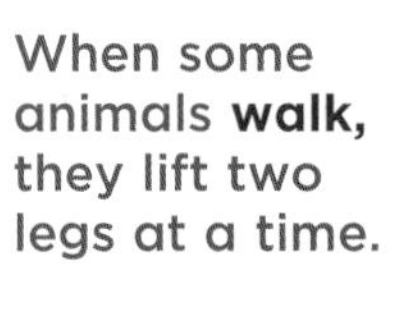

When some animals **walk**, they lift two legs at a time.

wall • walls

1. A **wall** is a side of a room: *Parker has a poster showing different whales on his bedroom **wall**.*
2. A **wall** can also separate one bit of land from another: *The stone **wall** around Grandma's garden has vines growing over it.*

want ▼ • wanted, wanting

If you **want** something, you would like to have it or to do it: *I **want** to buy a new computer game, so I have to save some money. Mandy **wants** to go to the zoo this weekend.*

Max is hungry and **wants** some food.

war ▼ • wars

War is a time when lots of people fight each other. Often two countries fight each other in a war: *The United States became a free nation after they won a **war** with Great Britain.*

warm • warmer, warmest

Something that is **warm** is not cold and has a feeling of heat without being too hot: *It was snowing outside, but in the house we were **warm** by the fire.*

The light **warns** ships of danger near the coast.

warn ▲ • warned, warning

To **warn** is to tell someone of something bad or dangerous that could happen: *The riding teacher **warned** Nicola not to walk behind the pony or it might kick her. She listened to his **warning** and walked in front.*

was

Was is a form of the word BE: *Bennet **was** the first runner over the finish line.* **Wasn't** is a shorter way of saying "was not": *Garth **wasn't** home when I called, so I left him a message.*

Soldiers in **wars** in ancient times often fought while riding horses.

Stephanie and Clayton help **wash** their father's car when it is dirty.

wash ▲ • washed, washing

To **wash** means to clean something with water and soap: *Gaby **washed** her doll's clothes in a bucket of water.*

waste • wasted, wasting

To **waste** something means to use more of it than you need to: *Don't **waste** electricity by leaving the TV on when you have finished watching it.*

Mom **waters** the garden to help the plants grow.

watch ▼ • watches, watched, watching

1. When you **watch** something, you look at it carefully for a while: *Brent **watched** some ants carry crumbs to their nest.*

2. A **watch** is a small clock that you wear on your wrist: *Natalie looked at her **watch** and saw that it was time to go home.*

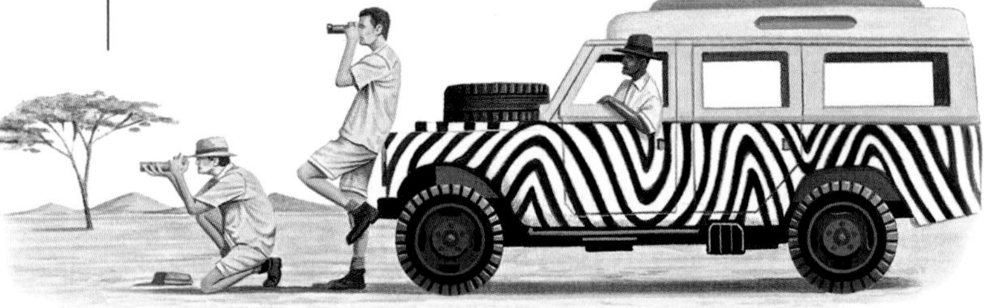

The men **watch** wild animals in the distance.

water ▼ • waters, watered, watering

1. Water is the clear liquid that falls from the sky as rain. The oceans, rivers, and lakes are made up of water: *When it was raining, the **water** quickly made puddles on the ground.*

2. When you **water** a plant or animal, you give it water: *I helped Grandma **water** her tomato plants.*

My sister and I have fun when **we** sing together.

wave • waves, waved, waving
1. To **wave** something is to move it up and down or from side to side in the air: *Hal **waved** good-bye to his dad from the bus as he left for camp.*
2. A **wave** is a part of the ocean that is going up and down as it moves along: *We had fun jumping in the **waves** at the beach.*

we ◀
You use the word **we** to speak about yourself and another or others with you: *Jane and I look alike because **we** are sisters. Our mom said **we'd** better come inside because it is starting to rain. **We'll** be going to our dance class this afternoon. We said **we're** too hungry to go just yet. **We've** got to eat something before we go.*

wax • waxes
Wax is something that is quite hard, but melts easily: *Candles are made of **wax** that melts as the candle burns.*

way ▼ • ways
1. How you do something is the **way** you do it: *The **way** you play a bongo drum is with your hands. Zane makes funny faces in **ways** that make me laugh.*
2. A **way** is also a path, road, or direction you take to get to a place: *This path is the **way** to the beach.*

Trees line the **way** through the country.

weak • weaker, weakest
1. Something that is **weak** could break or fall easily: *The old rope is too **weak** to hold up the swing anymore.*
2. Also, people or things that are **weak** are not strong: *The little kittens were too **weak** to stand up.*

weapon • weapons
A **weapon** is something that is used to fight with and hurt other people. A knife or a gun is a weapon.

wear ▶ • wore, worn, wearing
When you **wear** something, you have it on your body: *Julian **wears** his gloves, hat, and scarf in the snow.*

Sean **wears** a bright jacket and a helmet for safety.

weather

A weather report gives us information such as what the temperature is outside, if it is raining or snowing, and how stong the wind is blowing. Sometimes the weather changes very quickly.

In South America, the weather is often warm and there are many rain storms.

weather ▲

The **weather** is what is happening in the air outside. When you talk about the weather, you say what the sky is like and what the temperature is: *Today the **weather** is cold and cloudy, but I hope it will be a warm and sunny day tomorrow.*

The male spider climbs onto the female spider's **web.**

web ◀ • webs

A **web** is something that a spider makes from sticky, thin threads, to catch insects to eat: *A spider caught some flies in the **web** it made.*

Marissa and Angelo had a special cake made for their **wedding**.

wedding ▶ • weddings

A **wedding** is a special celebration where two people get married: *Ashley and Drew invited their family and friends to their **wedding**.*

weed • weeds, weeded, weeding

1. A **weed** is a plant that grows where it is not wanted: *Ingrid pulled the **weeds** out from around the flowers.*

2. To **weed** is to pull out plants you do not want: *Loretta helped her mother **weed** the garden to give the vegetables room to grow.*

week • weeks

A **week** is seven days in a row. The days of the week are Sunday, Monday, Tuesday, Wednesday, Thursday, Friday, and Saturday: *It has rained all **week**. Next Saturday and Sunday Dad wants to take us out on the boat, so I hope the **weekend** will be sunny.*

weigh • weighed, weighing

To **weigh** means to measure how heavy someone or something is: *Kathy **weighs** herself on the bathroom scale every morning.*

weight • weights

Weight means how heavy someone or something is: *The **weight** of this bag of potatoes is ten pounds.*

welcome • welcomed, welcoming

To **welcome** someone means to meet them in a friendly way when they have just arrived: *Grandma **welcomed** us with a big hug and a kiss.* Often people say "**you're welcome**" after you have thanked them for something.

well[1] • better, best

1. If you do something **well**, it means you do it in a good way: *Susie did **well** on her driving test and passed it the first time.*

2. Well also means being healthy: *My cousin was sick with a cold last week, but now she is feeling **well** again.*

well[2] ▼ • wells

A **well** is a deep hole that is dug to get water, oil, or gas from the ground.

The woman gets water from a **well**.

went

Went is a form of the word GO: *I **went** to the beach on Sunday.*

whales

Blue whales are the largest kind of whale, and they can be more than 100 feet long. All whales need to come to the surface to breathe air. Some whales are able to hold their breath and stay underwater for up to 20 minutes.

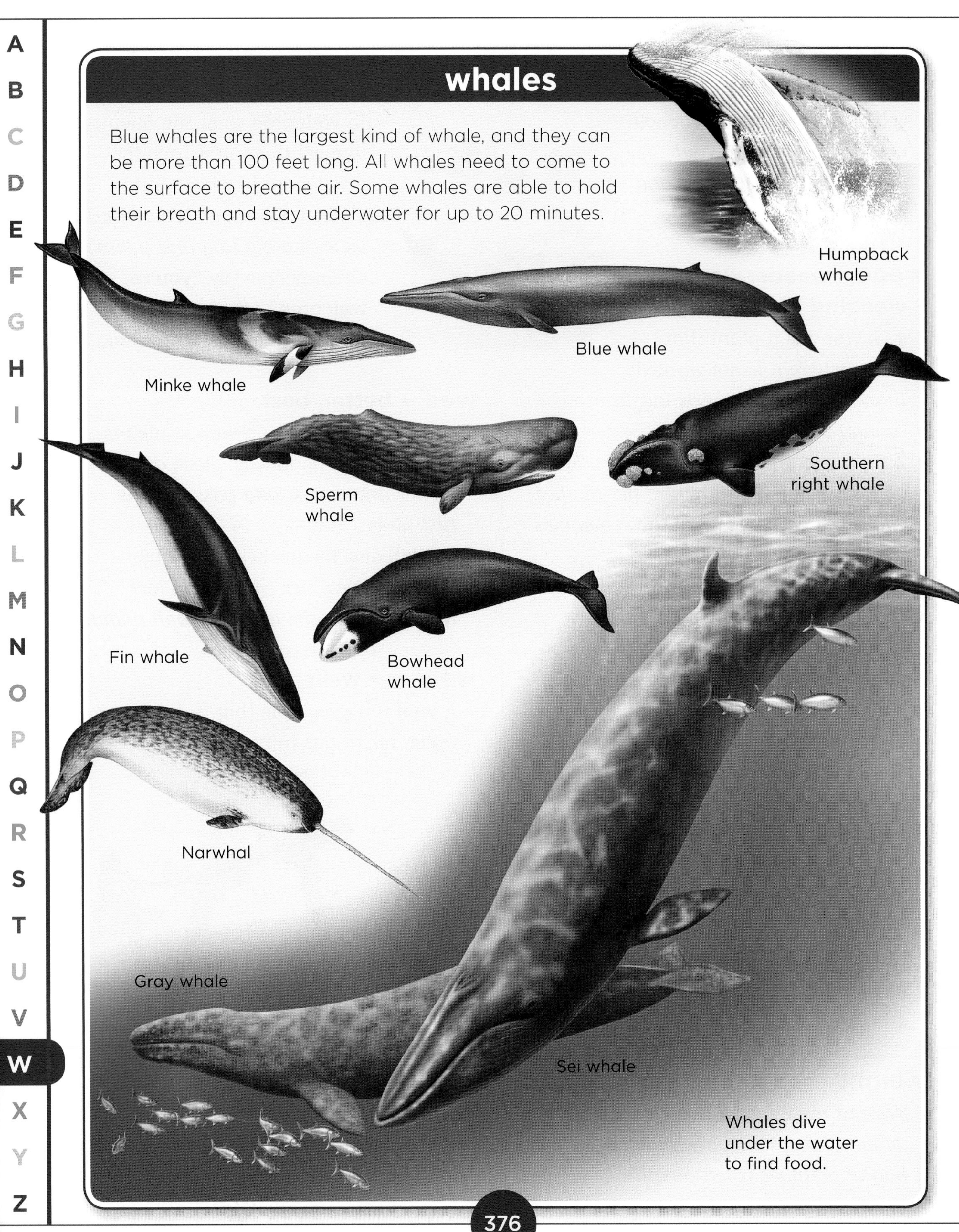

Whales dive under the water to find food.

Farmers use big machines to cut **wheat** in the field.

were

Were is a form of the word BE: *Mom and Dad **were** sad when my older sister went away to college.* **Weren't** is a shorter way of saying "were not": *They **weren't** happy because she had to go so far away.*

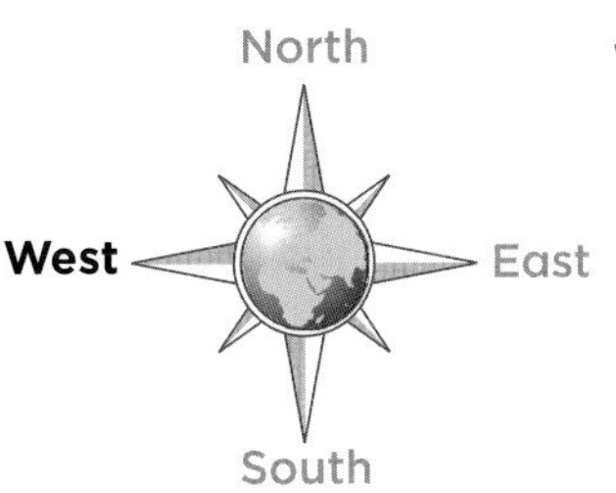

The compass shows the direction of **west**.

west ◀

West is a direction. If you look at the sun when it is going down at the end of the day, you are facing west. North, south, east, and west are the four main directions. The opposite of west is east: *The state of California is **west** of Arizona. Los Angeles is in the **western** part of the state, near the Pacific Ocean.*

The dog is **wet** after its bath.

wet ▶ • wetter, wettest

When something is **wet**, it is covered with water or another liquid: *Luke was really **wet** after he got caught in the rain without an umbrella.*

whale ◀ • whales

A **whale** is a very large animal that lives in the sea but is not a fish. Whales are mammals. They breathe air through a hole in the top of their head.

what

The word **what** is used when you want to ask questions about people or things: ***What** is your teacher's name? I didn't hear you—**what** did you say?*

wheat ▲

Wheat is part of a plant that is used for making flour. Wheat is used in many foods such as bread, cakes, and pasta.

Wheat comes from a word meaning "white" or "the white plant." This plant has white seeds and it is often made into flour, which is pure white in color.

wheel ▼ • wheels

A **wheel** is a round object made of wood, metal, or rubber with a hole in the middle. Wheels help things like cars, trucks, and bikes move over the ground.

The **wheel** will roll easily along the ground when you lift the handles.

Brendan plays basketball in his **wheelchair.**

wheelchair ▶
• wheelchairs

A **wheelchair** is a special chair with wheels. People who cannot walk use wheelchairs to move from place to place.

when
We use **when** if we want to know or say what time something happened or will happen: ***When*** *does the school play start? I was in first grade* ***when*** *my baby sister was born.*

where ▼
We use **where** if we want to know or tell about a place: ***Where*** *do you go to school? Be sure you put the cookies* ***where*** *the dog can't get them.*

whether
We use **whether** when we are trying to decide between two things: *I don't know* ***whether*** *I want to play in the park, or stay home and watch TV.*

Annika looks at a globe and finds **where** she will be going on vacation.

which
We use **which** when we want to know what one: ***Which*** *do you like better—basketball or baseball?*

while
1. While means during the time that something is happening: *Mom read a magazine in the waiting room* ***while*** *the dentist was cleaning my teeth.*

2. While also means a period of time: *We had to wait a long* ***while*** *at the airport.*

whisper • whispered, whispering
To **whisper** means to speak very softly: *We* ***whispered*** *quietly so that we wouldn't wake the baby.*

whistle ▶ • whistles, whistled, whistling
1. To **whistle** means to make a noise with your mouth by pushing your breath out of a hole you make between your teeth and lips: *I* ***whistled*** *and my dog came running back to me.*

This **whistle** makes a loud, high sound.

2. A **whistle** is a small pipe that you put to your lips and blow through to make a sound: *The referee blew a* ***whistle*** *for the game to begin.*

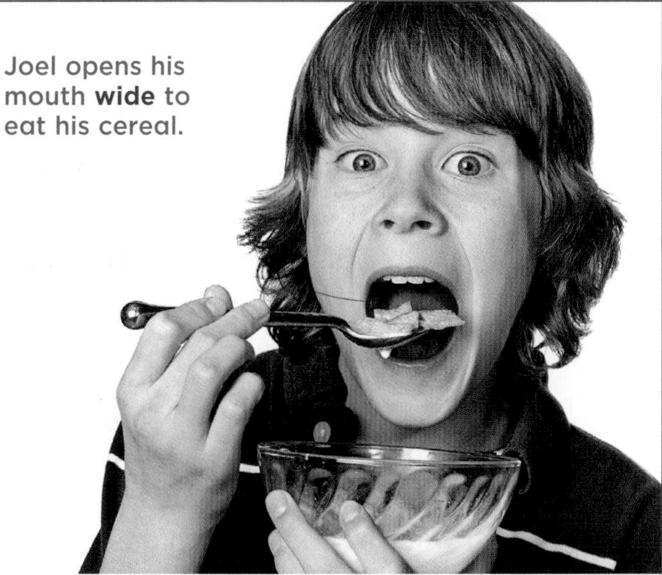

Joel opens his mouth **wide** to eat his cereal.

white • whiter, whitest

White is the lightest color. It is the color of milk and of snow.

who

We use **who** when we want to know which person: ***Who** is the star of that movie? Do you know?*

whole

When something is **whole**, it is complete with nothing missing: *Antonia and Felicity ate the **whole** chocolate cake by themselves. There was none left for Katherine.*

whose

We use **whose** when we want to know who the owner is of something: ***Whose** pencil is this? Is it yours?*

why

We use **why** when we want to know the reason for something: ***Why** isn't Patricia at school today? Is she sick?*

wide ◀ • wider, widest

Wide means having a large area from one side to the other: *The stream was too **wide** to jump over, so we walked across on the bridge instead.*

wife • wives

A **wife** is a woman who is married: *Mr. Robertson and his **wife** live next door to us.*

wild ▼ • wilder, wildest

Something is **wild** if it lives in nature without people to take care of it: *Tigers, elephants, and bears are **wild** animals that live in forests.*

Wild spider monkeys live in forests in Central and South America.

will

We use **will** when we say that we are going to do something later on: *I **will** finish my homework after dinner.*

win ▼ • won, winning

To **win** means to come first in something or to be the best at it: *Our hockey team is going to **win** the championship this year.*

wind[1] • winds

When the word **wind** rhymes with "pinned," it means the air that moves above Earth and blows things about: *At the beach, the **wind** blew sand in our face and all over our towels. It was a very **windy** day.*

wind[2] • wound, winding

When the word **wind** rhymes with "find," it means to make something work by turning a small handle around and around: *James watched Ted **wind** up the toy car to make it race across the floor.*

Betty is first across the line, so she **wins** the race.

Marcia opened the **window** to let in the cool breeze.

window ▶ • windows

A **window** is an opening in a wall for light and fresh air to come through. Windows are usually made of glass: *It was very hot in the house, so Diane opened a **window**.*

The word **window** comes from an old word meaning "eye of the wind." The glass of a window can look like an eye that opens to let in wind from outside.

The egret spreads its **wings** and flies away.

wing ▲ • wings

A **wing** is the part of an animal's body that is used to fly. Birds, bats, and insects have wings. Airplanes also have wings to help them lift off the ground and fly.

winter • winters

Winter is one of the four seasons in the year. Winter is the coldest season and comes between fall and spring.

wire • wires

A **wire** is a thin piece of metal that can be bent to make things like fences or cages. Wires are also used to carry electricity for things like telephones.

In the cartoon, the **witch** flies on a broom.

wise • wiser, wisest

When you are **wise**, you know a lot and you are able to decide what is the right thing to do: *Margaret was **wise** to go to bed early the night before her big race. A **wise** man named Henry David Thoreau once said, "Be true to your work, your word, and your friend."*

wish ▼ • wishes, wished, wishing

1. To **wish** means to really want something a lot: *I **wish** it were the last day of school today.*

2. A **wish** is something that you really want: *Billy closed his eyes and made a **wish** that he would get a new bicycle for his birthday.*

Simone **wishes** she could have a muffin now, but they are for the party.

witch ▲ • witches

A **witch** is a make-believe woman who has magical powers. In some stories, witches wear pointed black hats and can fly around on brooms.

with ▶

1. When you are **with** someone, it means that you are together in the same place, or that you are doing something together: *Gina watched TV **with** her brother Louis.*

2. With also means using something: *Dad cut the dead branch off the old tree **with** a saw.*

The man dances **with** the woman.

3. With can also mean having something: *The woman **with** the red hair is my teacher.*

without

Without means not having something: *I shared my sandwich with my friend Sophia, because she had come to school **without** her lunch.*

wolves

There are many kinds of wolves. Gray wolves hunt in large groups called packs. Together they can kill animals as big as a moose. Other wolves, such as the red wolf, hunt in smaller groups. Maned wolves usually chase small animals by themselves.

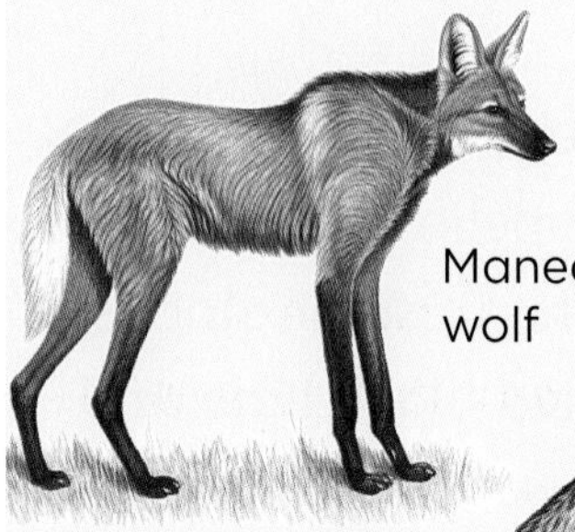

Maned wolf

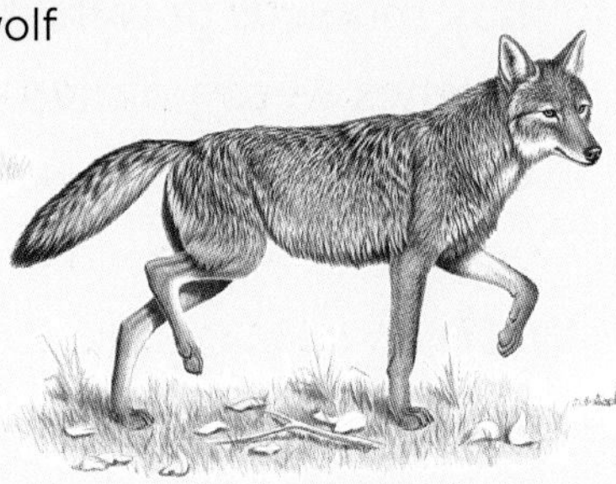

Red wolf

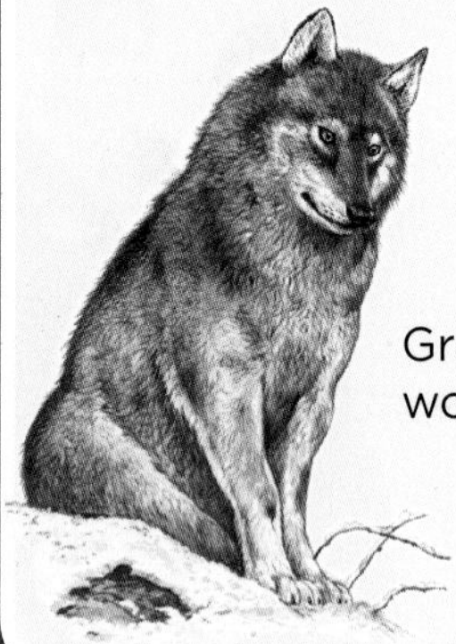

Gray wolf

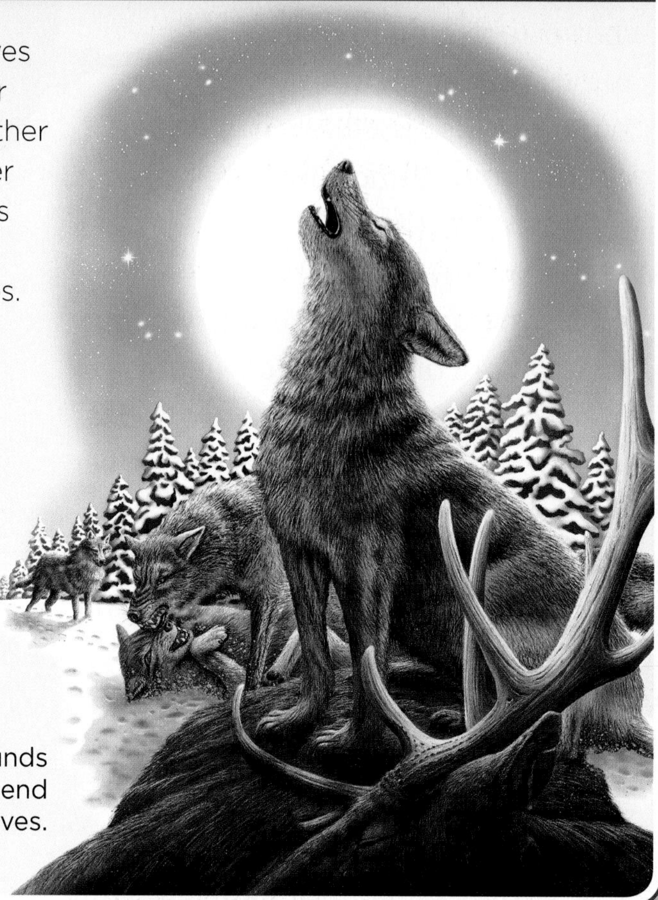

Wolves make loud sounds called howls to send messages to other wolves.

wolf ▲ • wolves

A **wolf** is a large wild animal that looks like a dog. Wolves live in groups, and together they hunt other animals for food.

woman • women

A **woman** is a grown-up female person: *Sally Ride was the first American* ***woman*** *to fly in space.*

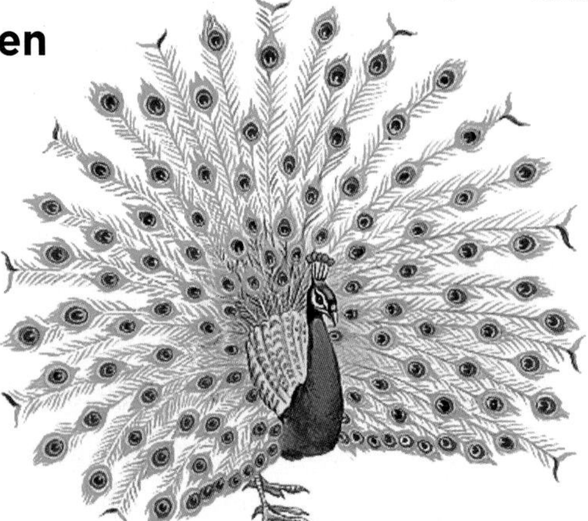

The male peacock spreads his **wonderful** tail.

wonderful ▼

1. **Wonderful** means something special, very different, or amazing: *We went to Europe on vacation and saw some* ***wonderful*** *old buildings and castles.*

2. **Wonderful** also means very good or excellent: *My mother is a* ***wonderful*** *cook.*

won't

Won't is a shorter way of saying "will not": *I* ***won't*** *be able to play softball on Saturday because I hurt my ankle.*

wood • woods

Wood is the hard material that trees are made of. You can use wood to build things, and you can also use wood to burn in a fire: *Dad used the **wood** from the old oak tree to build a big **wooden** table.* A large area of trees growing all together like a forest is sometimes called the **woods**.

wool ◀ • wools

This sheep has thick **wool** growing on it.

Wool is the soft, curly hair on sheep and some other animals. Wool can be made into cloth to make things like sweaters and blankets: *Grandma gave me a red hat made of **wool** for my birthday. Then she knitted me a red **woolen** scarf to match.*

word • words

A **word** is a group of sounds or letters that mean something. We use words every day as part of our language. We can say words or write them down: *The **word** "work" means "something you do to get money."*

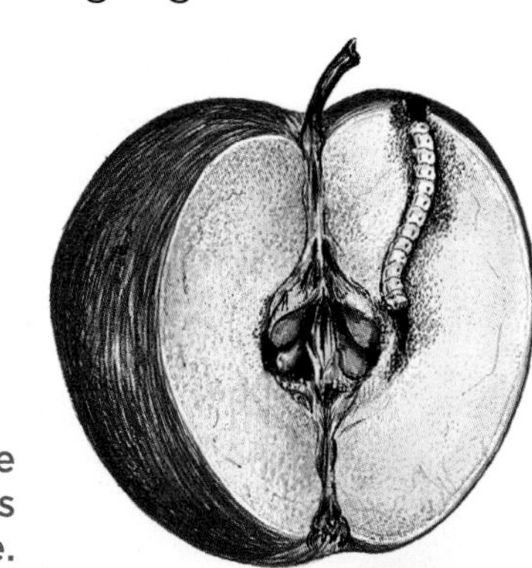

The **worm** made a hole and is inside the apple.

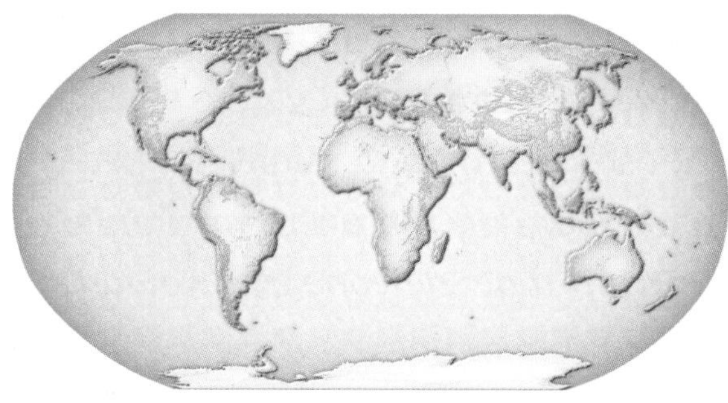

This map of the **world** is flat, and you can see all the continents.

work • worked, working

1. Work is the job that a person does to earn money: *Mom takes us to school on the way to her **work** at the office.*
2. To **work** means to do a job to earn money: *Daniel **works** as a teacher in an elementary school.*
3. To **work** also means to use energy to do something: *We **worked** hard all morning to get the house looking clean and neat.*
4. When something does what it is supposed to do, we say that it **works**: *This faucet isn't **working** right—there's no water coming out.*

world ▲ • worlds

The **world** is Earth and all the people and things on it: *Uncle Mark lives in Australia, which is a country on the other side of the **world** from where I live in Virginia.*

worm ◀ • worms

A **worm** is a long, thin, soft animal with no arms or legs. Worms move about by sliding along the ground like snakes.

worry • worried, worrying

To **worry** means to have the feeling that something bad might happen: *When our dog ran away, my family* ***worried*** *that someone else would find him and keep him.*

In **wrestling**, people sometimes pick each other up.

worse

Worse means even more than bad or unpleasant: *I got a bad mark for math, but a* ***worse*** *mark for spelling. An "F" is the* ***worst*** *mark you can get.*

would

Would is a form of the word WILL: *I told Mom that I* ***would*** *finish my homework after dinner.* **Wouldn't** is a shorter way of saying "would not": ***Wouldn't*** *it be great if there was no such thing as homework?*

wrap ▼ • wrapped, wrapping

To **wrap** means to cover something by folding paper or something else around it: *Lauren* ***wrapped*** *the birthday present in bright pink paper and put a bow on top.*

Long ago in Egypt, people **wrapped** dead bodies in cloth.

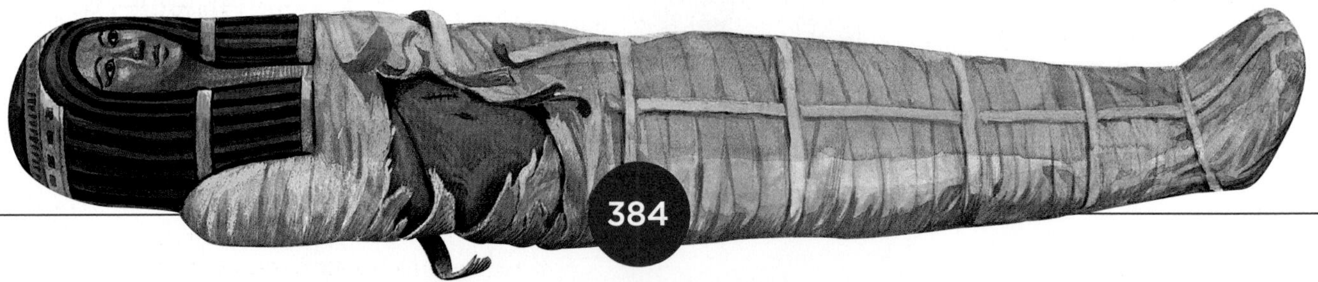

wrestling ▼

Wrestling is a sport or show where two people fight each other and try to throw the other person onto the ground and hold them there: *Dad and I love watching* ***wrestling*** *shows on TV. We each have a favorite* ***wrestler*** *that we like to watch.*

wrist • wrists

Your **wrist** is the part that joins your hand and your arm: *I wear my* ***watch*** *on my left wrist.*

write ▶ • wrote, written, writing

To **write** means to put letters, words, or numbers on something like paper: *I used a blue pen to* ***write*** *my name at the top of the page. Beth wrote a story about a kitten. Her teacher read it and said that Beth is a very good* ***writer****.*

Heidi **writes** a note to her friend.

wrong

Wrong means not true or right: *Eva thought that Los Angeles was the biggest American city, but that was* ***wrong****—it's New York. It was* ***wrong*** *of Zachary to borrow my bike without asking me first.*

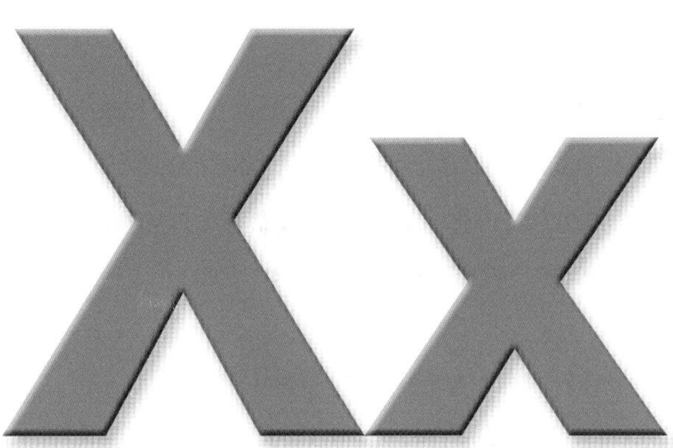

Xmas • Xmases

Xmas is a short form of CHRISTMAS: *My friend sent me a card that said "Merry **Xmas** and Happy New Year."*

X ray ▼ • X rays

An **X ray** is a photograph of the inside of something or someone. X rays are taken by a special machine that can see things we usually cannot see: *After Pierre fell and hurt his foot, his mother took him to the hospital for an **X ray** to see if any bones were broken. The doctor **X-rayed** his leg, just to make sure it was all right.*

In mathematics, X means "something that is not known." When the German scientist Wilhelm Roentgen discovered **X rays**, he gave them this name because people did not know about them before.

You can hold a hammer in each hand to play a **xylophone.**

xylophone ▲ • xylophones

A **xylophone** is a musical instrument that has a row of wooden or metal bars that you hit with a special hammer. Each little bar makes a different sound.

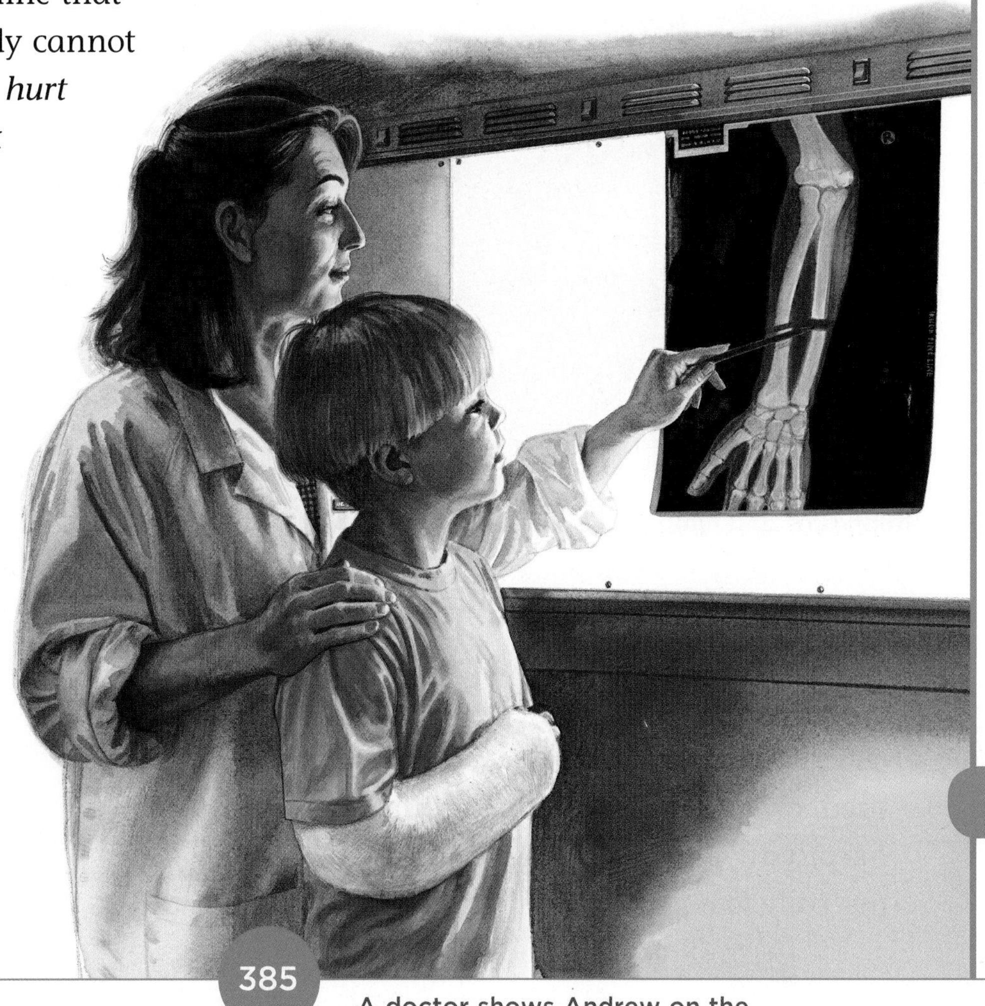

A doctor shows Andrew on the **X ray** where his arm was broken.

Rory's favorite toy is a **yellow** race car.

yard ▼ • **yards**

A **yard** is an area of ground around or beside a house, school, or some other building: *My brother and I went outside to play ball in the **yard**.*

Ralph runs and jumps in his **yard.**

yawn ▶ • **yawned, yawning**

To **yawn** means to open your mouth wide and take in a deep breath. You usually yawn when you are sleepy or tired, or not interested in something: *I kept **yawning** today because I stayed up really late last night.*

year • **years**

A **year** is a period of time that lasts for twelve months: *My big sister is going away to college for four **years**. Grandpa was born in the **year** 1941.*

yell ▶ • **yelled, yelling**

To **yell** means to shout out loudly: *I **yelled** out "stop!" to my dog who was about to run in front of a car.*

If someone **yells,** you can hear them from far away.

yellow ◀

Yellow is a color like gold, butter, or ripe lemons: *Bert used his orange and **yellow** pencils to draw a picture of the sun coming up in the morning.*

Maxine **yawns** because she has worked hard all day.

yes ▼

When you say **yes**, it means that you agree. Yes is the opposite of no: ***Yes** please, I would like some ice cream with my pie.*

Mom has a button that says **yes** from the last election.

yesterday

Yesterday is the day that came before today: *Mom and Dad came home from their vacation **yesterday**. Today they are very tired.*

yet

Yet means at this time or up until now: *Did you finish your homework **yet**?*

you ▼

We use the word **you** when we are talking to someone: *Are **you** taking the bus to school today? **You're** very late this morning. **You'd** better hurry up or **you'll** miss it. **You've** been late every morning this week.*

Emilio wants to take a photo of **you** with his camera.

Young penguins keep warm by staying close to their parents.

young ▲

Young means not very old: *The movie is really for **young** children and not for teenagers or grown-ups.*

your ▼

You use **your** when you mean that something belongs to you: *Did you finish **your** work all by **yourself**? I forgot to bring my pencil—can I borrow **yours**?*

To keep **your** dog healthy, you should take it for a walk every day.

The life jacket has a **zipper** down the front.

Zz

zebra ▼ • zebras

A **zebra** is a wild animal that looks like a horse with a black and white striped coat. Zebras live in Africa.

zero ▶ • zeros *or* zeroes

Zero means nothing: *After I spent all my money on a computer game, I had* ***zero*** *dollars left for the rest of the month.* Sometimes we use the sign for zero (**0**) instead.

There is nothing on the scale, so the arrow points to **zero**.

zipper ◀ • zippers

A **zipper** holds things like clothes and bags together. A zipper is made of two rows of teeth that you open or close with a sliding lock: *When he went outside, Tommy closed the* ***zipper*** *in his jacket to keep warm.*

There is an area with tame animals at the **zoo**.

zoo ▲ • zoos

A **zoo** is a park or large place where wild animals are kept for people to come and look at: *You can see lots of different animals at this* ***zoo****, such as monkeys, elephants, giraffes, and lions.*

The **zebras** are looking around for dangerous animals like lions.

Reference Section

United States of America

The United States of America is part of the continent of North America. The country has 50 states, and more than 300 million people live there. America's capital is Washington, D.C., and its largest city is New York City. Canada is the country to the north of the United States of America and Mexico is to the south.

KEY:

- ✪ National capital
- ★ State capital
- • Major city

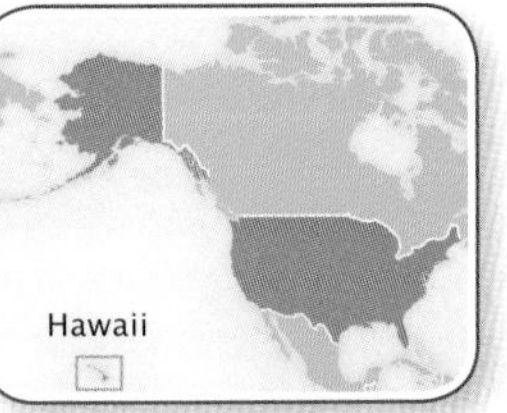

Golden Gate Bridge

Disneyland

Cactus

10 LARGEST CITIES IN AMERICA

New York, NY 8,214,000

Los Angeles, CA 3,849,000

Chicago, IL 2,833,000

Houston, TX 2,144,000

Phoenix, AZ 1,513,000

Philadelphia, PA 1,448,000

San Antonio, TX 1,297,000

San Diego, CA 1,257,000

Dallas, TX 1,233,000

San Jose, CA 930,000

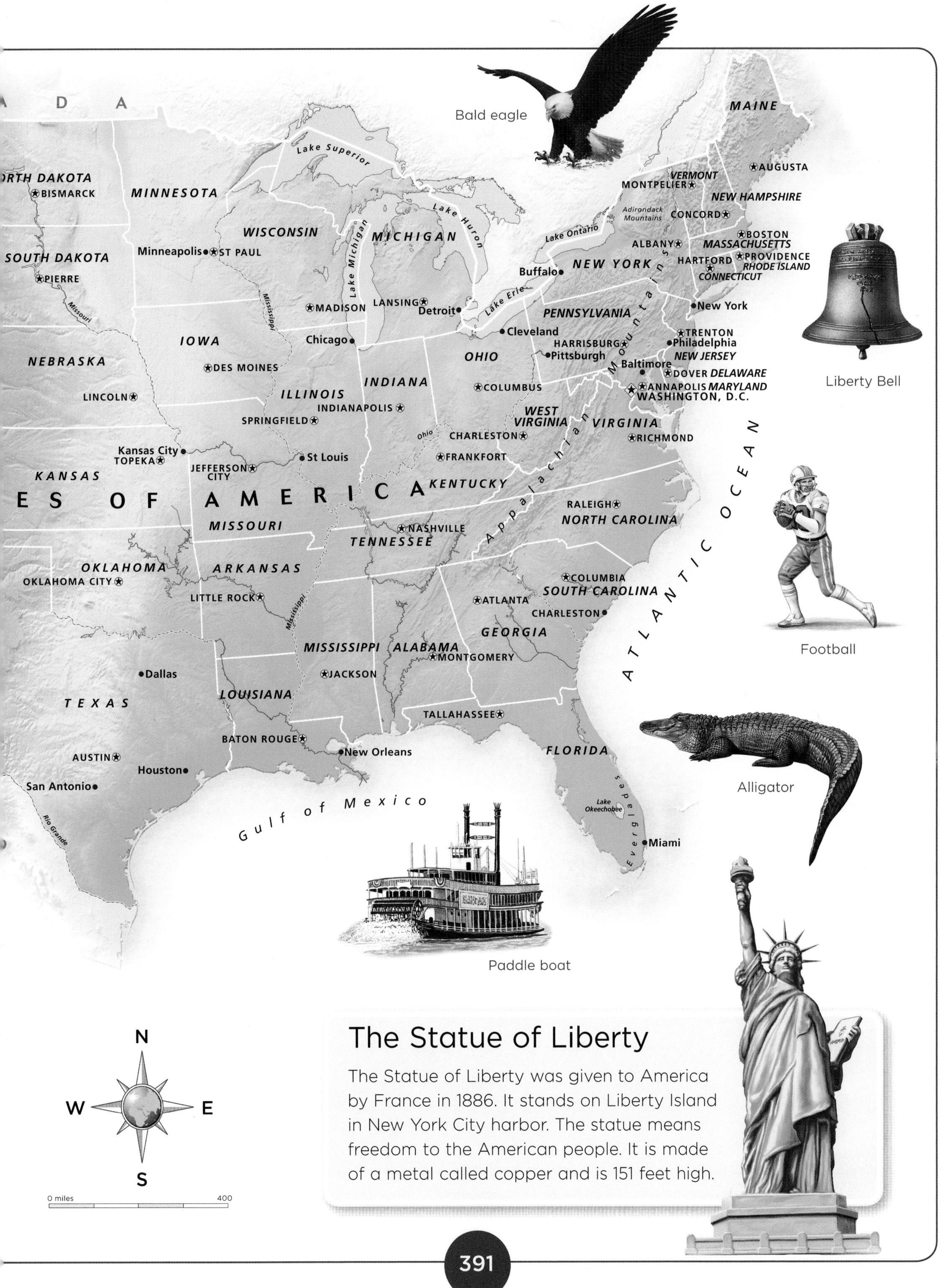

The Statue of Liberty

The Statue of Liberty was given to America by France in 1886. It stands on Liberty Island in New York City harbor. The statue means freedom to the American people. It is made of a metal called copper and is 151 feet high.

States of the United States

	National capital	Nickname	Population	Official flower	Official bird
	District of Columbia *DC*	Washington, D.C.	582,000	American beauty rose	Wood thrush

	State	Nickname	Capital	Population	State flower	State bird
	Alabama *AL*	The Heart of Dixie / The Yellowhammer State	Montgomery	4,599,000	Camellia	Yellowhammer
	Alaska *AK*	The Last Frontier	Juneau	670,000	Forget-me-not	Willow ptarmigan
	Arizona *AZ*	The Grand Canyon State	Phoenix	6,166,000	Saguaro cactus blossom	Cactus wren
	Arkansas *AR*	The Natural State	Little Rock	2,811,000	Apple blossom	Mockingbird
	California *CA*	The Golden State	Sacramento	36,458,000	Golden poppy	California valley quail
	Colorado *CO*	The Centennial State	Denver	4,753,000	Rocky Mountain columbine	Lark bunting
	Connecticut *CT*	The Constitution State	Hartford	3,505,000	Mountain laurel	American robin
	Delaware *DE*	The First State	Dover	854,000	Peach blossom	Blue hen chicken
	Florida *FL*	The Sunshine State	Tallahassee	18,090,000	Orange blossom	Mockingbird
	Georgia *GA*	The Peach State / Empire State of the South	Atlanta	9,364,000	Cherokee rose	Brown thrasher
	Hawaii *HI*	The Aloha State	Honolulu	1,286,000	Native yellow hibiscus	Nene (Hawaiian goose)
	Idaho *ID*	The Gem State	Boise	1,467,000	Syringa	Mountain bluebird
	Illinois *IL*	The Prairie State	Springfield	12,832,000	Native violet	Cardinal
	Indiana *IN*	The Hoosier State	Indianapolis	6,314,000	Peony	Cardinal
	Iowa *IA*	The Hawkeye State	Des Moines	2,982,000	Wild rose	Eastern goldfinch
	Kansas *KS*	The Sunflower State	Topeka	2,764,000	Sunflower	Western meadowlark

State	Nickname	Capital	Population	State flower	State bird
Kentucky *KY*	The Bluegrass State	Frankfort	4,206,000	Goldenrod	Cardinal
Louisiana *LA*	The Pelican State	Baton Rouge	4,288,000	Magnolia	Eastern brown pelican
Maine *ME*	The Pine Tree State	Augusta	1,322,000	White pine cone	Chickadee
Maryland *MD*	The Free State / The Old Line State	Annapolis	5,616,000	Black-eyed Susan	Baltimore oriole
Massachusetts *MA*	The Bay State	Boston	6,437,000	Mayflower	Chickadee
Michigan *MI*	The Wolverine State / The Great Lakes State	Lansing	10,096,000	Apple blossom	Robin
Minnesota *MN*	The North Star State / Land of 10,000 Lakes	St. Paul	5,167,000	Lady's slipper	Common loon
Mississippi *MS*	The Magnolia State	Jackson	2,911,000	Magnolia	Mockingbird
Missouri *MO*	The Show Me State	Jefferson City	5,843,000	Hawthorn	Bluebird
Montana *MT*	The Treasure State	Helena	945,000	Bitterroot	Western meadowlark
Nebraska *NE*	The Cornhusker State	Lincoln	1,768,000	Goldenrod	Western meadowlark
Nevada *NV*	The Sagebrush State / The Silver State	Carson City	2,496,000	Sagebrush	Mountain bluebird
New Hampshire *NH*	The Granite State	Concord	1,315,000	Purple lilac	Purple finch
New Jersey *NJ*	The Garden State	Trenton	8,725,000	Purple violet	Eastern goldfinch
New Mexico *NM*	Land of Enchantment	Santa Fe	1,955,000	Yucca	Roadrunner
New York *NY*	The Empire State	Albany	19,306,000	Rose	Bluebird
North Carolina *NC*	The Tar Heel State / The Old North State	Raleigh	8,857,000	Dogwood	Cardinal

States of the United States

	State	Nickname	Capital	Population	State flower	State bird
	North Dakota *ND*	The Sioux State / The Peace Garden State	Bismarck	636,000	Wild prairie rose	Western meadowlark
	Ohio *OH*	The Buckeye State	Columbus	11,478,000	Scarlet carnation	Cardinal
	Oklahoma *OK*	The Sooner State	Oklahoma City	3,579,000	Mistletoe	Scissor-tailed flycatcher
	Oregon *OR*	The Beaver State	Salem	3,701,000	Oregon grape	Western meadowlark
	Pennsylvania *PA*	The Keystone State	Harrisburg	12,441,000	Mountain laurel	Ruffed grouse
	Rhode Island *RI*	The Ocean State	Providence	1,068,000	Violet	Rhode Island red
	South Carolina *SC*	The Palmetto State	Columbia	4,321,000	Yellow jessamine	Carolina wren
	South Dakota *SD*	The Mount Rushmore State	Pierre	782,000	American pasqueflower	Ring-necked pheasant
	Tennessee *TN*	The Volunteer State	Nashville	6,039,000	Iris	Mockingbird
	Texas *TX*	The Lone Star State	Austin	23,508,000	Bluebonnet	Mockingbird
	Utah *UT*	The Beehive State	Salt Lake City	2,550,000	Sego lily	California gull
	Vermont *VT*	The Green Mountain State	Montpelier	624,000	Red clover	Hermit thrush
	Virginia *VA*	The Old Dominion / Mother of Presidents	Richmond	7,643,000	Dogwood	Cardinal
	Washington *WA*	The Evergreen State	Olympia	6,396,000	Coast rhododendron	Willow goldfinch
	West Virginia *WV*	The Mountain State	Charleston	1,819,000	Rhododendron	Cardinal
	Wisconsin *WI*	The Badger State	Madison	5,557,000	Wood violet	Robin
	Wyoming *WY*	The Equality State	Cheyenne	515,000	Indian paintbrush	Western meadowlark

Presidents of the United States

	President, term of office	First Lady	Vice President
1	**George Washington** 1789–97	Martha Washington	John Adams
2	**John Adams** 1797–1801	Abigail Adams	Thomas Jefferson
3	**Thomas Jefferson** 1801–09	Martha Jefferson	Aaron Burr 1801–05 / George Clinton 1805–09
4	**James Madison** 1809–17	Dolley Madison	George Clinton 1809–12 / *vacant 1812–13* / Elbridge Gerry 1813–14 / *vacant 1814–17*
5	**James Monroe** 1817–25	Elizabeth Monroe	Daniel Tompkins
6	**John Quincy Adams** 1825–29	Louisa Adams	John Calhoun
7	**Andrew Jackson** 1829–37	Rachel Jackson (died 1828)	John Calhoun 1829–32 / Martin Van Buren 1833–37
8	**Martin Van Buren** 1837–41	Hannah Van Buren	Richard Johnson
9	**William Henry Harrison** 1841	Anna Harrison	John Tyler
10	**John Tyler** 1841–45	Letitia Tyler (died 1842) Julia Tyler (from 1844)	*vacant*
11	**James Polk** 1845–49	Sarah Polk	George Dallas
12	**Zachary Taylor** 1849–50	Margaret Taylor	Millard Fillmore
13	**Millard Fillmore** 1850–53	Abigail Fillmore	*vacant*
14	**Franklin Pierce** 1853–57	Jane Pierce	William King 1853 / *vacant 1853–57*
15	**James Buchanan** 1857–61	Harriet Lane (niece)	John Breckinridge
16	**Abraham Lincoln** 1861–65	Mary Lincoln	Hannibal Hamlin 1861–65 / Andrew Johnson 1865
17	**Andrew Johnson** 1865–69	Eliza Johnson	*vacant*
18	**Ulysses S. Grant** 1869–77	Julia Grant	Schuyler Colfax 1869–73 / Henry Wilson 1873–75 / *vacant 1875–77*
19	**Rutherford Hayes** 1877–81	Lucy Hayes	William Wheeler
20	**James Garfield** 1881	Lucretia Garfield	Chester Arthur
21	**Chester Arthur** 1881–85	Ellen Arthur	*vacant*
22	**Grover Cleveland** 1885–89	Frances Cleveland	Thomas Hendricks 1885 / *vacant 1885–89*
23	**Benjamin Harrison** 1889–93	Caroline Harrison	Levi Morton
24	**Grover Cleveland** 1893–97	Frances Cleveland	Adlai Stevenson
25	**William McKinley** 1897–1901	Ida McKinley	Garret Hobart 1897–99 / *vacant 1899–1901* / Theodore Roosevelt 1901
26	**Theodore Roosevelt** 1901–09	Edith Roosevelt	*vacant 1901–05* / Charles Fairbanks 1905–09
27	**William H. Taft** 1909–13	Helen Taft	James S. Sherman 1909–12 / *vacant 1912–13*
28	**Woodrow Wilson** 1913–21	Ellen Wilson (died 1914) Edith Wilson (from 1915)	Thomas R. Marshall
29	**Warren Harding** 1921–23	Florence Harding	(John) Calvin Coolidge
30	**(John) Calvin Coolidge** 1923–29	Grace Coolidge	*vacant 1923–25* / Charles Dawes 1925–29
31	**Herbert Hoover** 1929–33	Lou Hoover	Charles Curtis
32	**Franklin D. Roosevelt** 1933–45	(Anna) Eleanor Roosevelt	John N. Garner 1933–41 / Henry Wallace 1941–45 / Harry S. Truman 1945
33	**Harry S. Truman** 1945–53	Elizabeth "Bess" Truman	*vacant 1945–49* / Alben Barkley 1949–53
34	**Dwight Eisenhower** 1953–61	Mamie Eisenhower	Richard Nixon
35	**John F. Kennedy** 1961–63	Jacqueline Kennedy	Lyndon B. Johnson
36	**Lyndon B. Johnson** 1963–69	Claudia "Lady Bird" Johnson	*vacant 1963–65* / Hubert Humphrey 1965–69
37	**Richard Nixon** 1969–74	Patricia Nixon	Spiro Agnew 1969–73 / Gerald Ford 1973–74
38	**Gerald Ford** 1974–77	Elizabeth "Betty" Ford	Nelson Rockefeller
39	**Jimmy Carter** 1977–81	Rosalynn Carter	Walter Mondale
40	**Ronald Reagan** 1981–89	Nancy Reagan	George H.W. Bush
41	**George H.W. Bush** 1989–93	Barbara Bush	James Danforth "Dan" Quayle
42	**William "Bill" Clinton** 1993–2001	Hillary Rodham Clinton	Albert "Al" Gore, Jr.
43	**George W. Bush** 2001–	Laura Bush	Richard "Dick" Cheney

The World

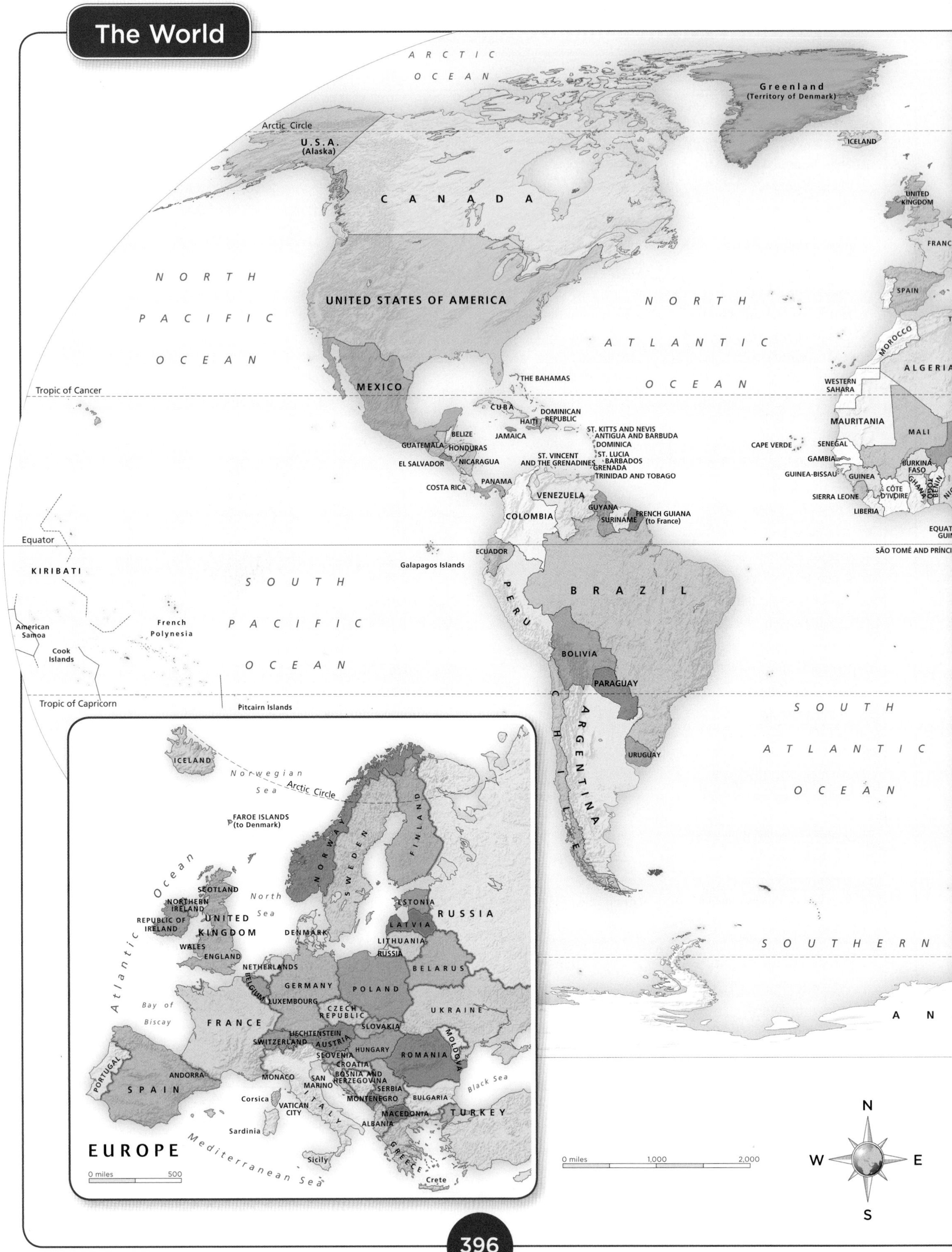

ARCTIC OCEAN
Greenland (Territory of Denmark)
Arctic Circle
U.S.A. (Alaska)
ICELAND
CANADA
UNITED KINGDOM
FRANCE
NORTH PACIFIC OCEAN
UNITED STATES OF AMERICA
NORTH ATLANTIC OCEAN
SPAIN
MOROCCO
ALGERIA
Tropic of Cancer
MEXICO
THE BAHAMAS
WESTERN SAHARA
CUBA
DOMINICAN REPUBLIC
HAITI
MAURITANIA
MALI
BELIZE
JAMAICA
ST. KITTS AND NEVIS
ANTIGUA AND BARBUDA
DOMINICA
GUATEMALA
HONDURAS
CAPE VERDE
SENEGAL
EL SALVADOR
NICARAGUA
ST. VINCENT AND THE GRENADINES
ST. LUCIA
BARBADOS
GRENADA
GAMBIA
BURKINA FASO
GUINEA-BISSAU
GUINEA
PANAMA
TRINIDAD AND TOBAGO
COSTA RICA
VENEZUELA
SIERRA LEONE
CÔTE D'IVOIRE
GHANA
LIBERIA
GUYANA
FRENCH GUIANA (to France)
COLOMBIA
SURINAME
Equator
ECUADOR
SÃO TOMÉ AND PRÍNCIPE
KIRIBATI
Galapagos Islands
SOUTH PACIFIC OCEAN
BRAZIL
PERU
American Samoa
French Polynesia
Cook Islands
BOLIVIA
PARAGUAY
Tropic of Capricorn
Pitcairn Islands
CHILE
ARGENTINA
URUGUAY
SOUTH ATLANTIC OCEAN
SOUTHERN
AN
0 miles 1,000 2,000
N
W
E
S
ICELAND
Norwegian Sea
Arctic Circle
FAROE ISLANDS (to Denmark)
NORWAY
SWEDEN
FINLAND
Atlantic Ocean
SCOTLAND
NORTHERN IRELAND
North Sea
ESTONIA
RUSSIA
REPUBLIC OF IRELAND
UNITED KINGDOM
LATVIA
DENMARK
LITHUANIA
WALES
ENGLAND
RUSSIA
NETHERLANDS
BELARUS
BELGIUM
GERMANY
POLAND
LUXEMBOURG
Bay of Biscay
CZECH REPUBLIC
UKRAINE
FRANCE
SLOVAKIA
LIECHTENSTEIN
MOLDOVA
SWITZERLAND
AUSTRIA
HUNGARY
SLOVENIA
ROMANIA
CROATIA
PORTUGAL
ANDORRA
BOSNIA AND HERZEGOVINA
MONACO
SAN MARINO
SERBIA
Black Sea
SPAIN
Corsica
MONTENEGRO
BULGARIA
VATICAN CITY
ITALY
MACEDONIA
TURKEY
ALBANIA
Sardinia
EUROPE
Mediterranean Sea
Sicily
GREECE
Crete
0 miles 500

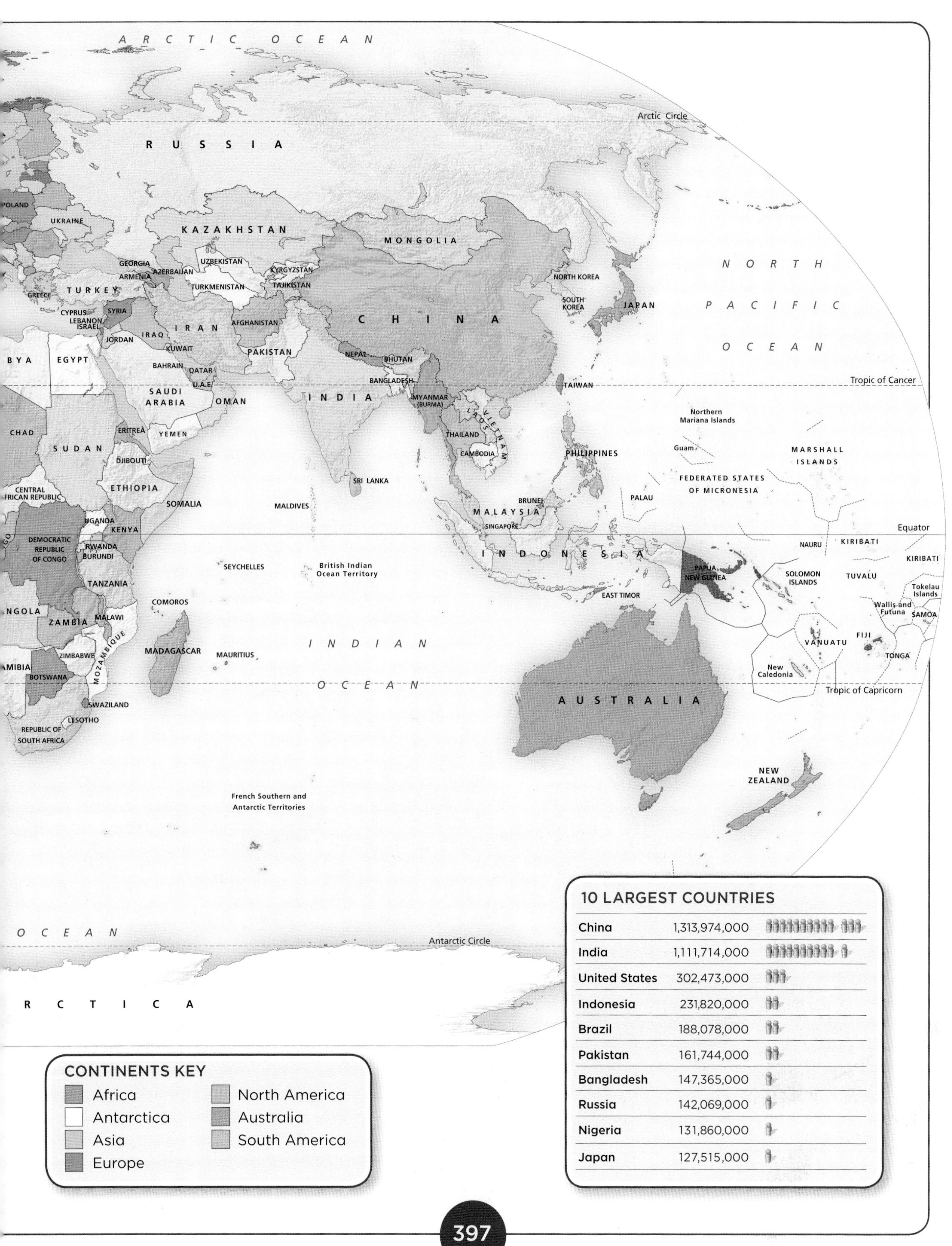

10 LARGEST COUNTRIES

Country	Population
China	1,313,974,000
India	1,111,714,000
United States	302,473,000
Indonesia	231,820,000
Brazil	188,078,000
Pakistan	161,744,000
Bangladesh	147,365,000
Russia	142,069,000
Nigeria	131,860,000
Japan	127,515,000

The Solar System

Scientists think the Solar System probably formed about 5 billion years ago, when a star exploded and made a cloud of dust and gas. This cloud fell in toward its center, and it became the Sun. Other material, such as rock, ice, and gas, came together to form the eight planets and their moons.

Jupiter
Size: 88,844 miles in diameter
Distance from the Sun: 484 million miles
Number of moons: 63

Venus
Size: 7,521 miles in diameter
Distance from the Sun: 67 million miles
Number of moons: 0

Mercury
Size: 3,032 miles in diameter
Distance from the Sun: 36 million miles
Number of moons: 0

Mars
Size: 4,220 miles in diameter
Distance from the Sun: 142 million miles
Number of moons: 2

Asteroid Be
Pieces of rock and met
known as asteroids, travel
an orbit around the Su
between Mars and Jupite

Earth
Size: 7,926 miles in diameter
Distance from the Sun: 93 million miles
Number of moons: 1

Sun
Size: 865,278 miles in diameter

Neptune
Size: 30,776 miles in diameter
Distance from the Sun:
2,794 million miles
Number of moons: 13

Uranus
Size: 31,764 miles in diameter
Distance from the Sun:
1,784 million miles
Number of moons: 27

Saturn
Size: 74,900 miles in diameter
Distance from the Sun:
887 million miles
Number of moons: 56

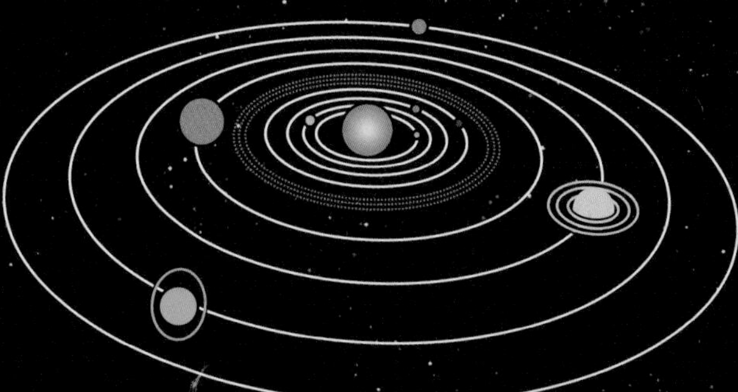

Each of the eight planets in the Solar System travels in its own path around the Sun. These paths, which are like circles, are called orbits. Earth takes a year to complete one orbit around the Sun. Mercury, the closest planet to the Sun, takes 88 days to complete one orbit. Neptune, the farthest planet, takes 165 years to travel around the Sun.

Credits and Acknowledgments

Illustrations Susanna Addario, Mike Atkinson/illustrationweb.com, Paul Bachem, Kenn Backhaus, Cy Baker, Alistair Barnard, Julian Baum, Andrew Beckett, Richard Bonson/The Art Agency, Anne Bowman, Peter Bull Art Studio, Danny Burke, Martin Camm, Dan Cole/The Art Agency, Leslye Cole/The Art Agency, Sam and Amy Collins, Tom Connell, Marcus Cremonese, Marjorie Crosby-Fairall, Barry Croucher/The Art Agency, Andrew Davies, Claire Davies/The Art Agency, Fiammatte Dogi, Sandra Doyle/The Art Agency, Levent Efe, Simone End, Christer Eriksson, Alan Ewart, Nick Farmer/Brighton Illustration, Rod Ferring, Cecilia Fitzsimons/The Art Agency, Giuliano Fornari, Chris Forsey, Lloyd Foye, John Francis/Bernard Thornton Artists UK, Luigi Gallante/The Art Agency, Lee Gibbons/The Art Agency, Tony Gibbons/Bernard Thornton Artists UK, Jon Gittoes, GODD.com (Marcus Junker, Rolf Schröter, Patrick Tilp, Robert Keller, Julian Krause), Mike Gorman, Ray Grinaway, Terry Hadler, Langdon G. Halls, Gino Halser, Gary Hanna/The Art Agency, Lorraine Hannay, David A Hardy/The Art Agency, Tim Hayward, Phil Hood/The Art Agency, Adam Hook/Bernard Thornton Artists UK, Christa Hook/Bernard Thornton Artists UK, Richard Hook/Bernard Thornton Artists UK, Robert Hynes, Mark Iley/The Art Agency, Inklink, Ian Jackson/The Art Agency, Gillian Jenkins, Janet Jones, Steve Kirk/The Art Agency, David Kirshner, Frank Knight, Mike Lamble, Alex Lavroff, Connell Lee, John Mac/Folio, David Mackay, Iain McKellar, James McKinnon, Martin Macrae/Folio, Stuart McVicar/Geocart, Robert Mancini, David Mathews, Peter Mennim, Siri Mills, David Moore/Linden Artists, Colin Newman/Bernard Thornton Artists UK, Kevin O'Donnell, Nicola Oram, Matthew Ottley, Darren Pattenden/illustrationweb.com, R. Spencer Phippen, Jane Pickering/Linden Artists, Sandra Pond/The Art Agency, Marilyn Pride, Tony Pyrzakowski, Oliver Rennert, Luis Rey/The Art Agency, John Richards, Edwina Riddell, Steve Roberts/The Art Agency, Trevor Ruth, Claudia Saraceni, Michael Saunders, Peter Schouten, Peter Scott/The Art Agency, Stephen Seymour/Bernard Thornton Artists UK, Christine Shafner/K.E. Sweeney Illustration, Nick Shewring/illustrationweb.com, Chris Shields/The Art Agency, Ray Sim, Marco Sparaciari, Spellcraft Studio e.K., Kevin Stead, Roger Stewart/Brighton Illustration, Irene Still, Roger Swainston, Kate Sweeney/K.E. Sweeney Illustration, Sharif Tarabay/illustrationweb.com, Claude Thivierge/Contact Jupiter, Steve Trevaskis, Thomas Trojer, Guy Troughton, Chris Turnbull/The Art Agency, Glen Vause, Jane Walkins/The Art Agency, Genevieve Wallace, Ross Watton/illustrationweb.com, Trevor Weekes, Rod Westblade, Steve Weston/Linden Artists, Simon Williams/illustrationweb.com, Ann Winterbotham, David Wood, David Wun

Photographs AdLibitum, Artville, Corel, Digital Stock, Getty Images, iStock International Inc., Andre Martin, Photodisc, Photolibrary.com, Shutterstock Inc.

Maps Map Illustrations

Flags Flag Society of Australia

The Publishers would like to thank the following people for their assistance:
Peter Bull, Michelle Burk, Simon Burk, Rebecca Jarvis, Elizabeth Louie, Danielle Parker, Angela Tootil